T0377002

STATE FORMATION, REGIME CHANGE, AND ECONOMIC DEVELOPMENT

Failed or weak states, miscarried democratizations, and economic underdevelopment characterize a large part of the world we live in. Much work has been done on these subjects over the latest decades, but most of this research ignores the deep historical processes that produced the modern state, modern democracy, and the modern market economy in the first place.

This book elucidates the roots of these developments. The book discusses why China was surpassed by Europeans in spite of its early development of advanced economic markets and a meritocratic state. It also hones in on the relationship between geopolitical pressure and state formation and on the European conditions that – from the Middle Ages onwards – facilitated the development of the modern state, modern democracy, and the modern market economy. Finally, the book discusses why some countries have been able to follow the European lead in the latest generations whereas other countries have not.

State Formation, Regime Change, and Economic Development will be of key interest to students and researchers within political science and history as well as to Comparative Politics, Political Economy, and the Politics of Developing Areas.

Jørgen Møller is Professor at the Department of Political Science, Aarhus University, Denmark.

"Recently social scientists have begun re-visiting historical processes of state formation, regime change and economic development. This book will be a must-read in this emerging and exciting field of study, providing an outstanding overview of past classics and current debates as well as offering promising and provocative insights into how scholarship might move forward."

Sheri Berman, *Barnard College, USA*

"If you haven't read the classics on state and regime formation, read Møller. If you have read the classics on state and regime formation, but need a brilliant synthesis and a thought-provoking independent argument, read Møller."

Jan Teorell, *Lund University, Sweden*

"This book provides a clear and concise overview of the classical and contemporary social science literature, both qualitative and quantitative, on the origins of the modern state, modern democracy and modern market economy. It is unmatched in its even-handedness, acuity of judgement and geographic coverage. In addition, it casts new light on the conditions that led to the emergence of representative institutions in medieval Europe. A must read for anyone interested in the current debates on the divergence (and recent convergence) in economic and political development between the West and Asia."

Thomas Ertman, *New York University, USA*

STATE FORMATION, REGIME CHANGE, AND ECONOMIC DEVELOPMENT

Jørgen Møller

Routledge
Taylor & Francis Group

LONDON AND NEW YORK

First published 2017
by Routledge
2 Park Square, Milton Park, Abingdon, Oxon OX14 4RN

and by Routledge
711 Third Avenue, New York, NY 10017

Routledge is an imprint of the Taylor & Francis Group, an informa business

© 2017 Jørgen Møller

The right of Jørgen Møller to be identified as author of this work has been asserted by him in accordance with sections 77 and 78 of the Copyright, Designs and Patents Act 1988.

All rights reserved. No part of this book may be reprinted or reproduced or utilised in any form or by any electronic, mechanical, or other means, now known or hereafter invented, including photocopying and recording, or in any information storage or retrieval system, without permission in writing from the publishers.

Trademark notice: Product or corporate names may be trademarks or registered trademarks, and are used only for identification and explanation without intent to infringe.

British Library Cataloguing in Publication Data
A catalogue record for this book is available from the British Library

Library of Congress Cataloging in Publication Data
A catalog record for this book has been requested

ISBN: 978-1-138-68280-1 (hbk)
ISBN: 978-1-138-68281-8 (pbk)
ISBN: 978-1-315-54488-5 (ebk)

Typeset in Bembo
by Apex CoVantage, LLC

CONTENTS

FIGURES

TABLES

PREFACE

The purpose of this book is to review and discuss works that have analysed historical processes of state formation, regime change, and economic development. These works contain a cornucopia of insights and enthralling observations. They show that when it comes to the past, only the imagination sets limits. The annals of human history contain stories of unfathomable cruelty and misery and of heroism and achievements. At different times, people have performed miracles of statecraft, social discipline, military exploits, and explorations of unknown lands. At other times, human folly has led them astray, and all too often a perusal of the past upholds the old saying that man is wolf to man. Human history contains both some of the greatest and some of the most heartbreaking stories ever told.

Most of these stories have taken place within and are about states. This association is not spurious. The invention of writing systems was probably a result of the need of the first states to manage their finances (Robinson 2009). The actual history – told directly or indirectly by people – is therefore a history of states. In recent centuries it has turned into a history about a particular kind of state as the European nation-state or territorial state has displaced other forms of political organization, including city-states and empires (Tilly 1990). Our contemporary international system is, as scholars of international relations like to remind us, a state-centred system.

It is therefore for good reason that the first words in the title of this book are 'state formation'. At the same time, the modern territorial state, which emerged over the course of the latest five hundred years, has been the basis for the democratization process that has characterized the period following the French and American Revolutions as well as for the modern market economy, which has come into its own in the same period. Only by understanding where states come from are we able to understand their contemporary appearance and characteristics. And only in this way are we able to shed light on the two next terms in the title of the book: 'regime change' and 'economic development'.

This illustrates how history sets the stage for the present. Cicero is credited with the remark that "History is the teacher of life" (*Historia magistra vitae*). In my view, it should also be the teacher of political scientists. Tellingly, scholars pondering the past have produced numerous interesting arguments about the advent of the modern state, modern democracy, and the modern market economy. Some of these arguments have stood the test of time; others have been proven wrong – or at least questioned – by later research. But even in the latter case, one is often tempted to recall one of Joseph A. Schumpeter's aphorisms: "We all of us like a sparkling error better than a trivial truth" (Swedberg 1991, 205).

Many of the theoretical intuitions of classical scholars such as Alexis de Tocqueville, Max Weber, and Joseph A. Schumpeter make us stop and reflect on the development of human societies, in spite of the fact that these scholars did not empirically corroborate their theoretical arguments in a way that would pass muster today, and even though later work has disproven parts of their arguments. These classical contributions tell us something about the development of the discipline and about aspects of the history of human societies which later work has tended to neglect in the search for clear-cut empirical regularities. Furthermore, they stand as a monument of the historical versatility and creativity of the founding fathers of what in this book is referred to as comparative historical analysis. Invoking Newton's aphorism, today's scholars stand on the shoulder of giants.

In the pages that follow, we will revisit the work of many of these giants. My hope is that readers will both be entertained along the way and feel that they have learned something which a pure focus on contemporary processes of state formation, regime change, and economic development could not have given them.

Why is this enterprise necessary? Basically, because much of the social sciences have been affected by a series of methodological trends that bias them to focus on the present. Most important are the quantification that has swept these disciplines and the increasing use of experiments, whether in the field or in the laboratory. With experiments, there is really no way to addresses causes that unfold over longer spans of time. At most, we can get at some of the contemporary implications. With respect to quantitative research, scholars are often hesitant to delve back in time to do historical analysis because they face a dearth of data. The 'presentist' bias of experiments underlines why this should be only one among a series of methods used by those studying development processes. The past makes up a quarry which social scientists need to mine if they truly wish to understand the way societies develop. It augurs well that, in recent decades, a new body of historical scholarship on state formation, regime change, and economic development has been burgeoning. Some scholars have gone so far as to proclaim this development a part of a new 'historical turn' in the social sciences (McDonald 1996; Capoccia and Ziblatt 2010).

If what follows serves to convince the reader about the merits of such a turn, then my writing this book will have been worthwhile. The book has a long history itself. It was originally conceived as a way of reading up the literature covered in Part II and Part III of the book. My idea was that if I set myself the challenge to summarize and discuss what, *inter alia*, Max Weber, Barrington Moore, and Theda

Skocpol had said about state formation, regime change, and economic development, it would force me to read their works systematically. A first version of the
book was published in Danish in 2012, followed by a revised and expanded second
edition in 2015. Those who have provided comments on the Danish texts are mentioned in the acknowledgements to these earlier editions. I thank my Danish editor,
Martin Laurberg at Hans Reitzels Forlag, for granting me permission to publish
an English version. Also, I thank my editor at Routledge, Andrew Taylor, for being
supportive when I first presented the idea of an English version, and I thank three
anonymous reviewers for valuable input and for their support of the project. Finally,
two disclosures. Chapter 3 draws on work I have done elsewhere with Svend-Erik
Skaaning (Møller & Skaaning 2016a), and the explanatory typologies produced in
Part III of the book draw on a methodological article that is also co-authored with
Svend-Erik (Møller and Skaaning 2016b).

INTRODUCTION

Modern social science was born as an attempt to account for the staggering modernization process that had propelled the West – or more particularly Western Europe and a number of European settler colonies – to world domination, and Western Europeans and North Americans to hitherto unknown levels of economic affluence, physical security, and intellectual accomplishments. This modernization process had three component parts: the advent of the modern state, modern democracy, and the modern market economy. This was the trinity that sociologists of the late nineteenth century grappled with (cf. Mills 1959, 152–153; Skocpol 1984a, 1; Goldstone 1998, 250; Pomeranz 2000, 3). Max Weber was but one among many to seek the roots of these astounding developments, which have been captured in formulas such as the question 'Why Europe?' and the phrase 'The Rise of the West' (Chirot 1985; Hall 2001).

Since then, social science has branched in many different directions. But the 'Why Europe?' question that gave the original impetus to the discipline has neither been forgotten nor forlorn. An entire research field, which is normally termed historical sociology, has been devoted to answering it, or at least to elucidating different aspects of it. This book revolves around a sub-discipline of this research field, namely comparative historical analysis (see Mahoney and Rueschemeyer 2003; Lange 2012). More precisely, it reviews and discusses three different strands within this body of literature.

The first consists of some of the most important classic contributions to this field. Authors here include Alexis de Tocqueville, Max Weber, Joseph A. Schumpeter, Otto Hintze, and Marc Bloch. This classic tradition began in the nineteenth century and culminated in the period between the two World Wars. Part II of the book covers this literature. After World War II, the classic tradition ground to a halt, partly because of a number of 'ahistorical' theoretical innovations within political science, sociology, and history to which we will return a number of times. However, towards the end of the 1960s, comparative historical analysis again began to stir.

Barrington Moore's *Social Origins of Democracy and Dictatorship* (1991[1966]) was the harbinger of a renewed focus on historical processes of development, particularly in the United States. Borrowing Mahoney's (2003a) term, I refer to this second body of literature as the 'Barrington-Moore research programme'. This literature – which is covered in Part III – also includes seminal contributions of Perry Anderson, Theda Skocpol, Charles Tilly, Brian M. Downing, and Thomas Ertman.[1]

The Barrington Moore research programme lasted well into the 1990s, but in the new millennium it has been superseded by a voluminous literature on state formation, regime change, and economic development, which is covered in Part IV. This literature includes contributions by scholars such as David Stasavage, Jack Goldstone, Victoria Tin-bor Hui, Jeffrey Herbst, Miguel Centeno, Daron Acemoglu, James Robinson, Philip S. Gorski, and Robert D. Woodberry. It is more fragmented than the Barrington Moore research programme in terms of choice of method, empirical focus, and theoretical approaches, and compared to the two other bodies of literature it is more inclined to draw on statistical methods and to focus on developments outside the Western world (Lange 2012, 33).

To set the stage for the critical readings and discussions of these three strands of work, Part I first details the puzzle that motivates the book, namely the origins of the trinity of the modern state, modern democracy, and the modern market economy. It then introduces the research field of comparative historical analysis in order to explain the focus and methods of this field, to delimit it within the broader discipline of historical sociology, and to explain the criteria for including and excluding prominent attempts to probe the 'Why Europe?' question.

We can also say that the book is structured as an attempt to answer a series of more particular research questions. First, what do the concepts 'state', 'regime', and 'economic development' actually cover? What is the subject matter of the analysis presented in the book? Second, how can we explain why the modern state, modern democracy, and the modern market economy emerged precisely in Europe? Which factors favoured this area, and to what extent do we find some of the same factors in other areas? Further along these lines, how can we explain that state formation, regime change, and economic development have also transpired outside of Europe in the period after the Age of Discoveries around the year 1500? Third, how can we explain the considerable variation that can be observed over the latest five hundred to one thousand years *within* Europe? Given that the factors that are capable of explaining the 'European miracle' (Jones 2008[1981]) cannot explain the European diversity, which factors can? Fourth and finally, to what extent do the European developments shed light on the considerable variation *outside* Europe in the latest five hundred years, and in the period after 1800 in particular?

Key themes

We can identify some main themes from among the profusion of insights contained in the reviewed attempts to probe these questions. The most important theme has to do with the relationship between geopolitical pressure and the development of human societies. A broad consensus, which spans the classic literature and the more recent literature, and which also pervades most of the Barrington Moore research programme, is that the existence of competing state entities within an interwoven whole was a prerequisite for the emergence of the modern state, modern democracy, and the modern market economy.

Some of the *bon mots* of comparative historical analysis testify to the importance of this theme. According to the German historian Otto Hintze, the story of Europe is one about *Schieben und Drängen* (push and pull). The English idiom 'when push comes to shove' is a neat rendering of Hintze's insight. Charles Tilly (1975, 142) said something similar in his laconic quip that 'war made the state, and the state made war'. As Samuel P. Finer (1997b, 1473) puts it, this pressure meant that 'Europe was always travelling but never arrived' – the rational restlessness that Max Weber's work revolved around. The point is that the European states, European regime forms, and European economies were forged in the cauldron of persistent geopolitical pressure. In the long run, the emerging European states could not – at least in Western and Central Europe – survive in this anarchic international system without some measure of state capacity, political legitimacy, and commercialization of the economy. This created momentum in European societies.[2]

The effects of geopolitical pressure on development can be seen as the master theme of this book. Geopolitical dynamics have been used both to explain the emergence of bureaucracies, market economies, and particular political regimes in some parts of the world and to account for the absence of such developments in other parts. In other words, the significance of geopolitical competition forms the common thread of the book.

However, several other themes also cut across most of the chapters. Most obviously, we find a shared premise about the importance of history. Two reasons for studying historical developments can be gleaned from the works reviewed and discussed in this book (see also Møller 2016b). First, history makes up a quarry of data that can be mined by social scientists interested in generating or testing theories about state formation, regime change, and economic development. A good illustration of this point is David Hume's (1987[1777], 566) claim that

> we should be for ever children in understanding, were it not for this invention. . . . A man acquainted with history may, in some respect, be said to have lived from the beginning of the world, and to have been making continual additions to his stock of knowledge in every century.

In this perspective, the past serves as a kind of laboratory in which we can investigate potential causal links. By harking back in time, we can enlist new data – that is, we can harness historical variation. More particularly, by embracing history, scholars can avoid the kind of truncated samples that plague much of social science (Boix 2011) and take advantage of the fact that many challenges of state-building and political change are generic (Tilly 2006). Historical analysis thus contributes to generating broad theories that advance knowledge and are not artefacts of – or at least only valid within – particular historical contexts. This is important because we cannot (or at least only to a very limited extent) test such relationships using experiments – unlike certain disciplines in the natural sciences or certain other subject matters of social science. Sometimes, history even contains developments that can be construed as 'natural experiments' – that is, situations where a certain stimulus has occurred at random – and its causal effects can thereby be ascertained (Dunning 2012).

Second, historical processes do not merely shed light on contemporary processes; they also constitute the point of departure for the latter. Processes of political change, state formation, and economic change are often either path-dependent or at the very least affected by initial conditions. That is to say, the effect of many historical factors is temporally lagged. The most striking example is probably found in deep patterns of state formation. Archaeological scholarship has documented how the Neolithic revolution occasioned the first states, beginning in the Fertile Crescent and soon spreading to what has been termed the 'Lucky Latitudes' (the belt north of the equator stretching from Japan in the East to Central America in the West and including all the great historical areas of civilization, from China to the Fertile Crescent over the Mediterranean region to Central America) (Morris 2014, 75–77). The areas that first saw the formation of states therefore got a head start, which has been difficult for the others to make up (Diamond 1999[1997], 2012; Petersen and Skaaning 2010).

Scholars have convincingly argued that the legacies of these state-formation processes have affected later patterns of economic development and democratization (Diamond 1999[1997]; Hariri 2012). To be sure, it has also been observed that large-scale colonization processes have at times been able to break the shackles of history in the sense that they have transplanted 'modern' institutions to pre-modern societies, thereby leading to state formation, economic growth, and democratization (see in particular Chapter 13). The most important example is the colonial transplantation of institutions to so-called European settler colonies or 'neo-Europes' after 1500 (Acemoglu et al. 2001). But colonization did not occur independently of deeper patterns of state formation. Researchers have shown that the old and consolidated states in areas such as the Middle East and East Asia were stronger and therefore able to keep the Europeans at bay in the period after the Age of Discoveries – which later inhibited the democratization of these regions (Hariri 2012). The European transplantation of institutions after 1500 was therefore in itself formed by prior development processes. In other words, history casts long shadows, which we need to understand to comprehend present-day dynamics of political change, state-building, and economic development.

The main thesis

In addition to these general themes, the book makes an independent contribution to the literature. This main thesis integrates insights from many of the reviewed works but also goes beyond them to elucidate the roots of the Rise of the West. The claim of the book, as presented in Part V, is that we must seek out the determining causes behind the uniqueness of Europe (or, rather, Western and Central Europe) in the High Middle Ages.

It is important for me to emphasize that readers can enjoy the general introduction to state formation, regime change, and economic development presented in this book without accepting (or even being interested in) this thesis. However, when an independent contribution exists, it seems best to present it in the introduction. The premise of the claim forwarded in Part V is the now well-established insight that the European representative institutions have had a decisive impact on the development of the modern state, modern democracy, and the modern market economy (cf. Stasavage 2010; Blaydes and Chaney 2013). These institutions originated and spread in the period 1200–1500, and they were not found anywhere else in the world until the proliferation of parliaments in the nineteenth and twentieth centuries (Myers 1975).

My key argument here is that the European representative institutions owe to a certain set of features which characterized Europe in the High and Late Middle Ages – i.e., in the period 1000 AD to 1500 AD. Medieval Europe was characterized by strong societal groups that had legal privileges that the authorities had to respect, at least formally. These estate or corporate groups – particularly the church, nobility, and urban elites – formed a counterweight to royal power. As the geopolitical pressure of wars intensified around 1200, kings and princes in Western and Central Europe had to negotiate with these groups in order to ensure tax bases capable of financing military clout – a prerequisite for surviving the anarchic European system.

This development led to the institutionalization of the wheeling and dealing between monarchs and estate groups in the representative institutions of the Middle Ages, where a pole representing the estates and a princely pole together accounted for the body politics. In the course of the thirteenth and fourteenth centuries, the representative institutions spread throughout all of Western and Central Europe, partly due to the influence of the Roman Catholic Church. In other words, the representative institutions are a reminder of the unique social, legal, and political context that characterized medieval Europe. This context, in turn, facilitated the later development of the modern European state, the modern market economy, and modern democracy.

Present-day implications

The main thesis reflects a rather simple point: the story of the modern state, modern democracy, and the modern market economy is above all a story about Europe,[3] albeit a story that involves detours to the other great civilizations of Eurasia. This story is fascinating unto itself. But it is also highly relevant to our time. Failed or weak states, unsuccessful democratization processes, and economic underdevelopment characterize much of the world we live in. Within the development aid sector and academia, there is a raging debate about how to achieve progress in these areas. The writings on these issues have been extensive in recent decades. Nevertheless, it is apparent that a blueprint for creating an uncorrupted and legitimate state apparatus, a well-functioning democracy, and an efficient economic system has yet to be found – whether we look to academic disciplines such as political science, sociology, or economics or the vast array of state and international institutions working with development aid.

This is where the historical processes covered in this book can assist us. The point about the shadow of the past, made above, naturally calls for reflections about the contemporary implications of the historical processes covered in this book. We can here start by returning to the master theme of the book, namely the importance of geopolitical pressure. In the absence of such pressure, it is very difficult to see how the modern state, modern democracy, and modern market economies might have come into being. As the book shows, above all else we find a relentless external pressure in the European state system that emerged in the High Middle Ages and was consolidated in the Westphalian Peace in 1648. If Europe, instead of competing territorial states, had been subjected to a form of imperial domination, the European continent would hardly have stood out from the other great Eurasian civilization areas in eastern Asia, the Indian sub-continent, and the Middle East.

The greatest difference between the history of state formation and political and economic development, which is set out in this book, and the corresponding processes in our time is found in this geopolitical pressure. In short, after World War II in general and the end of the Cold War in particular, geopolitical pressure has almost completely subsided. As a number of researchers have noted (e.g., Tilly 1990; Herbst 2000; Centeno 2003; Krasner 2005; Fukuyama 2010), stronger states no longer swallow up weaker states. Today, the international community largely prevents the competition between state entities that played a role in forming states internally up until the twentieth century. The elites in many developing countries therefore have no external (geopolitical) incentive to establish an efficient state apparatus, a well-functioning market economy, and a political system based on responsiveness to popular demands.

For this reason alone, the Eurasian state-formation processes of the past – and the European state-formation processes in particular – are fundamentally different from such processes today. This is further compounded by the elites in many developing countries having access to natural resources, most importantly oil, which renders it possible to finance the state apparatus without depending on the resources of citizens (Herbst 2000; Ross 2001). In this book, we will discuss two works that deal with this very issue in an attempt to understand the course of the development in Latin America and Sub-Saharan Africa since decolonization (see Chapter 15). These analyses reveal that the survival mechanisms of the past, which take up so much space in this book, are far less relevant today, perhaps except in East Asia.

The next point we can make about contemporary developments is entangled in this. It is hardly an overstatement to say that the majority of the analyses of state formation in Europe point towards a number of unique 'internal' conditions in European political units – or more precisely Western Christendom –[4] which have been decisive for the development of the modern state, modern democracy, and the modern market economy. I have already mentioned the importance of a social context pervaded by strong, autonomous groups, including the nobility, the clergy, and townsmen.

A more analytical point can be drawn by combining these external and internal factors, namely that the path to the modern state, modern democracy, and the modern market economy was paved by two distinct dynamics (see also Hui 2005): the external competition that is attributed to the geopolitical competition between state entities within a relatively stable multistate system and which we have already touched upon above, and a corresponding internal competition between the authorities and the citizens – or state and society, if you will. Today, we would most likely think of this in terms of the existence of a strong civil society that is capable of resisting transgressions by the powers that be (Gellner 1994; Oxhorn 2003).

These two dynamics or mechanisms make it possible to weave the threads together. The claim made in the book is that they have been decisive for state formation, regime change, and economic development. Which implications for contemporary development processes can we then draw on this basis?

First and foremost, some rather sobering implications. State formation, regime change, and economic development are sluggish processes. Moreover, while we find these developments in many different places, the modern state, modern democracy, and the modern market economy would appear to have resulted from a concatenation of special circumstances in Western and Central Europe. This obviously implies that progress along these dimensions is not automatic – at least not if these modern-day European developments make up the standard to be achieved. In fact, democratization, economic development, and the development of effective states have historically been exceptions, while legal arbitrariness, mismanagement, abuses of power, and economic stagnation have been the norm (North et al. 2009). Elites have commonly fought tooth and nail against the introduction of uncorrupted state apparatuses, effective economic structures, and being held politically accountable by the citizens. Furthermore, such dysfunctional bureaucratic, political, and economic structures are extremely difficult to change because of path dependency (Ertman 1997, 320).

More generally, we must confront the following question: why would rulers ever be willing to accept limitations on their power (Holmes 2004)? It follows from what has been said above that elites can be expected to do this – thereby introducing effective and reliable administrative, political, and economic institutions – only if they are forced (Carothers 1998, 96; Przeworski 2009; Levitsky and Way 2010, 23). More specifically, the comparative historical analyses reviewed in this book suggest that the basis for such admissions is either external or internal pressure – or preferably a combination of both.

Now, is it possible, based on this observation, to identify the formula for development success in the contemporary world? This question is not dealt with systematically in this book, which primarily uncovers the aspects of the past that must be understood in order to make such an attempt. However, the overall message that forms is that it is not possible for the West – or for developed countries more generally – to simply graft administrative, political, and economic development onto other countries. Genuine development must come from within, historically as a general consequence of competition – external and internal alike – but in our time more than anything else due to an efficient balance of domestic power between competing groups. The somewhat disheartening conclusion is that it is difficult to imagine successful state-formation processes in many regions of the contemporary world. As far as timeliness is concerned, this book may above all cast light on some of the limitations in this respect in the developing countries of our day.

Notes

1 For a relatively similar historical overview of comparative historical analysis – or, rather, the works covered in Parts II and III – see Lange (2012, Chapter 2).
2 Later in the book we shall become acquainted with a revisionist agenda that – among other things – sees this restlessness as evidence of the failure of the West as civilization (e.g., Wong 1997). From this perspective, both the Chinese and the Islamic civilizations are superior to the European civilization, as they have created stable social orders that precisely do not change; they were at ease with themselves, so to speak, whereas the West could never be comfortable in its own surroundings. Here, the Chinese introversion and conservatism are viewed as a strength rather than a weakness (cf. Hall 2001, 493).
3 Including the European settler colonies in North America and Oceania.
4 'Western Christendom' refers to the area that has historically referred religiously to the Papacy in Rome – that is, the Roman Catholic and later also Protestant regions of Europe. This area is thus distinguished from the part of Europe that was converted to Christianity from the east and which today constitutes the 'Orthodox' or 'Eastern' Christendom. Geographically, in other words, the distinction is between Western and Central Europe, on the one side, and Eastern Europe and the Balkans, on the other.

PART I

Big questions

1

STATE FORMATION, REGIME CHANGE, AND ECONOMIC DEVELOPMENT

In the introduction, I made clear that the aim of this book is to answer – or at least partially answer – some of the 'big questions' of social science (cf. Mahoney and Rueschemeyer 2003, 7; Skocpol 2003, 409). More particularly, the book revolves around three general questions:

(1) What are the causes of the state-formation process that has culminated in the modern territorial state/nation-state?
(2) What are the causes of the regime change process that led to the introduction of representative institutions and later culminated in modern democracy?
(3) What are the causes of the economic development that has culminated in the modern market economy?

To further substantiate and narrow down these three questions, this chapter considers the key concepts of state, regime, and market economy.

The state

Most people probably feel about the state like Augustine felt about time; we instinctively seem to know what the word covers, but when asked directly we struggle to provide a clear definition. The most important distinction in this area is between 'minimalist' and 'maximalist' definitions of the state. The minimalist definition of the state renders it possible to trace the first states six thousand years back in time (Diamond 1999[1997]). According to this view, the state is any organization of society that is more sophisticated than a tribe. Charles Tilly (1990, 1), to whom we will return in Chapter 9, has formalized the minimalist definition as follows: states are 'coercion-wielding organizations that are distinct from households and kinship groups and exercise clear priority in some respects over all other organizations within substantial territories'.

Max Weber offers a more maximalist definition of the state as an entity that possesses a monopoly on the legitimate use of force within a specific territory. This definition, at the very least, includes a monopoly on force internally, territoriality, and sovereignty externally (Poggi 2013, 64–65). This might not initially appear particularly demanding, but the legitimate monopoly on force implies 'modern' organs such as the military, the bureaucracy, the courts, and the police. The legitimacy of the modern, territorial state means that the citizenry normally follows its rules, partly because these rules are embedded in a rule-of-law mind-set and partly due to the presence of a common political community (Held 2006[1987], 131; see also Poggi 2013). This kind of power apparatus has not existed in the vast majority of the states that fit the minimalist definition. What Weber has in mind is the modern, territorial state as it has emerged in Europe since the High Middle Ages (Poggi 2013, 64).

Various scholars base their work on Weber's definition, although many add specific elements that they claim are underspecified in Weber (see, e.g., Skocpol 1985, 7; Gill 2003, 2–6; O'Donnell 2010, 51–53).[1] If we accept Weber's definition, the state is a relatively recent (Western) European invention. A brief foray into the etymology of the word illustrates this.[2] The word 'state' is terminologically the same throughout pretty much all of Western Europe. The Italians use *stato*, the Spanish *estado*, the French *état*, and the Germans *Staat*.[3] All these words stem from the Latin STATVS. With the rediscovery of Roman Law in the High Middle Ages, this word was first used to describe the legal position of certain corporate groups, such as the nobility, the king, the church, and later the townsmen. However, the word STATVS lost its attachment to status groups and was instead linked to the power apparatus and legal order in society – that is, what we today understand as the state.[4]

A common observation is that the modern European state distinguishes itself from all others in terms of its basic legalism (Finer 1997a, 1300–1301). Here, it is interesting to compare the word with the corresponding Russian, *gosudarstvo*, meaning 'rule'. As Hosking (2001, 91) points out, there is no distinction in the Russian use between personal ownership and political authority. In other words, the state is something that is more general and impersonal in Western political thought. It is this sense – that is, the state in this *gestalt* – that Weber attempts to capture with his celebrated definition.

This modern territorial state or nation-state can to some extent be seen as the negation of the much looser feudal state of the Middle Ages (Poggi 1978). The state-like entities of the Middle Ages did not distinguish between public and private authority and had fluid territorial boundaries (because vassal relations cut across nascent borders). The modern state, on the other hand, is defined by the distinction between public and private affairs and by its territoriality (Finer 1997b, 1265; Poggi 2013). As Gill (2003, 4) points out, the Weberian state actually distinguishes itself from all other – earlier – state forms in its ability to penetrate society. At the same time, it is both externally and internally sovereign (Gill 2003, 5).

The former entails that the modern territorial state is part of a relatively stable state system. As mentioned in the introduction, this external pressure has been crucial for the emergence of the state. The latter, Weber observes, means that the state has an internal monopoly on the legitimate use of physical force. The point is that the modern state is not marked by internal conflicts between competing groups or by the presence of armed groups within the territory, as was the case in the European Middle Ages. No other organizations within the state – for example, mafia groups – have a legitimate right to use coercive means. But this internal power monopoly is couched in international competition with other states (Held 2006[1987], 130). This geopolitical competition is at the core of Otto Hintze's (1975[1906]) pioneering understanding of the emergence of the modern state, to which we will return in Chapter 5.

The emergence of this modern, Western European form of the state is the primary focus of this book, but I will occasionally use the minimalist definition in order to trace the state further back in time. That is, the book makes use of two different definitions of the state – first, a minimalist definition, which sees a state as any territorial organization that is more sophisticated than a tribe (cf. Tilly's definition above). Explicit mention will be made in the text when this definition is applied. All other instances refer to the Weberian definition of the modern, territorial state.

The explanatory quest is, then, to understand the process that, in Weber's words, has rationalized state power. In this context, it is important to note that the Weberian definition is agnostic in relation to the regime. In short, whether a state is democratic or not has no bearing on whether it is modern (Gill 2003, 6). This brings us to the second general research question of this book.

The regime

The easiest way to distinguish between state and regime form is to remain with Weber. Mazzuca (2010a) uses Weber's body of writing to establish a relatively simple distinction, which is important in this context: the state is defined by the *exercise of power*; the regime, by *access to power*. That the exercise of power is the core of the state is apparent in the section above. However, the control over the state power apparatus is regulated via the regime. In other words, in an autocracy there is one set of rules for access to power; in a democracy, another. Ertman (1997), who is discussed in Chapter 9, captures this two-dimensional distinction in a four-fold table (see Table 1.1).

TABLE 1.1 Ertman's typology over states in eighteenth-century Europe

		Political regime	
		Absolutist	*Constitutional*
Character of state infrastructure	Patrimonial	Patrimonial absolutism	Patrimonial constitutionalism
	Bureaucratic	Bureaucratic absolutism	Bureaucratic constitutionalism

The point Ertman (1997, 6–10) makes is that both constitutional and autocratic regimes can be combined with different state types – in this case, respectively, a bureaucratic and a patrimonial one (another distinction borrowed from Weber). Ertman's constitutional regime is defined by the parliament acting as co-legislator together with the ruler (see also Finer 1997b, 1307). This regime form has also been termed the 'polity of Estates' (Myers 1975).

A voluminous literature has touted the representative institutions (aka polity of Estates) described by Ertman as a necessary condition for the nineteenth- and twentieth-century advent of modern democracy. These institutions – the Estates or parliaments and diets of the High Middle Ages – represent the first part of Brian M. Downing's (1992, 10) definition of 'medieval constitutionalism'. As presented in Chapter 9, Downing traces modern representative democracy back to these institutions. Robert A. Dahl (1989, 215), the greatest democracy theorist of the twentieth century, has phrased it in the following way:

> The first successful efforts to democratize the national state typically occurred in countries with existing legislative bodies that were intended to represent certain fairly distinctive social interests: aristocrats, commoners, the landed interest, the commercial interest, and the like. As movements toward greater democratization gained force, therefore, the design for a 'representative' legislature did not have to be spun from gossamer fibers of abstract democratic ideas; concrete legislatures and representatives, undemocratic though they were, already existed.

The representative institutions/Estates originated around the year 1200 on the Iberian Peninsula and spread in the following centuries throughout Western and Central Europe – an area also referred to as Western Christendom in this book (Myers 1975, 24). Tellingly, the entire period 1200–1789 has been referred to as the age of the 'polity of Estates' by some scholars (e.g., Myers 1975).

In recent years, there has been a strong focus on the importance of representative institutions for state-building, regime change, and economic development (Stasavage 2010; 2011; 2014; Van Zanden et al. 2012; Blaydes and Chaney 2013). In this connection, scholars have taken note of some crucial differences within the category. An older distinction, which goes back to Otto Hintze (1962[1930]), has been made between strong bicameral parliaments, such as the English case and weak three-chamber parliaments (*Dreikuriensystem*) as found in, e.g., France (see also Ertman 1997). Stasavage (2010) has more specifically identified the meeting frequency and prerogatives of the representative institutions, including whether or not they had a veto over the imposition of taxes and the right to audit the monarch's use of the resulting revenues. These distinctions play a major role in Ertman's (1997) and Stasavage's (2010) respective explanations of the influence of representative institutions on state formation and deficit finance in the High and Late Middle Ages.

The representative institutions are thus important for the state formation processes in the European past as well as the democratization that unfolds after 1800.

Both processes are of interest in this book. However, the slightly narrow focus on representative institutions means that the political gains of the twentieth century, including equal and universal suffrage, lie beyond the scope of the book. Another feature of modern democracy with roots in the Middle Ages, namely constitutionalism, *is* relevant, however. The constitutional element – as indicated by the qualifying adjective in the term '*liberal* democracy' (Sartori 1987) – is historically peculiar to Western Christendom and can, as mentioned above, be traced all the way back to the High Middle Ages (Hintze 1975[1931]; Downing 1992; Sabetti 2004). This unique feature is placed in relief by the fact that even the absolute states of Europe (with the exception of Russia) were legalistic and marked by the presence of corporative barriers blocking the exercise of power (Finer 1997b, 1298–1303, 1419).

In constitutional regimes, the exercise of power is subject to constitutional barriers. In contemporary parlance, this means that there are hard and fast rules for how laws are to be formulated and passed, and that a higher law (the constitution) guarantees certain basic rights (Sartori 1987, 308). Until the rise of the modern constitutions towards the end of the eighteenth century and the beginning of the nineteenth century, these barriers were not based on written laws, but the logic was basically the same. If we supplement the constitutional element with the demand for political competition over the power to rule[5] – through a form of election to representative institutions, albeit often based on a very limited suffrage – and the existence of modern freedoms such as freedom of expression, association, and assembly, we have more or less captured modern democracy as it emerged in nineteenth-century Western Europe. The point is that the elements of this regime form can be traced all the way back to the Middle Ages (Dahl 1989).

To sum up, the primary purpose of the treatment of regime change in this book is to shed light on the development of representative institutions and constitutionalism that has marked Europe since the Middle Ages and that not even the advent of absolutism after 1600 could erase.

The market economy

The book reviews a number of studies that aim to explain the emergence of the modern market economy in Western Europe.[6] The common premise of these analyses is that the market economy has caused the explosive growth in recent centuries (see, e.g., North and Thomas 1973, 1) and brought about today's global disparity in prosperity levels. North and Thomas (1973, 1) see this concept as essentially defined by the protection of private property and ownership rights, as economic efficiency is practically automatic when private property is protected. Jones (2008[1981], 245) touches on the same idea but formulates it in more general terms when he points to the eradication of legal arbitrariness as essential for the modern market economy. In Western Europe, arbitrariness was replaced by stable law enforcement, which rendered it possible to invest and harvest the fruits of these investments. Landes (1998, 59) also thinks along these lines when he explains effective, market-based competition with the abolition of the arbitrary exercise of power (265).

There is much more about this in Chapters 12 and 13. In general, we can say that from the perspective of these authors, the market economy will unfold when the authorities ensure the framework for rational economic behaviour. If labour is free of barriers created by, for example, serfdom or guild privileges, and if the authorities prevent attacks on private property, productivity increases will ensue. This situation guarantees that the 'invisible hand' described by Scottish economist Adam Smith in *The Wealth of Nations* can come into effect. The consequences include increased market activity based on a division of labour. When this situation extends across national borders, it is possible to harvest the comparative advantages accruing from trade as described by economist David Ricardo. The market economy can be defined more technically as an economic form of organization in which decisions about production, investments, and distribution are based on supply and demand and where the market mechanism spontaneously sets the prices for goods and services (i.e., without public intervention).

Weber goes beyond this point, yet again serving as the best guide. As Collins (1986, 85) has pointed out, Weber was interested in explaining the emergence of a market economy that operated as predicted by the neo-classical economists, Smith and Ricardo in particular. However, in contrast to these economists, Weber did not regard this market economy as a universal model of economic interaction. In his view, it was a historical product that had recently emerged in the West. On that basis, Weber distinguished between different forms of capitalism. A more traditional kind of market exchange is found in all societies, but a market economy capable of meeting the needs of all of its citizens on a daily basis is found only in the West from the mid-nineteenth century (Weber 2003[1927], 276). For Weber, this is modern capitalism, defined by a rational organization of labour and the lifting of restrictions on economic interaction (2003[1927], 313). This kind of a rational capitalism first and foremost rests on calculability, which again presupposes the existence of the previously described modern state and its systematic and impartial enforcement of laws (339). This rational capitalism – the modern market economy – constitutes the field of investigation for the last question addressed in this book.

Conclusions

Three major questions form the framework of this book. The first concerns the emergence of the modern state, the second the emergence of representative institutions and ultimately modern democracy, and the third the emergence of the modern market economy. In this chapter, I have attempted to define the subject area for each of these three questions. My guide here was above all Max Weber. It is no coincidence that Weber figures prominently in this context. As we shall see in Part II, he also occupies an important position in the attempt to analyse the posed questions. Subsequent authors have obviously not accepted Weber's answers uncritically. However, they have largely taken over his questions (together with many of his concepts). Weber's greatest scientific legacy is thus that his research question has proven far more durable than his answer – as should be the case in so far as science is cumulative.

This book very much adopts Weber's focus. Recall here that Weber's great endeavour was to understand why Europe had modernized politically, economically, and with respect to the state. This European modernization or – in Weber's terms – rationalization process has brought about the modern world. Samuel Finer, in his three-volume *The History of Government* (1997b, 1475), categorically declares that all the common 'features of the modern state are, without any exception whatsoever, derived from the West'. This entity – the European nation-state or territorial state – has in turn shaped the world as we know it, as it has displaced all other forms of government, including in particular city-states and empires (Tilly 1990). Much the same can be said of the European development of democracy and the modern market economy, both of which today set the standard for developing countries (Møller and Skaaning 2013). To understand the modern world – or at least the aspirations of people in the modern world – we need to elucidate the European roots of the modern state, modern democracy, and the modern market economy. That is, we need to answer the question, 'Why Europe?'

However, before we are able to do so in earnest, another introductory exercise is necessary. As Mahoney and Rueschemeyer (2003, 7) point out, the 'big questions' are closely tied to a specific field of research: comparative historical analysis. The next chapter provides an account of this field, within which we shall identify analyses that attempt to answer the three big questions posed above.

Notes

1 Technically speaking, this can be seen as that which Collier and Levitsky (1997) refer to as *precising* a definition. The point is that Skocpol and others argue that Weber implicitly also had these enhancements in mind – or at least that his definition only makes sense if other things are included. Therefore, they do not conceptually change the Weberian definition by bringing these additions to light.

2 As Sartori (1984, 41) has pointed out, there is a considerable amount of historical data in the etymology (see also Pocock 2003[1975], 3–80).

3 The English *state* is also terminologically identical, but semantically it has a slightly different meaning, since *government* is often used to refer to that which in Continental Europe is referred to as 'state'.

4 The term 'state' did not develop directly from STATVS but rather developed from the derivative Italian *stato*. According to many researchers, we first encounter the term in this sense in Machiavelli's *The Prince* where the noun *lo stato* appears 115 times (Hansen 1998, 138). However, as Skinner (1989) has pointed out, *stato* refers only to the government for Machiavelli, not the political community in the more general sense. On that background, Skinner argues that Bodin and Hobbes are the first to use 'state' (*Estat/state*) in the modern sense. Others have challenged even this interpretation by pointing out that Bodin uses the word in reference to the constitution or form of government (monarchy, aristocracy, and democracy), whereas he refers to the political community as *République*. Moreover, Bodin sometimes uses *Estat* in the older sense of 'estate' (Hansen 1998, 107, 138–141). However, it is beyond dispute that Hobbes uses 'state' in the modern sense in the preface to *Leviathan* and that Montesquieu also does so in *The Spirit of the Laws*. More generally, we can note that the term 'state' was clearly tied to the modern concept of the state around 1750 (Hansen 1998, 108–112).

5 The classic formulation is found in Schumpeter (1974[1942], 269).

6 In addition to Max Weber's seminal analysis, which will be discussed in Chapter 4, these contributions include North and Thomas (1973); Landes (1998); Clark (2007); Bernstein (2008), and Jones (2008[1981]). A number of these works are discussed in Chapter 12.

2

COMPARATIVE HISTORICAL ANALYSIS

The works we shall consider in this book belong within the research field referred to as 'comparative historical analysis' (Mahoney and Rueschemeyer 2003; Lange 2012). Such analysis is by definition both comparative and diachronic. This is a common feature of all of the analyses in the genre. It is hardly surprising that attempts to answer big questions about state formation, regime change, and economic development are normally based on large-scale historical comparisons. As we shall see in this chapter, however, different authors have very different approaches to such comparisons. Moreover, in what follows I argue that the research field is broader than it is often given credit for.

Historical sociology and comparative historical analysis

Comparative historical analysis constitutes a subset of the genre of historical sociology (cf. Mahoney and Rueschemeyer 2003, 11). Historical sociology is concerned with how human societies have developed throughout history. The focus is on complex processes, and the aim is to explain a host of different phenomena, from war to the character of the state to economic disparities. A number of well-known names in the social sciences have contributed to this research agenda. In fact, the first steps in the social sciences were taken within this genre. Among the first generations of sociologists, we thus encounter the renowned trio of Max Weber, Karl Marx, and Émile Durkheim. A bit further back in time, we find the French political scientist Alexis de Tocqueville. A selection of the most influential researchers in recent times includes the quartet consisting of Charles Tilly, Michael Foucault, Michael Mann, and Norbert Elias. One might even argue that Niccolò Machiavelli's work belongs within historical sociology – possibly even that he was responsible for it in the first place (Coppedge 2012, 130).

I do not include Machiavelli's work in this book. From the more recent quartet as well as the older quartet, we will deal only with Tocqueville, Weber, and Tilly.

Neither Marx, Durkheim, Foucault, Mann, nor Elias belongs to the subset of historical sociology that I refer to as comparative historical analysis. These otherwise formidable theorists do not in the same manner establish and test systematic causal relationships using empirical comparisons across time and space. Instead, they have a tendency either to expound theory without applying it based on empirical comparisons or, alternatively, to use more narrative or interpretive methods. The sole use of the historical narrative falls outside comparative historical analysis for the simple reason that no systematic use of comparisons is attempted; interpretative methods – particularly of the more recent, postmodern kind – fall more generally outside of the field because they do not in the same manner seek to identify cause-and-effect relationships (Mahoney and Rueschemeyer 2003, 15; Lange 2012, 5). Moreover, some of the aforementioned authors do not deal as clearly with specific historical processes as the authors examined below. This is most obvious in Durkheim, who often focuses on more general processes that are not rooted in time and space in the same manner.[1]

If we turn this negative delimitation around, we find ourselves with a definition of comparative historical analysis. According to Mahoney and Rueschemeyer (2003, 6), the field revolves around three things: analyses of causal relationships, historical processes, and a relatively limited number of cases. Tilly (1984) phrases it in the following way: the purpose is to get close to cases (*concrete analysis*) and consider the significance of sequences (*historical analysis*). In other words, comparative historical analysis should be seen as a general research approach – not a common theoretical base or the use of a specific research technique (Skocpol 2003, 419; Mahoney 2003b, 337; Coppedge 2012, Chapter 5).

In this context, the timing of events is crucial. As Tilly (1984, 14) famously put it, '*when* things happen within a sequence affects *how* they happen'. In this sense, we are products of the past, as former outcomes affect future outcomes. This point is echoed in several of the analyses in Parts II–V of the book.

Skocpol's division

What does this negative delimitation mean in practice? In the first half of the 1980s, American political scientist Theda Skocpol went to great lengths to describe the contents of and diversity within historical sociology (Skocpol and Somers 1980; Skocpol 1984b; 1984c; see also chapter 12). Skocpol started with the observation that this entire research agenda – represented by the great classics mentioned above – was almost shelved as a result of the behavioural revolution after World War II (Skocpol 1984b, 5). Instead of producing concrete historical analyses, most researchers tried to apply Talcott Parson's systems theory in general and Gabriel Almond's so-called structural functionalism in particular (Lange 2012, 27–28).

Parson's treatment of Weber is telling. As Anderson (1990, 53) has pointed out, Parsons concluded his strongly Weber-inspired *The Structure of Social Action* from 1937 by lamenting Weber's interest in comparative historical analysis. According to Parsons, this derailed Weber from developing more general analytical theories of social action. Parson's assessment is illustrative for the approach to history that prevailed in political science in the decades after World War II. In this period, researchers tended to either ignore the major macro-historical questions or view them in the light of ahistorical, functionalistic theory (cf. Mahoney 2003a, 151).

In the 1960s and 1970s, there was a reaction against this ahistorical approach to social processes (see, e.g., Mills 1959). As described in Chapter 6, Barrington Moore paved the way with his *Social Origins of Democracy and Dictatorship* (Ross et al. 1998, 4–7; Lange 2012, 30). In the 1970s, Charles Tilly followed up on this contribution, and, in the 1980s, historical sociology suddenly became a blossoming field (Skocpol 1984c, 356). But it was also a diverse field. Skocpol and Somers (1980) divide historical-sociological analyses into three categories:

- *Parallel comparative history*: in this approach, a theory is first presented and subsequently demonstrated to be in accordance with a considerable number of historical cases. All other differences between these cases are used to emphasize their theoretically relevant consistency. This is a purely deductive method, as it begins with the presented theory, while the empirical data makes its appearance only to demonstrate the validity of the theory.
- *Contrast-oriented comparative history*: the point here is that the comparisons – particularly comparisons with established ideal types – are used to show how each case is unique. The intention is, so to speak, to respect the integrity of the historical cases, and there is no direct attempt to generalize. Rather, the aim is to shed light on the limitations of generalizations. This purely inductive method, which begins with the existing historical discrepancies, comes closest to the historians' practice.
- *Macro-analytic comparative history*: in this third approach, systematic comparisons of historical events are used to test existing hypotheses/theories or to develop new generalizations. This is a combination of deductive and inductive elements, as the researcher shifts back and forth between cases and hypotheses. The starting point is always a concrete research question – a why – and the objective is to establish configurations (i.e., combinations of characteristics) of causal factors which can explain it.

There are almost no existing analyses that are completely pure examples of any of the three approaches. Characteristically, Skocpol and Somers place a number of authors somewhere between the points in a triangle consisting of these three points. Nevertheless, with Skocpol's help, let us try to label the categories. With reference to the best-known studies, S.N. Eisenstadt's (1963) *The Political Systems of Empires*, Perry Anderson's (1974b) *Lineages of the Absolutist State*, and Charles Tilly's (1990) *Coercion, Capital, and European States AD 990–1990* come closest to Skocpol and Somers' first category. Within the second category, we find several of Rheinhard Bendix's major works, including *Kings or People* from 1978. Tilly (1984) rather aptly refers to this approach as 'individualizing analysis' – that is, a desire for the individual or the specific. Finally, the third category includes a string of prominent analyses, including Skocpol's (1979) own *States and Social Revolutions*, Barrington Moore Jr.'s

(1991[1966]) *Social Origins of Dictatorship and Democracy*, and more recent analyses such as Brian M. Downing's (1992) *The Military Revolution and Political Change* and Thomas Ertman's (1997) *Birth of the Leviathan*.

The three approaches and comparative method

In Part II and III we will return to a number of these studies. Here, I will instead focus on the methodological differences between the three approaches. As mentioned, they all deal with a plurality of historical cases. That said, they do not make use of comparisons in the same manner. This much becomes clear when we consider the following point: we normally make comparisons in order to control – that is, to hold alternative ('competing') causes constant (Sartori 1991). However, this logic does not characterize all three approaches.

In fact, *contrast-oriented comparative history* is characterized by the absence of comparative control. The point here is actually that we can never keep causes constant through comparisons as any similarities effectively drown in the fundamental differences. Thus, the individual cases say nothing about other cases, for which reason it is not possible to approximate the experimental logic of control through comparisons. Paradoxically, the same goes for *parallel comparative history*. Here, cases are selected for the very reason that they fit the theory. In other words, there is no attempt to 'keep all other things equal' by systematically testing alternative explanations. The empirical data serves to demonstrate the general validity of the theory – not to test it. *Macro-analytic comparative history* alone rests directly on the logic of comparative control.

Between the idiographic and nomothetic extremes

One way of understanding this difference is to plot two extreme points, the idiographic and the nomothetic. We can do this, perhaps a little unconventionally, with the help of references to two renowned works of literature. In Milan Kundera's *The Unbearable Lightness of Being* (2004[1984]), 7–8, 216, the narrator repeatedly circles around the opportunity to use comparisons to generalize. His clear position is that such comparisons do not make sense outside of the natural sciences, including human life and history:

> We can never know what to want, because, living only one life, we can neither compare it with our previous lives nor perfect it in our lives to come. . . . There is no means for testing which decision is better, because there is no basis for comparison . . . *Einmal ist keinmal.* What happens but once, says the German adage, might as well not have happened at all. . . . History is similar to individual lives in this respect. There is only one history of the Czechs. . . . If Czech history could be repeated, we should of course find it desirable to test the other possibility each time and compare the results. Without such an experiment, all considerations of this kind remain a game of hypotheses.

This is a purely idiographic approach to the social sciences and history. Any social event is unique and therefore cannot be used to say anything about other incidents – for which reason we can never generalize, only describe.

Let us look at the opposite position. In Ivan Turgenev's *Fathers and Sons* (1972 [1861], 160), the anarchist Basarof repeatedly expresses a pure faith in the possibility to use the sciences to construct societal regularities. At one point, he says:

> All men are similar, in soul as well as in body. Each of us has a brain, spleen, heart and lungs of similar construction; and the so-called moral qualities are the same in all of us – the slight variations are of no importance. It is enough to have one single human specimen in order to judge all the others. People are like trees in a forest: no botanist would dream of studying each individual birchtree.

The understanding here is diametrically opposed to that which we encounter in the passage from Kundera. For Basarof, no social event is unique; to the contrary, they are characterized by fundamental uniformity. This is the nomothetic extreme, where we are exclusively working with general considerations and the individual cases in and of themselves can teach us nothing. As Gerring (2004, 351) points out, the consequence of the two extreme points is more or less the same with respect to comparative method. In the idiographic extreme, we cannot use the individual cases to cast light on other cases, for which reason we can never do anything other than describe the basic differences in the world around us. In the nomothetic extreme, we would never choose to deal with specific cases, as there are no cases that claim more attention than others.

Comparative historical analysis

The important point here is that the use of the comparative method, including comparative historical method, is based on an intermediate position between these two extremes (Lange 2012, 2). More succinctly, the social sciences cannot aspire to the ideal from the natural sciences about establishing general 'laws' capable of explaining individual events (see Kitschelt 2003, 54). The comparisons, at most, provide an opportunity to make *middle range* generalizations (see, however, Coppedge 2012).

Let us use the two examples to illustrate this. Obviously the history of the Czechs – or individual life, for that matter – cannot be repeated. Kundera's narrator is correct as far as that goes. However, from the perspective of the social sciences we would still disagree with his message. It is possible to compare Czech history with that of other countries – or Czech history at different points in time. Doing so, we approximate a comparative logic of control, as the various cases we are comparing are characterized by a combination of similarities that we are able to hold constant and a number of differences that (by definition) vary. This is the opposite of Basarof's position. For the point is not that the two cases are completely identical; were this the case, we would get nothing out of comparing them, as there is no variation. The point is merely that they are similar enough so that we are to some extent able to control – again, that they display a combination of similarities and differences.

This brings us back to the three approaches. As Skocpol and Somers (1980) point out, cases can never confirm theories in, respectively, *contrast-oriented comparative history* and *parallel comparative history*. As regards the former, the whole point is that the fundamental historical differences rule out generalizations. As regards the latter, the historical cases can only illustrate the theory, as alternative explanations are not ruled out via comparisons. In this book, we are not interested in following either of these two paths. When I refer to comparative historical analysis, it will first and foremost be what Skocpol calls *macro-analytic comparative history*. Elsewhere, she actually refers to this approach as comparative historical analysis (1979, 36; 1984b, 384), exactly like Mahoney and Rueschemeyer (2003) twenty years later.

It is thus first and foremost the analyses that are based on genuine empirical comparisons that will be treated in Part III of this book. This makes it possible to include two other categories of works in addition to the authors mentioned above. First, a number of classics: particularly the authorships of Alexis de Tocqueville, Max Weber, Joseph A. Schumpeter, Otto Hintze, and Marc Bloch, most of whom Mahoney and Rueschemeyer (2003, 3) also place in this field. These authorships distinguish themselves by their use of the comparative method, and we will discuss some of the resulting contributions in Chapters 3–5. Second, a number of more recent contributions that attempt to explain either the emergence of modern capitalism in Europe and its spread beyond the European continent (Chapters 11–13), the emergence of representative institutions in the High Middle Ages in Europe (Chapter 10), state formation outside of Europe (Chapters 14–15), or the effects of Protestantism on state-building and regime change (Chapter 16).

However, as suggested above, Skocpol and Somers exaggerate the positions to some degree. We find a telling example in Perry Anderson's *Lineages of the Absolutist State* (1974b). Skocpol and Somers place Anderson's work somewhere between *contrast-oriented comparative history* and *parallel comparative history*. There are a number of good reasons for placing Anderson here: he wants to demonstrate the validity of his general theory, while at the same time noting the particular characteristics of the individual cases in terms of a number of established theoretical ideal-types (feudalism and absolutism). That said, as presented in Chapter 7, we find at least two attempts at genuine empirical comparisons for the purpose of control in the work. In other words, some of the analyses that Skocpol and Somers categorize under *contrast-oriented comparative history* and *parallel comparative history* cannot entirely be detached from the comparative logic of control. We thus find this way of thinking to be a secondary strategy, even among many of the authors claiming to shy away from the comparative method. For this reason among others, I will confront some of these analyses with the logic of comparative control in Parts II and III – thereby also including them in the field of comparative historical analysis.

I also go beyond Skocpol and the limitations found in Mahoney and Rue-schemeyer (2003) in another, very important, sense. I have already made clear that these researchers emphasize that comparative historical analysis investigates relatively few cases in depth. In fact, Mahoney and Rueschemeyer (2003, 15) go so far as to exclude, per definition, statistical analysis from the field. Coppedge (2012, Chapter 5) has recently accepted this limitation in a fascinating examination of the field. In my opinion, however, it is not possible to sustain this position (see also Lange 2012, 3–4). As we shall see in Part IV of this book, statistical analysis has been the most common method for recent scholarship on state formation, economic development, and regime change. At the same time, it is difficult to see the rationale in this limitation as statistical methods draw upon the same basic logic of control as comparative methods. I will therefore include analyses that make use of statistical methods – often on a relatively large number of cases – in the examination of comparative historical analyses presented in this book that attempt to answer the three big questions. More particularly, the book discusses such works by David Stasavage (see Chapter 10) and Daron Acemoglu and James Robinson (see Chapter 13).[2]

Finally, another issue deserves mentioning. An oft-used procedure in comparative historical analysis has been to shift back and forth between concepts, indicators, and scores in order to change the concepts after having become more acquainted with the empirical variation. This has actually been hailed as one of the great advantages of comparative historical analysis (e.g., Mahoney 2004, 95). Coppedge (2012) has objected that this renders it impossible to carry out actual tests of the theories that have been developed within this tradition. A scientific analysis requires that the theories are tested against new empirical evidence instead of merely changing the theory so that it fits with the analysed empirical data. Seen from this perspective, comparative historical analysis merely amounts to theory-generating exercises that do not in themselves include some form of test of their arguments (Coppedge 2012, 148–149).

One of the criterions for comparative historical analysis established above is that it actually – via empirical comparisons – appraises the validity of theories. For that very reason, it is worth keeping Coppedge's objection in mind. That said, his criticism goes too far. It may well be warranted in the light of Mahoney's (2004) unsustainable methodological position, and there has undoubtedly been a certain tendency towards tailoring theory to the facts in comparative historical analysis. But the persistent endeavour to apply theoretical claims by studying historical developments cannot be written off as purely theory-generating exercises. We are surely dealing with – admittedly imperfect – attempts at testing theories on empirical data.

Structuralism and its critics

Enough about the methodological logic! A couple of words about the theoretical approach behind comparative historical analysis are also warranted and will allow us to say something about the development in the field. Mahoney (2003a, 151–152) has rightly pointed out that comparative historical analysis is permeated with the approach he refers to as 'structuralism'. According to Mahoney, we can trace this approach back to Moore's (1991[1966]) pioneering work, which we will study more closely in Chapter 6. Skocpol (1973) argues that Moore's renowned book is best understood as a Marxist analysis (see also Rothman 1970, 62; Femia 1972, 40–42). This point is readily understandable, as Moore links class struggle based on the relations of production to the political superstructure (democracy versus dictatorship) and vehemently rejects any and every kind of cultural explanation, including those of Max Weber. Nevertheless, it is still better to say that Moore 're-discovers' Marx's structural approach (more on this in Chapter 6).

It is for this very reason that, as Mahoney (2003a) points out, it would appear to be more correct to talk about a meta-approach – structuralism – that emphasizes how combinations of social structures set the framework for the choices made by agents (see also Coppedge 2012, Chapter 5). In addition to class structures, Mahoney highlights the state infrastructure and international structures. This structural focus dominates at the expense of cultural explanations and agency explanations, respectively (Mahoney 2003a, 151–152). Perry Anderson (1990, 72) says something similar when he points out that much of modern historical sociology – he is thinking about Giddens, Mann, Runciman, and Gellner – challenges Marxism but does so via a systematic dialogue with the same approach.

That structuralism prevails is no wonder, given that comparative historical analysis deals with general processes that measure time in centuries. A good way to put this into perspective is to go back to the basic problem of political science: the structure–agency problem. Most people can probably come up with a number of battles that are touted to have changed the course of history. A selection of such battles would likely include the renowned 'last stand' of Leonidas and the three hundred Spartans against the army of Persian king Xerxes at Thermopylae in the year 480 BC, Karl Martel's victory over the troops of the Umayyad caliph at Poitiers (Tours) in 732 AD, and the Swedish warrior king Gustav Adolf's victory over the Habsburg troops at Breitenfeld 1631 and Lützen 1632. The Battle of Thermopylae allowed the Greek army to evacuate to the Peloponnese, after which the Athenian statesman Themistocles lured the Persians into a game-changing naval battle in the Salamis Bay, thereby derailing Xerxes' effort to subjugate Greece. The Battle of Poitiers put an end to the Muslim advance on Western Europe. And, finally, Gustav Adolf's intervention in the Thirty Years' War prevented the Counter-Reformation from sweeping through Northern Europe as it was to sweep through Central Europe in the same period.

In all these cases, the course of history would appear to have balanced on a knife's edge – and the intervention of certain actors to have been decisive. Based on these examples, some might even be tempted to launch a kind of 'great man in history' thesis capable of explaining the course of history on the basis of the existence of formidable personalities and their decisions.

The important point is that all of these analyses in Part III shy away from such an agency perspective. Though class relations is the only structural factor that is included in almost all of the studies in this genre (Coppedge 2012, 135), comparative historical analysis – as a whole – has traditionally applied a strong structural focus whereby the actors are at most seen as a kind of intermediate variable that serves to shed light on the causal mechanism on the individual level. Gregory M. Luebbert (1991, 306), in *Liberalism, Fascism, or Social Democracy*, which is not included in this book (but see Møller and Skaaning 2013, Chapter 8), captures this approach with the following categorical assessment: 'One of the cardinal lessons of the story I have told is that leadership and meaningful choice played no role in the outcomes'.

To be more precise: the comparative historical analysis included in this book applies such a form of structuralism. In the past decade, there has been a reaction against such structuralism. We find a recent attempt set this agenda in a special issue of *Comparative Political Studies* edited by Capoccia and Ziblatt (2010) about the 'historical turn' in democratization research. Basically, the aim here is the same as described above – that is, to manoeuvre between structures and agents. But for Capoccia and Ziblatt – and the other contributors to the special issue – the main emphasis is clearly on the latter (946).

Capoccia and Ziblatt (2010) call for a shift in the focus of comparative historical analysis from class structures[3] to religious and ethnic cleavages – at least in relation to democratization in Europe over the last two hundred years. Next, Capoccia and Ziblatt (2010) contend that we need to analyse the role played by ideas, including how ideas are transferred from one context to another. Finally, they argue that we can only genuinely understand the history of democracy in Europe if we understand how parties mediated and activated the structural divisions.

Against this background, Capoccia and Ziblatt (2010) recommend that we view regime change – but presumably also state formation or economic development – as 'an inherently long-run chain of linked episodes of struggles and negotiations over institutional change' (957). According to this perspective, democratization is not something that follows from an automatic 'translation' of background structural conditions of political development but rather a matter of the interaction between the actors within a context created by these structures. It is only by analysing the perceptions and actions of the actors in the critical phases that we are really able to get close to the causal mechanism (942). This can be seen as an attempt to understand the significance of actors' strategic choices, including their interpretations of the ideas of their day, while also appreciating coincidences that take place in connection with historical turning points.

What can we say about Capoccia and Ziblatt's (2010) new research agenda? This is an extremely interesting contribution, which will possibly revolutionize how comparative historical analyses are carried out.[4] The attentive reader will notice that I have not made 'structuralism' a defining feature of comparative historical analysis (cf. also Mahoney and Rueschemeyer 2003, 6): in principle, there is nothing to prevent the field from being re-oriented around a focus on agency. Indeed, in Part IV we will at least be dealing with a single work that clearly builds on an agency-perspective (see Chapter 14). For the time being, however, this is still a fledgling research agenda, and for this reason this book will above all deal with analyses characterized by different variations of Mahoney's structuralism.

Comparative historical methods

A few words on the more particular methods used in comparative historical analysis are also warranted. As Lange (2012, 180) puts it, one of the great advantages of comparative historical analysis is its 'methodological pluralism'. The works reviewed and discussed in this book do indeed use very different methods. Insofar as there is a common ground, it is that most authors combine some kind of cross-case method with some kind of within-case method. Indeed, this combination has been used to define comparative historical analysis (Lange 2012).

As already made clear, I also include works that do not explicitly carry out within-case analysis. Instead, I see the attempt to situate a historical analysis somewhere between the idiographic and the nomothethic extremes as the key requirement of comparative historical analysis. The included works do this in different ways. The cross-case methods include simple 'most-similar' (MSSD) and 'most-different' system designs (MDSD), explanatory typologies, and various statistical methods. The within-case methods include simple illustrations of causal mechanisms and variables, historical narratives, and genuine process-tracing.

This is not a book about methods, and I will not detail each of these methods.[5] With respect to the cross-case methods, the important thing is that they represent different ways of harnessing the logic of comparative control. MSSD and MDSD, two methods that were seminally described by John Stuart Mill (1843), do so via a simple logic of classification. If two cases are situated in the same class on a particular variable or condition, say, the level of affluence, this variable or condition is held constant (Sartori 1991). Explanatory typologies are based on the same logic but expand the 'property space' beyond the simple MSSD and MDSD – e.g., by operating with more than two outcomes on each condition. This allows typological analysis to identify configurations of causes or conditions that produce a particular outcome (see Møller and Skaaning 2016b). Finally, statistical analysis uses a mathematical logic to achieve a similar aim – that is, to investigate the effects of one or more variables while controlling for others. In the recent literature reviewed and discussed in Part IV, these analyses also make uses of so-called instrument variables, which are used to alleviate concerns about endogeneity.

The within-case methods focus on the causal mechanisms that underpin cross-case relationships. The simple illustrations can be seen as a way of rendering these mechanisms plausible via telling, case-specific examples. Historical narratives represent an attempt to make sense of a particular case-specific development by narrating it with a particular theoretical argument in mind in order to see if facts and theory fit. Finally, process tracing can be seen as an attempt to actually investigate the empirical purchase of causal mechanisms by probing evidence that must be present for the mechanisms to be operating.

Conclusions

Only a single point is left to mention, which we have already discussed in Chapter 1. The comparative method is obviously relevant not only for comparative historical analysis but for many other fields of social science. However, the research field covered in this book distinguishes itself from common practice in at least one respect. As Mahoney and Rueschemeyer (2003, 7–8) make clear, researchers in this field are often not interested in using the cases they are working with as a basis for wider generalizations. Skocpol (1984c, 376) also emphasizes this point when she makes clear that comparative historical analysis attempts to avoid 'the dogma of universality', instead merely attempting to draw generalizations within a specific context (cf. Lange 2012, 18).

For instance, a number of analyses in Parts II–IV only claim to be valid within Europe, parts thereof, or specific areas outside of Europe (e.g., Latin America or Sub-Saharan Africa). Such analyses do not aim to infer from a random sample to a more general population, as is the case in other branches of the social sciences. This enables scholars to choose cases on the basis of prior knowledge (instead of doing so randomly or at least on the basis of the independent variable[s]) – for example, by using rather simple comparative methods (Mahoney 2003b, 351). In other words, we should always clarify the 'scope conditions' for the generalizations in the comparative historical analyses.

Notes

1 It is this objection that keeps Durkheim's work out of this book. Durkheim thus definitely attempted to test his theories empirically; indeed, he did so from an arch-positivist position (see Smelser 1976; Ragin and Zaret 1983).

2 Lange (2012, 6) argues that Acemoglu and Robinson shy away from within-case analysis and therefore does not include them in the field of comparative historical analysis. However, this is to a large extent a matter of degree as some appreciation of the within-case level is surely present. It is telling that, elsewhere, Lange seems to find room for this work within the genre (e.g., 36–37).

3 It must be added here that Capoccia and Ziblatt (2010) are too one-sided in emphasizing the following three defining features of the earlier analyses in the field: (i) to explain long-term regime changes, (ii) to emphasize the internal variables at the expense of external, and (iii) further along these lines, above all else, to deal with class structures. This fits with the three analyses to which they refer, namely Luebbert (1991), Moore (1991[1966]), and – partly – Rueschemeyer et al. (1992). As we shall see in Parts II and III, however, external geopolitical pressure in particular is very prominent in the other 'classics' in the field, just like the church, the state, or civil society are often included as variables. Mahoney's more general 'structuralism' therefore appears more comprehensive.

4 Although personally I am rather critical about some of the core building blocks of this new contribution (see Møller 2012).

5 Readers who are interested in the intricacies of these methods are referred to Lange's (2012) recent book on the topic.

PART II

Classic comparative historical analyses

3

THE CLASSIC ANALYSES I

Tocqueville

Tocqueville has been called the first modern social scientist (Elster 2009). Many would probably disagree that the French aristocrat-cum-democrat deserves this title. It seems less controversial to argue that Tocqueville is the first modern social scientist who practiced comparative historical analysis in a systematic way. Tocqueville did this in his two famous works, *The Old Regime and the Revolution* (henceforth *OR*) and *Democracy in America* (henceforth *DA*) (Lange 2012, 23–24). Tocqueville set out to understand the forces driving the staggering democratization process that had transformed Western societies. The aim of this chapter is to present and discuss Tocqueville's analysis of regime change, including the notion of the general ascendancy of democracy and the particular juncture of the French Revolution.[1]

Tocqueville's notion of causality

The stepping stone for understanding Tocqueville's work is to understand his views on causality. Here, we can begin with what is surely one of the most quoted passages from Tocqueville's oeuvre, from his autobiographical fragment *Recollections*:

> I have come across men of letters, who have written history without taking part in public affairs, and politicians, who have only concerned themselves with producing events without thinking of describing them. I have observed that the first are always inclined to find general causes, whereas the others, living in the midst of disconnected daily facts, are prone to imagine that everything is attributable to particular incidents, and that the wires which they pull are the same that move the world. It is to be presumed that both are equally deceived.
>
> *(Recollections, I.i.1)*

Tocqueville here eloquently conjures up images of the two positions I termed nomothetic and idiographic in Chapter 2. As the quotation indicates, Tocqueville opts for a middle-range position. Elster (2009) sees this combination of deductive insights and empirical observations as the great strength of Tocqueville's work. By walking the line between these two positions, Elster argues, Tocqueville was able to glean a number of general causal mechanisms from the material he studied; mechanisms that according to Elster are as relevant today as when Tocqueville put quill to paper.[2]

But to fully understand Tocqueville's take on causality we need to scale the nomothetic-idiographic dimension with another equally important divide, namely the structure-actor dimension. Here, another quote, this time from the last pages of *DA*, is helpful:

> Providence has not created mankind entirely independent or entirely free. It is true that around every man a fatal circle is traced beyond which he cannot pass; but within the wide verge of that circle he is powerful and free; as it is with man, so with communities. The nations of our time cannot prevent the conditions of men from becoming equal, but it depends upon themselves whether the principle of equality is to lead them to servitude or freedom, to knowledge or barbarism, to prosperity or wretchedness.
>
> *(DA, II.iv.8)*

This quotation not only introduces Tocqueville's great theme – that modern democracies can develop in the direction either of servitude or of freedom – it also shows how Tocqueville positioned himself with respect to structure versus agency. In a nutshell, Tocqueville tries to cut the Gordian Knot of the structure-agency problem by arguing that there is a place for voluntarism, albeit delimited by structural context. The aim of the new social science that Tocqueville saw himself as creating (see *DA*, I.Intro) was hence twofold: first, to understand the deep structural factors that created the context within which actors navigated; second, to understand how actors might make a difference within this circle.

What, more precisely, are the causal factors that constrain human action? Hewing to Montesquieu, Tocqueville primarily stresses two deeper factors, namely mores (*moeurs*) and institutions. Mores are a rather inclusive category which comprises the moral and intellectual abilities of a people (*DA*, I.ii.10). Institutions include constitutional rules in general and a number of more particular political institutions, *inter alia,* elections, parliaments, communes, townships, and courts of law.

However, both *DA* and *OR* are somewhat frustrating reads on this point – for two reasons. First, Tocqueville is rather vague with respect to what counts as mores and institutions, respectively. For instance, at some point in *DA* he groups religion as an institution, whereas he normally treats it as part of the mores of society (*DA*, I.ii.10). Second, Tocqueville sometimes argues that mores affect institutions; sometimes, that institutions can alter mores. Elster (2009, 97–98) tries to rescue Tocqueville from the charge of inconsistency by arguing that mores and institutions are interdependent – i.e., that Tocqueville conceives their relationship in terms of circular causality. Be that as it may, it is clear that to Tocqueville mores normally beat institutions with respect to explanatory power. To quote from *OR*: 'The belief that the greatness and power of a nation are products if its administrative machinery is, to say the least, shortsighted; however perfect that machinery, the driving force behind it is what counts' (*OR*, iii.4; see also *DA*, I.ii.10).

Tocqueville's questions

Taken together, mores and institutions constrain but do not dictate actors' choices. Against this background, Tocqueville attempted (in *OR*) to identify the causes that had brought about the French Revolution and (in *DA*) to understand how liberty might be preserved in the face of ascending social equality. Here, it is worthwhile to once again stress that Tocqueville did not see human action as fully determined by the social and institutional context. Indeed, Tocqueville is adamant that it takes deliberate action to avoid the modern scenario that he feared most, the concatenation of social equality and lack of liberty that he normally refers to as 'democratic despotism'. If humans did not fight the tendency of social levelling to undermine liberty, modernity was apt to be characterized by societies of equal but unfree persons. As such, human action made all the difference – social development was not preordained, even if it was constrained.

The attempt to understand the explanatory power of mores, institutions, and actors' choices, respectively, show that Tocqueville's aim was not to rehearse events but to explain them. But the reason that Tocqueville figures as my first example of a modern scholar practicing comparative historical analysis is that he did not simply present these explanations to be accepted on the basis of the truth value of the statements or backed up by a few empirical illustrations (as was the conventional model in much early social science). He constantly probed them via historical or contemporary comparisons, whether within countries or across countries, and when working out his ideas he often altered preconceived hunches when these did not fit the evidence (Smelser 1976; Welch 2000, 255).

Raymond Aron (1965, 184) goes so far as to proclaim Tocqueville the comparative sociologist *par excellence*. Most of Tocqueville's comparisons rest on a simple MSSD logic as he contrasts two rather similar cases with different outcomes, seeking to identify the explanatory factor that has produced the difference. For instance, in *DA* he notes that the work ethics differ completely on the two sides of the Ohio River, in Ohio and Kentucky, respectively. There are a number of similarities between these two adjacent states, which obviously cannot explain this divergence in outcomes. But there is also a key difference, namely the institution of slavery, which in Tocqueville's day was present in Kentucky but not in Ohio. Furthermore, one can make a plausible case for slavery influencing the work ethics, not only of slaves and slave owners but also of non-slave-owning whites in Kentucky. On this basis, Tocqueville attributes the different outcomes to slavery (see also Jardin 1988[1984], 174).

More generally, the main comparison in *DA* is between France and the United States, whereas in *OR* it is between France, England, and Germany. But in both books, Tocqueville also enlists a series of within-case comparisons, such as the one between Ohio and Kentucky just described (see Smelser 1976). Tocqueville's use of comparisons was backed up by more in-depth methods, including interviews (particularly in *DA*) and archival studies (particularly in *OR*). Tocqueville even collected rudimentary statistics of, e.g., government expenses. In all these ways, his work is a harbinger of the modern social science that was to come into its own in the decades following his death in 1859, at fifty-three years.

There is an additional reason why Tocqueville's work belongs in this book. He constantly posed the kinds of 'big questions' that I described in Chapter 1. Indeed, his two famous books, *DA* and *OR*, treat one and the same big question from different angles. The endeavour in *DA* is to understand how and why freedom has been combined with democracy in the United States, whereas in *OR* it is why this combination has not materialized in France during Tocqueville's own lifetime (Aron 1965, 185). In other words, what Tocqueville set out to understand was whether – and, if so, how – liberty might be preserved in the context of the ubiquitous democratization that was affecting the entire Western world.

In this sense, there is an important normative dimension to Tocqueville's work. Some of his biographers go so far as to refer to his work as political pamphlets (e.g., Brogan 2006, 561–563). Tocqueville is often invoked to the effect that liberty has intrinsic value – e.g., with reference to the following quote from *OR*: 'He who seeks freedom for anything but freedom's self is made to be a slave'. But he was deeply concerned that the new equality in conditions would undermine liberty: 'I would have loved liberty in all times, I think, but at the present time I am inclined to worship it' (*DA*, II.iv.7). Indeed, to Tocqueville the default position of the modern age is one of equality without liberty. It would take an assertive endeavour in the form of human action to preserve the liberty that had historically been associated with aristocracy in the new context of democracy. As we shall see, deeper structural factors made this easier to achieve in some contexts than in others – say, in America than in France.

Understanding Tocqueville's key concepts

Even this brief introduction of Tocqueville's big question is apt to have created some confusion. For what is meant by 'democracy' and 'aristocracy', respectively, and how do these concepts relate to 'social equality'? More particularly, what is 'social equality' and what is 'liberty'?

To answer these questions, we first need to recognize that we are here faced with what is surely the biggest weakness of Tocqueville's work, namely the vagueness and apparent contradictions that characterize both his use of key concepts and his insights about causal relationships (Elster 2009). Let us try to cut through the maze. By 'democracy', Tocqueville means different things at different points in his work. Sometimes the term denotes social equality; at other times, a democratic political regime. However, the former understanding is by far the most common in both *DA* and *OR* (Swedberg 2009, 14–15; Mansfield 2010, 19). What, then, does Tocqueville mean by social equality? The French expression is *égalité des conditions*, and it is normally rendered as 'equality of conditions' in English. However, as Brogan (2006, 275) points out, a better translation would be 'equality of status'. The term thus denotes the absence of the kind of judicial and political privileges which are associated with the medieval and early modern European society of orders (see Poggi 1978; Zagorin 1982). It follows that democratization consists of the upending of the birth right to political influence or economic privileges. These privileges had traditionally rested with nobles and the clergy, and, albeit to a lesser extent, with townsmen.

Aristocracy is the exact opposite, namely a system of inequality of status where formal positions of power are inherited and where judicial and economic privileges pervade society. It follows that for Tocqueville social equality (and hence democracy) does not in any way denote equality of material conditions – i.e., it does not denote economic equality. On the contrary, Tocqueville is unwavering that economic inequality cannot undermine equality of status (Aron 1965, 187, 192). To illustrate, according to Tocqueville, the United States, England, and France were all democracies in the 1830s (as he worked on *DA*), in spite of the presence of huge material inequalities and the absence of equal and universal suffrage (Brogan 2006, 351). What Tocqueville attempts in *DA* and *OR* is to compare these different instances of democracy to understand the causes of their differences (Aron 1965, 183–184).

This brings us to the concept of liberty or freedom. For this is the most crucial way in which modern democracies differ. Again, there is quite some vagueness in Tocqueville's use of this concept. However, the core meaning seems to be what is often termed negative liberty – i.e., the absence of state restrictions on individual actions (Brogan 2006, 354; Richter 2006, 247). This is interwoven with the understanding that power is exercised via law, not arbitrarily. That is, to Tocqueville, genuine liberty is law-based (Aron 1965, 190; Brogan 2006, 522). Finally, Tocqueville also deals with liberty in a more cultural sense, namely as the preparedness to engage in public affairs and speak truth to power (Welch 2000, 52–54). Historically, such liberty had been the preserve of (and been preserved by) the nobility which via a series of 'intermediate institutions' had kept the monarchs in check. As mentioned above, the modern scenario Tocqueville fears most is one where social equality is realized at the expense of such liberty, what he normally terms 'democratic despotism' (Jaume 2013, 18). In other words, the modern choice, after the passing of aristocracy, is democracy with or without liberty (*DA*, I.ii.9).

We finally need to understand what Tocqueville meant by another key concept – viz., 'civil society'. There is today a vibrant 'neo-Tocquevillian' literature on the effects of civil society (see Berman 1997a, 1997b). As the name says, these authors regularly invoke Tocqueville's work, principally *DA*. For instance, in *Making Democracy Work*, Robert Putnam (1993, 182) flatly claims that 'Tocqueville was right'. The 'neo-Tocquevillians' are principally concerned about non-political voluntary civil organizations, including the bowling clubs that have occasioned the title of Putnam's (2001) other great tome on the virtues of civil society, *Bowling Alone*.

Tocqueville did indeed take note of the American tendency to associate at all levels of society and also attributed positive effects to this (e.g., *DA*, I.ii.4, II.ii.5). However, his main understanding of civil society – or at least the gist of civil society – was a different one. What Tocqueville honed in on were local political structures, including townships, communes, and parishes (e.g., *DA*, I.i.5; see also Jardin 1988, 214). These were important because they created a bulwark against the central power of the state (see Welch 2006). In other words, Tocqueville's key insight was that these local political structures were functional equivalents of the bygone aristocratic 'intermediate institutions', thereby providing a check on the (central) powers that be (Welch 2006, 229–236).

The point de départ

Thus equipped, we are ready to probe Tocqueville's causal statements. The most general one is anchored in his notion about the importance of the *point de départ*, or what today's scholarship refers to as 'initial conditions'. In both *DA* and *OR*, Tocqueville draws on the notion that origins shape developments (Aron 1965, 193). In *DA*, the point of departure explains both why American democracy has progressed so much more than, e.g., French democracy and why it has successfully been combined with liberty (as French democracy has not, or at least to a much lesser extent). Tocqueville associates these developments with the pattern of colonization of the states that were to become the United States. The original colonists hailed from England, and therefore brought along the free English institutions and the mentality of liberty. Furthermore, they were mostly poor, which increased equality and hindered the establishment of a native aristocracy. Finally, in religious terms many of the colonists were puritans who sought freedom of conscience on foreign shores and who practiced a religiosity that was in itself beneficial for both equality and liberty.

In *OR*, Tocqueville's point of departure is that the character of the French Revolution can only be understood with reference to the 'medieval' or 'feudal' political and judicial institutions that characterized all of Western Europe before early modern state-building began (*OR*, i.4). As we shall see below, it was the fact that these medieval institutions had been emptied of content but still existed as empty shells that both triggered the French revolution and made it so very radical. In fact, the medieval institutions even had consequences for the American democratic experience. In a famous passage of *OR*, Tocqueville thus explains how the self-governing medieval parish was 'transported overseas' to the American colonies, here appearing in the form of the New England township which plays such an important role for preserving liberty in the context of social equality (*OR*, ii.3).

Tocqueville's is thus a somewhat peculiar version of path dependency – not path dependency in the form of contingent events triggering a path with deterministic properties, as some social scientist today define this concept (e.g., Mahoney 2000). Tocqueville does not rid the longer-term development of the impact from actors' choices. But the explanation is path dependent in the sense that these initial conditions constrain the choices of actors and condition the effects of their actions. Here, we can hark back to the insight about the causal priority of deep social mores. These mores can be seen as the texture that makes up the initial conditions, and in turn conditions both institutions and actors' choices.

Centralization and revolution

Most discussions of Tocqueville's work both start with *DA* and place most emphasis on it (e.g., Brogan 2006; Elster 2009). There is of course a certain chronological logic to this in that *DA* is the early work and *OR* the late work. Furthermore, *DA* remains by far the most famous and influential of Tocqueville's two books. However, if we look at the books shorn of considerations about fame or dating, it seems natural to start with *OR*. Here, too, we can invoke chronology as *OR* deals with the deep historical developments that ultimately paved the way for the democratization of the eighteenth and nineteenth centuries. Moreover, *OR* serves to place some of the insights of *DA* in relief, most notoriously the role of state centralization. Finally, most scholars agree that *OR* beats *DA* if measured up against criteria of good social science (e.g., Elster 2006, 64).

OR is basically a tale about monarchical centralization during the old regime. Tocqueville's first insight is a negative, namely that centralization was *not* begun with the French Revolution but rather centuries earlier by the Valois and Bourbon monarchs. In other words, Tocqueville stresses the continuity of modern French history (Brogan 2006, 453). The revolution of course changed things but mostly by intensifying a centralization that had already progressed pretty far (*OR*, i.2). This might not sound like a revolutionary insight, if you pardon my choice of words. But at the time *OR* was written, in the 1850s, that was exactly what it was. Until then, virtually anyone who had written about the French Revolution had stressed it being a clear juncture – and argued that it was the revolution that had created the modern French state. After *OR*, this 'radical' view has never been completely rescued, even though Tocqueville's postulates about the scope and intensity of Bourbon state centralization have been challenged (Brogan 2006, 562).

Tocqueville dates the start of the royal centralization all the way back to the introduction of the first royal tax that did not require consent, the *taille*, in 1439 (Elster 2006, 55). This undermined the key barrier against despotism, namely the requirement of consent for taxation. The nobility was 'bribed' to accept this because the nobles were exempted from the new tax – thereby weakening their incentive to insist on their traditional veto against taxation (*OR*, ii.10). Monarchical centralization gathered further momentum following the religious wars of the sixteenth and seventeenth centuries, particularly under the Bourbon kings. To Tocqueville, the increasing sway of the Royal Council and the royal agents that were sent to administer most French regions, the so-called *intendants* and their *subdélégue*, were the main means of the royal centralization, orchestrated by powerful and skilled statesmen such as Richelieu and Mazarin.

One of the manifestations of this centralization was the increasing importance of Paris. Indeed, by the end of the old regime, Paris *was* France (*OR*, ii.7). This was reflected in the nobility now flocking to Paris – and to Versailles – to put on a show of conspicuous consumption, rather than staying at and tending to their estates in rural France (*OR*, ii.12).

The other side of the coin was a steady erosion of the local, 'medieval' institutions, now increasingly disempowered by royal centralization. Before this royal centralization, the French nobility (and to a lesser extent the clergy) had, Tocqueville argues, functioned as a surrogate state power in several ways: first, directly on their estates where the nobles both expended justice and provided a rudimentary social safety net; second, indirectly via a series of 'intermediate institutions', including regional and national Estates, courts of law, parishes, and – later in the day – the special courts of law called *parlements* (Brogan 2006, 352). All of these functions were steadily undermined by state centralization. So was the autonomy of towns; albeit this development only really began at a somewhat later stage, by the end of the seventeenth century (*OR*, ii.3).

Centralization and liberty

Tocqueville's aim with his book about the old regime and the revolution was not simply to show that French centralization preceded the revolution. It was to explain both the timing and the character of the French revolution and to more generally account for why liberty had not flourished in modern France, before as well as after the revolution. On both accounts, centralization is key.

If we begin with the latter point, centralization steadily eroded liberty under the old regime (Brogan 2006, 564). Tocqueville follows Montesquieu in seeing the roots of Western liberty in the aristocratic counterweight to the monarchy in medieval and early modern Europe. More precisely, it was the aristocratic 'intermediary institutions' that provided an aegis of liberty. Even long after royal centralization had swept away many of these barriers, remnants could still to be found. Tocqueville hence notes that even into the eighteenth century, 'though as far as administration and political institutions were concerned France had succumbed to absolutism, our judicial institutions were still those of a free people' (*OR*, ii.11).

But the ultimate consequence of state centralization was to remove even this last barrier against royal despotism. Tocqueville thus parts way with Montesquieu in seeing the 'intermediary institutions' in general and the French *parlements* in particular as an effective aegis of liberty, at least when royal power became overwhelming. At the end of the day, the Bourbon monarchy succeeded in destroying the aristocratic counterweights. Tocqueville deduces a more general law from this: 'whenever a nation destroys its aristocracy, it almost automatically tends towards a centralization of power' (*OR*, ii.5).

Centralization and revolution: the Tocqueville paradox

OR was a product of Tocqueville's attempt to understand the character of the French Revolution. As he announces on the very first page of the foreword, this focus forced him back in time because one needs to understand the old regime to understand the revolution. The important point here is that centralization also figures as the main culprit behind the revolution, albeit in a more indirect way than with respect to its effects on liberty.

To understand this, we need to understand the frustration that was brewing towards the end of the old regime. By far the most violent part of this frustration was directed at the nobility. Indeed, the French nobility was much more reviled than the nobility of countries such as England and Germany, and the main aim of the French revolutionaries was to eliminate the 'feudal' institutions (OR, i.5). At first sight, Tocqueville notes, this seems paradoxical. For the state centralization described above had rendered the French nobility politically impotent. In fact, by the late eighteenth century, social equality had progressed further in France than elsewhere in Western Europe. Serfdom had long vanished, and the French nobles had by and large lost the political and judicial power they had once had, making the peasants their social (though of course not their economic or cultural) equals in many respects (OR, ii.1).

However, this development was achieved by a form of *quid-pro-quo* where the monarchs had politically neutered the nobles but allowed them to retain economically lucrative and socially decorative privileges, including exemptions from taxation and a series of economic demands on the peasantry linked to the soil and to agricultural production (OR, ii.1). The end result was that the nobility became a closed caste of parasites. They had lost all their functions as surrogate state power, including even the military functions which had originally prompted their tax exemptions. But they kept their economic benefits both directly via their claims on the peasantry, including ground rent and the demand that peasants take their corn to the nobleman's mill, and indirectly via the sale of offices such as judges.

It was this pernicious combination of political impotence and social prominence that paved the way for the radicalness of the French Revolution. To use Huntington's famous metaphor (1991, 137), Tocqueville's insight here is that 'the halfway house does not stand'. The destruction of some medieval institutions made the rest all the more hated (OR, ii.1). Tocqueville corroborates this insight via two sets of empirical comparisons. First, he contrasts the parts of France where this development had been most extreme – the region around Paris (*Ile-de-France*) – with the parts of France where it had been least intensive, namely Western France. It turns out that the revolution found much more backing in the former place; whereas the nobility actually mobilized to defend the king in the latter place (OR, iii.4). Second, Tocqueville shows that a similar pattern characterizes Germany. The French Revolution thus infested the Western parts where seigneurial rights had long vanished, whereas it made little headway further to the East where more aspect of the 'medieval institutions' still functioned, including seigneurial rights (OR, ii.1).

There is yet another dimension to the paradox. As Tocqueville points out, France had experienced accelerated economic development in the decades preceding the revolution. Moreover, progress had been most steep in the central areas around *Ile-de-France* (*OR*, iii.4; see also Swedberg 2009, 259). According to Tocqueville, the minute the crisis began, this further fuelled the frustration. Tocqueville here makes the shrewd observation that people will often put up with tyrannical rule for years, only to revolt as soon as repression is diminished. His more general point is that an evil which seems inexorable is accepted whereas a lesser evil is seen as unbearable the very instant people conceive of the idea that things could be different (*OR*, iii.4). This is sometimes referred to as the 'Tocqueville Effect', and it has been very influential in later studies of revolution (see, e.g., Davies 1962).

The full causal chain

Elster (2009, 49) in his review of OR divides the causes of the revolution into preconditions (1439–1750), precipitants (1750–1787), and triggers (1787–1789). My account instead distinguishes between deep versus proximate causes (cf. *OR*, III.i). The deep causes are to be found in the monarchical centralization which steadily eroded medieval constitutionalism. Among the more proximate causes we find the 'Tocqueville Effect' as well as a series of inauspicious actors' choices. But we also find a particular Zeitgeist, which according to Tocqueville imbued all of France in the eighteenth century. This Zeitgeist inculcated a 'vision of a perfect state' (*OR*, iii.1), based on uniformity and brought into being via a total transformation directed from above by state power.

Tocqueville finds this best expressed by an influential group of eighteenth-century economists, the so-called *physiocrats* (*OR*, iii.3). Their writings were characterized by contempt for each and every established institution and a yearning for radical change. They wanted to abolish all hierarchies and differences of rank in order to make all alike, and they wanted the state to orchestrate this transformation. In other words, they yearned for a 'form of tyranny sometime described as "democratic despotism"' (*OR*, iii.3). We are here back at the great bogeyman of modernity, which the French Revolution heralded in, and which had been so popular in France in Tocqueville's own time.

Democracy and liberty

In what remains of this chapter, I use these insights to unfold and understand Tocqueville's more renowned analysis of civil society and modern democracy. Tocqueville is today closely associated with these two concepts. This is quite fitting as the most important premise of his work is the inexorable march (or ascendancy) of democracy – and as civil society makes up the bulwark that can potentially hinder democracy from showing its despotic face.

Let us go step by step. Recall that Tocqueville normally means equality of status when he refers to democracy. On this basis, he traces the early beginning of democratization all the way back to the High Middle Ages – viz., to the moment non-nobles began to be admitted to the clergy. But Tocqueville is keen to add that democratization has intensified in the period following the French Revolution (Mansfield 2010, 18–19). In his own lifetime it has therefore spread to all of Western Christendom, which is the empirical scope that his work covers.

Recall that democracy (social equality) can take two different guises: one where it is combined with liberty and one of democratic despotism. Tocqueville was surely not alone in seeing a ubiquitous process of democratization engulfing the Western world. But he was among those who saw most clearly that despotism might come riding on the tailcoats of this democratization (Jardin 1988, 275).

The main purpose of *DA* is to understand how, in the United States, the former rather than the latter combination has triumphed. Tocqueville here operates on two different levels. First, he identifies a number of institutions which are propitious to liberty. These include the federal constitution, the communal or municipal institutions, and the way judicial power is structured. It is here we can return to Tocqueville's notion of civil society. It is the local political structures – including townships, communes, and parishes – that safeguard liberty. To Tocqueville, these institutions are functional equivalents of the aristocratic 'intermediary institutions' that protected liberty under the old regime, before being swept away by state centralization, at least in France. In American democracy, the local political structures similarly made up barriers against state centralization by creating vigilant citizens who organize and engage politically.

Second, Tocqueville traces these institutions, or at least the vibrancy of these institutions, to a set of deeper mores. In particular, he emphasizes the importance of religion. The puritan Protestantism of North America has benefited freedom in several ways, most importantly by breathing life into the local political structures. Tocqueville goes so far as to refer to American Protestantism as republican and democratic (*DA*, I.ii.9; see also *DA*, I.i.2). Indeed, even the Catholic faith has had similar effects in America because it has been severed from both pope and state. Catholicism thus also facilitated political engagement on a local and national level. More generally, Tocqueville construes Christianity[3] as a powerful force for liberty (Jardin 1988, 365).

This combination of mores and institutions together explains why liberty has flourished in the American democracy Tocqueville encountered during his travels. The other side of the coin is that such an amalgamation is not necessarily to be expected elsewhere (*DA*, I.Intro.). *OR* can very much be understood as a diagnosis of why Tocqueville's own France had been unable to develop or at least sustain this combination – as illustrated by the *coup d'état* of Napoleon Bonaparte's nephew, Louis-Napoleon, on 2 December 1851 (Brogan 2006, 572). This coup was yet another manifestation of the democratic despotism that Tocqueville saw lurking in modernity.

Tocqueville had already anticipated as much in *DA*. The second part of *DA* concerns the often perverse effects of democracy writ large, including the possible pernicious effects on liberty. Already in the first part of *DA*, Tocqueville had vented his fear of majority tyranny. But in the second part, which – in spite of the title – does not as such concern the United States but rather concerns democracy more generally, he ventures much further (Jardin 1988, 251). First and foremost, Tocqueville is concerned about the individualism and conformism that characterizes democracy. To understand this, it is once again worthwhile to revisit *OR*. Democratization basically entails sundering the bonds that connected individuals and groups in the context of Aristocracy (*DA*, II.ii.2). Democracy thereby creates an atomism that facilitates despotism by weakening social opposition to the powers-that-be.

It is of course exactly this problem that strong local political structures mitigate. But in the France that is always implicitly at the centre of Tocqueville's thoughts,[4] this has not occurred. *Au contraire*, in Tocqueville's own lifetime France has been caught up in a pernicious cycle of revolutions and reactions, which have steadily undermined liberty. Here, it is well to recall Tocqueville's premise that actors' choices matter even if they are constrained by structures. It takes an assertive defence of liberty to secure the American combination of social equality and freedom. But such assertiveness is most likely if the champions of liberty stand at the battlements of strong local institutions thereby being able to hold off the modern age in arms, that is, the forces of centralization (Jardin 1988, 268–269).

Influence and criticism

Tocqueville's writings have been hugely influential. Indeed, save Weber, his is the most influential body of work to be covered in this book. A list of famous works influenced by Tocqueville starts with John Stuart Mill's *On Liberty* and includes Friedrich Hayek's *The Road to Serfdom*, the work of the mass society theorists of the 1940s and 1950s (Lederer 1940; Kornhauser 1959), James Davies's (1962) J-curve of revolution, some of Seymour Martin Lipset's (e.g., Lipset et al. 1956; Lipset 1963) and Robert A. Dahl's (e.g., 1956) works, as well as the huge 'neo-Tocquevillian' literature on civil society that has been so influential in recent decades, including the work of Robert D. Putnam (1993; 2001).

But Tocqueville has also been criticized. I have already noted the most conspicuous problem of Tocqueville's works in general and *DA* in particular, namely the vague concepts and many apparent contradictions (Elster 2009, 2). More could be added. If we start with *OR*, some have objected that the description of centralization under the Bourbons is overdrawn, indeed that it is sometimes close to a caricature. This has been called the 'Tocquevillian Myth' (Brogan 2006, 564). Others have pointed out that Tocqueville – as a French aristocrat – simply did not get the modern parties that were emerging in the United States, and thus did not understand their role in modern, representative democracy (Brogan 2006, 160). Tocqueville instead seems to have taken the direct democracy of the New England township as his model of the American system, in spite of this already being a curiosity rather than the umbilical cord of the American democracy (Brogan 2006, 160–161). Finally, Tocqueville's use of the comparative method has also been severely criticized (Smelser 1976).

Nonetheless, the positive influence obviously trumps the criticism in the case of the gentleman political scientist that Alexis de Tocqueville was. Since World War II in general and since the breakdown of communism in particular, Tocqueville's work has received remarkable attention within social science. Both *DA* and *OR* are today standard references in political science, sociology, history, and to a lesser extent philosophy. In 1997, Sheri Berman declared Tocqueville to be nothing less than 'the theorist of the decade' (1997b, 401).

Indeed, the only field within social science where his influence has been relatively minor is economics. It says a lot about the attention presently devoted to Tocqueville that Swedberg (2009) has recently written an entire book about the French aristocrat's contribution to the dismal science. In this connection, Swedberg (2009, 252) proclaims Tocqueville to be a pioneer within the tradition of 'fiscal sociology', which is normally associated with the work of Joseph A. Schumpeter, and which we return to in Chapter 5. Likewise, the Nobel laureate in economics Elinor Ostrom (2000, 281–283) recommends *DA* and *OR* as basic reading to anyone caring about the future of democracy.

Conclusions

Tocqueville is the first modern scholar to practice comparative historical analysis on a large scale. Doing so, Tocqueville marshals both within- and cross-country comparisons in order to probe causes, and he uses historical analysis to understand the causes of the French Revolution as well as the difficulties, in France, of having liberty temper social equality. The most telling illustration of Tocqueville's success is the extent to which his works, principally *DA* and *OR*, have influenced later social scientists.

In this chapter, I have paid special attention to the way in which *OR* and *DA* makes up one coherent research project, the ambitious aim of which was to understand the causes and character of the democratization process that had engulfed Western societies in Tocqueville's own lifetime. By reading *DA* with *OR* in mind, this project is easier to understand. In particular, this approach serves to highlight Tocqueville's ideas about the importance of the *point de départ*, of deep social mores, and of the decentral political institutions that balance central power. Tocqueville's analysis is thus very much historical. However, as I have also made clear, Tocqueville does not rid the equation of the importance of actors' choices. Let me end this chapter by quoting one of the most heartening of his many lyrical passages:

> For my part, I detest these absolute systems, which represent all the events of history as depending upon great first causes linked by the chain of fatality, and which, as it were, suppress men from the history of the human race. They seem narrow, to my mind, under their pretense of broadness, and false beneath their air of mathematical exactness. I believe (pace the writers who have invented these sublime theories in order to feed their vanity and facilitate their work) that many important historical facts can only be explained

by accidental circumstances, and that many others remain totally inexplicable. Moreover, chance, or rather that tangle of secondary causes which we call chance, for want of the knowledge how to unravel it, plays a great part in all that happens on the world's stage; although I firmly believe that chance does nothing that has not been prepared beforehand. Antecedent facts, the nature of institutions, the cast of minds and the state of morals are the materials of which are composed those impromptus which astonish and alarm us.

(Recollections, II.i)

Notes

1   Tocqueville's three main works – *DA, OR,* and *Recollections* – exist in very many different editions. For this reason, my references in this chapter are not to page number but to the relevant book (e.g., I), part (e.g., i), and chapter (e.g., 1). This way, the reader will be able to locate the quotation or point referred to in any of the numerous editions available.
2   John Stuart Mill said something similar when he reviewed *DA* in *London and Westminster Review* and noted that the great strength of the work was Tocqueville's ability to combine specific observations with general insights about society. According to Mill, *DA* thereby inaugurated 'the beginning of a new era in the scientific study of politics' (Swedberg 2009, 13).
3   Tocqueville elsewhere claims that Islam is hostile to freedom (Jardin 1988, 322).
4   Jaume (2008, 4) goes so far as to claim that *DA* is really about France, not the United States.

4
THE CLASSIC ANALYSES II
Weber

Anyone who has read Homer's *Iliad* will have noticed the hierarchical character of Greek society in the Bronze Age. The heroes of the story are kings, the foot soldiers are largely ignored, and the common Hellenes and Trojans can only hope for the benevolence of the gods. The society of the day was largely constructed in this manner because bronze was a precious resource. Kings and chieftains alone could afford proper equipment for war, meaning that they had a solid grip on the monopoly on violence. The advent of iron technology turned this society upside-down. Iron was cheaper to produce than bronze, and, with these new weapons in hand, tradesmen, peasants, and shepherds alike could suddenly join the fray. The monopoly on violence previously enjoyed by the elite was simply broken, and the democratic city-states, *poleis*, replaced the kingdoms, at least in many parts of ancient Hellas (cf. Hintze 1975[1906], 183–184; McNeill 1982, 5–20; see also Finer 1996, 281–282, 453).

In fact, Aristotle describes his preferred version of democracy – *Politea* – as a form of hoplite constitution. Under such a constitution, the political power is in the hands of the class of citizens who are capable of paying for their own military equipment and therefore act as foot soldiers, hoplites, in the army of the *polis*. In this sense, the hoplite constitution provides a reminder of how the ancient polis originally democratized[1] (see, however, Finer 1996, 332–333). It is possible to identify a corresponding development at roughly the same time in China, although here the military development did not bring about genuine democracies but 'merely' undermined the monopoly on power of the warring aristocracy and reinforced the power of the rulers (see Hansen 2000, 63).

In other words, the development in military technology has had very significant repercussions on both the state and the regime form. We owe the formulation of this insight to, among others, Max Weber (2003[1927], 324–325) (see Collins 1986, 98; Bobbit 2002, xxii). *Naturally*, one is tempted to say. In this chapter, we will see that Weber formulated a series of the relationships that have subsequently attracted attention in the literature.

The classic comparative historical analyses

An entire chapter is devoted to Weber, as he towers so high above everyone else in the literature. But the next chapter will show that the relationship described above between geopolitical pressure and state formation and regime change occupied a central position in the comparative historical literature written some one hundred years ago.

This literature – the classic comparative historical analyses, as I refer to them – is first and foremost a continental European phenomenon; in particular, a number of German researchers contributed to it. Moreover, the classic literature has a greater tendency to cut across different academic disciplines than the later literature. In this and the next chapter, we will thus touch upon contributions from the economist and sociologist Weber, the historians Otto Hintze and Marc Bloch, and the economist Joseph Schumpeter. The fact that researchers from such different disciplines have contributed to one and the same research agenda reflects that the differences between economics, sociology, and history were more blurred one hundred years ago than now.[2]

As Swedberg (1991; 1998) has described in books on Schumpeter and Weber, powerful forces in economics made attempts to integrate economic theory, economic sociology, and economic history in one and the same field: what Weber labelled *Sozialökonomik*. Weber was – *naturally*, one is again tempted to say – the driving force behind this attempt to formalize an interdisciplinary field. It is telling that, throughout his career, he saw himself as an economist whereas posterity primarily views him as a sociologist (Swedberg 1991, 93).

Weber and the quarry

Weber's courage to grapple with historical developments across time and space have left a veritable quarry that anyone with an interest in the social sciences would have an interest in visiting, pick in hand. In an interview about his career, the late political scientist Juan J. Linz tellingly stated: 'Whenever I start working on something, I usually look to see whether Weber has anything to say on that theme' (Munck and Snyder 2007, 182).

However, the quarry metaphor should not merely be regarded as an expression of the weight and extent of Weber's contribution; the image also refers to Weber's research agenda being fragmented, partly conflicting, therefore difficult to summarize, and that the individual contributions often lie hidden in remote corners of Weber's extensive writings. As Collins (1986, 10) puts it, Weber's authorship is multidimensional to the point that it is 'somewhat schizophrenic'; in other words, there is not one single 'Weber'; there are several 'Webers' (11). For this reason, I will not attempt to provide a general overview of Weber's writings or a comprehensive overview of his contributions to comparative historical analysis. Instead, I will single out a number of points that are especially relevant for this book.

Weber's questions

Weber distinguishes himself from other researchers in terms of how he posed the biggest and – at least in relation to the subject matter of this book – most interesting questions. In the introduction, I presented his general inquiry as 'Why Europe?' More than anything else, Weber wanted to uncover the causes behind the rationalization process that in his opinion was distinctive for the Western World (Collins 1986, 69; Weber 2003[1927], 312; Poggi 2006, 53). In other words, why has Western culture – as opposed to all other cultures – assumed a systematic, rational character?

According to Weber, this European rationalization process can be traced all the way back to ancient times but really took off in the period from the High Middle Ages and onwards. Subsequently, it has spread like rings in water and, thus, had an impact on the rest of the world (Poggi 2006, 53). What does Weber mean more specifically by 'rationalization'? It is difficult to give a short, concise answer. Ultimately, he wanted to explain the emergence of rational capitalism (Weber 2003[1927], 276), but he noted that this development was entangled in a number of other rationalization processes, particularly the rationalization of the law and state power, including the bureaucracy (Collins 1986, 90; Poggi 2006, 78).

At the centre of this rationalization is the steady expansion of the notion that life is calculable – a process that is unique to the Western world and can be seen in the emergence and triumph of modern science (Held 2006[1987], 127). In more specific terms, Weber attempted to explain the origins of 'calculability, formal and fixed rules, written notations, social coordination, intellectual systematization, and professionalization' (Collins 1986, 69). According to Collins, Weber conceived of these using a family resemblance logic; at one place, Weber emphasizes the Western rationalization of music, as reflected in harmony and the division of the octave in twelve (compared to five in other cultures) (Collins 1986, 62–69).

This attempt to describe the contents of rationalization brings out the complex – and ambiguous – character of Weber's body of work. On a general level, his rationalization process can be regarded as the rise of modern science, the modern state (including the predictable and impartial enforcement of the law), and the modern market economy. While Weber sees these things as being difficult to separate,[3] what is most important in relation to this book is the emergence of rational capitalism, which, as touched upon in Chapter 1, is based on an effective organization of labour and the lifting of restrictions on economic interaction backed by the power of the rational-legal state, which is anchored in a rule-bound bureaucracy and universal civil rights. Weber dates the former to Western Europe in the middle of the nineteenth century (Weber 2003[1927], 276), while the latter stretches further back in time and is one of a number of the conditions for the emergence of capitalism.

Weber's method

Weber's work is characterized by a tension between the emphasis on the peculiarity of historical cases and the use of comparisons to test more general relationships (cf. Collins 1986, 131). Weber did not necessarily see this as a contradiction. His renowned use of ideal types can be understood as an attempt to place himself in an intermediate position between the idiographic and nomothetic extremes, as described in Chapter 2. On the one hand, the ideal types make it possible to shed light on the fundamental differences of historical events; on the other, they do so based on general concepts/types (Poggi 2006, 26).

For Weber, the use of ideal types is exactly what unites the social sciences and at the same time distinguishes them from the natural sciences (Swedberg 1998, 193). Ideal types make dissimilar objects comparable, thereby paving the way for generalizations (Smelser 1976, 54–55). More specifically, Weber usually sets up typologies consisting of several (but rarely many) ideal types, where each case/society can be positioned close to one of the types. In this manner, Weber is able to capture variation without losing himself in diversity. With respect to causal relations, the point is that Weber acknowledges that chance plays a role but at the same time limits the number of possible outcomes (Poggi 2006, 33; see also Poggi 1991, 92).

Moreover, Weber uses the method he refers to as *Verstehen*. As the word suggests, it is about empathy – setting oneself in the place of the historical actors and understanding the world as they understood it (Collins 1986, 42). This aligns with Weber's emphasis on methodological individualism – that is, the fact that causal propositions must make sense on the individual level in order to be convincing. The best-known example of both is Weber's (1995[1904–05]) attempt at understanding the Protestant ethic and the spirit of capitalism by delving into the minds of the first generations of Calvinists and Puritans. This is empathy with a vengeance, but it also enables Weber to move back and forth between the societal level (the emergence of Protestantism and capitalism, respectively) and the individual level (the believer's relationship to religion and business) (Swedberg 1998, 131).

Weber is rightly famous for his use of *Verstehen*, but he is also famous for his grand comparisons. How can the two things be reconciled? Smelser (1976, 60–67) explains that Weber had a dual aim with respect to method: interpretations of social situations were to be followed up with causal verification. In other words, the endeavour to understand social situations should be backed by the use of comparisons. Causal relationships must therefore be rooted in both causal mechanisms on the individual level and correlations established on the macro-level via the logic of comparative control. In this sense, one can argue that Weber is almost scarily modern, as his methodological approach match what is today termed 'mixed methods', which is becoming increasingly common in contemporary social science (see, e.g., Hall 2003; Lieberman 2005).

This point is further underlined when we consider the character of the causal relationships Weber formulated and tried to prove. Weber's comparisons almost never take the form of simple 'Most Similar System Design/Most Different System

Design' (MSSD/MDSD) (Swedberg 1998, 143–144). Instead, Weber at a minimum combines these two methods (Smelser 1976, 143). More generally, he uses comparisons to show how a number of factors have interacted to produce a certain outcome – what is more technically referred to as interactive or *conjunctural* causality (Smelser 1976, 123; see, e.g., Weber 2003[1927], 275–369).

According to Weber, these relationships are rarely or never universal – operating across time and space – they are only valid under specific conditions. In fact, Weber repeatedly shows that we must deal with equifinality (that one and the same effect can result from different combinations of causes). 'Combinations' is to be taken quite literally, as Weber almost always ends up stressing that it is a set of causes – not a single cause – that makes the difference (Smelser 1976, 142–144).[4] This can be understood as a form of typological theory (Elman 2005; George and Bennett 2005; Møller and Skaaning 2016b). Such complex typological comparisons across historical eras and historical societies can seem overwhelming. But this is exactly where we find Weber's great strength. In Collins' (1986, 130) words:

> We ought to recognize that this is Weber's strength and our weakness, not vice versa. For comparisons are the basis of any science, and sociology can establish its most powerful generalization only by seeing the conditions under which events occur.

Religion and rationalization

More than anything else, Weber wanted to explain the rise of rational capitalism in Western Europe and North America. He dealt with this issue for most of his career. For posterity, however, his little essay on *The Protestant Ethic and the Spirit of Capitalism*, published in 1904–05, stands as his most famous attempt to answer this question.

The Protestant ethic and capitalism

As indicated by the title, Weber adopts a sociology-of-religion perspective. The premise for his work is that ideas play an independent and often very important role in history. More particularly, the essay represents something of a break with Marxist analysis, which rests upon the notion that the driving forces in world history have a material basis – and that ideas merely reflect this (see Rothman 1970, 65).

Weber begged to differ. While he does indeed point out in the last section of the essay that it is necessary to investigate both the significance of ideas and material conditions, Weber undoubtedly places greater emphasis on the former than the latter in *The Protestant Ethic and the Spirit of Capitalism*. In fact, he directly uses a set of logical considerations to raise objections against the materialist analysis. Weber describes the spirit of capitalism with a quote from Benjamin Franklin, who preaches that time is money, that being careful with one's money and being sober and honest is a virtue, and that one should always attempt to make the most of one's efforts here on earth. Weber then immediately draws attention to how this ethical norm for the conduct of life was present before modern capitalist development started. As an *effect* cannot precede a *cause*, we must reject the materialistic causal chain (1995[1904 05], 31).

What then explains the emergence of capitalism? Weber finds a decisive impulse in ascetic Protestantism. He begins with an apparently consistent empirical regularity. Business statistics in religiously mixed countries indicate that shareholding, corporate governance, and the skilled sections of the working class are overwhelmingly dominated by Protestants – regardless of whether these make up the majority or the minority of the population (1995[1904 05], 20). This can be seen as an attempt to establish a general relationship using a combination of MSSD and MDSD (Smelser 1976, 145–147).[5]

Weber uses the rest of the essay to explain this correlation historically. His *Verstehen* method consists of decoding the influence of the various Protestant denominations on how their proselytes live their lives. Weber argues that it is not the formal religious institutions, such as church discipline, that make the difference but rather the subjective appropriation of ascetic religiosity that affects behaviour. Weber traces the first beginnings back to Luther, whose sense of religious vocation provides secular life with an independent meaning that is foreign to Catholicism. These are merely the first beginnings, however, as Luther also emphasizes how everyone ought to be content with their lot in life (Weber 1995[1904–05], 50–55; Poggi 2006, 69–70).

The stricter, ascetic Christianity of the Calvinists had greater repercussions. Calvin's teachings rested on the idea of selection for grace or predestination – that is, the notion that God has pre-selected those who are to be saved and those who are damned, and that neither faith nor good works can change anything. It might seem rather paradoxical, but this teaching, which might be expected to breed some measure of apathy, motivated Calvin's disciples to behave like secular monks. The knowledge that only few are chosen and that this was predetermined was unbearable. The early generations of Calvinists therefore started looking for signs that they were predestined to make it through the needle's eye. They believed that a virtuous life lived in this world might reflect that they were selected for grace in the afterlife. Consequently, to ape this, they systematized and rationalized life – also in the economic sphere (Weber 1995[1904–05], 72–79).

This is obviously an example of unintended consequences of human action. None of the Protestant reformers encouraged a specific economic behaviour (Weber 1995[1904–05], 56). Nonetheless, the spirit of capitalism was the result of their work. The rationalization that was derived from the Protestant ethic, which can also be viewed as the final expulsion of magic from the world (68), was further supported by the two reformed movements referred to as Methodism and Baptism in the Anglo-Saxon world. Here again, the theological doctrines were converted into a methodological, worldly asceticism. The wealth of the self-made man – as long as he does not fritter it away on idle pursuits – became testament to his faith (and grace). Particularly in the British colonies, parts of Great Britain, Switzerland, and the Netherlands, and to a slightly lesser degree in Scandinavia and Northern Germany, these psychological effects made themselves felt. Over the years, this Protestant ethic was freed from its religious roots and established itself instead as a secular ethics of bourgeois vocation, which was, strictly speaking, irrational. Even though the Puritan ethic is long gone, rational capitalism is therefore here to stay (Weber 1995[1904–05], 121).

Weber's work has been so influential that Protestantism has subsequently been used to explain almost anything and everything. For example, a number of analyses in recent years have coupled the rise of modern democracy, the development of the rational state, and the fight against corruption to Protestantism (see Gorski 2003; Møller and Skaaning 2010; Woodberry 2012). Weber briefly touches upon the first relationship in the preface to the little essay. The theoretical point is – slightly simplified – that the personal relationship to God fosters individualism, which renders democratic rights easier to establish. At the same time, this individualism counteracts corruption in the form of, for example, nepotism.

There has also been extensive criticism, however. Joseph Schumpeter, whose work is discussed in the next chapter, early on pointed out that the capitalist spirit could already be found in fifteenth-century Italy – that is, among Catholics before the Reformation. Others have wondered why Puritan Scotland wallowed so long in an economic standstill. On a more fundamental level, a series of class analyses, including Barrington Moore's work (1991[1966]), which we shall examine in Chapter 6, argue that ideas such as the Protestant ethic are epiphenomenal – that is, they reflect the production relations and class constellations in society (see Rothman 1970, 62–65). More generally, the assessment in the literature would appear – in Barrington Moore's words – to be that it is 'by no means clear whether Max Weber's famous contribution in *The Protestant Ethic and the Spirit of Capitalism* constituted an important breakthrough or a blind alley' (quoted in Swedberg 1998, 129; see also Collins 1986, 52). As Swedberg (1998, 132) puts it, the theory is 'not proven'.

The study of world religions

The 'Weber thesis', as Collins (1986, 47) calls it, has often been misunderstood. Weber did not claim the Protestant ethic to be *the* ultimate (or deep) cause of rational capitalism. Doing so would go directly against his general approach to causality, as described above. Rather, in his usual style, this was an ideal-typical focus on one among many factors that contributed to the development of rational capitalism (Smelser 1976, 136; Collins 1986, 53; Weber 1995[1904–1905], 63).

In his more general work on the sociology of religions, Weber investigates the more general relationship between material factors and ideas (Bendix 1962[1946], 481; Poggi 2006, 61). Here – as in other parts of his work – he focuses on the conflict between social groups and the independent impact of religious beliefs. Weber engages in an extremely ambitious analysis of the emergence of the great world religions and their economic consequences. In addition to Christianity, Weber is interested in Judaism, Hinduism, Confucianism, and Islam. The basic aim is again to shed light on why the rationalization processes, of which the emergence of capitalism is merely a single element, did not make themselves felt to the same extent outside Western Christianity (Swedberg 1998, 133; Poggi 2006, 78). Weber investigates how materialistic factors – notably the social stratification and the ensuing conflict between social groups – affected the formation of religious ideas and how they in turn affected the ethical notions and economic behaviour of the faithful (Bendix 1962[1946], 84).

Weber's ultimate purpose is to uncover the extent to which the religions themselves have been rationalized, which includes giving up magical elements and placing the believer in a personal relationship to God (Smelser 1976, 115, 143). This kind of rationalization process undermines the extent to which religion explains the meaning of life and replaces an enchanted world with one in which understanding and predictability render humankind capable of asserting itself over nature (Held 2006[1987], 127–128). In Weber's eyes, this requires the existence of an organized clergy preaching the message that the will of God predetermines the course of events. This last message – often initially opposed by the organized priesthood – is communicated by prophets whose messages are based on divine revelation rather than tradition. This prophetic revelation clashes, head on, with tradition as something sacred that must be respected at all costs (Bendix 1962[1946], 89–90).

Weber died before completing the project, but he did manage to analyse Judaism, Hinduism, and Confucianism. As was his wont, Weber combines a *Verstehen* approach with systematic comparisons. He ventures well beyond the actual sociology of religion, particularly by appreciating the significance of material factors (Poggi 2006, 77). According to Weber, China is the area outside of the West that has historically had the best conditions for rationalization. Confucianism, which is not an actual religion but rather a set of prescriptions for how to live life, thus included a strong emphasis on meritocracy, particularly in the imperial bureaucracy. In addition, China led the world technologically for quite some time (Poggi 2006, 83). However, it was lacking in other crucial areas. Above all else, there was no room for a personal relationship to God along the same lines as in Christianity (Protestantism in particular). Nothing corresponding to the Protestant ethic therefore developed, nor was the traditional role of the family undermined. On the contrary, the prevailing religious ideas regarding ancestry worship contributed to making clan ties even more constricting.

Moreover, the Chinese cities never acquired the autonomy that characterized the cities in medieval Europe. The bourgeoisie was therefore unable to become an independent, corporative power that could push through the rationalization of economic life (Bendix 1962[1946], 99–100). Most importantly, according to Weber, is the absence of an organized clergy and a prophetic revelation. The secular ruler (the emperor) was, at least formally, the direct contact to the cultic worship, and there was never a 'battering ram' strong enough to turn the faithful away from their family and towards an alternative source of religious authority. To make matters worse, the more popular religious currents that emerged – Taoism being the most important – had a magical character that prevented economic rationalization by resisting innovation (Bendix 1962[1946], 131–139). In Weber's eyes, China therefore appeared to be stuck in a 'semi-rationalized' state from a very early point in its history. A bureaucratic state apparatus existed side by side with a number of traditional characteristics (Collins 1986, 124), and, via its Confucian ideology, this bureaucracy guarded the almost sacrosanct nature of ancestral bonds.

In India, the religious ties were even more constricting. Above all else, the caste system – the pivotal point of the societal structure – stood in the way of rational capitalism (Collins 1986, 115; Weber 2003[1927], 344). The caste system created direct links between religious ideas and social status, and its significance in relation to world history corresponds to that of the Confucian bureaucracy in China (Bendix 1962[1946], 142–143). More generally, Hinduism – and later also Buddhism – turned the attention of the faithful away from secular matters and towards an inner mysticism. As such, a prophetic revelation capable of instilling religious meaning upon everyday labours never emerged. Hinduism in general and the caste system in particular thereby prevented economic development (Bendix 1962[1946], 194–199). This is put into relief by that fact that, in some periods, India actually had commercially strong cities that could have laid the groundwork for capitalism. However, just as in China these cities were lacking a very important feature of medieval European cities, namely the notion of citizenship (Collins 1986, 115). In China, clan ties prevented the emergence of a bourgeois estate group; in India, the caste system was a similar suppressor (Bendix 1962[1946], 194–198).

Finally, Judaism plays an important role in Weber's account of rationalization. In fact, Weber studies the Jewish religion in order to find the roots of the differences between the Christian rationalization of secular life and the oriental worship of mysticism and magic (Bendix 1962[1946], 200). Judaism was the first religion to drive magic out of its belief system (Swedberg 1998, 141; Weber 2003[1927], 360). According to Weber, the cultural impact of the work of the Jewish prophets was the critical impulse behind the development of Western civilization (Bendix 1962[1946], 233). The prophets' interpretation prevailed because the groups to which it appealed prevailed in the Jewish class struggle. Judaism was thus shaped by the social conflicts in and around Palestine in Biblical times.

The prophets established the notion that the believer had a moral obligation to live in accordance with religious law.[6] The premise was that the world was ruled by Yahweh's will rather than by coincidence or magic. This focus on law instead of magic and on ethically correct behaviour contributed to the rationalization of the Jewish way of life – the first step towards the rationalization of Western civilization (Bendix 1962[1946], 247–256). Moreover, Judaism overcame both the clan ties that constituted a barrier for capitalism in China and the caste system that helped prevent capitalism in India. The notion of being a chosen people repealed the distinction between family members and other Jews – that to which he also refers as the internal ethic. But Judaism could never create more than a 'pariah capitalism' because of the difference in ethics that kept them apart from Gentiles (Collins 1986, 88). This 'external' ethical barrier was only overcome by Christianity (Weber 2003[1927], 322).

Weber never completed his planned work on Christianity. On the basis of his other work, however, three successive breakthroughs have clearly had landmark economic significance over time (cf. Collins 2000). Weber found the first breakthrough in the rise of Christianity. Jesus admonished his disciples that they leave their families and follow him. As such, he was the first major religious figure to reject the unique status of the family. The individual should not grant more ethical consideration to family members than to its neighbour. That was important. For in this manner, the Christians bridged the divide between 'the tribe' and the outside world – that is, abolished the aforementioned barrier between the internal and the external ethic (Collins 2000, 105).[7]

The second breakthrough occurred in the Early Middle Ages. In the East, secular and religious power were united. It was the Byzantine emperors and later the Russian tsars who ruled over church matters (Caesaropapism). The exact opposite occurred in the West. The papacy found itself in an on-going conflict with the Holy Roman Emperors and later with the French kings. At times, the Pope was on top. The penance extended by Emperor Henry IV to Canossa in 1077 was an example of how the Church in its heyday was able to humiliate the crowned heads of Western Europe. At other times, the Pope was left holding the short end. The exile in Avignon in the fourteenth century is an example of how a strong king – in this case the king of France – could put the thumbscrews on the Church. According to Weber, the conflict between the two paved the way for the emergence of an independent group of lawyers – for secular law. This cornerstone of the enforcement of law – and of a non-religious political authority – was thus established in the West but not in the East.

Finally, a third new breakthrough with the Protestant Reformation followed. According to Weber, the teachings of the papacy – Roman Catholicism – were ceremonial rather than psychological and moral. As we have already seen, Calvinism and the other Puritan creeds instead encouraged the faithful to live an almost monastic life (see also Weber 2003[1927], 365–367). Work – going about one's business conscientiously – was perceived as nothing less than a vocation or a call. The same was the case with veracity with respect to contractual obligations. This paved the way for capitalism, which is based on the profit motive – as opposed to consideration to family or clan – guiding business life and based on the notion that contracts must be respected.

Agrarian sociology

The material factors are thus hardly absent in Weber's sociology of religion. And in other parts of his writings, they dominate completely. I have already touched upon Weber's thoughts on the relationship between military technology, state formation, and democratization (Collins 1986, 98). However, the purest example is found in Weber's agrarian sociology, a subject with which he worked from the very beginning of his career. His second book (published in 1891) thus addresses the significance of Roman agrarian conditions for public and private law.

Weber revisited this subject twenty years later in a more general work on agrarian sociology, which revolved around the relationship between geographic, political, and economic factors. Above all else, Weber's theory of 'hydraulic bureaucracy' has become famous (Swedberg 1998, 153; see also Weber 2003[1927], 57). Weber noted that the most centralized and bureaucratized states in the ancient world formed in river valleys. Egypt of the Pharaohs, organized around the Nile, offers the most typical example. The Middle Eastern state formations along the Tigris and Euphrates as well as the Chinese empire, which first formed around the Yellow River, are other examples. In Weber's eyes, it was the resources of and dependence on the fickle rivers that created these great empires. The river valleys made intensive agricultural production possible. This required large-scale irrigation systems and dams that had to be built and maintained, which required strong, centralized state power. The rivers were meanwhile the sinews that connected the empire (Weber 2003[1927], 57). In this manner, the rivers paved the way for bureaucratization (Collins 1986, 97).

This theory was later adopted by Karl August Wittfogel (1957),[8] who combined Marx and Weber in his work on 'oriental despotism'. Wittfogel identified an 'Asian' mode of production, the economic basis of which could be found in Weber's hydraulic theory, while the superstructure was bureaucratized despotism. Wittfogel first and foremost found this form of social organization in China. He explains it in terms of the need for large-scale irrigation systems, which in turn require that the labour supply is organized by a strong bureaucracy.

Weber's theory has a form of *prima facie* plausibility, and the intensive agriculture in the river valleys and centralized state power have undoubtedly been mutually reinforcing. But archaeological studies have identified a fundamental problem – the irrigation systems appear to have been developed prior to the bureaucratized state authority (see Diamond 1999[1997]). More generally, scholarship has convincingly established that institutions that can manage common pool resources – in the face of collective action problems – have arisen 'from below' in very many different social contexts and have often proven surprisingly effective even when not backed by state power (e.g., Ostrom 1990). Further along these lines, there has been widespread agreement in the literature that Wittfogel's version of the 'hydraulic' theory is not valid (Bodde 1956, 79; Swedberg 1998, 153, fn. 34).

Free cities as a characteristic of the West

Another example of Weber's understanding of material factors is found in his analysis of the city. More precisely, Weber singled out the autonomous or free cities that emerged in and came to characterize Western Christianity in the Middle Ages.

Weber touches on this subject in a number of his writings, and he viewed the emergence of these cities to have important consequences for world history.

Most European cities had disappeared or declined to mere shadows of their former selves in the course of the Early Middle Ages, but they slowly began growing again around the year 1000. As indicated by many place names, this development often occurred on sites where the cities of antiquity had been located. For instance, the German city Cologne (*Köln*) is a vulgarization of the Latin Colonia. This was the first of three phases that brought into being the free cities of the High Middle Ages. The second phase consisted of the development of informal institutions for self-government in the resurgent cities. This development formed the basis for the third phase, where these institutions were formalized, either as cities won privileges of self-government or when the authorities conferred such privileges on them. In addition to the institutions of self-government, the autonomous cities were characterized by other prerogatives such as the right to defend themselves militarily, the right to impose taxes on their own citizens, and the right to pass and enforce their own laws (Stasavage 2014, 6–7).

According to Weber, the free cities are a unique feature of Western civilization (Poggi 2006, 30). What made these cities unique was the notion of legal citizenship. Such rights are found in the Western world alone, although some precursors can be identified elsewhere (Weber 2003[1927], 323; Poggi 2006, 316; see also Finer 1997a, 538–539, 775). Here, Weber's analysis entwines with the aforementioned point on military technology, as he points out that the city militias in the Occident were often able to resist the armies of princes – in contrast to the situation in the Levant and the Orient (Collins 1986, 92; Weber 2003[1927], 320–321). But Weber is more interested in the effects than the causes.

As usual, his purpose is to explain the emergence of rational capitalism. Weber repeatedly emphasizes how the legal institutions that made capitalism possible – especially contractual relations – were developed in the Middle Ages (Swedberg 1998, 95–98; Weber 2003[1927], 341–342). More specifically, they were developed in the free cities, where the merchant class had a clear interest in a rule-based (non-arbitrary) commercial system. These innovations were possible because the more general test of strength between the kings/emperors and the Catholic Church (Collins 1986, 113) enabled the cities to operate independently of both. For instance, this helped to provide the independent sphere for the legal science that arose in medieval Italy.

To demonstrate the empirical purchase of this explanation, Weber carries out a number of large-scale historical comparisons. In his analysis of Confucianism and Hinduism – which as mentioned deals with much more than just religion – he repeatedly emphasizes the absence of autonomous cities (Collins 1986, 119; Poggi 2006, 83; see also Hintze 1975[1931], 342–343; cf. also Finer 1996, 445, 538–539). A veritable 'who's who' of researchers has since picked up on Weber's analysis of the free cities (Hintze 1975[1931], 342–343; Poggi 1978; Chirot 1985, 185; Stasavage 2014). For instance, Hall (1985, 136) declares without hesitation that Weber was correct in attributing importance to these cities.

Conclusions: Once causal chain?

We have seen that Weber touches upon a number of different causes in his attempt to explain the rationalization of the West, including the emergence of modern capitalism and the modern state. It makes sense to stop and ask whether these explanations can be combined into a single whole.

I already mentioned in the beginning of this chapter that Collins (1986) describes Weber's authorship as almost schizophrenic. Nevertheless, the very same Collins has attempted to draw up a causal model based on Weber's body of work. Generally speaking, Collins sees Weberian rationalization as being caused by a considerable number of factors, some of which are very deep factors while others are much more proximate to the effect (1986, 89).[9] It is difficult to reproduce this causal model for the very reason that it is composed of so many different elements. Collins emphasizes that the balance between the many elements has paved the way for rationalization. In other words, the causes have interacted with one another to produce rationalization (95–97).

The most general conclusion is therefore that Weber shows how an interweaving of economic, political, and religious factors (which might be impossible to place in one equation) are behind the rationalization process in the West (Swedberg 1998, 18–21). Methodologically, Weber is constantly identifying necessary but unto themselves insufficient conditions by using comparisons to show how these conditions also operate outside the West.

What then does Weber more precisely bring to the subject matter of the book: state formation, regime change, and economic development? C. Wright Mills (1959, 125) once noted that there are hardly any interesting ideas in the social sciences that cannot be traced back to the classic sociologists. If we were to highlight just one of these authors, Weber would be the one. I already mentioned in Chapter 2 that Weber has to a large extent formulated the questions we are wrestling with on these pages. But he was also a pioneer in the endeavour to answer them. His methodological approach – to generalize about the causes of historical developments within certain scope conditions – continues to characterize the field one hundred years later. And a number of his major contributions have been picked up and developed by later researchers.

This brings us back to where we started – that is, Weber's quarry, which anyone with any interest in history would be advised to visit, pick in hand. The next chapter examines a number of other classic contributions to comparative historical analysis before we return to the question why this rich literature emerged when and where it did, more than one hundred years ago in Continental Europe.

Notes

1 My thanks to Mogens Herman Hansen for drawing my attention to this.
2 Although in recent decades we have again experienced an increasing dialogue across disciplines, especially between political scientists and economists. An example of this is examined in Chapter 13.

3 In fact, Weber sees the modern state, rational law, and modern science as basic conditions for the modern market economy (capitalism) (Weber 2003[1927], 313).

4 See, for example, Weber's (2003[1927], 354) empirical conclusion about the catalogue of causes that was necessary for the emergence of rational capitalism.

5 Smelser interprets it solely as a MDSD, but the MSSD logic is also put to use by Weber on these pages.

6 Which also meant that the religious law – Mosaic Law – to some extent checked the kings of Juda. Weber links this point to rationalization alone. Others have linked it to political dynamics. From this perspective, Judaism created a regime form in which the monarchy did not have the power to pass laws but only to administer Mosaic Law. This development points towards the conceptions in the Christian Middle Ages about the authorities being bound by higher laws – and therefore also to a kind of limited monarchy (see Finer 1996, 254–263).

7 Moreover, scholars have argued that the Catholic Church broke clan bonds in a more specific sense in the Middle Ages via religiously endorsed inheritance practices. For an appraisal, see Hall (1985) and Fukuyama (2011).

8 Just as it was used – albeit qualified – by Otto Hintze (1975[1931], 331).

9 Collins is mainly building on the closing chapters of Weber's (2003[1927], 275–369) *Wirtschaftsgeschichte*, but it is worth remembering that this work builds on students' notes from Weber's last great series of lectures, where he has undoubtedly simplified his reading of the emergence of capitalism more than he would have in a carefully composed manuscript.

5

THE CLASSIC ANALYSES III

Schumpeter, Hintze, and Bloch

'Schumpeter was Weber's most noteworthy successor as an economic sociologist and historian'. So wrote Alfred Chandler in 1971 (see also Hughes 1958; Swedberg 1991). As this chapter shows, Schumpeter the economist was not alone in following in Weber's footsteps. The historians Otto Hintze and − less directly − Marc Bloch also did so. Schumpeter and Bloch differ from Hintze with respect to their extensive influence on the social sciences. In Schumpeter's case, this goes without saying. But Bloch has also, via the so-called *Annales* school, had an impact on the social sciences, in addition to his massive influence on the study of history (see Hobsbawm (1997[1978]).[1] His importance to Barrington Moore, Wallerstein, Anderson, and Tilly deserves to be singled out because it points towards later chapters in this book (Chirot 1984, 23).

Hintze's work has been more overlooked, at least outside the German university milieu (Gilbert 1975), although Barrington Moore (1991[1966], 415), in his renowned *Social Origins of Dictatorship and Democracy* (to which we will return in Chapter 6), builds on Hintze in a short passage on feudalism. But Hintze has enjoyed a renaissance in recent decades. Some of his important works were translated into English in 1975, and in 1985 Theda Skocpol introduced her attempt to bring the state back in with special emphasis on Hintze's earlier contribution (see Chapter 8). Likewise, Thomas Ertman draws extensively on Hintze in his book *Birth of the Leviathan* from 1997 (which we return to in Chapter 9).

More generally, the following pages will identify a number of interesting relationships and observations in the bodies of writing left by these three scholars − insights that are best understood in light of the review of Weber's writings in the previous chapter.

Schumpeter and Weber

Schumpeter, Hintze, and Bloch did not blindly accept Weber's conclusions. Schumpeter, for example, traced the origins of capitalism further back in time than did

Weber and he rejected the Protestant ethic explanation, directing attention instead to the modern banking system. Prior to the modern age, capitalism was static, as it had not really been possible to pursue new ideas by means of capital increases. However, the opportunity to loan money made it possible for the first time for entrepreneurial individuals and groups to expand and make investments, Schumpeter argued. This contributed to genuine growth, albeit repeatedly interrupted by recessions (Swedberg 1991, 36; Hawthorn 1992, 15–16).

Schumpeter is famous for this economic analysis of the dynamic character of capitalism, which rests upon his celebrated theory about the almost heroic entrepreneur who creates the dynamic element in the market economy via his or her ability to innovate (Schumpeter 1911; Swedberg 1991). However, in this chapter we will concentrate on two of Schumpeter's other contributions, both of which can be seen as efforts of Schumpeter as sociologist and both of which point towards some of the most prominent issues in today's democratization literature.

Schumpeter's fiscal sociology

At the summit of World War I, Austria was more or less bankrupt. Schumpeter (1991[1917/1918]) set out to diagnose the social consequences of this situation, which led to the essay *Die Krise des Steuerstaates* (the crisis of the tax state). While the immediate purpose was to analyse Austria's financial problems, Schumpeter took this opportunity to recommend the more general approach that sociologist Rudolf Goldscheid (1958[1925]) a few years earlier had dubbed 'fiscal sociology' (*Finanzsoziologie*). Schumpeter (1991[1917/1918], 100) approvingly cited Goldscheid's remark that 'the budget is the skeleton of the state stripped of all misleading ideologies', adding his own, equally lyrical claim that he who listens to fiscal history 'here discerns the thunder of world history more clearly than anywhere else' (101).

Schumpeter's aim was to capture the social processes that are reflected in the state budget.[2] According to Schumpeter, Western Christianity made a mighty leap forward when feudal states were replaced by 'tax states' in the High Middle Ages. Prior to this transition, the princes, kings, and emperors of Western Europe had financed the state with the surplus from their own domains. An explosion in the costs of warfare rendered this financial model unsustainable in the thirteenth century. The military technology of the day built on the use of mercenaries, and the European regents did not have the means to hire them. A similar pattern therefore repeated itself throughout Western Christendom in the period 1200–1500: the regents pleaded with the Estates (parliaments and diets) to impose taxes so that they could hire mercenaries for offensive or defensive campaigns. As a sweetener, the rulers offered to establish certain liberties and political representation for the privileged classes. The elite groups in society struck a bargain with the regent: taxes in exchange for rights and law enforcement.[3]

The tax state to which Schumpeter refers in the title of his essay – the forerunner of Max Weber's rational-legal state – was born out of this 'common exigency'

(106). The geopolitical pressure that caused it also served to rationalize adminis-tration and ensure the rights of the elite. Here, Schumpeter's analysis fits squarely into the war-made-the-state tradition, which first Hintze (more on this later in the chapter) and subsequently Tilly (see Chapter 9) have made such a key feature in comparative historical analyses and which constitutes a recurring theme in this book. However, Schumpeter's greatest contribution was to demonstrate that the emergence of the Weberian state can be analysed using fiscal sociology. Schumpeter here presents a historically grounded explanation as he situates these processes in time and space, beginning with Europe in the High Middle Ages.

Fiscal sociology never became what Schumpeter had hoped. Indeed, the disci-pline faded into oblivion after the 1920s (see Moore 2004). However, it appears to have made a comeback recently. Generally speaking, the influential theory about the 'resource curse' (Ross 2001) builds on similar ideas. Resource curse theory is best understood as an attempt to explain why a number of wealthy countries, particularly in the Middle East, are undemocratic despite the well-established link between modernization and democratization (Lipset 1959; Ross 2001; see Møller and Skaaning 2013, Chapter 7). Researchers have pointed out that the power elite in many countries in Africa and the Middle East finance themselves through the sale of resources that did not play any role in the European state formation process, not least oil, metals, and foreign aid. The more technical term is 'rentier states' – i.e., states that build on 'rents', which make the authorities independent of tax revenue collected from the citizenry. As a consequence, the authorities have little or no incentive to democratize or build a rational-legal state apparatus.

Some of the scholars working on the resource curse have directly suggested resurrecting fiscal sociology (see, e.g., Moore 2004; Møller 2007). In other words, Schumpeter's almost one-hundred-year-old ideas have proven highly productive in terms of explaining political change in contemporary developing countries.

Schumpeter's theory of imperialism

If there is one 'law' in political science, it is that liberal democracies do not engage in war with one another (Kant 1995[1795]; Sørensen 2008). With respect to the companion of modern liberal democracy – the free market economy – the tones are rather different (McDonald and Sweeney 2007; Møller and Skaaning 2010, 280–286). In the first half of the nineteenth century, liberal French economist Fred-eric Bastiat described the relationship between the market economy and peace as follows: 'When goods do not cross borders, soldiers will'. However, the outbreak of World War I has been used as smoking gun evidence against the peace-promoting consequences of the market economy. And Lenin, in *Imperialism, the Highest Stage of Capitalism*, went so far as to claim that capitalism and free trade are conducive to war and conflict.

Does it really make sense to see capitalism and imperialism as two sides of the same coin? Or does it make sense to establish a cause-and-effect relationship between the two? In the years following World War I, Schumpeter (1991[1919]) launched into a criticism of the Marxist coupling of capitalism and imperialism (Swedberg 1991, 99),[4] and his thoughts differ significantly from the mainstream.

What is imperialism, really? That was Schumpeter's introductory question in an essay titled *The Sociology of Imperialism*. He arrived at a clear answer: imperialism is a perpetual aggression – and corresponding territorial appetite – for aggression's own sake; literally, it is an 'aimless' aggression. A state is imperialistic when it has a persistent inclination to – without any 'rational' reason – lead wars of conquest (1991[1919], 143). More particularly, imperialism is the result of either a dominant war machine, war-like instincts in society, or what Schumpeter calls export monopolism (cf. Doyle 1986, 1152).

Schumpeter found an early but striking example of the first two elements among the Assyrians, who fought their neighbours simply because the god Assur 'demanded' it. The holy character of war meant that it was waged with the greatest imaginable cruelty; captured cities were burned to the ground; conquered enemies were crucified, were impaled, or had their eyes gouged out; often these were wars of extermination. But Schumpeter could reassure his readers that a culture can only display such aggression when it does not rest upon its own efforts. Where the daily grind at the plough or in the workshop is essential for perpetuating the system, the desire for conquest is suffocated by everyday practical chores (1991[1919], 173).

This brings us to the relationship between capitalism and imperialism. As should be clear, Schumpeter summarily dismisses the notion that capitalism prepares the ground for imperialism akin to that of the ancient Assyrians. The basic premise of the market economy is precisely that survival and prosperity can be achieved only by one's own efforts. At the same time, Schumpeter draws political elements into his explanation as he emphasizes the interaction between capitalism and democracy. The ordinary citizen in a capitalist society gets nothing out of a military adventure and will therefore turn against the parties advocating imperialistic policy (see also Doyle 1986, 1152).

Schumpeter traced the imperialistic tendencies of modern Europe – and in particular the numerous wars fought upon the continent itself – back to the age prior to the emergence of capitalism, to absolutist monarchy (1991[1919], 188). Take France, a country and nation that was forged by the sword. The medieval French kings legitimized themselves with a military ideology. The king was the first (and greatest) warrior, a status he constantly had to prove. Characteristically, the high nobility were referred to as the 'nobles of the sword' (*noblesse d'epée*). This legacy lingered long after the king – and for that matter the nobility – had stopped playing a practical role in warfare. The lust for war therefore survived the advent of capitalism. However, Schumpeter observes, the days of this aggressiveness were numbered. The capitalist form of production not just removes the basis for imperialism; it promotes a peace-friendly culture. In Schumpeter's own words:

> In a purely capitalist world, what was once energy for war becomes simply energy for labor of every kind. Wars of conquest and adventurism in foreign policy in general are bound to be regarded as troublesome distractions, destructive of life's meaning, a diversion from the accustomed and therefore

'true' task. A purely capitalist world therefore can offer no fertile soil to imperialist impulses. That does not mean that it cannot still maintain an interest
in imperialist expansion. We shall discuss this immediately. The point is that
its people are likely to be essentially of an unwarlike disposition. Hence we
must expect that anti-imperialist tendencies will show themselves wherever
capitalism penetrates the economy and, through the economy, the mind of
modern nations – most strongly, of course, where capitalism itself is strongest,
where it has advanced furthest, encountered the least resistance, and pre-
eminently where its types and hence democracy – in the 'bourgeois' sense –
comes closest to political dominion.

(192)

In these lines, Schumpeter is describing nothing less than a social mechanism on
the individual level – a mechanism linking capitalism with anti-imperialism or even
pacifism. This is interesting unto itself, for when the opposite claim is advanced
(that capitalism leads to imperialism) it is often with reference to the dark structural forces – a logic of exploitation inherent to the market economy, the demand
for natural resources or something of that ilk. Here, it is appropriate to repeat the
methodological message that also infuses Weber's work: a cause-and-effect relationship lacking a basis on the individual level is always questionable. Add to this that
Schumpeter's explanation is relatively easy to support with examples, one of which
he provides himself in his essay. Pacifism is, Schumpeter writes, a child of capitalism. The principle of embracing peace is obviously older than that, but only small
religious sects embraced it before our time (192).

The biggest objection to Schumpeter's analysis is his method, which, strictly
speaking, also characterizes the essay on the tax state. He describes this method as
an endeavour to analyse imperialism using historical examples that can be regarded
as 'typical'. By identifying the core features shared by these cases, which otherwise
differ enough that Schumpeter talks about *imperialisms* in plural instead of *imperialism* in the singular, he believes it is possible to capture the sociological essence of
imperialism (144). Schumpeter thus shies away from using controlled comparisons.

This does not alter the fact that he presents a genuine contribution to the literature. His theory about imperialism supports the economic element in the democratic
peace thesis (see Doyle 1986) – an element that, as mentioned, constitutes the Achilles' heel of the peace thesis. More generally, Schumpeter's fiscal sociology and his
theory of imperialism are two extremely interesting attempts at understanding the
uniqueness of the West. On this point in particular, Schumpeter followed the example
of Weber. As presented in the pages below, this was also Hintze's great undertaking.

Hintze and Weber

For much of his career, Otto Hintze was primarily occupied with Prussian history
and wrote extensively on the Hohenzollerns (Gilbert 1975, 10). Later in life he
began working with European history in general. This re-orientation can largely
be attributed to Weber's influence (Gerhard 1970, 32, 39; Gilbert 1975, 20–21).[5]

Hintze was inspired by Weber's great research questions as well as his findings and methods. In fact, the 'late' part of Hintze's work can be read as an attempt to continue Weber's efforts to explain the European uniqueness (Gerhard 1970, 24; Gilbert 1975, 22). As we shall see, Hintze ultimately produced a related but somewhat different answer to the question 'Why Europe?' In order to understand this, it is necessary to examine more carefully two points in Hintze's authorship: his geopolitical theory of state formation and his more specific analysis of the emergence of representative institutions in Europe.

Before we get that far, a few words about Hintze's method are in order. Like Schumpeter and Weber, Hintze was able to transcend disciplinary boundaries. Especially in his later analyses, he attempted to combine history and sociology (Gilbert 1975, 21). In fact, Hintze argued that mastering history, precisely because it deals with both general development tendencies and specific events, requires knowledge of other aspects of the social sciences (Gilbert 1975, 21). As in the case of Weber, this did not mean that Hintze attempted to uncover a kind of meta-historical logic capable of explaining the course of history. Instead, his objective was to unearth theoretically based empirical relations that were valid under specific conditions.

This requires historical comparisons. It is interesting to follow how Hintze's use of the comparative method develops over time. In his early analyses of European history, he used comparisons to illustrate how certain developments were repeated in numerous countries (Gilbert 1975, 14) – somewhat similar to Schumpeter's attempt to understand 'typical' cases. However, inspired by Weber, Hintze gradually embraced the use of the controlled comparisons, as he contrasted cases with and without certain theoretically relevant characteristics, such as feudalism. We will return to this in the discussion of Hintze's attempt to explain the emergence and spreading of representative institutions.

Geopolitics as the locomotive for state formation

> It is one-sided, exaggerated, and therefore false to consider class conflict the driving force in history. Conflict between nations has been far more important; and throughout the ages, pressure from without has been a determining influence on national structure.

These lines are from a famous essay Hintze (1975[1906], 183) wrote about the relationship between military relations and the character of the state (*Staatsverfassung und Heeresverfassung*). This relationship was not something that he had plucked out of thin air. The whole idea of the primacy of foreign policy (*Das Primat der Aussenpolitik*) dominated the writing of Prussian history and can be traced back to Leopold von Ranke, the founder of the modern academic study of history (Waltz 1959[1954], 7, 124; Gerhard 1970).

Hintze's historical work is first and foremost a kind of 'political history'. It focuses on the impact of governments and rulers on society – not on the social and economic structures that are derived from political developments (Gilbert 1975, 13). The more general point is that the European states emerged and were shaped in a world of *Schieben und Drängen* (pushing and shoving), which affected both the state apparatus and the form of government. Historically speaking, war has had two very important political consequences. First, warfare – depending on its regularity – has strengthened the centripetal forces in society at the expense of the centrifugal forces; war has consolidated state power. Second, warfare, depending on its character, has changed the internal balance of power in society, and thus has had very tangible political consequences.

As regards the former, the point is that the threat from foreign powers – and the related need to prepare for war – has traditionally strengthened central power and has often forced it to rationalize itself. 'War made the state and the state made war', as American sociologist Charles Tilly (1975) would later put it (see Chapter 9). Geopolitical pressure paved the way for the as yet rather pristine state apparatuses of the High and Late Middle Ages. In addition, geopolitical competition has had political effects. As we have already touched upon in the discussion of Schumpeter, the intensive warfare of the Middle Ages created a persistent financial need to pay for mercenaries, among other things (Hintze 1975[1906], 193). The privileged groups in society accepted taxation but demanded political and civil rights in return, including the regular summoning of Estates or parliaments. With the advent of universal conscription in the wake of the Napoleonic wars, these privileges gradually became universal, as the consent of commoners became critical for military success. In other words, this extension of the original bargain eliminated the privileges of the corporative elite groups that had dominated the medieval body politics (Hintze 1975[1906], 206–208; see also de Ruggiero 1927, 4).

However, this process did not unfold in the same manner throughout Europe. Hintze uses the character of geopolitical pressure to explain why England never developed an absolutist state (see also Ertman 1997, 11–12). The British Isles were simply not subjected to the same intensive pressure as the continent (Hintze 1975[1906], 199); at least not after the conclusion of the Hundred Years' War (1337–1453). Here, Hintze touches upon an issue that Brian M. Downing (1992) later took up in *The Military Revolution and Political Change* (see Chapter 9).

According to Hintze, the absolutist state was merely a temporary interruption in the process that – as a result of geopolitical pressure – created increasingly comprehensive political and civil rights. Hintze seemingly presents this as an analytical relationship that is valid across time and space. As we saw with Weber in the previous chapter, he traces it all the way back to Ancient Greece and the Roman Republic (183–184), noting that this relationship would also appear to characterize contemporary Russia, where representative institutions were being developed (212–213).[6] From the essay, it is difficult to tell whether Hintze actually perceived this as a universal relationship. If so, it would be at odds with his later writings.

Hintze's geopolitical theory constitutes a premise for his subsequent attempts at understanding the emergence of representative institutions in Europe. But here, the basic condition is expressly the European state system, which in Hintze's eyes was unique.

Feudalism and representative institutions

The uniqueness of the West is primarily attributable to the representative institutions that emerged in medieval Europe and later developed into modern parliaments, although the absolutist period temporarily interrupted this process in many countries. This summarizes Hintze's general reading of European history (1962[1929], 119; 1962[1930], 120; Gerhard 1970, 34; Gilbert 1975, 22; 1975[1931], 347–348).

These representative institutions are to be traced back to the medieval 'polity of Estates'. This distinguishes itself from modern states, which are characterized by an overall *Staatspersönlichkeit*, in terms of its fundamental dualism (cf. also Finer 1997a, 1029). Two separate halves faced each other, a princely/monarchical pole and a pole consisting of the Estates (representative institutions). The Estates represented the clergy, the nobility, and the autonomous/free cities. This basically meant that private and public law were intermingled as the legal system was characterized by privileges, not civil rights (Hintze 1962[1930], 120–124). Hintze distinguishes more specifically between two different forms of polity of Estates: a bicameral system, as we know it from the English parliament, and the more classic assemblies of estates with three chambers (tricurial assemblies), as known from France (124–129). The monarchical pole was generally stronger in the latter systems, while the estate pole was usually stronger in the former (139).

The difference between the bicameral and tricurial systems is important, as we shall see in Chapter 9. But even more important are the similarities: representative institutions distinguish Western Christendom from all other areas. In other words, the West began its unique journey towards the modern state as the medieval constitutionalism and the representative institutions (Estates) associated with them emerged after 1200 (see Myers 1975). This response to 'Why Europe?' obviously begs the question, 'Why representative institutions?' Hintze focused on this question in three consecutive essays: *Wesen und Verbreitung des Feudalismus* (1929), *Typologie der ständischen Verfassungen des Abendlandes* (1930), and *Weltgeschichtliche Bedingungen der Repräsentativverfassung* (1931). The three essays can basically be viewed as parts I, II, and III of a single work, which I summarize below.

As mentioned above, the very premise for Hintze's analysis is the existence of the European multistate system, where no omnipotent power centre (e.g., an empire) is able to prevent the competition between the entities in the system (more on this state system in Chapter 12). This paved the way for the rationalization of the state – born out of consideration for military survival – which according to Weber is unique to the West (Gerhard 1970, 32; Hintze 1975[1931], 313, 345–346). Hintze's three essays can be seen as an attempt at explaining the emergence of this system in general and the polity of Estates specifically.

The development of the European state system was strongly affected by the competition between state and church – that is, the fact that the papacy often stood in opposition to the emperors, kings, and princes (Hintze 1975[1931], 312). The origins of the state system should be dated more precisely to the High Middle Ages, as the Investiture Controversy between church and emperors and the prior Gregorian Revolution were preconditions for the church being able to defy the secular rulers (317; see also Fukuyama 2011).

According to Hintze, inter-state competition does not automatically bring about representative institutions. Two more specific factors must be present. We find the first in European feudalism. Hintze (1962[1929], 89–95) defines feudalism rather broadly (see Møller 2015a) and identifies feudalism both inside and outside Europe. Within Europe, feudalism characterized the Frankish successor states, England, and Southern Italy (i.e., what we today generally refer to as 'Western Europe'), but not Poland, Hungary, and Scandinavia (102–103). Outside Europe, Hintze finds feudalism in Russia, the Islamic states, and Japan, which, from a historical perspective, constitutes a 'strange parallel' (*merkwürdige Parallelismus*) (99). In keeping with the spirit of Weber, Hintze thus compares Europe directly with a number of Asian state formations (see also Hintze 1975[1931], 327–328).

On the one hand, Hintze is clear when it comes to the relationship between feudalism and the representative institutions. The latter grew out of the former as the polity of Estates simply institutionalized (and formalized) the political privileges of feudalism (1962[1929], 118; 1975[1931], 308; see also Gilbert 1975, 22). In other words, the polity of Estates is an institutionalized version of the balance of power between secular rulers and the corporative groups inherent to feudalism (Hintze 1975[1931], 350). On the other hand, for Hintze feudalism is neither a necessary nor a sufficient condition of the polity of Estates – for two reasons: there are areas with feudalism without parliaments (e.g., Japan), and there are areas with parliaments without feudalism (e.g., Poland).

Hintze therefore draws attention to another factor, namely the influence of the Catholic Church (Hintze 1975[1931], 308). The Church not merely – via the conflict with secular rulers – helped bring about the state system; the Church also contributed directly to the creation of the Estates via its attempt to ensure corporative representation for the clergy. Moreover – and above all else – the Church was essential to the dissemination of representative institutions to the parts of Western Christianity that did not have feudalism (318, 341). In these areas – Scandinavia and parts of Central Europe – it was the Church's demands for corporative privileges that extended similar privileges to other estate groups, particularly townsmen and the nobility. Strictly speaking, for Hintze the Catholic Church therefore emerges as the primary cause for the emergence of the Estates, the later representative institutions, and thus ultimately for explaining the uniqueness of the West (344–345). However, just like Weber, Hintze is not looking for monocausal explanations, and he therefore maintains that it was precisely the combination of feudalism, the independent Roman Church, and the European state system which produced the polity of Estates. More generally, the Western representative institutions are the product of a 'unique constellation' of factors characterizing medieval Europe (Gerhard 1970, 35). This constellation is in turn both necessary and sufficient, and it is best understood using a form of typological theory. Weber couldn't have said it better himself!

History seen as a whole: Bloch and the *Annales* School

The name Marc Bloch is associated with the so-called *Annales* School, which he established together with Lucian Febvre in France in the 1920s and 1930s, and which was later continued by researchers such as Fernand Braudel, Georges Duby, and Jacques Le Goff. The *Annales* School, which was built around the journal *Annales d'Histoire Economique et Sociale*, were the Young Turks rebelling against the historical establishment of the day. As indicated by the title of the journal, the rebels were out to expand the perspective of the historians – or at least their subject area. Instead of 'merely' sticking to historiography – that is, narrowly documenting the events of the past[7] – Bloch and his followers wished to draw on insights from and instruments used within fields such as sociology, geography, law, anthropology, and economics (Chirot 1984, 22). For instance, it was necessary to understand the collective mentality at different times and in different locations.

Good historians should be able to navigate the intersection between the social sciences; they must be able to do 'total history' (Burke 1992, xvi). This aim permeates Bloch's writings. Later, we shall see how Bloch used the *Annales* approach in his best-known work, the two-volume *Feudal Society* (*La société féodale*). The 'total history' agenda is nicely illustrated by the selected collection of Bloch's articles, which was translated to English in 1967. Article headings such as 'Technical change as a problem of collective psychology' speak for themselves, and Bloch repeatedly returns to the collective mentality in the societies he describes.

Indeed, as Eugen Weber (1982, 76) points out, the reader is practically blown away by the sheer scale of Bloch's academic interests: he reviewed works on Africa, China, Japan, and naturally Europe and switched back and forth between ancient slavery and match stick production in the twentieth century, alternating between anthropology, sociology, political science, linguistics, geography, and psychology.

The comparative method

Bloch's acquaintance with sister disciplines also formed the basis for his grand campaign to provide historians with an understanding of the comparative method. Bloch was a declared opponent of the tendency to shy away from historical comparisons, whether across time or space (du Boulay 1967, vii; Sewell 1967). His essay 'A contribution towards a comparative history of European Societies' illustrates the unfortunate consequences of attempting to understand particular historical cases independently of other cases.

In this article, Bloch notes that there are a series of monographs that attempt to shed light on the transition to regional representative assemblies in various parts of Western Europe in the High Middle Ages. These monographs have a tendency to emphasize a series of 'local' causes, including the choices made by significant actors. Bloch draws attention to how such assemblies sprang up *throughout* Western and Central Europe at this time. Obviously, such a general phenomenon can be explained only by general causes – that is, causes that are present *throughout* Western and Central Europe in this period (Bloch 1967, 55–56). As Rustow (1970, 350) once put it, individual case studies leave us unable to distinguish between the factors that represent the general trend and those that merely represent 'the national idiosyncrasies of Monographistan'. There might well be regional variations, but conditions that only characterize a single area, including the choices made by specific actors during a crisis, obviously cannot explain why the other areas also acquired assemblies at roughly the same time.

Bloch offers a number of similar examples, all of which are destructive for the attempt to understand a single case without situating it in comparative perspective. More generally, his purpose in the article is to demonstrate the indispensable value of the logic of comparative control mentioned in Chapter 2. The precise character of the comparative methods he recommends is not entirely clear (see Bloch 1967, 45–48). However, in his practical examples, Bloch is clearly thinking in terms of MSSD and MDSD logics. For instance, he uses an MSSD to explain why the relatively similar city-states of Genoa, Florence, and Venice did not begin issuing gold coins at the same time. Bloch first rejects prosperity as the cause, pointing out that Venice was richer than Genoa and Florence but issued gold coins a generation later than its two poorer peers. Instead, Bloch finds the crucial difference – the explanatory factor – in the positive trade balance between Genoa and Florence, on the one hand, and the Orient, on the other. This trade balance provided Genoa and Florence with an abundance of gold that was not found in more prosperous Venice, where silver from Western Europe flowed in large quantities (Bloch 1967, 209–210; cf. Sewell 1967, 209–210). In other words, the comparison allows Bloch to hold constant a number of similarities between the three cities, including prosperity, while singling out the crucial difference.

Conversely, Bloch's example of the origins of the Estates is a clear example of an MDSD. Here, we have the same outcome across a number of European cases, which are otherwise marked by regional differences (the local causes). The task is to identify the crucial uniformity that has created Estates despite the differences (i.e., to identify the general causes). Bloch grants that the same outcome in different cases does not necessarily prove that the same causes operate: 'imitation' is another possible explanation. But imitation in itself can only be identified by analysing multiple cases.

Bloch's understanding of the comparative logic similarly runs like a common thread through his incomplete *The Historian's Craft* (*Apologie pour l'histoire ou Métier d'historien*) from 1949. Here, he actually goes one step further, pointing out that comparisons are not merely necessary to uncover the causes; they are also required to carry out proper source criticism and to do historiography (Bloch 1954[1949], 119–122). Historians must generalize, both descriptively (using classifications) and by providing explanations.

Bloch's thoughts about how to periodize and demarcate historical entities are likewise intertwined with his thoughts on comparative method. Bloch went to great lengths to discuss how to define the temporal unit of historical investigations. He rejected that it automatically makes sense to think in centuries, decades, or the rule of individual monarchs. As he points out, there is no historical rule that years ending with a '0' or a '1' are more important than other years – just as rulers' spells might not in a meaningful sense demarcate historical periods. Bloch's alternative was to operate with either generations or civilizations (Bloch 1954[1949], 150–154; Chirot 1984, 35–36) – that is, two very different systemic wholes. Similarly, Bloch used his ideas about comparisons to expose the folly in automatically allowing territorial boundaries to demarcate cases (Bloch 1967, 71). This is above all misleading in the case of medieval Europe, where state boundaries were still in their infancy. But it is also possible that we should think more in terms of local regions than in countries in later periods. This point might be said to anticipate the current 'subnational turn' in comparative politics – i.e., the increasing focus on comparing different units below the country level (Snyder 2001).

Feudalism and estates

Bloch's greatest work is surely his two volumes on feudal society, *La société féodale*, from 1939. This work is in keeping with the best *Annales* tradition as Bloch (1971a[1939]; 1971b[1939]) attempts to capture the characteristics of an entire civilization. He crosses shamelessly back and forth between psychological, social, legal, military, and political spheres, and he analyses the medieval mentality, clan structure, contract law, class structure, vassal relations, and political organization.

Bloch's basic question is this: which characteristic feature of this part of the past provides reason to focus on it (1971a[1939], xx)? As a result of his broad approach, he arrives at a very broad answer. His definition of feudal society involves serfdom, fiefs, a specialized military elite, vassal relations that tie men to other men, fragmented authority, and finally the continued existence of other forms of organization, such as the family (1971b[1939], 446). In this sense, Bloch's definition is extremely comprehensive. It covers political, legal, economic, and social characteristics, and it even includes characteristics that are relics from other ages, such as ties of kinship.

One would expect that there are very few cases of 'feudalism' in this quite demanding version. Bloch does indeed point out that only the Frankish successor states really count as pure specimens (1971b[1939], 445–446). Paradoxically, however, he identifies a number of other cases. As far as Europe is concerned, we find feudalism throughout Western Europe in the High Middle Ages. Around the year 1100, feudalism was at its peak, and it gradually started disappearing around the year 1300 (Bloch 1971b[1939], 448). Just a few hundred years later, however, we find an almost equally pure specimen of feudalism in Japan (447). On this basis, Bloch – just like Hintze – emphasizes that feudalism is not an isolated case but rather a social process multiple areas have undergone.

The reason this is paradoxical is that scholars with a more strict definition usually only find feudalism in medieval Europe (Cantor 1993[1963], 196). How can we solve this paradox? Bloch would appear to use a kind of 'family resemblance' logic in order to identify instances of feudalism (see Herlihy 1970, xix; cf. Collier and Mahon 1993). This logic turns the more common Aristotelian logic – where each defining feature is necessary and the number of cases therefore decreases every time the definition is expanded – on its head. A member of the family (hence the name) is identified by the fact that they exhibit some of the features that define the family. The more features – defining characteristics – the more family members (Collier and Mahon 1993). It is only in this manner that Bloch's analysis makes sense.

There is an inherent danger that the use of such broad concepts can establish false historical analogies. Elsewhere I have demonstrated that this risk is especially great for scholars who use the feudalism concept to answer Weber's question, 'Why Europe?' (Møller 2015a). Here, I will merely note these objections and instead focus on the most important historical relationship in Bloch's work.

Bloch was concerned with the contractual character of feudalism – or, rather, vassal relationships (1971a[1939], 228). Lords and vassals were placed in a hierarchy where higher positions always carried more privileges than the lower positions. But even the lowest vassal had certain rights, which the lords could not ignore if they wanted to have the courts on their side. According to Bloch, these relations were inevitably extended to the political sphere over time. The resulting social contract, which can be traced all the way back to the Oaths of Strasbourg[8] in the year 842, was reflected in the limited duty of obedience and the corresponding right of rebellion. In the High Middle Ages, this 'ruling contract' found its institutional manifestation in the many charters of liberties, forced upon the regents in Latin Christianity by their nobles. The *Magna Carta* from 1215 is the best known. However, as Bloch points out, we find charters of liberties throughout Western and Central Europe in the thirteenth and fourteenth centuries (1971b[1939], 451–452). This prepared the way for the Estates, which were formed in the High Middle Ages (1971b[1939], 451–452).[9]

More generally, we can connect the 'contractualness' of the Middle Ages to the unique legalistic character that the state came to assume in Western Christianity (cf. Finer 1997b, 1298–1307). Like Hintze, Bloch thus emphasizes the link between feudalism and both political representation and the rule of law.

Conclusions

Two general points begin to form. First, the classic comparative historical analyses can generally be understood as an attempt at answering the question 'Why Europe?' Second, this research agenda transcended disciplinary boundaries in a manner that for long afterwards was inconceivable in the social sciences but might be making a comeback (see Part IV). Weber, Schumpeter, and Hintze all mastered economic theory, sociology, and history – mainly because the boundaries between academic trades and professions were more blurry one hundred years ago (Swedberg 1991, 93).

Another reason was that especially German academic environments at the time of Weber, Schumpeter, and Hintze emphasized the ability to operate in the intersections between different academic disciplines.

Schumpeter, for example, repeatedly emphasized that a good economist had to have an extensive historical knowledge. Swedberg (1991, 106) even claims that Schumpeter had greater historical versatility than later historical sociologists like Barrington Moore, Charles Tilly, and Theda Skocpol, as Schumpeter worked in an environment with an entirely different and deeper understanding of history than anyone today. This is probably an exaggeration, but there is little doubt that no living economist is able to operate on the level of Schumpeter and Weber[10] with respect to historical knowledge.

Weber's and Schumpeter's attempt to develop *Sozialökonomik* can precisely be understood as an endeavour to integrate different disciplines (Swedberg 1991; 1998). More specifically, *Sozialökonomik* was Weber's proposed solution to the renowned German *Methodenstreit*. This was a dispute between the advocates of economic history (led by Gustav von Schmoller) and the advocates of economic theory (led by Carl Menger). Weber's point, which Schumpeter adopted, was that economic history and economic theory were both necessary but that they ought to co-exist and communicate as parallel disciplines on the same level. *Sozialökonomik* was, thus, a more general field that included economic history, economic theory, and sociology. This ability to cross between fields paved the way for the major comparative historical analyses described in Chapters 4 and 5 – the likes of which the social sciences have not seen since!

Notes

1 Hobsbawm (1997[1978], 237, 242) mentions that Bloch was already regarded as one of the greatest living medievalists in 1930s Cambridge (see also Weber 1982).

2 Tellingly, Schumpeter (1991[1917/1918], 101) noted that 'even greater than the *causal* is the *symptomatic* significance of fiscal history'.

3 Schumpeter is not alone in making note of this relationship. Multiple generations of liberal thinkers have done the same. John Carteret, one of the great English statesmen of the eighteenth century, put it aptly in his observation that '[t]he Security of our Liberties are [sic] not in the Laws but by the Purse being in the Hands of the People' (quoted in Brewer 1989). We encounter something similar in Montesquieu's (1989[1748], 220) *The Spirit of the Laws* in phrasing that is repeated almost verbatim in Guido de Ruggiero's (1927) excellent history of European liberalism. To quote the latter: 'As a general rule, heavier taxes can be raised in proportion as the subject enjoys more liberty; as liberty decreases taxes must be diminished. In free States heavy taxes are counterbalanced by liberty; in despotic States the lightness of the taxes is a compensation for the loss of liberty' (54–55).

4 Schumpeter's essay was written against the Austrian Marxists Rudolf Hilferding and Otto Bauer more than against Lenin. Indeed, Schumpeter was probably not even aware of Lenin's writings from 1917 on capitalism as the highest stage of imperialism (Swedberg 1991, 99). But as Lenin built on similar Marxist ideas as Hilferding and Bauer, this makes little difference.

5 Hintze's steadily deteriorated eyesight would also appear to have played a role. The wear on his eyes rendered it impossible to continue his work in the archives, which compelled

Hintze to turn his attention towards the bigger lines in European history (Gilbert 1975, 20f.).

6 Remember that Hintze's essay is from 1906 – that is, the year after the 1905 revolution in the wake of which a national Duma (parliament) was established and a multi-party system was allowed. This presumably made an impression on him.

7 The purest formulation of this narrow view of the field of history is found in von Ranke's renowned dictum that it is not the historian's responsibility '[. . .] das Amt die Vergangenheit zu richten, die Mitwelt zum Nutzen zukünftiger Jahre zu belehren, sondern bloß zu zeigen, *wie es eigentlich gewesen*'.

8 Charles the Bald and Louis the German pledged allegiance to one another at Strasbourg in the year 842 in an alliance against their third brother, Lothar I. The Oaths of Strasbourg are famous because they contain the following provision: if one of the brothers broke his oath, his soldiers – who were also sworn – were free to abstain from assisting their king. Many therefore trace the germ of popular sovereignty to the Oaths of Strasbourg.

9 Note, however, that already in the beginning of the fourteenth century, the English Parliament would appear to play a more important role than the continental Estates (Bendix 1978, 193). In this sense, it can be argued that the English development is unique.

10 In Weber's case, this is entirely obvious. In *Wirtschaftsgeschichte* (2003[1927]), the reader is struck by the combination of grandiose historical comparisons and detailed historical knowledge. One moment, Weber is comparing medieval Europe with China, India, or ancient Egypt; the next moment, the reader is presented with information about agrarian conditions in Celtic Ireland, Scandinavia in the Viking era, or German areas during the Germanic migrations. And these are merely transcribed copies of students' notes from Weber's lectures! The quality of the notes also reveals how Weber's students had an entirely different knowledge of history than contemporary students.

PART III

The Barrington-Moore research programme

6

BARRINGTON MOORE AND THE REBIRTH OF THE DISCIPLINE

All fields of research in the social sciences have their classics, but few of these classics occupy as prominent a position as Barrington Moore's (1991[1966]) *Social Origins of Dictatorship and Democracy* (hereafter *Social Origins*) does in comparative historical analysis. The reason is twofold. First, a great number of subsequent analyses relate to Moore's results (see Kitschelt 1992). Thus, Downing (1992), to whom we will return in Chapter 9, writes in *The Military Revolution and Political Change* that it 'is no overstatement to say that every page of this study was written with attention to Barrington Moore's classic study of the same questions' (241).

Secondly and even more importantly, Moore's work revived the classic field of research, which we – via visits to Tocqueville, Weber, Hintze, Schumpeter, and Bloch – have discussed in the previous chapters (cf. Skocpol 2003, 408). Stephens (1989, 1020) points out that *Social Origins* 'is one of the most widely read and cited books in social science' (see also Mahoney 2003a, 137). Skocpol (1979, xv), in the preface to *States & Social Revolutions* (discussed in Chapter 8) declares that her greatest debt is to Moore and his *Social Origins*. Downing acknowledges the same debt when he gives thanks to Moore in the preface to *The Military Revolution and Political Change* for 'posing an important question twenty-five years ago, and for boldly advancing an answer that cut against the grain' (xii). For these two reasons, I follow Mahoney (2003a, 137–152) in referring to the works discussed in Part III as 'the Barrington Moore research programme'.

Let us return to the second Downing quote. Exactly how did Moore go against the tide? He did so in multiple ways. As mentioned in Chapter 2, at the time when Moore was working on *Social Origins*, ahistorical theories of social action, particularly Talcott Parson's functionalism, dominated political science. In Mahoney's words (2003a, 151), researchers either avoided the major macro-historical questions or dealt with them using Parson's very abstract (hence ahistorical) theory.

Moore's contribution was to create a turnaround in the discipline, and with his emphasis on structural factors, he defined the meta-approach referred to in Chapter 2 as 'structuralism' (Mahoney 2003a, 151–152). An example from the literature illustrates this. Hall (1985, 1) describes how his history teachers at Cambridge had taught him that social structures play no role – that the course of history is determined by actors. His 'encounter with Barrington Moore's *Social Origins of Dictatorship and Democracy* therefore amounted to, as the French so nicely put it, *la scène de seduction*'.

Finally, *Social Origins* can be read as a reaction against the modernization literature that was so prominent in the 1960s. The modernization literature was analytical in the sense that its basic claim was the existence of a positive relationship between economic wealth and democracy (Lipset 1959), independent of time and place. As indicated by the subtitle of Moore's book, *Lord and Peasant in the Making of the Modern World*, he did not believe that things were so simple. Moore draws attention to the structure of land ownership (iix). Already in the preface, he declares that the book can be seen as an attempt to 'understand the role of the landed upper classes and the peasants' (xxiii) in the creation of the paths to democracy and dictatorship in the modern world. Moore's general message is that the political effects of industrialization are historically specific, as they are determined by the encounter between these agrarian classes and the nascent bourgeoisie. Modernization via capitalism therefore has very different political effects than modernization via a planned economy.

Femia (1972, 21) accordingly interprets *Social Origins* in terms of a modernization theory arguing that democracy is the result of a *certain kind* of modernization, namely the Anglo–American variant. There is something to be said for this interpretation. However, precisely because the existing modernization theory was inspired by Parson's ahistorical functionalism, *Social Origins* represented something of a showdown with conventional wisdom.

If we are to gather the threads, it would be fair to say that, when considering the classic status of *Social Origins*, the fact that Moore set a new course weighs much heavier than his actual findings. In fact, the number of scholars who have subsequently accepted Moore's results is rather limited (see Mahoney 2003a, 137–138). One reason for this is that it is difficult to scrutinize Moore's work, as he is often rather vague, sometimes almost opaque (Coppedge 2012, 142). This vagueness is partly due to the breadth of the spectrum he covers and partly due to his emphasis on the timing of the events. But it is also due to his open, Socratic approach. Moore learns as the story in the book unfolds; he is not tied to a pre-established model (Smith 1984). This is an admirable characteristic in any researcher (cf. Hirschman 1970). However, as touched upon in Chapter 2, this can also be argued to undermine Moore's ability to subject the relationships with which he is working to a scientific test. Moreover, attempting to summarize and retest Moore's results is a rather frustrating endeavour because his theory, due to its vagueness, has a tendency to slip through the fingers.

Moore's questions

Moore worked on *Social Origins* for around ten years. The book is probably the last great comparative historical analysis where the author has read virtually all relevant literature on the subject, usually in the original languages. Moore hails from the era when well-educated Americans still mastered foreign languages. In college, he had learned Latin, Greek, French, German, and Russian and was then able to read academic literature in these languages (Munck and Snyder 2007, 88). Few Americans (or for that matter Europeans) of my generation can say the same. Here again, Moore points back towards the classic tradition in comparative historical analyses described in the preceding chapters.[1] For example, Schumpeter had learned perfect German, English, French, Latin, and ancient Greek in high school, linguistic skills which he maintained his entire life. He died with *The Iliad* (in the ancient Greek) in front of him. Marc Bloch's linguistic abilities were even more impressive; he read scientific literature written in German, English, Spanish, Italian, Flemish, Latin, and multiple Scandinavian languages, and he wrote and published in five of these languages (Weber 1982, 73–74). The broad, classic cultural schooling these generations of researchers had with them is difficult to find today.[2] In this sense, there is hardly any doubt that we are indeed (to once again use Newton's renowned expression) standing on the shoulders of giants.

Back to Moore (1991[1966]) and *Social Origins* – the book is intended to uncover the most prominent paths to democracy and dictatorship:

> The first and earlier route through the great revolutions and civil wars led to the combination of capitalism and Western democracy. The second route has also been capitalist, but culminated during the twentieth century in fascism. . . . The third route is of course communism.
>
> *(xxi–xxii)*

The first destination is democracy, while the other two, apropos the title of Moore's book, are different instances of dictatorship. For Moore, this is the decisive political distinction (Smith 1984, 329–330). It is therefore worth establishing from the outset exactly what Moore means by 'democracy'. As Stone (1967) writes, Moore classifies his countries in relation to the dependent variable based on institutional and legal standards. More precisely, Moore's definition is as follows: democracy represents efforts '1) to check arbitrary rulers, 2) to replace arbitrary rules with just and rational ones, and 3) to obtain a share for the underlying population in the making of the rules' (1991[1966], 414).

Some researchers have argued that Moore is equating democracy and 'liberal democracy' (Femia 1972, 22). However, his is a rather narrow, minimalistic definition of democracy, which requires neither equal nor universal suffrage. This means that Moore is able to identify a number of democracies in the nineteenth century. These were political systems in which political competition and later the parliamentary principle made inroads without it necessarily leading to all citizens of a certain age being accorded the right to vote and stand for election (Przeworski 2009). More generally, one might claim that Moore's dependent variable has more to do with constitutionalism and limited political competition than with democracy per se. As presented below, part of the criticism of Moore's work follows from other researchers applying a broader (more maximalist) definition of democracy (see also Møller and Skaaning 2013, Chapter 8).

Another important part of the criticism relates to the period Moore studies. Stone (1967), among others, has pointed out that Moore's differences on the dependent variable gradually 'disappear' after World War II. Contemporary Germany and Japan are thus democracies today – in fact, they were already democracies when Moore wrote his book. One might therefore question whether or not Moore has identified relevant, long-term differences or if he is merely studying a transition phase. This does not mean that Stone (1967) is of the opinion that Moore's work is irrelevant. He argues that there are actually some other questions in *Social Origins* that are more relevant than the general question about different paths of regime change. More specifically, Stone draws attention to Moore's efforts to shed light on the roots and consequences of revolutions as well as his attempt to identify the pre-conditions for modernization and industrialization. We will return to both later in this chapter.

Moore's approach and method

In *Social Origins*, Moore conducts an endogenous class analysis, where the class struggle is reflected in a particular form of government. This approach has had a huge influence in comparative historical analysis. Later work, such as Luebbert (1991) and Rueschemeyer et al. (1992), use much the same approach (cf. also Capoccia and Ziblatt 2010, 933–934).[3] Against this background, it is worthwhile pondering whether Moore's analysis qualifies as a (neo)Marxist analysis? A number of scholars claim this to be the case (Rothman 1970; Femia 1972, 40–41; Skocpol 1973). Rothman (1970, 62) is the most categorical, as he emphasizes that Moore's analysis rests on two 'neo-Marxist' assumptions: the relations of production determine the ideology of the social classes as well as the political structure, and the primary objective of ruling classes is always to exploit the masses.

As a result, Rothman points out, cultural factors become epiphenomenal; that is, they follow directly from the material conditions (and therefore lack any independent explanatory power), and revolutions are always a consequence of the power-elite exploiting the lower classes to the point where it triggers a violent response (1970, 62). In this connection, Rothman (65) reasons that *Social Origins* can be seen as a break with Weber's emphasis on the significance of cultural factors (cf. also Femia 1972, 41–42) – what is occasionally referred to as 'Weberism' (Hall 1985, 16–17, 19–21). Skocpol (1973) concurs that the analysis in *Social Origins* is neo-Marxist, first and foremost in order to point out that Moore overlooks the significance of state structures.

The interpretations presented by Rothman, Femia, and Skocpol make sense, up to a point. Moore clearly sees class struggle as the force driving political change and just as obviously rejects cultural explanations (1991[1966], 486). Nevertheless, it is more apt to say that Moore is expanding Marx's structural approach. He thus deals with the timing of the commercialization of agriculture, and the working class plays no role in his analysis. In fact, one of his important points is that the communist revolutions occurred in agrarian societies, not industrialized societies – a circumstance Marxist class analysis struggles to explain. Similarly, it is rather obvious that Moore, in the course of his analysis, draws in numerous other explanatory elements that again do not fit in a neo-Marxist analysis.[4] In fact, Moore's analysis contains at least one partly cultural element: much is determined by which social group achieves hegemony over the others.

It therefore seems better – with Mahoney (2003a, 151–152) – to credit Moore as the man behind the meta-approach 'structuralism'. We have already discussed this in Chapter 2, and providing a comprehensive description would lead to unnecessary repetition. Suffice it to highlight the main point – that combinations of structures (particularly the class structure, the state infrastructure, and international structures) weigh heavier than, and set the framework for, cultural factors and actors' choices.

Nor is it entirely clear whether Moore's analysis should be understood as a deterministic structuralist theory. Femia (1972, 37) argues rather convincingly that this was not Moore's intention, while Rothman (1970, 62) interprets Moore in this manner. It does seem reasonable to assume, however, that the theory – if not the actual analysis – is conceived in terms of deterministic rather than probabilistic causation.

With respect to the methodological tools, the secondary literature disagrees on what Moore is doing more precisely in *Social Origins*. Stone (1967) finds a clear application of comparative method and praises Moore for this, claiming that nobody had ever previously used the comparative method in such a large-scale study. Others have highlighted Moore's savvy use of case studies. This debate can be concluded by noting that Moore combines intensive case studies with comparisons across cases (Smith 1984, 317). In other words, he uses the logic of comparative control (see, e.g., Moore 1991[1966], xix–xx) but at the same time attempts to understand the details in the individual country developments – how analogous processes play out in different places and at different times – in order to confirm his established causal chain. Smith (1984, 347) refers to this particularly demanding combination as the 'great strength' of Moore's work.

Moore's explanation

Moore uses these tools to uncover the three aforementioned paths to democracy, fascism, and communism, respectively. As already touched upon, these paths can also be regarded as three different ways of undergoing large-scale industrialization/modernization (Rothman 1970, 61) – with significant political consequences.

The democratic track is the most important for Moore, and he emphasizes that it runs via 'bourgeois revolutions': the English Civil War, the French Revolution, and the American Civil War. These revolutions weaken the agrarian aristocracy, strengthen the middle class, and mark the final 'disappearance' of the peasantry as a class. As Stone (1967) points out, the bourgeois revolution is crucial for the democratic track; according to Moore, democracy is born of a violent rupture of the traditional structures (see Moore 1991[1966], 505–506). Secondly, Moore exposes another route according to which industrialization is carried out 'from above' via an alliance between state power and a weakened bourgeoisie. The result of this alternative capitalist route, which in his own words runs through 'abortive bourgeois revolutions' (xxiii), is fascism. Moore's third route is characterized by a strongly centralized state power, a weak middle class, and therefore a great revolutionary potential among the subjugated peasantry. For Moore, an important point here is that the misery of the peasants does not in itself lead to revolution – he finds impoverishment in all of the three routes (xix–xx) – what is crucial is their relationship to the agrarian upper class.

As these descriptions suggest, it is difficult to single out a set of independent variables that systematically explain the three routes. As Stephens (1989, 1022–1023) emphasizes, Moore's explanatory factors are presented in a very vague way in *Social Origins* (cf. also Mahoney 2003a, 137). Tellingly, the literature has very different ideas about what the content of Moore's explanation actually is (Mahoney 2003a, 138). According to Skocpol's (1973, 10) early attempt to capture Moore's model, it is possible to identify three variables. First, a strong 'Bourgeoise Impulse' is necessary and sufficient for democracy. No other factors are individually necessary or sufficient. Skocpol furthermore observes that the 'Bourgeoise Impulse' is an unexplained, given premise in Moore's analysis, but one that determines which alliances can be entered into. The second variable is whether agriculture is commercialized or not. Here, Skocpol distinguishes between the categories 'labour-repressive' and 'market'. We find the market-based form in the democratic path, while both paths to dictatorship run via the labour-repressive category. The third variable measures 'Peasant Revolutionary Potential'. The path to fascism is only possible if the bourgeois revolutions did not remove this revolutionary potential while no peasant revolutions interrupted to lead the country to communism.

In relation to what I have earlier said about Moore's break with modernization theory, it is rather odd that Skocpol's interpretation is easily set in a modernization perspective. The first path thus seems more 'modernized' on the first two variables. And the hierarchy can be extended to the two other paths in the sense that a medium-high level of modernization leads to fascism, while a low level leads to communism. Before we accept this interpretation, however, it is worth emphasizing that other researchers have interpreted Moore very differently. Femia (1972, 23) identifies five necessary conditions for democracy in *Social Origins*. Stephens and Kümmel (2003, 46) distinguish between no less than five more general independent variables; I will bring the three most important of these together in an explanatory typology at the end of this chapter.

Smith (1984, 328–329) goes so far as to argue that it makes no sense to think in a set of independent variables because Moore's three routes are merely analytical categories, not genuine combinations of variables. As we shall also see below, there are thus important differences within the individual routes. According to Smith, this finds expression in the way Moore distinguishes between the routes based on the outcome – democracy, fascism, and communism – rather than the causes.

It is nevertheless possible to identify a set of general patterns in Moore's mosaic. As Mahoney (2003a, 138–139) points out, there is widespread consensus that two general hypotheses can be derived from *Social Origins*: first, the famous 'No bourgeois, no democracy' (1991[1966], 418) – that is, the point that the middle class or the bourgeoisie is one of the *condiciones sine quibus non* of democracy. The democratization processes in Britain, France, and the United States succeeded because the middle class avoided becoming an appendage of the agrarian aristocracy, Moore argues. The second is the conclusion that the same agrarian aristocracy – the large landowners – has historically been democracy's number-one enemy. This is also referred to as the 'Moore-Gerschenkron thesis', as economic historian Alexander Gerschenkron had previously stressed this relationship (Mahoney 2003b, 364–365). In the fascist cases, Germany and Japan, democracy was prevented by the alliance between the landowners and the middle class and by their combined ability to let the peasants feel the iron fist. In the communist cases, Russia and China, it was the landowners' reluctance against commercializing agriculture that rendered the communist revolutions possible.

Criticism

Let us begin the critical appraisal of Moore by asking whether or not these two hypotheses have found support in the literature that developed in the wake of *Social Origins*? Generally speaking, there is more or less consensus that much is to be said for the second hypothesis, whereas the first hypothesis has received considerable criticism (Therborn 1977; Stephens 1989; Mahoney 2003a). This criticism points to some more general problems with Moore's analysis. As Mahoney (2003a) recounts, later empirical tests of Moore's paths have provided little support to the analysis in *Social Origins*. Table 6.1 attempts to illustrate this with the help of Stephens' (1989) and Stephens and Kümmel's (2003) expanded appraisal of Moore's relationships.

As illustrated above, Moore's analysis appears somewhat battered and bruised after Stephens (1989) and Stephens and Kümmel (2003) attempt to retest it on a larger sample of countries. Only nine of the twenty-one countries fit Moore's predictions. This table goes to show that Moore's analysis has not proven particularly strong empirically.

But, we must ask, is it at all reasonable to carry out such an expansion? There is hardly any doubt that Moore – for example, by including India and China – presents his relationship as general, possibly even universal (Rothman 1970, 73; Femia 1972, 23). However, in *Social Origins* he emphasizes that 'small' countries do not work as proper test material, because the most important impulses in the political development of these countries are exogenous – that is, follow from the development in the large countries that Moore includes in his analysis (1991[1966], x; see

TABLE 6.1 Moore's implicit explanatory typology with additional countries (based on Stephens 1989 and Stephens and Kümmel 2003)

		Strong agrarian elite		Weak agrarian elite	
		Bourgeois politically important but less strong than the agrarian elite	Bourgeois not politically important and less strong than the agrarian elite	Bourgeois politically important but less strong than the agrarian elite	Bourgeois not politically important and less strong than the agrarian elite
Outcome: authoritarian regime	Absence of revolutionary juncture	Austria Estonia Hungary Poland Portugal Romania Spain	Germany Italy		Greece
	Presence of revolutionary juncture				
Outcome: democratic regime	Absence of revolutionary juncture	Czechoslovakia			Belgium Denmark Finland Ireland Netherlands Norway Switzerland Sweden
	Presence of revolutionary juncture		Great Britain		France

Note: As mentioned earlier in this chapter, Stephens and Kümmel (2003) operate with no less than five explanatory conditions, but only the three included into the typology seem to be necessary based on a closer reading.

also Mahoney 2003a, 139). Stephens (1989) convincingly argues that this premise cannot be sustained (see also Femia 1972, 39). Add to this (see Table 6.1) that, according to recent analyses, the greatest problems with Moore's theory actually owe to the countries he used in *Social Origins* (cf. Mahoney 2003a, 139, 145).

Further along these lines, it has been pointed out that England, France, and the United States, the three countries that have moved along the democratic path, differ in several ways. As Skocpol (1973) points out, the path via bourgeois revolutions is very much a residual category, as there are great dissimilarities between the three revolutions – revolutions that are, mind you, crucial for Moore's theory.

This brings us back to Moore's two theses. Stephens (1989, 1028, 1068) points out that it was only in large countries, such as France, that an actual revolution was required to remove the barriers formed by the agrarian aristocracy on the way to democracy. The small European countries did not have a similarly strong land-owning class. Stephens hastens to add that the landed aristocracy – with the Prussian Junkers as the most paradigmatic example – have been the most consistently undemocratic class. Luebbert (1991, 308–309) has criticized this conclusion on the basis of a detailed analysis of the areas in which the undemocratic parties secured their support (see also Mahoney 2003a, 142; 2003b, 364–365). Nevertheless, there is general agreement that this is the most empirically durable aspect of Moore's analysis (cf. Mahoney 2003a, 147).

It is a very different situation with Moore's first – and most famous – hypothesis: 'No bourgeois, no democracy'. A string of scholars have shown that, historically, the middle class has at best been ambivalent about democracy (Therborn 1977; Stephens 1989, 1065; Rueschemeyer et al. 1992). Instead, these scholars have identified the working class as the locomotive of democratization. Stephens (1989, 1030–1034, 1064) thus shows how World War I strengthened the working class at the cost of the other classes and thereby helped pave the way for democracy: a relationship that both Moore and Lipset (1959) – the latter in his modernization theory – ignore.

This criticism misses the mark to some degree. As described above, Moore's definition of democracy is relatively minimalistic in the sense that it does not require equal and universal suffrage. However, the analyses that have criticized Moore on this point do. It is therefore possible for both parties to be right, at least up to a point. As several of the critical analyses show, the middle class has historically fought for its own political inclusion and the rule of law and constitutionalism, whereas it has been more reluctant (often downright hostile) when it comes to extending political rights to the lower classes (see particularly Therborn 1977). The criticism therefore loses much of its force if we draw a systematic distinction between minimalistic and maximalist definitions of democracy (Møller and Skaaning 2013, Chapter 8; see also Mazzuca 2010b).

Another way of putting this is that much of the criticism really concerns the fact that Moore does not take developments in the second half of the nineteenth and the first half of the twentieth centuries particularly seriously. This is why Stephens (1989, 1019) can declare that while his own empirical results confirm parts of Moore's analysis, Moore underestimates the role played by the working class because he 'stops too early'. The devil, as the saying goes, is in the details. Nevertheless, there is still reason to underwrite Mahoney's (2003a, 145) conclusion that Moore's analysis cannot be maintained in the light of recent research, as also demonstrated in Table 6.1 (see also Femia 1972, 23).

Finally, it makes sense to distinguish here between the 'early' and 'late' criticism of *Social Origins*. The criticism so far summarizes the latter category, which has attempted to retest Moore's paths empirically. The early criticism was directed at more specific points in Moore's work.[5] For example, it was pointed out that the revolutionary junctures along the democratic path were not nearly as violent as Moore makes them out to be. In particular the English 'enclosures' did not mark a radical restructuring of the agrarian structures (see Stone 1967; Rothman 1970, 67–70; Femia 1972, 25; Moore 1991[1966], 28–29). Similarly, many scholars have questioned Moore's claim that the American Civil War was necessary to prevent an alliance between the capitalists in the North and the Junker-like plantation aristocracy in the South – an alliance that, according to Moore, would have led to American fascism (Rothman 1970, 73; Femia 1972, 30).

There is also a methodological aspect to this criticism, namely that Moore commits 'confirmation bias' in the way he processes narrative historical evidence to test his explanation (Goldthorpe 1991; Lustick 1996). For instance, in his analysis of the English case, he relies heavily on Tawney (1912, 1941), whose thesis is rather similar to Moore's in a very important respect, namely the role of the English bourgeoisie in the English revolution (see Goldthorpe 1991; Lustick 1996, 608–610; Lange 2012, 147). It is therefore hardly surprising that, based on Tawney, Moore is able to empirically corroborate his theoretical arguments.

However, the early criticism was most strongly directed at the flat rejection of the independent significance of culture and ideas. Femia (1972, 45) expresses the frequent and almost shocking objections when he notes that Moore

> can explain French and American democracy without reference to Enlightenment thought, discuss the origins of Nazism in isolation from German Romanticism and Idealist philosophy, neglect the role of nationalism as a prime force behind the Chinese Revolutions of the twentieth century, and underestimate the implications of Western and Soviet models for the Third World.

As Smith (1984, 335) points out, this is a rather strange approach for a researcher whose first book, on Soviet policy, was sub-titled *The Role of Ideas in Social Change*.

Conclusions

Barrington Moore's *Social Origins of Dictatorship and Democracy* is undoubtedly the most important 'modern' work in comparative historical analysis. It might therefore appear slightly paradoxical to have learned that subsequent research has disproven rather than confirmed Moore's conclusions about the routes to democracy and dictatorship. The criticism of Moore's approach has at times been very harsh; some critics even call Moore's position 'intellectually and morally untenable' (Rothman 1970, 82). Indeed, it seems fair to say that *Social Origins* is one of the most controversial recent works in the social sciences. The most vehement rejections probably concern Moore's conclusion that an abrupt, violent revolution is necessary for democracy. Or, according to Rothman's (1970, 80–81) interpretation: the normative message that a radical revolution serves liberty and development better than a gradual development.

So why does Moore's book nevertheless enjoy a status as *the* modern classic of the discipline? Above all else because with *Social Origins*, Moore 're-discovered' the approach that Weber and Hintze excelled at some one hundred years ago. This is not to say that Moore builds on Weber and Hintze. As mentioned, he actually rejects the 'Weberist' emphasis on the independent role played by ideas (Rothman 1970, 64–65); and though he refers to Hintze in passing when he discusses feudalism (Moore 1991[1966], 415), he does not use the German historian's work actively in *Social Origins* either. Moore's most important contribution is his insistence that the comparative historical analysis of a limited number of countries – based on structural variables – has its place in social science and that the timing of events often affects their causes.

I have already described how, each in their own way, Skocpol, Hall, and Downing emphasize that their works would be almost inconceivable without Moore. More generally, the 'Barrington Moore research programme' has taught us much about deeper factors of democracy and dictatorship. Moore's greatest contribution is thus that he has inspired others to follow suit (Mahoney 2003a, 138). This slightly ambivalent relationship to Moore's work also permeates this book. As we shall see in the chapters that follow, few subsequent analyses draw directly on Moore's substantial points. However, the aim of this book – taking comparative historical analyses seriously – would almost be unthinkable without Moore's pioneer work.

Notes

1 Moore also reminds us of his great predecessors in another sense. At a time when political science is engaging in ever larger and more expensive research projects with ever-increasing numbers of participants, it is rather refreshing to hear the laconic quip he gave shortly before his death (in 2004) when asked which facilities and resources he required for his research: 'I just need transportation to the library and transportation back home again, that's it' (see Munck and Snyder 2007, 108).

2 It is of course possible to make up for this educational deficit on one's own. Thomas Ertman, to whom we return in Chapter 9, thus reads more than ten different languages.

3 Paradoxically, the same is not the case in earnest for Perry Anderson (1974a; 1974b), who – as we shall see in the next chapter – claims to carry out a pure Marxist analysis.

4 Rothman (1970, 62) also points this out but sees it primarily as an indication that Moore is not always consistent.

5 Stephens (1989, 1020) refers to this early criticism when he writes that Moore's theory has yet to be tested in a multiplicity of cases despite the extensive debate about the book.

7

PERRY ANDERSON ON THE ABSOLUTIST STATE

In 1974, English sociologist Perry Anderson published two books: *Passages from Antiquity* (1974a) and *Lineages of the Absolutist State* (1974b). In these two works, Anderson introduced a historical-materialist analysis of the course of events that over time led 'the West' to capitalism and to what he would probably refer to as bourgeois democracy. Time was ripe for such a Marxist interpretation of European state formation, and, with these two books, Anderson made a significant impact on the fields of history, political science, and sociology. For example, Charles Tilly (1990) started with a quote from Anderson's book, which is presented on the next page, when he attempted a similar analysis of the development in Europe (see Chapter 9).

More specifically, Anderson attempts to explain two sets of empirical variation: a general gap between Europe and the rest of the world and a more specific gap between Western and Eastern Europe. For Anderson, the second point serves to show that the historical breakthrough to communism should have happened in Western Europe, whereas Eastern Europe, Russia in particular, was not at all geared to such a revolution.[1] Pursuant to this, Anderson's purpose is to explain the growth of the bourgeoisie within the framework of the absolutist state – a class whose destiny is to abolish this state and establish capitalism upon its ruins (Lachmann 2002, 85), which, in turn, will be abolished by communism.

Anderson never completed his grand project. The third and fourth planned volumes – announced in the preface to *Lineages* (Anderson 1974b, 11) – about the great bourgeois revolutions and the capitalist state that followed have never been completed, and the analysis therefore stops provisionally with the advent of the absolutist state. It is this part of Anderson's project that we focus on here.

The absolutist state

Anderson sets the stage for his analysis by stating that it is

> necessary to recall one of the basic axioms of historical materialism: that secular struggle between classes is ultimately resolved at the *political* – not the economic or cultural – level of society. In other words, it is the construction of States which seal the basic shifts in the relations of production, so long as classes subsist.
>
> *(1974b, 11)*

Thus, the revamping of the state marks the pivotal shifts in the economic conditions, and the character of 'the state'[2] therefore becomes the dependent variable in Anderson's analysis. In *Lineages* (1974b, 15), he is more specifically interested in explaining why feudalism was replaced by absolutism in the centuries following the Black Death (and the associated economic crisis) – that is, from the fourteenth century onwards. Here, it is important to remember that Anderson's main causal mechanism is class struggle. The crisis weakened the nobility at the expense of the peasantry, which gave the nobles an interest in replacing the direct exploitation of the serfs with the sale of offices and sanctioning of private property by the absolutist state. In other words, with the transition from feudalism to absolutism, exploitation of the peasants shifted from the local level to a centralized and militarized state centre (Anderson 1974b, 18–19; Lachmann 2002, 85). This took place in different ways in Western and Eastern Europe, however, and Anderson is interested in uncovering this difference – rather than the character of the state as such.

Approach and method

In Chapter 2, I outlined the contours of the approach that Mahoney (2003a) refers to as 'structuralism'. Anderson's analysis provides a good occasion to return to this issue. As mentioned, structuralism is more than a mere class perspective. That said, most of the work included in this book to some degree and in some manner draws on historical materialism, understood as the notion that the economic basis of society affects its political superstructure.[3] A good example is Tilly's (1990) distinction between state-building via 'capital' and state-building via 'coercion', which we shall examine more closely in Chapter 9.

Perry Anderson goes all in by claiming to carry out a genuine Marxist analysis. However, though Anderson is occasionally constrained by his Marxist framework, he also retains a certain flexibility to stray from it. As we shall see, external geopolitical pressure is an important driving force in his model; in fact, it is the crucial impetus behind the formation of states in Eastern Europe. Recall in this connection that Hintze (1975[1906], 183; see Chapter 5) presented an emphasis on external pressure as the direct opposite of Marxist internal class analysis. Bearing this in mind, I will argue that Anderson's analysis – despite declared intentions – is yet another example of structuralism in Mahoney's (2003a) sense rather than of a Marxist analysis as such.

In Chapter 2, we established that Anderson's method is a rather strange concoction. Anderson is trying at one and the same time to produce abstract theory (about general structures) and to uncover historical differences (about concrete cases). This much is clear when, on one of the first pages of *Lineages*, he writes that

> the aim of this study is to examine European Absolutism simultaneously 'in general' and 'in particular': that is to say, both the 'pure' structures of the Absolutist State, which constitute it as a fundamental historical category, and the 'impure' variants presented by the specific and diverse monarchies of post-mediaeval Europe.
>
> *(1974b, 7)*

Skocpol and Somers (1980, 187–189) argue that Anderson first presents his theory and then simply shows how it is empirically in accordance with a number of cases – using empirics to illustrate rather than test his theory. That is, he shows that each case is unique in relation to the building blocks (particularly feudalism and absolutism) that make up his theoretical edifice (cf. also Fulbrook and Skocpol 1984, 180–184).

As was briefly mentioned in Chapter 2, this characterization does not entirely hold true. It is correct that there is in a general sense no variation on Anderson's 'dependent variable', as he constantly focuses on instances of absolutism. And his Marxist analytical apparatus can indeed be used to understand all cases – which is certainly his starting point. That said, *Lineages* contains at least two obvious attempts at making comparisons in order to control. The first is Anderson's general comparison between Western Europe and Eastern Europe, which serves to explain why the nature of absolutism differs in these two areas. This can be regarded as a form of MSSD, as Anderson finds the explanation in the varying character of the preceding feudalism.

Next, Anderson compares Europe with Japan in order to illustrate the impact of feudalism (1974b, 435–461). This can be regarded as two different sets of comparisons: first, a form of MDSD, where the point is that we find feudalism in both places and therefore also, later, capitalism in both places (despite the significant differences between the two areas); second, a form of MSSD, where the point is that the legacy from antiquity is only found in Europe (not Japan), that genuine absolutism could therefore only make inroads in Europe, and that capitalism therefore arises endogenously in this area. In contrast, capitalism emerged in Japan as the result of an exogenous shock in the form of interactions with European powers. However, as feudalism had existed earlier it was possible to absorb and channel this shock in the direction of capitalist development.

In my opinion, the far greater methodological problem is that Anderson, in his empirical analysis, is unfaithful to his conceptual definition of feudalism (which, as mentioned, leads to absolutism in his model). It is precisely on this point that Anderson's tension between pure theoretical types/structures and 'impure' empirical cases raises problems. We will return to this below.

Anderson's explanation

What, then, is Anderson's take on the historical breakthrough that led to liberal democracy and capitalism in the West? Anderson summarizes his answer in the following one-liner: 'what rendered the unique passage to capitalism possible in Europe was the *concatenation of antiquity and feudalism*' (1974b, 420). As we shall see, this is precisely Anderson's general finding. Nevertheless, it is still rather surprising that he resorts to such unambiguous wording, as Anderson's project is marked by a curious duality. On the one hand, his pen is extremely elegant, especially considering the rather cumbersome Marxist conceptual apparatus he is using. On the other hand, like Moore he does not present his explanation in a particularly systematic manner.

The vague character of Anderson's explanation is reinforced by the fact that the third and fourth volumes – on the bourgeois revolutions and the capitalist states that followed – have never materialized. As readers, we are moving towards a destination that never comes into shape, which is somewhat frustrating. Nevertheless, with these caveats in mind, it is possible to crystallize a set of causes and effects from the work. With the main volume, *Lineages*, Anderson (1974b) attempts to explain how feudalism was transformed into absolutism after the great economic crises of the fourteenth and fifteenth centuries (15). According to Anderson, the absolutist state – as later capitalism – is a uniquely European phenomenon and must therefore be explained using factors that are only found in Europe.

The beginning: The feudalism of the Middle Ages

Anderson finds the roots of the uniqueness of Europe in medieval feudalism – as mentioned above, the first volume is titled *Passages from Antiquity to Feudalism* – which thus appears to be the actual independent variable.[4] Within the Marxist tradition (see, e.g., Wickham 1984, 6), feudalism has ordinarily been defined as what the Germans term *Grundherrschaft* (in English *the manorial system* or *landlordism*): in other words, the economic basis or mode of production that characterized at least part of Europe in the High Middle Ages. A competing definition, the political, which Max Weber helped create, construes feudalism as the combination of divided sovereignty and vassal relations (see Bendix 1962[1946], 360–384; Poggi 1991; Cantor 1993[1963], 196). Here, the focus is on the medieval representative institutions and the legal privileges of corporative groups – such as autonomous cities or the Church. That is, feudalism is construed as a form of rule rather than something relating to economic structures.

Anderson rejects the conventional Marxist definition, which makes feudalism something that is found many different places at different points in time (1974b, 400–402; cf. also Strayer (1987[1965], 13; Finer 1997a, 871). With his own wonderful metaphor: 'Feudalism, in this version of materialist historiography, becomes an absolving ocean in which virtually any society may receive its baptism' (Anderson 1974b, 402). To put it bluntly, if we are to understand feudalism narrowly as *Grundherrschaft*, a number of non-European societies will also be instances of feudalism – which renders it impossible to explain absolutism (and later capitalism) from this perspective.

However, with his Marxist approach, Anderson cannot choose Weber's solution and merely operates on the political level. He therefore defines feudalism as the combination of the economic basis and political-legal superstructure. Feudalism, then, is a kind of 'landlordism' combined with fragmented sovereignty. How does Anderson – from a Marxist perspective – defend this augmented definition? His argument is that all other 'production forms' than capitalism are based on non-economic exploitation and that this can only be captured by including the superstructure (1974b, 404). As Fulbrook and Skocpol (1984, 183–184) point out, fragmented sovereignty – that is, an element in the 'superstructure' – would in fact appear to be the core element in Anderson's definition of feudalism.

Feudalism so defined is a hallmark of Europe (408–409). How do we explain its origins? In *Passages*, as indicated by the title, Anderson (1974a) traces the development back to late antiquity. Feudal societies emerged in the areas where a '"Romano-Germanic" fusion' (160) occurred after the fall of the Roman Empire – that is, current-day France and Germany. More specifically, this meant the merger of tribal-based (German) and slave-based (Roman) modes of production, both of which were in the process of disintegrating in the period leading up to this fusion (214). However, it was not the modes of production alone that tied feudalism to antiquity. As Hall (1989, 553) points out, Anderson resorts to ideological factors on this point. The Catholic Church is the glue that binds the ancient period with the Middle Ages in Western Europe. To use Anderson's (1974a, 131) own unforgettable image – the Christian Church constituted 'the main, frail aqueduct across which the cultural reservoirs of the Classical World now passed to the new universe of feudal Europe, where literacy had become clerical'.

Feudalism then began to spread, partly due to Western colonization, to the rest of the continent with the exception of the Balkans, where first the Byzantines and then the Ottomans ruled and kept it at bay. In other words, the eastern part of Europe was not originally characterized by the Roman-German fusion. But the eastern half of the continent – with the exception of the Balkans – could not avoid adopting elements of Western European feudalism given that the two halves of Europe were so closely interwoven (1974a, 229). Anderson justifies this by again referring to how feudalism was based on political and not economic exploitation: 'conquest, not commerce, was its primary form of expansion' (1974b, 197).

From feudalism to absolutism

As mentioned, Anderson's explanation of the shift from feudalism to absolutism begins with the great economic crisis of the High Middle Ages (1974a, 252). According to Anderson, this crisis arose because the feudal form of production had exhausted itself. However, in the absence of a bourgeoisie, the crisis could not lead directly to capitalism, and the aristocracy's reaction to the crisis was absolutism.

Here, Eastern Europe fundamentally distinguishes itself from Western Europe. In the west, absolutism emerged from within. It killed serfdom, as exploitation now occurred via different mechanisms. England and the Netherlands are partial exceptions, as the bourgeoisie stood so strong that the bourgeois revolutions came (too) early (cf. also Ertman 1997, 16–18). In France, Spain, and parts of Germany, however, the *quid pro quo* between aristocracy and monarchs created absolute states that sold offices to the upper class. The exploitation of the lower class inherent to feudalism was thus reproduced in absolutist trappings. In other words, the absolutist state is an apparatus that caters to the interests of the feudal aristocracy – it is not a product of an alliance between rulers and bourgeoisie or between aristocrats and bourgeoisie, as many others have claimed (Anderson 1974b, 15–17).

In Eastern Europe, absolutism was also a means to ensure the interests of the aristocracy, but it was a consequence of an external shock rather than an endogenous development. It was Sweden – 'the Hammer of the East' (Anderson 1974b, 198) – that provoked the consolidation of state power in Prussia and Russia. In the brief period between 1630 and 1720, Swedish cavalry rode victoriously through no less than five eastern capitals: Moscow, Warsaw, Berlin, Dresden, and Prague. This forced these as yet rather inchoate polities to introduce and implement absolutism from above (1974b, 198–202). In other words, it was war as opposed to class struggle that drove the development towards absolutism in the east, although absolutism was also in the interests of the aristocracy here. More generally, Anderson's diagnosis is that Eastern Europe distinguished itself from Western Europe in the sense that the development in this area was not based on the passages from antiquity in general and the Roman-German fusion in particular. This means that the features that constituted the institutional manifestation of the political level of feudalism in Western Europe were lacking. Eastern Europe was thus characterized by weak or non-existent Estates and weak or non-existent autonomous cities (1974a, 252). In the west, these elements were largely derived from the prior existence of autonomous cities and Roman Law in antiquity.

In the Foreword to *Lineages*, Anderson (1974b, 9) points out that his purpose is to 'suggest a regional *typology* that can help to clarify the divergent trajectories of the major Absolutist States of both Eastern and Western Europe'. Based on the discussion above, such a typology might look something like what we see in Table 7.1.

We shall return to Scandinavia, which does not fit this model very well. Note here that Anderson classifies the countries in the region – or at least Sweden – as exemplifying Western European absolutism even though feudalism did not emerge from within via a Roman-German synthesis between modes of production based

TABLE 7.1 Anderson's typology of different forms of absolutism

		Roman-German synthesis	
		+Synthesis	−Synthesis
	+External push		Exogenous absolutism (Eastern Europe)
Geopolitical competition	−External push	Endogenous absolutism (Western Europe)	

Source: Anderson, 1974b.

on slavery and tribalism, respectively. Nor does the model in itself answer why England and Holland were able to skip absolutism and go directly to the bourgeois revolutions (Ertman 1997, 18).

However, Anderson's most important point is that the difference between east and west resulted in two different kinds of absolutism. Precisely because Eastern Europe was lacking free cities and Estates, absolutism was more 'pure', as there was nothing to oppose it in these societies. In a slightly broader perspective, it was the absence of these elements that prevented the emergence of a bourgeoisie. The opposite was the case in the west, where the presence of these elements over the years made room for a bourgeoisie, as corporative rights rendered it difficult to suppress this class (Lachmann 2002, 87). In Anderson's own terms, the logic is that Eastern Europe was forced to develop the political superstructure (absolutism), even though the economic basis was not yet mature. Instead of private property and the opportunity to purchase offices, the nobility got a more solid grip on the peasants (serfs) in return for strengthening central power (1974b, 195). While serfdom came to an end in Western Europe, it intensified in Eastern Europe. At the same time, the service nobility of Eastern Europe seized a role in the state apparatus similar to what the nobility – via the sale of offices – occupied in the west.

The explanation of the historical distinction between East and West was thus the 'uneven development of feudalism within Europe' (1974b, 197), which in turn determined the state structures. This qualitative difference in absolutism points forward towards the later difference between Western and Eastern Europe – a difference that ultimately paved the way for the triumph of capitalism in the West, and that Anderson had planned to pursue in the two additional volumes announced in *Lineages*. For in Anderson's eyes, the differences in absolutism explain the later economic, political, and legal differences (cf. Lachmann 2002).

Problems with Anderson's explanation

How far does this bring us in relation to understanding the uniqueness of the West? Generally speaking, Anderson successfully isolates some uniquely European factors by merging the economic and political levels of feudalism. He has been criticized for letting feudalism – intended as an analytical category – become an empirical description of Western Europe, and particularly France, at a certain point in time

(Fulbrook and Skocpol 1984, 182–187). But the fact remains that there are no other areas – as mentioned, according to *Lineages*, Japan is a partial exception – with this same historical point of departure and that no other areas therefore become characterized by absolutism and later capitalism.

Anderson furthermore offers a fairly clear explanation of the difference between Western and Eastern Europe (the latter has historically lagged behind the former both politically and economically). He argues that it is the uneven development of feudalism, reproduced under absolutism and in a sense a result of the transition from antiquity, that makes the difference. As Knudsen and Rothstein (1994, 205) point out, it is widely recognized in the literature that within Europe there is analytical value in thus distinguishing between 'Eastern' and 'Western' paths to the modern state.

These strengths certainly deserve mention. But they do not change the fact that there are significant problems with the explanation. If we disregard the view that classes are homogenous entities with collective interests – and the practically conspiracy-like treatment of the mésalliance between the monarch and the nobility bringing about absolutism – one particular problem deserves to be highlighted. As mentioned, Anderson wishes to develop a theory about pure structures and reveal how the individual cases distinguish themselves from these 'ideal types'. However, for his explanation to be valid, the individual cases (countries) must fit into the categories presented, such as feudalism and absolutism, in at least a general sense. As Fulbrook and Skocpol (1984, 194–196) point out, France is really the only country that fits Anderson's definition of absolutism; all other Western European countries distinguish themselves on crucial points from the conceptualized type (see also Ertman 1997, 18).

Indeed, Sweden plays the most important role in Anderson's explanation. This is 'The Hammer of the East', which triggered a rather different form of absolutism in the area between the Elbe and the Don. In other words, Eastern absolutism owes to the pressure from more advanced Western absolutism. But Sweden is very far from the pure definition of Western absolutism, meaning that it is not really the sophisticated Western model that sparks the Eastern European development but instead a country on the Western European periphery, which by the way is not characterized by the initial Roman–German fusion and never became absolutist (cf. Downing 1992; Fulbrook and Skocpol 1984, fn. 49).

The same problem applies regarding feudalism. As mentioned, Anderson explains the emergence of the absolutist state partly by combining the two faces of feudalism: the economic and the political. But as is clear when reading the country chapters in *Lineages* – and as a number of great historians and sociologists pointed out in the nineteenth and early twentieth centuries (e.g., Myers 1975, 19) – Eastern Europe was not at all characterized by feudalism on the political level. In Russia in particular there was neither fragmented sovereignty nor legal privileges, which also explains why free cities and Estates never emerged (Møller 2015b).

To sum up, Anderson cannot have his cake and eat it too. With respect to the Russian case, he is only able to save his explanation by returning to a narrow definition of feudalism as landlordism. Anderson stretches his otherwise adequate definition of the concept when he allows Eastern Europe to be characterized as feudal. The attempt to safeguard the explanation by introducing the pressure from Sweden only dilutes it. For this shows that absolutism – in the uniquely European sense – can emerge even if the deeper causes (feudalism) are absent. In other words, it is actually the variation in factors such as war, the spread of autonomous cities, and the Estates that explain the differences between Western and Eastern Europe (Lachmann 2002, 87).

Numerous researchers have pointed out that it is hardly a coincidence that Anderson has never written the third volume about the major bourgeois revolutions. According to Lachmann (2002, 88), Anderson lacks an explanation for why bourgeois interests differ from those of the aristocracy when the former emerge from the aristocratic niches of the absolutist state. One could also merely point out that Anderson's explanation does not point towards the most important later empirical dividing lines within Europe. Most importantly, Anderson cannot explain the later differences *within* the eastern half of the European continent, namely the difference between East-Central Europe, where the political level of feudalism is present to some extent, and Eastern Europe proper where the same did not apply. This difference is obviously important for the bourgeois revolutions in 1830 and the period 1848–1849, which rather characteristically covered East-Central Europe but not Eastern Europe.

In any case, treating all of Eastern Europe as a single homogenous category is a very crude simplification. It is not only that there are crucial 'medieval' differences with respect to the Estates and autonomous cities that were found in Central Europe but not in Eastern Europe; we also find a subsequent difference with respect to absolutism. While absolutism did indeed make inroads in Prussia and Russia, Anderson downplays the fact that it never actually made itself felt in Poland and Hungary (Downing 1992; Ertman 1997, 18). It is also worth noting that Prussian absolutism was far more legalistic and characterized by constitutional barriers than Russian absolutism (cf. Finer 1997b, 1405–1419, 1455).

We return to this in Part V. Here, I will merely add that Anderson's explanation also fares less well with respect to Scandinavia – Sweden in particular – which (as Scandinavian researchers have pointed out) is situated somewhere between the Western and Eastern paths (Knudsen and Rothstein 1994, 206–208). Add to all of this that Anderson does not actually put his theory to any kind of systematic test. Instead, as Skocpol points out, he spends his time showing how it sheds light on countries that have to some degree been selected because they fit the theory. No genuine attempt to probe the explanation empirically is carried out in *Passages* and *Lineages*.

Conclusions

We are left, then, with an explanation that includes some relevant explanatory factors but reduces a number of important differences to one and the same inexorable path towards the absolutist state. Lachmann (2002, 91) praises Anderson for his consistent use of class struggle to explain social changes. This conclusion is some-what paradoxical, considering that it is really other factors that account for the difference between Western and Eastern Europe (see also Hall 1989, 553; Ertman 1997, 18). I have already mentioned that Anderson must fall back on the Catholic Church as the glue that binds antiquity and the Middle Ages together. However, more than anything else the geopolitical dimension clashes, head-on, with the Marxist approach. Here, Anderson is entirely in line with Leon Trotsky, who once declared that war is the locomotive of history. It should be clear to the reader of this book that there is a lot to this idea. But it fits poorly with Marxist orthodoxy. The mere fact that Anderson must introduce the Swedes as a kind of *deus ex machina*[5] in order to explain deep societal developments in multiple Eastern European countries indicates that the one-sided focus of historical materialism on the class struggle is not an adequate explanation, even in the rather nuanced presentation of *Passages* and *Lineages*. Anderson simply bites off more than he can chew.

Notes

1 Anderson writes about the past in order to understand the present. His political purpose, which is not otherwise treated in this chapter, is to argue for the West having had unique conditions for an actual Marxist revolution. However, this revolution must build on a democratic foundation (as opposed to the Bolshevik Revolution) (Fulbrook and Skocpol 1984, 179f.).
2 It is all the more paradoxical that Anderson's definition of the state is not very easy to capture. However, this does not cause major problems since it is obvious what he wants to explain, as described below.
3 This is an interpretation of historical materialism that Hobsbawm (1997[1969], 192) criticizes as vulgar Marxist. But there is much precedent for it: see, e.g., Rothman's (1970) and Femia's (1972) respective interpretations of Moore (1991[1966]), described in Chapter 6.
4 Merely by using the term 'independent variable', I am in a sense violating Anderson's explanation. Anderson shies away from the logic of comparative control and conceives of historical development in a more systemic manner (Fulbrook and Skocpol 1984, 191–192). Feudalism is not an independent variable, as such, but rather in itself a product of a deeper legacy from antiquity and the Germanic tribal communities. In this chapter, the term is used in an attempt to break down Anderson's explanation and make it more manageable.
5 David Gress suggested this wording to me.

8

SKOCPOL

Revolutions and the state

If Barrington Moore rediscovered comparative historical analysis, Skocpol is the discipline's whip and organizer. In the 1970s, directly inspired by Moore's *Social Origins* (Munck and Snyder 2007, 653), Skocpol threw herself into comparative historical analysis. She has described how difficult it was at the time to devote scientific work to large-scale historical comparisons (Munck and Snyder 2007, 658–659). However, in 1979 her *States and Social Revolutions*, an incredibly ambitious historical comparison of the French, Russian, and Chinese revolutions, was published. This book has become a classic in the genre, and the main purpose of this chapter is to discuss it.[1]

In the first half of the 1980s, Skocpol further pursued this research agenda before turning to other areas in political science. First, she formed a network of researchers in order to organize comparative historical analysis as a discipline (see Munck and Snyder 2007, 670–672, 699). This organizational work resulted in, among other things, the book *Vision and Method in Historical Sociology* (1984). Second, she made a heroic effort to describe the methodological strategies used in the field (Skocpol and Somers 1980; Skocpol 1984b; 1984c), arguing in this connection for the logic of comparative control. Third, Skocpol was the driving force behind the renaissance of state theory in the 1980s. Together with Peter B. Evans and Dietrich Rueschemeyer, she published a book in 1985 with the rather telling title, *Bringing the State Back In*. Skocpol's state theory is a good place to begin this chapter, as it runs like a common thread throughout her theory on social revolutions.

Skocpol's state theory

An important premise for Skocpol's approach to comparative historical analysis is that the state apparatus has an independent impact on social, political, and economic processes. She appears to have acquired this insight rather early on. The emphasis on 'the state' thus plays an important role in the review article of Moore's *Social Origins*, which Skocpol published in 1973. As mentioned in Chapter 6, Skocpol criticized Moore for neglecting the way an autonomous state apparatus could affect political development. This point plays an important role in her theory on social revolutions where the character of the state apparatus is presented as one of the key independent variables in *States and Social Revolutions*.

In *Bringing the State Back In*, Skocpol further details her state theory. After World War II, American political science had largely ignored the importance of state structures.[2] Instead, approaches such as Gabriel Almond's (Almond and Powell 1966) so-called 'structural functionalism' and David Easton's systems theory attempted to establish a more general conceptual apparatus capturing the basic functions of society (including political socialization, recruitment, and communication). *Bringing the State Back In* is a reaction against this very abstract focus. The book includes contributions from different scholars, including Charles Tilly, but Skocpol is clearly in charge, and her introductory chapter includes a programmatic version of the new state theory.

An interesting point in relation to this book is that Skocpol (1985, 9) explicitly construes her state theory as an attempt to return to the 'Weberian–Hintzean perspective'. Skocpol's point is that state structures were attributed great significance in the continental European – particularly the German – scientific community, which flourished one hundred years earlier and which we have studied in Chapters 4 and 5. Now that the state structures are again being taken seriously, Skocpol points out, it is

> perhaps not surprising that many researchers are relying anew – with various modifications and extensions, to be sure – on the basic understanding of 'the state' passed down to contemporary scholarship through the widely known writings of such major German scholars as Max Weber and Otto Hintze.
>
> *(7)*

More specifically, Skocpol directly adopts Weber's definition of the state (see Chapter 1), particularly as a means to point out that the state in the Weberian sense must be an entity that has an independent impact on society (7). Via Hintze, she emphasizes that the state is always a part of a system of competing states and that this shapes the state structures and increases their autonomy in relation to, for example, class structures (8). Skocpol emphasizes that she does not have a general state theory to offer. Her main aim is to make two points that, in her eyes, have been neglected in American political science: the importance of state autonomy and the capacity of the state to influence political life. Both points pervade Skocpol's theory on social revolutions. As we shall see, Skocpol identifies a divide between the state and societal groups, pointing out that, for example, the political power of the upper class is influenced by existing state structures. Finally, geopolitical competition also plays a key role in her model as a scope condition of social revolution.

States and social revolutions

Skocpol's (1979) explanation can be summarized as follows: social revolutions result from the combination of weak state apparatuses and agrarian structures that encourage peasant uprisings in 'agrarian bureaucracies', which are incorporated in an international system with geopolitical competition, where other players are more developed.

Let us attempt to unfold this explanation. According to Skocpol, there are two basic conditions for social revolution in a country: it must be an agrarian bureaucracy (that is, a non-industrialized, non-commercialized economy with a traditional state apparatus), and it must be part of a multistate system in which it lags behind more developed competitors. In the case of France in 1789, the more developed competitor was Great Britain; in 1917, Russia could generally look towards the more developed countries of Western and Central Europe; and twentieth-century China was lagging behind Japan, which the Chinese had always regarded as inferior (77). The resulting geopolitical competition contributes to the pressure on the state apparatus. In particular, military defeat has often opened the floodgates of revolution (23).

These conditions are necessary but not sufficient. We find a considerable number of cases that have fulfilled these conditions without it setting the stage for social revolutions. Skocpol therefore introduces two additional conditions: first, the existence of weak state apparatuses suffering latent crisis, typically staffed by the sons of the landed gentry – as opposed to the meritocratic bureaucracy we find in countries such as Japan and Prussia (100–103). Here, it is important to recall Skocpol's basic point that the state is an autonomous entity and that its internal conflicts and convulsions can pave the way for a revolution (29). The fundamental problem in all three cases of social revolution was that the monarchical state apparatuses in the periods preceding the upheavals were unable to carry out the reforms necessary to assert themselves in the international competition (50). The landed aristocracy had excessive influence on the state apparatus, which therefore lacked sufficient autonomy, and this was a crucial weakness because it arrested the necessary reforms (110). Finally, the degree of prior centralization of state power is important: the most radical changes took place where the absolute state had centralized power the most. In countries where power was spread out more, the collapse of the central power did not threaten the existing social order in the same manner.

Second, Skocpol sees peasant uprisings as a necessary condition for social revolution (112–113). The important feature of these uprisings is that they are national – not merely local. Local peasant uprisings can practically be found at all times and in all places, but there are at least two requirements for national uprisings: the peasant communities must be relatively autonomous (143–147) and the state structures must collapse to leave space for mobilization (133). Skocpol finds a good example of the latter in her comparison of the situation in Russia in 1905 and 1917. In both cases, the country had suffered defeats in war – against Japan and the Central Powers, respectively – and in both cases these defeats led to revolutionary situations.

However, in 1905 the military was intact and able to re-establish the status quo in the rural areas after returning from the Far East. In 1917, it virtually disintegrated at the front.

These two factors are therefore sufficient for social revolutions in agrarian bureaucracies that are incorporated in geopolitical systems with more advanced participants (Mahoney 2003b, 349). More generally, we can say that Skocpol's (1979, 14) theory rests upon three principles: the necessity of a structural perspective on revolution, an appreciation of the international context, and an emphasis on the state as a potentially autonomous actor. We have already touched upon the latter two points. Skocpol uses the structural perspective to challenge virtually all other theories on revolution. Her major point is that these theories are based on the character of political protest in liberal democracies/capitalist societies (1979, xiii). These alternative theories are not applicable in predominantly agrarian countries with monarchical state apparatuses and agrarian-dominated social structures (xiv).

The consequences

But what are social revolutions, really? Skocpol combines two elements in her definition: rapid and comprehensive changes to the socio-economic structure and the political institutions, and class struggle from below. Political revolutions – such as the English revolutions (1640–1660 and 1688) or the major liberal revolutions in the mid-nineteenth century (1831 and 1848) – thus do not qualify as social revolutions (1979, 4). This is a crucial point for Skocpol. Political revolutions may well be thought to result from other causes than social revolutions, which can again have other causes than failed social revolutions (5).

This brings us to our next point. Skocpol's book consists of two parts: the causes of social revolution and the consequences of these revolutions. The common consequence in the three instances of social revolution is the abolishment of political and economic privileges for selected groups (the nobility in particular) and increases in the autonomy of the state. A tangible consequence of these revolutions is the significant growth of the bureaucracy (199, 263). The revolution thus strengthens the state in relation to its international competitors (161–162).

However, there are also important differences between the three social revolutions. As far as the substantive consequences are concerned, the French Revolution was more 'bourgeois' than the other two: it genuinely strengthened private property and the capitalist system, in stark contrast to the later Russian and Chinese Revolutions (162, 178). As far as the sequence or course of events is concerned, the revolution made itself felt most rapidly in Russia, it was most tardy in China, and France was somewhere in between.

Skocpol attributes these differences to the starting points in the respective countries. The state structures as well as the socio-economic legacies from the previous regimes contributed to the character and consequences of the revolutions in all three cases (164–171). More analytically, the point is that these differences result from the respective status of the three cases in relation to the independent variable

(Skocpol 1979, 234, 280). The French Revolution thus distinguished itself from the Russian Revolution by a less threatening geopolitical competitive situation and by agrarian structures that did not enable quite as radical peasant uprisings. The Chinese Revolution was more drawn out because the agrarian structures did not give the peasants the autonomy required for national uprisings in the event of crisis.

Skocpol's method

How does Skocpol establish these relationships? She is concerned to show that it is possible to carry out a systematic comparison of a few cases using the two methods earlier referred to as MSSD and MDSD (36).[3] Early in the book, Skocpol points out that it is often possible to combine these methods by comparing different cases with a certain outcome (using MSSD) and then contrasting these with similar cases without this outcome (using MDSD) (37). Skocpol's analysis largely follows these steps. She thus matches the three instances of social revolution – France, Russia, and China – in order to identify relevant, shared causes, such as weak state apparatuses. She compares each with relatively similar cases without social revolutions – for example, China with Japan, and Russia in 1917 with Russia in 1905 – in order to identify the causes that distinguish these cases (94, 136).

Both MSSD and MDSD serve to control for other factors. However, as a number of critics have pointed out, it is somewhat difficult to accept the logic of control in Skocpol's case. Sewell (1996, 258–260) notes that Skocpol's analysis rests on the three revolutions making up independent trials in a more general experiment. More specifically, according to Sewell, the analysis rests on two premises: that the revolutions are identical (*principle of equivalence*) and that they are independent of one another (*principle of independence*). According to Sewell, the basic problem, which applies to the use of the logic of comparative control in historical analysis more generally, is that it is difficult to fulfil both principles at the same time. There is an inherent danger that different cases affect one another. Independence is therefore best ensured by finding cases that are far apart in time and distance (say, a comparison of state structures in Central America and state structures in Eurasia prior to Columbus discovering the New World). However, this makes it less convincing that the cases are identical.

Sewell's criticism threatens the very basis of the logic of control used in comparative historical analysis (but see Møller 2015a). The first thing to note here is that Skocpol is well aware of the limitations. She acknowledges that the MSSD and MDSD can never be applied in their pure form, as the relevant cases are never sufficiently similar/different. According to Skocpol, it is therefore often necessary to carry out strategic guesses about causes (39). She also concedes that the cases investigated are not actually independent of one another, as MSSD and MDSD require. For example, the French Revolution indirectly (as a source of inspiration) affected all subsequent revolutions, and the Russian Revolution directly (via the Soviet assistance to the Chinese communists) had an impact on the Chinese

Revolution (39). Here, Skocpol introduces what she refers to as *world time* as a variable that in itself undermines the uniformity of the various cases (see also Mann 1986, 167–174).

Purely on methodological grounds, the combination of MSSD and MDSD is thus not particularly convincing. How, then, can Skocpol's work enjoy the recognition that it does? There are a number of reasons why. We have already touched upon the ambitious and courageous character of her entire project. Another weighty reason is that *in practice* Skocpol compensates for the described methodological problems. As several scholars have pointed out, Skocpol does not rely on Mills' comparative methods alone.

Mahoney's (2003b) general overview of the methods used in comparative historical analysis illustrates this point. Mahoney first notes that Skocpol, who features prominently in this overview, uses ordinal divisions of her variables to show that 'the degree' of the different causal factors effected the degree of social revolution, with France's as the most moderate and Russia's as the most radical (2003b, 358; see Skocpol 1979, 280). We have already touched upon this in the discussion of the consequences above. Next, Mahoney shows that Skocpol also uses *process tracing* to eliminate alternative causes. For example, she uses this method to show that ideologically radicalized elites, such as the Russian Bolsheviks, were not a key cause of social revolutions (Skocpol 1979, 164–173; 2003b, 364), even though we would accept them as such based solely on comparative control. Finally, Skocpol uses the method normally referred to as historical narratives (Mahoney 2003b, 366; cf. Sewell 1996; Lange 2012). This method breaks different courses of events in sequences and shows how the same dynamics play out in these courses of events, notwithstanding that they take place in different places at different times.[4]

In other words, Skocpol (1979) puts the full palette of qualitative methods to use. *States and Social Revolution* is actually the only work Mahoney includes under *all* of the methods he identifies in the literature – even though, as he also notes (2003b, 359), the book is renowned for its use of Mill's simple methods. Skocpol's supplement to MSSD and MDSD thus does not merely consist of 'strategic guessing' but also consists of systematic analysis with other methods to support this 'guesswork'. This might be the greatest strength of this work, and it underlines how good a social scientist Skocpol really is. She is actually applying these other methods without declaring that she does so, all the while claiming to base her analysis on MSSD and MDSD.[5]

Criticism

Even though Skocpol (1979, xiii, 6–14) with her book issued a broadside against virtually all established theories on revolution, her work has not attracted as much criticism as, for example, Moore's *Social Origins*. Three forms of objections are worth mentioning, directed against her method, the substantive assessments, and the generalizability of the arguments.

As far as method is concerned, we find two different points of criticism in the literature. We have already mentioned the first one: that Skocpol applies a much broader range of methods than she appears willing to admit. The other point accepts that Skocpol's analysis actually depends on MSSD and MDSD but then launches a radical attack on this logic of inference. I have already mentioned how Sewell (1996), with direct reference to Skocpol's analysis in *States and Social Revolutions*, dismisses the logic of comparative control (see also Mann 1986, 167–174). Abbott (1991, 227–228) has similarly fiercely criticized the very idea that the logic of control can be put to use in historical sociology. Abbott acknowledges that Skocpol appears to use analytical narratives: 'But her methodological language betrays the dream of somehow generating "causal explanations" that are abstracted from actors and stories' (228). According to Abbott, this is a problem because Skocpol is hereby 'forgetting the basic insights of process-oriented theorizing in social science' – that is, that the significance of an event depends on how it fits together with an ensemble of other events:

> There is therefore no abstracting 'causes' out of their narrative environments. . . . The search for typical narratives becomes the first and perhaps the only means for generalization.
>
> *(Abbott 1991, 228)*

The second criticism stems primarily from historians who object that Skocpol does not respect the historical integrity of the three cases (see Munck and Snyder 2007, 671). Skocpol obviously builds on the primary and secondary work of historians, but many historians feel that she has misread or misrepresented their works in certain areas in an attempt to force the three cases into more general categories (e.g., Kiernan 1980; Perry 1980). This criticism is hardly surprising, and one might argue that it can be raised against almost all comparative historical analyses. It first and foremost shows that history as a discipline is more idiographically oriented than political science (Lange 2012, 12–13; see also Chapter 2).

Third, a number of political scientists have questioned whether Skocpol's results can be generalized beyond her three cases. Stephens raises this form of criticism (1989, 1073) when noting that the cases of Spain and Italy demonstrate that a strong state is not – as Skocpol appears to assume – a prerequisite for an authoritarian outcome. According to Stephens, a strong state is only necessary in order to carry out a 'revolution from above'. Goertz and Mahoney (2005) have tested Skocpol's explanation in more general terms. Their test can be summarized using the explanatory typology we see in Table 8.1.

Goertz and Mahoney's analysis suggests that Skocpol's explanatory model has a more general purchase. Compared with the typological replication of Moore's analysis in Chapter 6, Skocpol's model proves to be more robust when additional cases are enlisted to test it.[6]

TABLE 8.1 Skocpol's implicit explanatory typology with additional countries

	+State breakdown		−State breakdown	
	+Peasant rebellions	*−Peasant rebellions*	*+Peasant rebellions*	*−Peasant rebellions*
+Revolution	China France Russia II (1917)			
−Revolution	Poland- Lithuania	Austrian Empire Austria-Hungary England India Japan Netherlands Ottoman empire Portugal Prussia Spain Sweden	Russia I (1905)	Germany

Source: Based on Goertz and Mahoney (2005).

Conclusions

As with Moore, it makes sense to situate Skocpol's analysis in relation to Marxism. As she points out herself (Munck and Snyder 2007, 688), many of her colleagues painted her as a (neo-)Marxist researcher, and Skocpol's analysis in *States and Social Revolutions* clearly incorporates elements from the Marxist approach to revolutions (cf. Kiernan 1980, 639). But Skocpol also emphasizes that the Marxist understanding of revolution is inadequate, as it lacks an appreciation of the potential autonomy of the state from economically dominant classes. Indeed, Skocpol's analysis has been interpreted as clear criticism of the strong focus in historical materialism on the significance of economic structures (Alsted 2001, 41–42).

Whether we accept this or not, Skocpol obviously breaks with the Marxist understanding of history to a greater degree than Moore. On one point, however, Skocpol is completely in agreement with Marx, namely that the social revolution – with Marx's famous phrase about the French Revolution – represented a 'giant broom' that swept away 'the medieval trash' (Skocpol 1979, 174). In the next chapter, we will become acquainted with an analysis that indirectly criticizes this point by coupling modern democracy to the constitutional legacy of the Middle Ages.

Notes

1 Which should hardly raise any eyebrows considering the relevance of these three revolutions. Finer (1997b, 1517) thus calls the French Revolution the most important single event in the history of government, only to add that we must proceed to the Russian Revolution to find anything that comes close in importance.

2 The neglect of the state as an analytical object was less prevalent in European political science (Keating 2009, 312).

3 Skocpol describes this as an attempt, when analysing only a few cases, to draw inspiration from the multivariate methodological logic she had been schooled in more generally (see Munck and Snyder 2007, 666).

4 Skocpol has recently reported how she learned from Barrington Moore's seminars that it is possible to compare historical sequences across time by identifying identical analytical processes that take place independent of the chronology (see Munck and Snyder 2007, 622).

5 Note the similarity with Bartolini's criticism that Tilly's (1984) methodological prescriptions are lacking but that his practice compensates for this. More generally, one can apply this combination of praise and criticism to a wide range of works discussed in this book.

6 Additionally, there has been far less criticism of Skocpol's 'scoring' of her cases than of Moore's (see Chapter 6). Mahoney (2003b, 352) points out that Skocpol is so familiar with her cases that it is not a problem that her MSSD and MDSD methods rest on a deterministic causality (which implies that measurement errors can potentially be destructive).

9

WAR, STATE FORMATION, AND REGIME CHANGE

Tilly, Downing, and Ertman

Historically speaking, war and preparations for war – as we know from several of the preceding chapters – have had an impact both on the character of the state and on the political regime. In Part IV of this book, we shall see how military competition – at least in Europe – has also had important economic consequences. In gist, geopolitical pressure is a premise in most comparative historical analysis. Nevertheless, it is hardly wrong to say that it was partially forgotten as the classic literature ended after World War II. At the same time, it is striking that Barrington Moore, when he resurrected the field, failed to include military competition in his analysis of the paths to democracy and dictatorship (see Chapter 6).

Both Perry Anderson (Chapter 7) and Theda Skocpol (Chapter 8) did incorporate it into their theories. In this chapter, we shall see how the classic insights of Weber, Schumpeter, and Hintze have since been systematized, above all in the writings of three important authors, Charles Tilly, Brian M. Downing, and Thomas Ertman. These three authors all included geopolitical competition as a key causal factor in analysis of state formation and regime change,[1] and this is why these works are discussed in a single chapter.

Charles Tilly

Up until his death in 2008, Charles Tilly was possibly the most influential living American sociologist. He had also left a significant mark on political science, and even historians read the American *polymath* with great enthusiasm. In this chapter, we shall discuss two of Tilly's great contributions to comparative historical analysis – one substantive and the other methodological.

First, the substantive – from the 1970s onwards, Tilly (1975; 1985; 1990) revolutionized the study of the emergence of the European territorial states. His 'puzzle' was the following: why did the European states, in the course of the latest four hundred to five hundred years, become the most important political centre of power? Parallel to this, Tilly – particularly in the 1980s – worked to get the social sciences to invest more energy in the analysis of 'big' events that unfolded over lengthy periods of time. He did this partly in works on methodology (e.g., Tilly 1984) and partly by setting a practical example worth emulating. In his 'later'[2] research, Tilly usually strives to make use of historical narratives and to uncover causal mechanisms rather than causal relationships (see, e.g., McAdam et al. 2001, 81–84). His general message is that the best way to go about this is to allow the sequences to play out over time – as opposed to using simple statistical correlations within a specific area at a specific point in time.

The intersection between time and space is also relevant for understanding some of the weaknesses in Tilly's methodological guidelines. As mentioned, he is in a sense a better craftsman than methodologist (Bartolini 1993; Pierson 2000). His renowned recommendation is to focus on processes that play out across time, but in his own research he constantly supplements this focus with a keen understanding of variation across space. At a more general level, Tilly's focus on historical narratives and mechanisms has much to offer, but sometimes it creates more confusion than clarity.

To be sure, simple renderings of causal relationships often pervert reality. However, as a tool for understanding a particular development, they are difficult to replace with intricate mechanisms that are rarely directly useful for in-depth studies. It is hardly a coincidence that in his best works – *Coercion, Capital, and European States AD 990–1990*, which we will primarily discuss in this chapter, is possibly the most telling example – Tilly ignores his own guidelines and presents something reminiscent of general causal relationships. Tilly himself writes that the book is marked by a 'compulsion to order and simplify' (1990, ix), and to some extent I will use the logic of control to assess the relationships presented in the book, despite Tilly's methodological caveats.

Tilly's early explanation

Tilly (1975; 1985; 1990) is renowned for having 're-discovered' and systematized the *war-makes-states* theory, which we have already met in the writings of Weber, Schumpeter, and – in particular – Hintze. In fact, this relationship is directly imprinted in Tilly's conception of the state. In Tilly's (1985) unforgettable image, the state is an outsized mafia that runs a protection racket and that specifically needs protection money in order to fend for itself in an anarchic international system.

Tilly used this understanding of the state in his 1975 essay 'The Formation of National States in Western Europe'. Here, Tilly presented an overall model of the development of the European states according to which all (European) states went through the same transition towards bureaucratization and absolutism due to the pressure of warfare. He would later refer to this as his 'unilinear story – one running from war to extraction and repression to state formation' (1990, 12). However, Tilly's original approach could not explain the multiplicity of state types found in

Europe over the past one thousand years. There is also a methodological dimension to this objection: that we require variation in the outcome in order to be able to test our explanations – at least by means of the logic of comparative control (cf. also Spruyt 1994, 3–21).

Tilly began adding new explanatory elements rather quickly. In the course of the 1980s, and particularly in the essay 'War Making and State Making as Organized Crime' (Tilly 1985), he introduced the conditions for tax collection as a conditioning variable. Tilly maintained that a direct relationship exists between the cost of war and the need to construct a central authority and bureaucracy. However, he also pointed out that such a centripetal force is inversely proportional to the commercialization of the economy. In those areas where, because of economic modernization/commercialization, there are readily available resources to tax, the relationship between war, bureaucratization, and absolutism does not develop to the same degree (1985, 172, 181–182). The state-building dynamics in the commercialized economies of England / Great Britain and the Netherlands therefore differ from those in, e.g., France and Prussia. We have already encountered a slightly rougher version of this argument in Hintze's work (see Chapter 5), and, as we shall see, Downing (1988; 1992; see also Ertman 1997, 13–15) has elaborated on this claim.

Tilly's more sophisticated geopolitical explanation

This more refined relationship is the starting point for Tilly's *Coercion, Capital and European States* (hereafter *Coercion*), from 1990. In *Coercion*, Tilly emphasizes that the war-makes-states relationship is general, while his theory on 'coercion' and 'capital' is specifically European (1990, 15–16) – and therefore able to account for European diversity. One might also say that the war-makes-states mechanism is a premise for the theory (14). War is a catalyst for the European development, but it cannot by itself account for the European diversity (cf. also Ertman 1997, 317).

It is important to understand precisely what Tilly wants to explain. Tilly's dependent variable is the European territorial state and the corresponding multistate system. But most crucial is why Europe has been characterized by different paths to state formation, which have led to (i) empires, (ii) city-states, and (iii) nation-states (31). In other words, Tilly classifies states according to their organizational structure (Kestnbaum and Skocpol 1993, 666). One might say that Tilly wants to explain the difference in the timing of certain elements in the state formation process (Mahoney and Rueschemeyer 2003, 12). All three tracks lead to the territorial state, but depending on explanatory factors they do so at different points in time!

Tilly's general model in *Coercion* is based on a rather simple observation: the character of the state formation process depends on which resources and coalition partners are available to those building the states (Tilly 1990, 15; see also Alsted 2008). In other words, the variation in economic relations drives the original difference between empires, city-states, and territorial states, while the ability to survive explains the recent convergence towards the latter (Kestnbaum and Skocpol 1993,

663). The socio-economic organization of the economy prior to the occurrence of geopolitical pressure therefore determines under which conditions state formation takes place. This is where the distinction between 'coercion' and 'capital' comes to the fore. Coercion is best understood from a 'top-down' perspective: it implies consolidating the state from above. Conversely, capital requires a 'bottom-up' perspective on the groups in society and their resources (cf. Hui 2005, 40–41). The important point is that coercion and capital vary across the European space over the course of the one-thousand-year period that Tilly is analysing.

In order to simplify the causal model, we can then say that the independent variable measures the distinction between coercion and capital, that the dependent variable measures the timing of certain forms of state, and that the mechanism is preparation for war and bargaining over taxes (see, e.g., Tilly 1990, 100). Capital is most commonly found in the cities, which explains why the construction of states via capital first and foremost occurred in the European 'city belt'. Here, state-builders allied themselves with merchants, artisans, and sometimes financiers, partners who provided ample access to capital. The Netherlands, parts of Western Germany, and North and Central Italy are the best examples of such areas.

Where capital was scarce, state-builders had to resort to coercion. In these areas, the landed gentry – who controlled the peasants, whether serfs or not – were the obvious coalition partners. Russia in particular, but actually all of Eastern Europe, is an example of such an area. Third, Tilly draws attention to the areas where coercion and capital could combine. These were states that both included cities of a certain size and large rural areas with strong landowners. Tilly refers to England and France as examples of such countries, and this third route came to leave its mark on Europe (183). This leads to the following three paths (see also Tilly 1997, 405–406):

(1) *Coercion-intensive*: often empires such as Russia, but in reality all of Eastern Europe and Sweden.
(2) *Capital-intensive*: Italian, German, and Swiss city-states, but also the Netherlands.
(3) *Capitalized coercion*: over time territorial states or nation-states, particularly France and Great Britain, but also Spain and Prussia.

Eventually, all European state-builders felt compelled to follow the third track, which simply proved to be militarily superior, particularly with respect to the ability to organize a standing army (Kestnbaum and Skocpol 1993, 664). This meant that the territorial state gradually came to stand tall (Tilly 1990, 183). However, Tilly stresses that even after the convergence, the states retained characteristics from previous paths, such as the character of the representative institutions (1990, 31). This is probably where he most clearly transcends his stated focus on the state and conflates it with or at least highlights aspects of the regime form (see also 187–188).

Finally, Tilly identifies the European uniqueness that made the advent of the territorial state possible. Roughly speaking, he finds this in capital: it is the clout of the cities that distinguishes Europe from other areas. Here, Tilly draws direct comparisons with China (127–130), where such cities were not found. In other words, capital is specifically European and therefore becomes the most crucial variable in the analysis. Tilly's explanation implies that the presence or absence of capital determined which of the three aforementioned tracks materialized, once coercion was put to use (133).

Criticism

Tilly's analysis of the European state-formation processes is certainly worth reading, and the distinction between coercion and capital exposes important differences within Europe, particularly the line dividing Western and Eastern Europe, which we have mentioned in several of the previous chapters (see also Knudsen and Rothstein 1994, 205). Tilly's analysis has been criticized from multiple angles, however. Spruyt (1994) has pointed out that warfare is not the only important historical force driving European state formation. Historically, non-military aspects of the efficiency of institutions have also been a part of the competition between the states.

Another criticism is that Tilly's relationship between capital, coercion, and the construction of states is overly analytical. Tilly ignores – entirely deliberately, it would seem – Weber's distinction between free and autonomous cities and other types of cities (see Chapter 4). In Tilly's sense, both must provide capital, as it is otherwise not possible to procure capital outside of Western Christendom (and he includes Orthodox Christendom in the analysis). An obvious objection here is that it was not the quantity of capital but its specific quality (autonomy and legal privileges) that distinguished Europe from, say, China, as well as Western Europe from Eastern Europe. Finally – and to some degree further along these lines – it has been pointed out that Tilly is unable to explain the later differences between the European territorial states (Kestnbaum and Skocpol 1993, 671). This last point will become clearer when we move on to Downing's and Ertman's analyses, where the analysed cases are distinguished both in terms of the state apparatus and the regime.

Brian M. Downing

Western Christendom has had unique conditions for developing modern democracy. This Protestant and Roman Catholic area – Europe excluding Orthodox Eastern Europe – developed a set of constitutional characteristics in the Middle Ages in the form of representative institutions/Estates, free cities, and the notion of rule of law in general. We do not find any such historical legacy anywhere else, and this historical heritage has laid the foundations for modern democracy.

This is Brian M. Downing's (1989; 1992) general response to Max Weber's great question 'Why Europe?' in *The Military Revolution and Political Change* from 1992. The book can be understood as a reaction against the modernization theory that dominated American political science in particular in the decades after World War II (see Lipset 1959; Rostow 1960; Almond and Powell 1966). The basic claim in modernization theory is that all countries move along the beaten track from the traditional to the modern – that is, they transform themselves in a Western image over time. Downing's objection here is palpable: this perspective completely overlooks the unique beginnings of the European path in the constitutionalism of the Middle Ages (see also Downing 1989; Møller 2015b).

However, as indicated by the book's title, *The Military Revolution and Political Change*, this is only one half of his analysis. Downing also sets out to elucidate the internal diversity in Western Christendom (see also Downing 1988). By the end of the Middle Ages, this entire area was characterized by constitutionalism, and each area within it had the potential for developing towards modern democracy. However, in the sixteenth and seventeenth centuries, the so-called 'military revolution' intervened, turning many states and regimes upside-down. The 'military revolution' is Downing's term for the process whereby the crowned heads of Europe replaced the decentralized feudal military – where vassals were obligated to serve their lords in war with a specific number of men over a short period of time – with standing armies of increasing size and professionalism (1992, 10; see Parker 1996[1988]).

Such a development costs money, and the military revolution forced the fledgling European territorial states to develop a strong civil service capable of taxing their citizens. Or, rather, it forced geographically vulnerable states, such as France and Prussia, to tread this path once geopolitical pressure had intensified. In these exposed places, continual survival demanded that the economy was mobilized for warfare. This could not occur voluntarily, and the French and Prussian monarchs therefore abolished the medieval constitutional institutions. Instead, what Downing refers to as a military-bureaucratic complex was established, and absolutist monarchy, where the monarch stands above the law, took hold (Downing, 1992, 11–13).

Where war was only sporadic or where it could be financed without mobilizing the economy, constitutionalism survived. The geographically protected British Isles belong to the former category, as the British could make do with a navy and the occasional expeditionary force. In the latter category we find the highly developed Netherlands, which was able to extract the required resources from its commercialized economy, and poorly developed Sweden, which collected taxes outside of Sweden itself (particularly in the occupied areas of northern Germany). In none of these countries did the absolutist monarchy and the associated bureaucracy materialize, and constitutionalism was therefore gradually replaced by modern, liberal democracy (Downing, 1992, 9–10).

A similar development is found in a few states that were actually vulnerable and therefore experienced intensive warfare, Poland offering the best example, Downing (1992, 140–156). Here, the nobility refused to surrender their medieval privileges. In fact, these privileges were strengthened during the military revolution, such that an individual member of the Polish parliament, *Sejm*, via his *liberum veto* (the free right to veto), could prevent the passage of new legislation. Consequently, Poland lost out in the struggle with its absolute neighbours. The country was repeatedly overwhelmed and divided. It has been pointed out that Poland was not liquidated – it simply committed suicide (Palmer 1970, 21).

It is relatively simple to illustrate Downing's theory as an explanatory typology (Møller and Skaaning 2016b, see Table 9.1). The basic condition for the theory is medieval constitutionalism, and the two independent variables are the intensity of the warfare after the military revolution (+/−) and the access to resources to conduct warfare. Finally, the dependent variable consists of the distinction between 'military-bureaucratic absolutism' and 'preservation of constitutionalism'. The first independent variable − the intensity of the warfare − becomes a constant in the course of the analysis, as all of Western Christianity became involved in large-scale warfare after the military revolutions of the sixteenth and seventeenth centuries. Access to resources to finance warfare therefore is − or at least becomes − the crucial variable. Constitutionalism was replaced by absolutism only in the regions where it was necessary to mobilize the national economy because no other sources of financing were available.[3]

The shaded areas are those that fit Downing's theory. Only Poland falls in an unexplained type. The theory therefore receives substantial backing on the cross-case level. However, Downing does more than rely on this general use of comparisons; his book also contains a series of within-case analyses of the polities presented in Table 9.1.

Note that Downing's explanation is purely structural. It is not deterministic as the elites can be 'naive' − as in the Polish case − and fail to read the writing on the wall. However, in most countries, king, nobility, and bourgeoisie reacted exactly as expected based on the structural conditions. Downing is therefore able to explain why modern democracy emerged in Europe as well as why some European states in the centuries after the military revolution became absolutist while others proceeded directly to liberal democracy.

Downing is not only critical of modernization theory. He deliberately writes up against Barrington Moore's renowned explanation of the rise of democracy and dictatorship. As described in Chapter 6, one of Moore's most important conclusions has been summarized in the phrase 'No bourgeois, no democracy' − that is, democracy is inconceivable without a bourgeoisie or middle class. Downing sheds light on why some European countries could move towards democracy

TABLE 9.1 Downing's theory as explanatory typology

	+Intensive warfare		−Intensive warfare	
	Necessary to mobilize domestic economy	Availability of alternative of finance	Necessary to mobilize domestic economy	Availability of alternative sources of finance
Military-bureaucratic absolutism	Prussia France			
Preservation of constitutionalism	Poland	England II (1688–1713) Dutch Republic Sweden		England I (until 1648)

Source: Downing (1992), cf. Møller and Skaaning (2016b).

without such a middle class. The reason is precisely medieval constitutionalism, and Sweden is Downing's example *par excellence*. He is brash enough to summarize his analysis of Sweden in the following paraphrase of Moore: 'No bourgeois, yet democracy' (Downing, 1992, 245).

Criticism

This is all very convincing. But a couple of problems warrant mention. First, it is rather interesting that, even in countries such as France and Prussia, absolutism was replaced by constitutionalism and democracy in the nineteenth and twentieth centuries. Hintze (1975[1931], 348) goes so far as to observe that absolutism was a temporary transition after which the representative principle of the Middle Ages reasserted itself in the form of modern parliaments. If we follow Downing's reasoning, this indicates that maintaining medieval constitutionalism was not a necessary condition for the development of liberal democracy. Downing points out that it is difficult to imagine a large-scale diffusion of democracy to areas outside the European constitutional heritage. However, just as his book was published in 1992, the so-called 'third wave of democracy' (Huntington 1991) began to flood large parts of the world (see Møller and Skaaning 2013, Chapter 6). On that point, then, we can firmly establish that Downing overestimated the long-term historical significance of medieval constitutionalism for modern democracy.[4]

Secondly, the linking of absolutism and bureaucracy is not unproblematic. As Ertman (1997) has pointed out, the absolutist regimes were very different from one another on this point. In Prussia, actual bureaucracies that fit the 'Weberian' model were developed under absolutism. In France and the rest of southern Europe, the absolute kings established more primitive, patrimonial state apparatuses in which offices were sold to private entrepreneurs, who then carried out the executive and legal functions of the state.

There are also other – slightly more specific – problems with Downing's categories. I have already mentioned that Prussia and France are both cases of military-bureaucratic absolutism. However, this absolutism broke down much earlier in France than was the case in Prussia. Downing attempts to explain this with reference to how Prussia was more absolutist than France – that is, he opens up on this point for gradual differences within his otherwise dichotomous categorization (Coppedge 2012, 142). This is all well and good as far as these two cases are concerned, but it obviously raises the question whether we are dealing with homogenous categories as Downing's explanation otherwise implies.

Thomas Ertman

Thomas Ertman is a conscientious scholar. His only book to date, *Birth of the Leviathan*, was published in 1997. According to the foreword (1997, xi), he began mulling over the subject back in the late 1970s. In 1990, he defended his doctoral thesis, which is the basis for the book. As the reader quickly learns, this is thorough research. Ertman interchangeably refers to texts written in English, French, German, Spanish, and Italian – indeed, even in Danish and Swedish. It is telling that he is still working on the follow-up, *Taming the Leviathan*.

If Ertman's forthcoming book is of the same calibre as *Birth of the Leviathan*, it will be worth the wait. For *Birth of the Leviathan* represents a large-scale attempt at explaining the European state formation from the Early Middle Ages to the forerunners of the modern territorial state in the eighteenth century. Ertman begins by outlining how the European path distinguishes itself from all others in two ways, described by Max Weber (see Chapters 2 and 4): the development of the sovereign territorial state and the modern market economy (1997, 3–4). This unique combination can be attributed to a number of background conditions that are specific to Europe. Ertman draws attention to three of these: Europe's geography, the existence of many competing political entities, and the Christian cultural community (4; see also Ertman 2005, 166–169). These factors have created a fairly closed system in which war-based competition has forced various countries to follow suit when new forms of organization have proven superior (see also Chapter 12). The best example is how the territorial states outperformed the city-states and empires after the High Middle Ages (see the discussion of Tilly above).

These background conditions are constant within Western Christendom,[5] and they are therefore unable to explain the two sets of variations, which Ertman claims characterized this area in the eighteenth century (see Table 9.2). The first concerns the regime form. Some countries had absolutist regimes; others had constitutional regimes. The other concerns the character of the state apparatus. Some countries boasted a merit-based, rule-bound bureaucracy, while others had a more primitive administration, where nepotism and corruption flourished and titles were sold to the highest bidder (Ertman 1997, 6–10). I have already illustrated Ertman's typology of the dependent variable in eighteenth-century (western and central) Europe in Chapter 2.

Southern Europe, including France, combined absolutism with a kind of 'patrimonial' civil service. In Poland and Hungary, constitutionalism existed alongside a similar kind of state apparatus. The complete opposite situation developed in most of what later became Germany and in Denmark, where absolutism went hand in hand with a professional bureaucracy (see also Ertman 2005). Finally, constitutionalism co-existed with meritocratic administration in Great Britain and Sweden (Ertman 1997, 10).

TABLE 9.2 Ertman's typology over states in eighteenth-century Europe

		Political regime	
		Absolutist	*Constitutional*
Character of state infrastructure	Patrimonial	Patrimonial absolutism	Patrimonial constitutionalism
	Bureaucratic	Bureaucratic absolutism	Bureaucratic constitutionalism

Source: Erman, 1997, 5.

Ertman's preliminary explanation

How can we account for the emergence of this four-fold division? Ertman emphasizes that geopolitical pressure alone has not driven the development, as such pressure − cf. also the discussion of Downing above − is a constant in Western Christendom (1997, 317). Instead, he emphasizes two other factors.

First, inspired by Hintze (1962[1930]), Ertman draws attention to the characteristics of the representative institutions. The point is that constitutionalism gained a foothold in the countries where representative institutions took the form of territorially based bicameral systems, the best example being Great Britain. On the contrary, absolutist monarchy prevailed where the three-chamber systems (consisting of the bourgeoisie, nobility, and church) existed without any anchoring on the local level (Ertman, 1997, 20−25). The bicameral systems acted as a shield against absolutism, because the lower house, whose members represented territorially defined areas (e.g., cities), and not particular social groups (e.g., townsmen), could form a united front against the authorities − in contrast to the tricurial systems, where the legally defined classes (estate groups) could rarely find common ground due to their corporate divides (21−22).

This difference can be traced to the fall of the Roman Empire − or more specifically to the character of local administration in the first medieval phase of state formation. This brings us back to the Early Middle Ages. The three-chamber systems emerged in areas where the new polities of the Middle Ages were created on the foundations of the Roman Empire (e.g., in France and Germany). In contrast, the bicameral systems arose where the first state formation was made from scratch (e.g., in Poland and Hungary) (23−25). Ertman calls the former *administrative* local government and the latter *participatory* local government.

A good way of putting this into perspective is by re-invoking Tilly's analysis. Whereas Tilly emphasizes the socio-economic organization prior to the intensification of geopolitical pressure, Ertman instead stresses the political organization. Ertman then plays the war card, but with a twist. He underlines the importance of the timing of geopolitical competition in different parts of Europe. In those areas where the military competition intensified early on − as in France as a result of the Hundred Years' War (1337−1453) − there was no alternative to developing a primitive, patrimonial administration. Where military competition occurred later − for example, in the more isolated Prussia − it was possible to establish a proper bureaucracy because new administrative techniques had been developed in the interim period.

This is a 'timing' analysis of the finest kind. Ertman (1997, 26−27) is inspired by the economic historian Gerschenkron's (1962) observation that industrialization proceeded differently in Europe, depending on whether a country had undergone an 'early' or 'late' industrialization. According to Gerschenkron, the late industrializers − for example, Germany − were characterized by a greater involvement of the state and a more important role for banks than was the case in the earlier English industrialization. This speeds up progress, particularly with respect to heavy industry, as it is possible to 'borrow' modern technology in specific areas. For the same reason, Gerschenkron's theory has been summarized in the expression *the advantages of backwardness*, which goes all the way back to Torstein Veblen (Moore 1991[1966], 413–414). This notion refers to the advantages of being inspired in specific areas while avoiding expensive 'sunk costs' in other areas. Ertman shows that a similar relationship is relevant for the European state-formation processes. He argues that the developments in military technology and administration – the presence of university graduates, who could staff administrative structures – and the development of international financial markets rendered it possible to create a bureaucracy in the cases where geopolitical pressure kicked in late (after the year 1450). Conversely, it is the absence of these ingredients that made the choice of the patrimonial path necessary in the earlier instances (Ertman, 1997, 27–28).

Ertman emphasizes that it was very difficult to deviate from these paths once they had been chosen. In other words, these are *critical junctures*[6] (Ertman, 1997, 320–321). Countries such as France were therefore unable to professionalize an inefficient system, which rested on the sale of offices and was created as a result of the Hundred Years' War against England. In this manner, Ertman explains the position of most of the European countries. I have illustrated his argument in a typology in Table 9.3.

As presented in Table 9.3, the explanation (the shaded areas along the diagonal are predicted) has a relatively strong empirical fit as nine out of thirteen cases are correctly classified. The remaining four countries cause problems for Ertman. First, contrary to expectations, Great Britain developed a professional bureaucracy, in spite of it being the second part of the aforementioned Hundred Years' War. Second, Poland and Hungary never developed an efficient state apparatus, despite a late intensification of warfare. Finally, Denmark, which should have been in the same type as Sweden, is absolutist.

TABLE 9.3 Ertman's theory as explanatory typology (without the independent effect of parliaments)

	Onset of geopolitical competition before 1450		Onset of geopolitical competition after 1450	
	Administrative	*Participatory*	*Administrative*	*Participatory*
Patrimonial absolutism	France Naples Papal States Portugal Savoy Spain Tuscany			
Patrimonial constitutionalism				Hungary Poland
Bureaucratic absolutism			German Territorial States	Denmark
Bureaucratic constitutionalism		Britain		Sweden

Source: Based on Ertman 1997, 320–321; cf. Møller and Skaaning 2016b.

Ertman's more sophisticated explanation

Ertman proceeds by refining his explanation in order to account for the three most important of the four cases. The very fact that Great Britain, Poland, and Hungary had strong, locally based parliaments meant that the character of their respective bureaucracies was not shaped by warfare alone (Ertman 1997, 29–30). In Great Britain, the parliament forced monarchs to professionalize the bureaucracy. Conversely, the strong parliaments in Poland and Hungary, which were completely dominated by the nobility, prevented the weak monarchy from creating a well-functioning state apparatus. In other words, the strong parliaments became the one actor capable of breaking with the underlying structural conditions.

Note that Ertman is not introducing a probabilistic element in his analysis here. What he presents is an interaction in which the strong bicameral parliaments always attempted to change the character of the state apparatus (accordingly, as presented in Table 9.4, Sweden transforms into an unexplained case as a result of the introduction of this element). In Great Britain, the patrimonial state institutions had thus emerged *before* the strong parliament, which prevented the parliamentary elites from dominating it. In Poland and Hungary it was the other way around, as a strong parliament was in place when the state apparatus was first developed, for which reason the elites were able to colonize it (31–32). By getting involved in warfare early on, the elites in parliament therefore fought patrimonial tendencies (Great Britain), while they struggled against bureaucratic tendencies in those cases where this involvement was late (Poland, Hungary). These theoretical expectations can be illustrated as seen in Table 9.4.

TABLE 9.4 Ertman's theory as explanatory typology (with the independent effect of parliaments)

	Onset of geopolitical competition before 1450		Onset of geopolitical competition after 1450	
	Administrative	*Participatory*	*Administrative*	*Participatory*
Patrimonial absolutism	France Naples Papal States Portugal Savoy Spain Tuscany			
Patrimonial constitutionalism				Hungary Poland
Bureaucratic Absolutism			German Territorial States	Denmark
Bureaucratic constitutionalism		Britain		Sweden

Source: Based on Ertman 1997; cf. Møller and Skaaning 2016b.

This leaves Denmark and Sweden alone as unexplained cases. Both 'should' be cases of patrimonial constitutionalism, just like Poland and Hungary. Here, Ertman resorts to *ad hoc* explanations. In the Danish case, he points to an export of absolutism as well as bureaucracy from the German territorial states, Prussia in particular (see also Ertman 2005, 170–172). In the Swedish case, he emphasizes the successful campaigns of the Vasa Kings to bureaucratize the country after breaking away from the Danish crown (Ertman 1997, 32–33). In the Swedish case, Ertman thus identifies an actor that is actually able to break with the structures, meaning that he introduces a probabilistic element into his otherwise deterministic explanation (cf. Mahoney 2003b, 345).

Ertman makes a good deal of progress measured up against previous interpretations, including the analyses carried out by Perry Anderson (see Chapter 7), Charles Tilly, and Brian M. Downing mentioned above – at least if we accept his own definition of cases and periods. In fact, Ertman rejects these analyses as well as one of Hintze's theories (see Chapter 5) by pointing out that each of them leaves four of his cases as unexplained. Poland and Hungary in particular create problems, but Great Britain also falls through several of the competing theories (see also Mahoney 2003b, 345).

More specifically, Ertman (1997, 4–5, 13–19) identifies three problems in the theories of Anderson, Tilly, Downing, and (partly) Hintze. First, they do not appreciate the significance of different kinds of representative institutions (estate-based tricameral systems versus locally based bicameral systems). Second, they link absolutism and bureaucracy; that is, they see absolutist states as characterized by a large, well-functioning state apparatus, whereas constitutional states such as Great Britain had a limited state apparatus; just think of Downing's 'military-bureaucratic absolutism'. With reference to Brewer (1989), Ertman points out that the British state apparatus was actually larger than that of Prussia per capita – but merely decentralized. More generally, Ertman's point is that constitutional systems were sometimes bureaucratic. Third, the other side of the coin is that Anderson, Tilly, and Downing place insufficient emphasis on the significance of patrimonialism – that is, non-Weberian bureaucracies, which, as illustrated in Tables 9.2 and 9.3, were often found in absolutist systems.

Conclusions

In the 1970s, Tilly reintroduced the 'war-makes-states' relationship. In his initial version, the relationship was conceived as unilinear, a point of criticism Tilly later conceded. In the course of the 1980s and 1990s, the geopolitical explanation was further refined, partly via a systematic dialogue with the classic analyses in general and Hintze's in particular. The research breakthroughs achieved by Downing and Ertman are characterized by their 'rediscovery' of forgotten or at least forlorn arguments, which figured prominently in the classic analyses described in Chapters 3–5. The result is a growing body of empirical research that has taught us much about the significance of war for European patterns of state formation and regime change.

Downing has shown that the way war is financed often determines its political effects, and Ertman has convincingly argued that the timing of geopolitical pressure has implications for its effects on the state apparatus.

If we lift our gaze slightly, we can note that the war-makes-states relationship is found in two versions or, more precisely, is driven by two different mechanisms (cf. Kurtz 2013). First, the relationship is sometimes interpreted in such a manner that war directly leads to the transformation of institutions. This logic is described very well in Albert Einstein's famous one-liner: '*Necessity is the mother of all inventions*'.[7] Second, war can be seen as creating an evolutionary process of selection in the sense that the only states that survive are those that – possibly by pure chance – have developed effective institutions. Unpropitious institutions disappear over time as the strong states swallow up the weak. The misfortune of Poland is an obvious example of this logic in the sense that the Polish elites stubbornly refused to see the necessity to which Einstein referred – to read the writing on the wall – and failed to introduce the reforms that made neighbouring countries such as Prussia stronger.

It is not always entirely clear towards which of the two mechanisms Tilly, Downing, and Ertman are inclined. One reading is that they place emphasis on both mechanisms and might actually see them as mutually reinforcing. That would at least appear to be the logic in Downing's analysis. In other words, war leads to institutional reforms, which render some states militarily superior. Neighbour countries follow suit in most cases; should they refrain from doing so, they are wiped off of the face of the map. The result in both cases is that geopolitical pressure promotes more efficient state institutions.

Let us close the chapter with one last point of criticism: though the focus is on geopolitical pressure, which is ubiquitous in human history (Morris 2014), Tilly's, Downing's, and Ertman's explanations do not really work outside of Western and Central Europe. For instance, none of the countries in Eastern Europe proper – despite the late occurrence of geopolitical competition – were able to develop the well-functioning bureaucracies or the constitutional systems that Ertman links with a late intensification of warfare. Ertman would of course counter that this is because the European scope condition he lists at the beginning of his analysis makes up an essential part of the equation. But the conclusion is, then, that (Western and Central) Europe is so completely different that the most important features of European state formation cannot be found elsewhere. In some ways, the problems are even greater for Tilly, who attempts to include Eastern Europe in his analysis. Suffice it to say here that Tilly's large-scale analysis is a little rough around the edges. This is to be understood entirely literally, as his theory does a much better job of accommodating the development in the Western European core areas than in the periphery of the continent, including Scandinavia, Eastern Europe, and parts of Southern Europe (cf. also Ertman 1997). Conversely, we can note that Downing is better at explaining the general difference *between* Western and Central Europe and the rest of the world than the more concrete differences *within* Western and Central Europe.

These problems result from the broad focus of these three scholars, and they show that academic boldness and academic accuracy can never be completely reconciled. I will therefore conclude by stressing the scope of the contributions made by Tilly, Downing, and Ertman. Generally speaking, this is a set of analyses that remind us that history matters. History does not offer 'blank slates', as Downing remarks with words borrowed from the great Polish–British author Joseph Conrad. For better or for worse, we are a product of our past, and – one might inspired by Machiavelli add – even though societies can change, they can rarely be transformed.

Notes

1 This is most readily apparent in the case of Ertman, but Downing and Tilly also emphasize elements of both, just in a slightly less systematic manner.
2 Tilly also revolutionized historical sociology through his use of statistical methods – regression analyses in particular – in his 'early' work (cf. Hunt 1984), but this part of his authorship is not discussed in this chapter.
3 Downing actually operates with three – and not (as illustrated) two – classes on the 'resources for warfare' variable. In addition to the mobilization of the economy, he distinguishes between whether warfare is financed by taxing conquered areas (Sweden) or by taxing the commercialized economy (England II and the Dutch Republic). But as the effect is the same in both cases – namely, the preservation of constitutionalism despite intensive warfare – it is possible to collapse these two classes into a more general one (see Møller and Skaaning 2016b).
4 This statement applies above all to the 'electoral' dimension of the present wave of democratization. There is considerable evidence that the constitutional tradition for rule of law – the adjective in the term 'liberal democracy' – is far more difficult to export (see Fukuyama 2011). Downing may therefore have an important point but should have merely phrased his prediction more narrowly so that it applied to the rule of law instead of democracy (see Møller & Skaaning 2013).
5 Ertman applies the logic of comparative control in a very direct and therefore transparent manner, as he only compares territorial states within Western Christendom in order to keep as much as possible constant (see 1997, 5, fn. 13).
6 Note, however, that Ertman's explanatory model does not live up to the requirements about contingent actor choice, which is normally associated with critical junctures (e.g., Mahoney 2000).
7 Einstein virtually drew this phrase word for word from Plato's writings.

PART IV
Recent contributions

10

REPRESENTATIVE INSTITUTIONS
REDUX

In recent decades, the 'Why Europe?' question has attracted overwhelming interest in the social sciences. From having been a dusty, forgotten issue, primarily studied by historical sociologists, it is now a part of mainstream political science and economics. For example, over the last decade, the leading journal in political science, *American Political Science Review*, has published a series of articles that, often with the help of sophisticated statistical methods, address different aspects of the question (e.g., Acemoglu and Robinson 2006; Stasavage 2010; 2014; Hariri 2012; Woodberry 2012; Blaydes and Chaney 2013; Kokkonen and Sundell 2014). Similarly, the question has received attention from economists, an issue to which we return in Chapter 13.

It is thus hardly an exaggeration to say that much of contemporary social science – as in the late nineteenth and early twentieth centuries – revolves around the causes of the emergence of modernity in the West and the implications of this for the rest of the world. This new interest in old questions primarily seems to have been prompted by the following insight: only a historical perspective can enable us to understand the contemporary variation in economic prosperity and levels of democracy, particularly outside of Europe and the European settler colonies (e.g., Acemoglu et al. 2001; 2002a; Acemoglu et al. 2008; Hariri 2012). The more specific claim is that a series of medieval political institutions contributed to putting a leash on European monarchs and limiting their arbitrary exercise of power. These institutions were subsequently transplanted to some of the European colonies, where they facilitated economic growth as well as democratization.

What kinds of institutions have been attributed these tantalizing effects? As we shall see in Chapter 13, which addresses economic and political development outside of Europe, the answer to this question is not always clear. But it should be obvious that the representative institutions of the Middle Ages – Estates or parliaments and diets – form part of the core. Here, we can repeat Ertman's (1997, 19) observation from Chapter 2 that these institutions alone were able to limit the monarchy's exercise of power in a systematic manner.

The following pages are premised on this point. The purpose is to address a new body of literature on the origins and character of representative institutions. I have already reviewed Ertman's (ultimately, Otto Hintze's) account of why medieval representative institutions were stronger in some areas than others, and why they therefore had a varying impact on state formation and regime change. However, new research has been burgeoning in recent years. Most importantly, English political scientist David Stasavage has followed up on Hintze's and Ertman's analyses of the character and impact of the representative institutions in medieval Europe. Stasavage's work has thus far resulted in two books (2008; 2011) and four scientific articles (2007; 2010; 2014; 2016). This chapter discusses this work and sets the stage for the next chapters, which use this medieval legacy to explain contemporary variations in economic and political development.

Surveying representative institutions

To explain a phenomenon, one first has to capture it. With this in mind, Stasavage compiles a dataset tallying representative institutions in twenty-four European states in the five centuries between 1250 and 1800 – the period to which Myers (1975) refers as the Age of the Polity of Estates. Instead of distinguishing between the number of chambers and whether or not the representatives were representing estate groups or localities, as Hintze and Ertman do, Stasavage (2010) maps the following:

(1) Does a representative assembly exist?
(2) Does the representative assembly have a veto on taxes?
(3) Does the representative assembly audit government spending?

The first condition is fulfilled if a collective assembly is found on the national level, convenes with some regularity, and at a minimum is consulted by the monarch. We find assemblies of this kind throughout Western (or Latin) Christendom in the Middle Ages. They emerge at different points in time: relatively early in Western Europe and relatively late in Scandinavia and East-Central Europe (Poland and Hungary). The only states in Stasavage's dataset that do not live up to the first condition at any time in the period 1250–1800 are the duchies of Milan and Tuscany and, hardly surprisingly, Russia, which is the only state outside of Western Christendom that is tallied.

The second condition is more demanding as it requires that the assemblies have a veto on taxation. This was the core prerogative of most representative bodies, and this condition is fulfilled in the vast majority of the twenty-four states. In fact, among the states with representative institutions, Denmark and Naples are the only ones without.[1] The third condition is met if the representative institutions had a direct right to audit the monarch's expenditure and possibly even decide over public spending. There are very few cases in which we find this prerogative (eight of Stasavage's twenty-four states). In addition to city-states such as Siena and Florence, England after the Glorious Revolution in 1688 is an instance. Finally, Stasavage codes how frequently the representative institutions convene, 'annually' being the highest value and 'never' the lowest.[2]

Geographic barriers for representation

What explains the variation captured in Table 10.1? And what explains why the frequency of assemblies was so different across this universe: from the city-states, where the assemblies met many times annually, via the almost annual meetings in states such as Württemberg, Austria, and England, to the extremely rare gatherings in states such as Denmark and France?

Stasavage's attempt to answer this question begins with an apparent paradox. As we know from previous chapters, it is widely assumed that representative institutions made it easier to impose and collect taxes for the purpose of financing warfare,

TABLE 10.1 Stasavage's mapping of representative institutions

+Representative institutions	Cologne, Siena Florence, Netherlands, Württemberg, Genoa, Burgundy/ Flandern, Saxony, Austria, Piedmont, Naples, Venice, Portugal, Prussia, Denmark, England, Sweden, Hungary, Castille, France, Poland	
+Veto over taxation		Cologne, Siena, Florence, Netherlands, Württemberg, Genoa, Burgundy/ Flandern, Saxony, Austria, Piedmont, Venice, Portugal, Prussia, England, Sweden, Hungary, Castille, France, Poland
+Right to audit public expenditure		Cologne, Siena, Florence, Netherlands, Genoa, Sachsen, Venice, Prussia, England

Source: Based on Stasavage 2010.

and they have also been seen as easing public borrowing and promoting economic growth. If only some of these postulates are correct, then why did the representative institutions not win out throughout Europe? And why were many states so slow to introduce them? These are the questions raised by Stasavage (2010) in the article 'When Distance Mattered'.

The title hints at his answer. Boiled down to a single sentence, there were significant geographical barriers to representation. A myriad of researchers have linked democracy with the size of the political unit. This point is best illustrated by the direct democracies of antiquity, which required that all (male) citizens were able to participate in the popular assembly. But scholars have also been pointed out that many island states have been able to maintain democracy in the period following World War II, an observation that has been linked to their limited size, which has made it easier to create a sense of political community (Dahl and Tufte 1974).

The representative institutions of the Middle Ages were not particularly democratic (see Møller and Skaaning 2013, Chapter 4). However, Stasavage argues, this does not alter the fact that geographical barriers had at least as much significance for how they worked. In Europe of the High Middle Ages, traveling great distances was associated with exorbitant costs – measured in time as well as money. The network of Roman roads had fallen into disrepair in the Early Middle Ages. In fact, it was mostly the memory of them that remained by the year 1200, at which time the representative institutions were emerging. Some improvements were made around this time, but it was only really after 1800 that large-scale advances of European infrastructure began to occur. In other words, transport was extremely cumbersome throughout the period Stasavage analyses.[3]

Stasavage argues that this affected the impact of representative institutions on public borrowing. Here, he invokes economic theories about corporate finance. One of the key insights of these theories is that a common condition for being able to raise new funds for investments is that the borrower accepts external control or at least monitoring. However, such control can be so costly that potential investors pull back for this reason alone (2010, 625–626). Stasavage draws an analogical inference about the medieval representative institutions, the point being that the cities' representatives would only go along with raising funds for the monarch if they were allowed to monitor how he spent them, but that such *ex-post* control could easily become too costly if geographical barriers prevented the representatives from meeting with some regularity.[4]

Stasavage accordingly reasons that a state's geographical size will have an impact on (i) the existence of representative institutions, (ii) how frequently they were called, and (iii) whether or not they had the right to oversee public spending. Conversely, he does not expect to find a relationship between geographical size and a veto on taxation, as this does not require a high meeting frequency. Stasavage applies these expectations in a series of statistical analyses in which he supplements the information from the dataset above with a number of control factors, including indicators measuring the presence of external threats and the size of the population, respectively. The intuition behind the first control variable is that the threat of war can trigger the summoning of representative institutions – and for that matter bring about an expansion of the prerogatives of these assemblies. The reasoning behind the second control variable is that the per capita expenses related to warfare will be greater in areas where the population is smaller. Finally, Stasavage controls for urbanization by rerunning his analysis without the city-states that are included in the dataset – on the basis of the potential objection that the representative institutions in these states were peculiar.

Stasavage measures geographic barriers in several different ways, including the average distance any representative would have to travel – 'as the crow flies' – in order to participate in an assembly. More specifically, he tests his expectations in two different ways. The first analysis operates on the 'national' level – that is, across the national units described in Table 10.1 above. As a next step, Stasavage shifts the level of analysis to the regional level by repeating his analysis on the French regions that had separate representative institutions. That is, Stasavage investigates whether there were also geographical barriers to representation *within* France.

What do the analyses show? Stasavage finds that geographical size has a very consistent, statistically significant, and substantial effect: first, in terms of whether or not a representative assembly existed; second, whether it exercised oversight over public spending; and third and finally, on how frequently it met. For example, the assembles in the quartile of the smallest states in the dataset met on average more than once every second year, while the assemblies of the corresponding quartile of the largest states met less than once every third year. Conversely, as expected, there is no correlation between geographical barriers and whether or not the representatives have a veto on taxation (2010, 636–637).

Stasavage uses this baseline to predict how often the French regional Estates were convened. The model provides a reasonably good prediction of the meeting frequency in eleven of the thirteen regions. The two exceptions are Normandy and Brittany, where the regional Estates convened surprisingly often considering the large size of these units. Finally, Stasavage repeats his national analysis but substitutes the French regions for France. The results are again robust, which is reassuring in as much as it is rather artificial to work with 'national' units in the medieval world. France is thus not the only country with regional Estates. The same applies to the Holy Roman Empire, which had a single representative assembly (the Imperial Diet – *Reichstag*), but where Stasavage has instead coded the assemblies in the individual states (*Landtage*).

A final objection is that, over time, the political institutions might have an impact on how large a given state is (or, rather, becomes). If a certain kind of representative institution made it easier to borrow or charge money for warfare, this should make it possible to swallow up neighbouring states that did not have the same advantage – as money is the fuel of warfare. Conversely, one might imagine that authorities that are not accountable to a representative assembly would be able to engage in ambitious foreign policy more easily, which might provide opportunities to increase the size of the state in question. In both cases, this would undermine Stasavage's test of the relationship between geographical barriers and the characteristics of the political institutions. However, Stasavage also takes this into account in his test and dismisses this objection.

Representative institutions and public borrowing

In some ways, Stasavage's work on the geographical barriers of representation is merely a postscript to his work on the relationship between the characteristics of representative institutions and public borrowing (Stasavage 2008; 2011). His point of departure here is one of the classic claims in the literature on state formation: that representative institutions eased access to public credit in the High Middle Ages (see North and Thomas 1973; Schumpeter 1991[1917/1918]; Ertman 1997).

According to Stasavage, the relationship is not that simple. He observes that the emergence of representative institutions can only be tied to public borrowing in the European city-states. In the period 1000–1300, an economic revival throughout Western Europe made it possible for governments to finance warfare via borrowing (Stasavage 2011, 9). At the same time, the geopolitical pressure became more intensive from 1100 and henceforth, as exemplified by the Hundred Years' War (1337–1453) between France and England (25–26). This created pressure to raise the wherewithal for warfare. The problem with short-sighted loans was that they were normally associated with exorbitant interest rates. The state-builders therefore had an interest in creating a long-term state debt, which could be financed by a stable source of income (e.g., taxes) that could convince creditors about the wisdom of lending money at lower interest rates.

However, it was not the budding territorial states that took the lead in the efforts to establish a fixed public debt. Rather, the European city-states showed the way. They had already started experimenting with such instruments early in the High Middle Ages. Conversely, we find the first example of a territorial state that established a genuine government debt as late as in 1489, when Castile followed the lead of the city-states (30–32).

According to Stasavage, this pattern shows that it was not the representative institutions themselves that eased access to credit but rather two key features of certain representative institutions: that they were dominated by creditor interests and that they were able to meet regularly to oversee public spending (93). More specifically, it was the domination of the merchant class that made it possible for the city-states to establish a long-term public debt, particularly where the assemblies, because of the limited size of the political unit, could be summoned at short intervals. The 'merchants' financed the borrowing, and it was precisely because they – via the representative institutions – controlled the government that they could be sure that the state did not default on its loans.

Stasavage investigates this claim in two steps. The first consists of a statistical analysis of nineteen city-states and twelve territorial states in the period 1250–1750. The analysis confirms that the city-states established long-term state debt earlier than the territorial states and that even after the latter had followed suit, the former were consistently paying lower interest on their government loans. As we have already seen, however, the size of a state – and therefore the existence of city-states – may depend on their political institutions. In other words, the endogeneity problem rears its ugly head again. More specifically, to what extent did background conditions both lead to the establishment of city-states and ease their access to public borrowing (94)? A striking feature of Europe after the year 1000 comes in handy in this respect, namely the 'city belt' running from the Netherlands (initially in Flanders, later also including Holland), via the Rhine area in what is today western Germany and eastern France, over Switzerland to northern Italy. An older literature – represented by researchers such as Stein Rokkan and Charles Tilly – explains this belt of cities with reference to European geography. This scholarship places special emphasis on waterways (rivers), which allegedly render this specific part of Europe more suitable for commercial activity than others.

Stasavage prefers a rather different explanation, which he refers to as 'The Carolingian Partition Hypothesis' (95). This term refers to how the Frankish Empire was divided in the ninth century. In the Treaty of Verdun in 843, Charlemagne's possessions were divided in three parts: a western zone, which over time would become France; an eastern zone, which lay the foundation for the Holy Roman Empire of the German Nation; and a central zone – the so-called Lotharingia (preserved in today's 'Lorraine'), after Charlemagne's son, Lothar – which was never consolidated in earnest and for centuries existed as an unstable border area. Stasavage's point is that it was this political instability that fostered the growth of more or less independent city-states. A strong central power never surfaced in this area, which made it relatively easy for the city-states to assert their internal autonomy or direct independence, for example at the expense of the Holy Roman Emperor's formal sovereignty.

This 'political' explanation shares certain features with Weber's more general insight that the free cities were able to fill a niche created by the dispute between church and emperor (see Chapter 4). Stasavage uses 'The Carolingian Partition Hypothesis' as a lever to investigate whether or not it actually was the limited size and the merchants' domination of the city-states that accounted for the timing of public borrowing in the Middle Ages. He uses the distance to the so-called Meersen partition line, the foundation for the division of the Kingdom of the Franks, as an instrument.[5] Stasavage's point is as follows: if it is correct that it was the fragmented sovereignty and political instability of the border zone that created the basis for the independent city-states, then we can use this distance as an exogenous source of variation in the frequency of city-states. In other words, the distance to the Meersen partition line can only explain the conditions for the city-state autonomy, not the opportunities for public borrowing (with the exception of the direct impact via the economic and political structures of the city-states). The result of the subsequent statistical test confirms Stasavage's presumption that it is the character of the representative institutions in the city-states and not the representative institutions themselves that is crucial for public borrowing.

Can this explanation be further confirmed if we dig into specific cases? Stasavage investigates this in a qualitative comparison of three city-states (Cologne, Genoa, and Siena) and three territorial states (France, the Kingdom of Castile, and the Netherlands).

The analysis of the city-states corroborates that the establishment of credit-auspicious institutions eased access to public borrowing. These institutions made it possible for the creditor interests to oversee public spending. With respect to the territorial states, Stasavage shows not merely that they generally had more difficulty obtaining access to credit. He also uses internal variation to once again support his statistical results. He does so by comparing Castile and the Netherlands in the sixteenth and seventeenth centuries using the MSSD logic. From the outset, the two states were part of one and the same realm, namely the Spanish possessions of Charles V. In fact, Charles, who became the King of Spain in 1516 and Holy Roman Emperor in 1519, hailed from the Netherlands, and these provinces were the goose that laid golden eggs for him for a long time. In the 1560s, however, the Dutch provinces revolted against Charles' son and heir, Spanish King Philip II. The result was the so-called Eighty Years' War, which raged from 1568 to 1648. The war triggered a need for financing for the Spanish monarch and the Dutch rebels alike, but these financial needs were addressed very differently. The Dutch created a stable government debt with very low interest payments and an abundance of willing creditors, whereas the Spanish monarch struggled to raise loans, went bankrupt repeatedly, and therefore had to pay exorbitant interest rates.

Prior research has tended to attribute this difference to representative institutions. According to this claim, the contrast was due to the difference between (Spanish) absolutism and (Dutch) constitutionalism. According to Stasavage, this explanation does not fare well when scrutinized in depth. Indeed, the most important representative assembly under the Spanish crown – the Castilian *Cortes* – had a striking resemblance to its Dutch equivalent. They were both dominated by cities, which in turn were dominated by the merchant class, and they both had a veto on new taxes, which they also assisted in collecting (143–144). The most important difference is found in the geographical size of the two states, which made it easier for the Dutch representatives to meet frequently to audit public expenditure. Moreover, the merchant class was politically dominant in the Netherlands in a more general sense, meaning that creditor interests enjoyed a stronger political position than in Castile.

The qualitative analysis thus supports the results of the previous statistical analysis. What are the more general consequences of this? Stasavage shows, among other things, that territorial size was a mixed blessing in Europe of the High and Late Middle Ages. There were costs associated with size, as size prevented efficient public borrowing. Financing was the sinews of warfare, and this explains why the European city-states were long able to hold their own in competition with the territorial states that, at first glance, seem formidable. Next, it is worth noting that the representative institutions of Europe were far stronger – and more active – in the period 1250–1500 than after 1500. In other words, it was only when the initiative had conclusively passed to the territorial states that the representative institutions began the *déroute* that would ultimately lead to absolutism following the 'military revolution' between 1550 and 1650 (Downing 1992; Parker 1996[1988]).

Free cities and economic growth

Finally, Stasavage has revisited Max Weber's claim that autonomous cities contributed to the unique development of Europe. This work points towards the subsequent chapters, which address the historical conditions for economic growth. 'Was Weber Right?' is the telling title of Stasavage's (2014) article, which investigates whether the 'free' or autonomous medieval cities promoted economic growth. 'Yes and no' is his answer.

Stasavage first notes two opposing views in the literature as to whether or not the autonomous cities provided a favourable arena for economic activity (1–2). With reference to, e.g., Weber, one current emphasizes that the commercial activity in the free cities contributed to ensuring property ownership and thereby stimulating economic activity. The rationale is rather obvious. The elites in the cities had rid themselves of the yoke of the greedy feudal lords, and it was in their own interest to rid themselves of the kind of indiscriminate attacks on property that inhibited economic activity outside the city walls, including exorbitant taxes and the violation of property rights. Historically, commercial elites in cities have fought for the introduction of rule of law, while the landed aristocracy has often had an interest in transgressing the rights of others.

However, another current argues that the cities blocked efficient competition, principally by establishing guild privileges. The city autonomy fostered rights for citizens that did not apply to residents outside of the city walls. In addition, the cities were normally ruled by a merchant class that was organized in guilds. These guilds jealously guarded their own privileges and had an interest in establishing barriers to effective competition in order to reap monopolistic benefits.

Stasavage proposes to cut this Gordian knot in a simple way: perhaps both claims are correct? The advantages and disadvantages for economic growth might then cancel each other out, meaning that there is no net effect. However, Stasavage reasons, there is also a temporal dimension that must be taken into account. The advantages will be strong from day one (as a free city), because economic agents will immediately react to secure property rights and be more willing to engage in new and riskier or more long-term investments with potentially greater returns. Conversely, the consolidation of guild privileges primarily has a negative impact in the longer term – for example, by creating barriers to external impulses and competition. Or as Stasavage summarizes it: the political control of the guilds initially stabilizes ownership rights, but later on it acts as a barrier to competition. On this basis, he expects an asymmetrical relationship that looks something like this:

(1) For a certain period after a city has won or been granted autonomy, it will have higher economic growth than similar cities without these privileges.

(2) Over time, this lead will dwindle, and the day will come when the city will begin to grow more slowly than corresponding cities without these privileges.

In order to investigate whether these expectations hold, Stasavage has compiled yet another dataset. This covers all of the cities in Western Europe with a population of at least ten thousand in the year 1500.[6] In total, 173 cities fulfil this requirement. Stasavage maps which of these cities achieved political autonomy in the period 1000–1800 and when they did so. Stasavage codes autonomy in the following manner: first, there must be clear evidence that the city has institutions that were responsible for internal (municipal) self-government; second, these institutions must possess at least one of the following three competencies – the right to collect taxes, the right to legal autonomy, and the right to military defence.

Stasavage identifies eighty-one autonomous cities in Western Europe between the years 1000 and 1800. As reported in Table 10.2, virtually all of these cities achieved autonomy before the year 1300. In fact, seventy-three of the eighty-one cities won their 'freedom' in the twelfth and thirteenth centuries. Conversely, their demise is a more drawn-out affair, which really only begins after 1200 but continued until the French Revolution – thirteen of the cities in fact maintained their autonomy into the nineteenth century.

Stasavage measures economic growth in terms of population growth. He is aware that this is a somewhat problematic measure, but he is unable to find a better alternative and follows a considerable body of scholarship that uses this proxy. What does the dataset show about the growth rates in the autonomous and non-autonomous cities, respectively? At first glance, there is no difference. On average, both types of cities grow equally fast (or slowly) over the course of the period Stasavage is studying. However, as soon as he breaks the period down into sub-periods, these results change. Almost all models – and Stasavage runs many different specifications – confirm that the free cities first have a period in which they grow more rapidly than the non-free cities but that this is then followed by a period with slower growth. The specific results vary slightly between models. According to some of the

TABLE 10.2 Stasavage's overview of the development in autonomous towns

Period	Number of towns that achieve autonomy	Number of towns that lose autonomy	Total number of autonomous towns
– 1100	6	0	6
1100–1199	44	1	49
1200–1299	29	15	63
1300–1399	2	13	52
1400–1499	0	15	37
1500–1599	0	12	25
1600–1699	0	2	23
1700–1799	0	10	13
1800 –	0	13	0

Source: Stasavage 2014.

specifications, the turning point is 108 years after establishing autonomy; in others the turning point is after 160 years. But there is at least general evidence that the free cities had an advantage the first one hundred years, after which things begin to go downhill (2010, 11–12). A number of objections can be raised regarding this relationship, but Stasavage does exemplary work in terms of controlling for alternative explanations, including controls for regional effects.

Finally, he raises the following objection: is it possible that it was during the specific period in which cities were growing that they were able to become autonomous? The cities often had to fight for their privileges, and it seems plausible that this is easier when a city is growing larger and therefore stronger. At the same time, it is difficult to imagine that a city will stop growing at the very moment it achieves autonomy. In other words, a more rapid post-autonomy growth rate might reflect an underlying trend that *also* contributes to autonomy. To account for this, Stasavage carries out a placebo test, where he sets the date for autonomy one hundred years earlier than it actually is. The results disappear, and he concludes that there is no underlying growth trend that is driving the asymmetrical relationship.

According to Stasavage, these findings help explain why the free cities eventually disappeared (see Table 10.2). Earlier research has noted that the cities could not fend for themselves militarily in competition with the growing might of the territorial states. However, as other parts of Stasavage's research have shown, the city-states were long able to raise larger sums for warfare than the territorial states. Stasavage therefore reasons that the explanation for their demise might simply be that they gradually stagnated economically and therefore no longer offered advantages in the development race between political entities.

Criticism

If we go back to the distinction between idiographic and nomothetic approaches (see Chapter 2) – that is, the specific and the generalizing – Stasavage's work falls closer to the latter than the former pole. It is therefore hardly surprising that many historians have been critical of some of the details in his analysis (see, e.g., Prak 2012; Martoccio 2013; Tracy 2013).

Beyond the historical subtleties, at least three major objections are worth raising. First, some of Stasavage's datasets appear rather arbitrary when it comes to the delimitation and to some degree the scoring of the relevant cases. This particularly applies to the analysis of the geographical barriers to representation. As we have already seen, Stasavage has difficulties selecting the unit of analysis in a historical context where political entities are fragmented. It is especially interesting that while the German states are coded as independent units, this is not the case on the Iberian Peninsula, which is represented by 'Spain'. The truth of the matter was that Castile, Aragon, Naples, and Portugal – the latter disappears from the analysis after 1600, as Philip II of Spain won its crown in 1580 – were independent kingdoms under the same monarch (we can in fact draw further distinctions between them, as independent representative institutions also existed in, for example, Catalonia, Valencia, and Sicily). It is also telling that Stasavage compares Castile – not Spain – with the Netherlands in his qualitative analysis of public borrowing. Great Britain also appears as a single entity in the dataset despite the fact that Scotland had its own representative institution and was independent for a considerable period. Moreover, it seems rather curious that Russia is included in the analysis. As we know from the earlier chapters, representative institutions are found only in Western Christendom, and the size of Russia and absence of such institutions obviously make it easier to find the correlation between size and representation that Stasavage expects.[7]

It is also difficult to code the beginnings of representative institutions in the Middle Ages. Most researchers identify a particular assembly called by King Alfonso IX of Leon (in northern Spain) in 1188 as the first representative assembly. However, when we examine historical works, it is rather doubtful whether Leon in 1188 truly deserves this status (see Møller 2016a). More generally, the sources are so inadequate that a number of early convocations of parliaments are likely to have been overlooked. For example, it is difficult to code the early Iberian cases (see, e.g., Procter 1980; O'Callaghan 1989), and we find major differences in the few existing datasets and overviews (e.g., Myers 1975; Poggi 1978; Van Zanden et al. 2012). Bearing this in mind, there are limits to the extent to which we can rely on Stasavage's data.

The dataset covering the autonomous cities likewise appears to be problematic in certain aspects. It is important to keep in mind that Stasavage selects a certain (very narrow) range of autonomous cities, namely those with a significant population. He then compares these cities with other large cities within Western Christianity that do not have similar autonomy. Stasavage (2014, 6–7) himself points out that there are major differences within his category of autonomous cities – for example, between the completely sovereign Venice, which ruled over a large territory in northern Italy and along the Mediterranean shores, and Ghent in Flanders, which at least formally was part of the Duke of Flanders' possessions. But an even greater problem is found in Stasavage's category of non-autonomous city-states. In reality, most medieval cities enjoyed some kind of autonomy (see Bartlett 1993), which is where they distinguish themselves from cities in regions such as Russia and the Ottoman Empire or for that matter China. If we relate this to Max Weber's comparisons of civilizations, the important question is whether or not this difference meant anything in relation to the emergence of the modern market economy and rule of law as we know it today, not so much whether outright municipal independence did so. Stasavage's analysis does not tell us anything about this.

Second, does it make sense to interpret the political institutions of the city-states as being representative? Many of these political units had direct rule similar to the ancient city-states based on the drawing of lots (Manin 1997, 41–42) – a feature Stasavage (2011, 62) himself mentions. One could of course argue that the political institutions of direct rule are a functional equivalent of the representative institutions. Nonetheless, there is little doubt that Stasavage stretches his concept of 'representative institutions'. Most importantly, it cannot be ruled out that some of the more specific features of direct rule eased access to borrowing – that is, features that are not associated with more frequent meetings and the greater dominance of creditor interests.

This point can be further supported by touching upon one of the more general objections historians have made against Stasavage's causal mechanisms (e.g., Prak 2012; Tracy 2013). Historians generally accept Stasavage's argument that commercial interests (the merchant class) represented the relevant creditors in city-states and for that matter in a territorial state such as the Netherlands and that they dominated representative institutions. However, there was a similar overlap in numerous territorial states where the landed aristocracy and civil servants loaned money to the monarch and had the biggest say in the representative institutions. This holds for France as well as for numerous German states (Bavaria and Württemberg are some of the examples highlighted by historians). The problem is that this combination led to neither an early public debt nor low interest rates. On that basis, one can question whether it was really the creditor dominance or simply other features of the city-states that stimulated the extension of credit.

Conclusions

Stasavage poses the kind of 'big questions' around which this book revolves. In fact, his work on representative institutions and autonomous cities is a good example of the new research agenda that has emerged in recent decades. This research agenda raises big questions about state formation, regime change, and economic development but attempts to answer them using methods developed for entirely different purposes in economics, first and foremost formal theoretical models and econometric methods of analysis.

This kind of research shows why we cannot retain Mahoney and Rueschemeyer's (2003, 6–15) definition of comparative historical analysis as research that raises big questions, takes time seriously, is interested in generalizing, but does not use statistical methods. More generally, Stasavage's work shows that there is no contradiction between using the new methods introduced by economists and wrestling with questions such as those raised by Weber and his contemporaries. When these methods started to gain ground in political science, a common concern was that they only made it possible to analyse small and trivial questions. This objection was, for instance, voiced by American political scientist James C. Scott in an interview a couple of years ago. Scott refers to how one of his colleagues defended the use of these instruments – in this case, the use of experiments – by claiming that they created bricks that can later be put together to form a larger structure. Scott objected, 'I think you just get a pile of bricks' (Munck and Snyder 2007, 381).

This metaphor breaks down when we consider Stasavage's daring constructions. In Chapter 13, we will examine the research agenda that introduced the economic, theoretical, and analytical techniques to the field, namely Daron Acemoglu and James Robinson's work on the economic and political effects of colonization processes.

Notes

1 It is worth noting, however, that a veto on taxation was established relatively late in some places – e.g., after 1650 in Sweden.
2 Here, Stasavage deliberately removes part of the variation, as some of the city-states had assemblies that met extremely frequently.
3 We find a curious example of the significance of geographical barriers for the opportunities of elected representatives to convene in connection with the drafting of the Norwegian constitution in 1814. Representatives had been elected from virtually all of Norway, and they met at Eidsvoll from 10 April to 20 May 1814. However, not all elected representatives took part in the discussions, which led to the Eidsvoll Constitution, the most 'democratic' constitution of the day. Some of the representatives from northern Norway did not make it; or, rather, they only reached Eidsvoll *after* the constitution had been adopted.
4 No such problem existed in the small city-states, where most of the residents lived within walking distance of the place of assembly. As Stasavage mentions, the assembly in Siena was simply summoned by ringing a bell that could be heard throughout the city. A similar model was used in a number of autonomous medieval cities.
5 The Treaty of Meersen was signed in 870, but it maintained – with some minor changes – the tripartite Verdun-division of 843.
6 And which are included into the standard work on European cities, which Stasavage (2014, 2) uses as the basis for his coding.
7 Just as the relationship would be easy to remove if the small states outside Western Christendom were included.

11

THE WEST VERSUS THE REST

The debate on the great divergence

This book revolves around Europe in general and Western Europe in particular. There is a simple reason for this. In the modern era, Europe ran away from the other great civilizations of Eurasia with respect to affluence and technological development. The European head start made it possible for Europeans to colonize large parts of the rest of the world and, after the mid-nineteenth century, to dominate the few areas that had been able to resist European colonization. More specifically, in the last phase Europe ran from East Asia, which, at least economically, had been the most advanced region in Eurasia for the previous one thousand years.

On this the literature agrees. However, there is rampant disagreement as to when and why this break occurred. Chapters 11 and 12 address this disagreement. More specifically, we shall consider two competing perspectives on the breakthrough to modern economic growth. I refer to these two perspectives as the 'Eurocentrists' and the 'revisionists'.[1] The next chapter focuses on the Eurocentrists, who in my view continue to represent the main current in the literature. According to this perspective, the economic differences between Western Europe and Eastern Asia date far back in time, and they are a product of deep historical differences that at the latest started taking shape in medieval Europe. In this chapter, the main emphasis will instead be on the revisionist agenda, as represented by the so-called California School. This school argues that the European *sorpasso* occurred very late (approx. 1800) and that Europe was actually trailing behind the more advanced East Asia until around this time. The associated contention is that the subsequent break – 'the Great Divergence' (Pomeranz 2000) – is the result of small coincidences rather than profound differences that stretch far back in time (Goldstone 2000, 191).

The Eurocentrists and the dating of the break

In order to set the stage for the examination of the California School, it is necessary to anticipate the next chapter in one respect. We need to know what the established literature has to say about the point in time Europe started to distance itself from the other civilizations in Eurasia.

The main assumption – or claim – has been that China and the Islamic civilizations in Asia Minor, the Middle East, and Iran were ahead of Europe at least until the Age of Discoveries. In fact, according to Jared Diamond (1999[1997]), in the year 1450 the Chinese Empire would have presented the best bet for a forthcoming industrial revolution. Wallerstein (1974) makes a similar point in his extensive work on the world system. Historian William McNeill (1982) has gone so far as to advance the thesis that the Chinese technological revolution after the year 1000 AD 'tipped a critical balance in world history' (25), kicking off the unique economic development that took place over the next one thousand years. Technologically, the area along the Yellow River and the Yangtze was the most advanced in the world at the time. For example, paper, the printing press, gunpowder, and the compass were all invented in China. Similarly, around the year 1100 AD, China was on the verge of something resembling an industrial revolution in iron and steel production (45).

However, the listed scholars all agree that Europe in the centuries after the beginning of the Age of Discoveries (around 1500) started to pull away – or at least laid the foundations for the later lead on the rest of the world. Others go even further and question the claim that Europe had long lagged behind China economically. Jones (2008[1981], 41) thus points out that Europe was already far ahead of Asia prior to the Industrial Revolution. A similar claim has been made by Hall (1985), Landes (1998), and Clark (2007). These researchers – the California School's archetypical 'Eurocentrists' – assert that the Europeans were achieving slow but sustained technological and economic progress in the early High Middle Ages and were already in the process of overtaking the great Eurasian cultural areas (see also Hall 1989, 553–554; Mann 1986).

The California School

The revisionists have challenged the Eurocentrists. Jack Goldstone (2000, 175) has dubbed these challengers 'The California School' with reference to the institutional affiliation of most of the leading advocates of this perspective. The Californian connection at least applies to Kenneth Pomeranz, Bin Wong, and Goldstone himself, who this chapter focuses on.[2] These researchers agree on at least two general revisionist points.

The first is that the economic and technological gap between Europe (or just North-Western Europe) on the one side, and East Asia (or just China) on the other, was insignificant up until 1800 (Epstein 2002, 172; cf. Wong 1997; Goldstone 2000, 179–180; Pomeranz 2000). If anything, East Asia was leading well into the eighteenth century, whether we are looking at textile production, the size of commercial enterprises, the scale of the integrated markets, average standard of living, or state capacity. Likewise, the Chinese family structure was just as well suited as the European to prevent undesired family expansions – more mouths to feed blocking prosperity. Finally, it was the Chinese demand for American silver more than the European domination of trade that shaped the global system of trade until around 1800.

Indeed, it was the more advanced economy that allowed the Chinese to sell products such as porcelain, silk, and tea to the Europeans in exchange for silver coin retrieved from European colonies on the other side of the Atlantic. Conversely, the Chinese were not interested in purchasing lower-quality European products, and it was only when the English started exporting opium from India that the asymmetrical balance of trade shifted to some degree. Similarly, the Chinese state apparatus was in many ways more developed than the Western European one at the time. For example, the Chinese bureaucracy was better able to tax the agrarian economy, better at conducting systematic censuses, and vastly superior with respect to providing the citizenry with a safety net and influencing the opinions of the common man (Wong 1997, 182). Finally, it is worth noting that, until the mid-eighteenth century, the European colonial powers were only able to hold isolated points along the Eurasian coasts. Actual European colonization was, in other words, reserved for the Americas, Oceania, and the African coast (see Chapter 15),[3] as the Europeans were simply not strong enough to colonize the old civilizations in the Middle East, India, and East Asia. It was only in the period 1750–1850 that the global balance of power shifted decisively in favour of Europe (Goldstone 1998, 269).

It did so precisely because the Western Europeans at this time surpassed the Chinese in terms of technological, economic, and military technology and prowess. This brings us to the second major revisionist claim: that this sudden shift was caused by a number of differences, some of which might appear rather insignificant at first glance; that these differences occurred late; and that they were often caused by coincidences. In other words, the rise of Europe did not result from deeper – or systematic – differences between two societal orders, located at opposite ends of the Eurasian land mass. It therefore makes little sense to trace these differences far back in time, say, to developments in medieval Europe. Needless to say, there were a great many differences between Western Europe and China in the Middle Ages and in the centuries following the Age of Discoveries. But it is very difficult to connect these differences causally to a gap that only began to form in earnest in the nineteenth century (Wong 2002, 448). Instead, we need to understand what happened during and just before the Great Divergence – that is, in the period leading up to 1800.

The California School links these issues to a number of methodological points. Goldstone (2000, 176–177) formulates it rather provocatively by stating that the European colonizers have colonized history. European scholars, from Karl Marx and Max Weber onwards, have written the history of the 'winners' at the expense of the 'losers'. They have done so by, retrospectively, emphasizing certain conditions in Europe without worrying excessively about the corresponding conditions in East Asia. This myopic perspective on the course of history calls for a correction; that is, it calls for more balanced comparisons that, without considering recent developments and without scrutinizing China from a European perspective, establish differences and similarities between Europe and East Asia in the period 1500–1800 (see, e.g., Wong 1997, 1–4; Goldstone 2000, 176–177). In other words, it calls for what Pomeranz (2000, 8–9) refers to as reciprocal comparisons (cf. Hall 2001, 491). This methodological advice reminds one of Marc Bloch's (1954[1949]) classic instruction to reading history forwards and not backwards in order to avoid interpreting differences in the light of later developments – thereby potentially inferring from effects to causes.

What happens when we apply such a balanced perspective and read history forwards? According to the California School, a picture begins to form of a world that was polycentric as late as around 1800 – that is, a world in which economic centres in Western Europe and East Asia were equally advanced (Pomeranz 2000, 5). All of the Eurasian centres of civilization – and for that matter the European settler colonies in North and South America and in Oceania – were by this time very similar agrarian societies. In Goldstone's (1998) phrase, these were 'advanced organic societies', permeated by markets based on specialization and individual enterprise but which had yet to learn to exploit fossil fuels on a large scale. These societies faced a number of fundamental barriers to economic growth, whether we are speaking about the most advanced Western European country in the seventeenth century (the Netherlands) or East Asia's most advanced area around the lower part of the Yangtze River Delta.

This was a world where there were essentially two paths to productivity improvements and increasing prosperity. The first was by increasing market interaction based on the division of labour. This was the mechanism which Adam Smith described in *Wealth of Nations*, and we find such specialization and market-economic expansion in Western Europe as well as East Asia (Wong 1997; Pomeranz 2000). The second was by cultivating new land, something that the Europeans did in their colonies and to some degree in the peripheral areas of Europe, whereas the Chinese did so in China's outer spaces. Both paths were thus trodden at both ends of the Eurasian landmass, but there were limits to how much they could increase prosperity. The Western Europeans and the Chinese were hitting their heads against the agrarian barrier: the ecological resources and technological contributions to productivity increases were limited.

Goldstone, Pomeranz, and Bin Wong all observe – with ill-concealed delight – that Adam Smith assumed that there was a ceiling on the potential economic growth accruing from the division of labour and that wages must repeatedly fall to subsistence levels as the result of population growth. In other words, Smith was in line with his pessimistic colleague Thomas Malthus, to whom we return in the next chapter, in his economic perspectives on the agrarian world. It follows that the onset of capitalism, even in a sophisticated variant, does not explain the ascent of Europe. Here, we are touching on the difference between growth based on market relations and growth based on technological revolution (Epstein 2002, 172–173). Just a few centuries ago, there was therefore no indication that the shackles of the agrarian world would be broken (cf. Hall 2001, 490).

However, Adam Smith would be proven wrong, as Western Europe broke the agrarian ceiling in the centuries after his death, partly due to technological advances such as the steam engine and partly due to fossil fuels, coal in particular. When it comes to explaining this breakthrough, the agreement in the California School comes to an end (cf. Goldstone 2000, 180). In the following we shall examine the different explanations provided by Pomeranz and Goldstone for this divergence.[4]

Pomeranz: The great divergence

With *The Great Divergence*, Kenneth Pomeranz (2000) has written the principal work of the California School. Pomeranz concentrates on comparing parts of Western Europe with parts of China and Japan while at the same time glancing to other areas in Eurasia. He acknowledges that this approach potentially neglects important conditions in, for example, the Middle East, but he convincingly argues that China, in a historical perspective, is the great 'Other' of the West. The book has two main messages: there were no differences of significance between Europe and East Asia until 1800, and the European overseas expansion was the source of the differences that began to accumulate around this point in time (3–4).

Pomeranz thereby writes up against two established points among the 'Eurocentrists': that the European resources and/or the European institutions were more conducive to economic activity than those in East Asia (in particular, Eurocentrists argue, private property was more secure, at least in North-Western Europe).

The problem with the former point – regarding European resources – is that industrial capital first emerged in earnest after 1800; indeed, outside England, industrialization was quite limited until 1860 (16). More specifically, Pomeranz rejects Eric Jones' claim, which I touched upon above, that Western Europe was pulling ahead of East Asia early on. On the contrary, *The Great Divergence* documents that the East Asians

- had life expectancies that were at least as long,
- had birth rates that were no higher than the Europeans,
- had better sanitary conditions, especially in the cities (46).

In certain respects, East Asia actually appears to be far more modernized. For example, around 22% of the Japanese lived in cities in the nineteenth century compared to 10–15% of the West Europeans (35).

With respect to the latter point, Pomeranz focuses on basic market institutions. His slightly surprising conclusion is that markets in eighteenth-century China and Japan were more akin to Adam Smith's ideal type than Western European markets. Labour was more mobile and free in East Asia. The Chinese, for example, were far more willing to migrate great distances, whereas the European guilds, all the way up to the French Revolution, created a number of barriers to efficient markets

(70–87). In short, there is no indication that institutions provided any advantage to Western Europe – to the contrary.

The sudden elimination race after 1800 is therefore difficult to explain on the basis of prior differences. According to Pomeranz, the great divergence should instead be attributed to a set of proximate circumstances. First – and most important – was the dividend from the European overseas possessions. It was resources from the colonies that allowed Europe to expand economically. The flow of such resources increased gradually – partly because the trade between Europe and most of its colonies was based *not* on the market relations described by Adam Smith (264) but, in most places, on the colonial slave economy. It was slave labour that enabled the Europeans to reap such great benefit from the colonies (296–297). The exception was the British settler colonies in, for example, North America, which traded on much more equal conditions, but what is important here is the important supply of timber to England, which was essential to the British naval domination.

The windfalls derived from the colonies included foodstuffs, natural resources, and precious metals. The latter were especially important, as the Chinese were in the process of changing their monetary system to one based on silver and were therefore the willing consumers of metals from the New World. But foodstuffs were also essential, as it helped free up European labourers, who were able to find their place in the nascent industrial enterprises of Europe. In the absence of these overseas resources, the Western Europeans would have been forced to tread a much more labour-intensive path, as was the case in China at the time.

Pomeranz uses the small North European country of Denmark to illustrate this point. Denmark was in a crisis in the eighteenth century. Centuries of intensive agriculture coupled with the expansion of the Danish fleet had led to deforestation and soil depletion. The reaction was a number of labour-intensive measures, including trench digging, establishing dykes to reclaim new land, a move to grow clover, and an increase of almost 50% in average working hours. These measures prevented an ecological catastrophe, but they did not foster economic growth. All they did was stabilize the population and the average standard of living, which was now 'sponsored' by a longer working day (2000, 212, 223, 239–240).

The resources from the colonies made it possible to escape this labour-intensive strategy – first in England and later in the rest of Western Europe. In other words, the windfalls from the colonies allowed an entirely different use of the labour in Western Europe than would otherwise have been possible. This is the most important part of Pomeranz' explanation, but he adds an extra dimension, the abundant and easily accessible English coal supplies. These deposits were a precondition for the advent of the steam engine in England, a development that was thus based on a geographical coincidence (67–68). Pomeranz goes so far as to speculate how history might have unfolded if the Chinese coal deposits had not been concentrated in the economically backward north of the country (63–64; cf. Hall 2001, 490). On this point, Pomeranz' explanation might be said to set the stage for Goldstone's writings, which are the next stop on our journey through the fascinating wings of the California School.

Goldstone: The English miracle

Goldstone aligns himself with Pomeranz and Bin Wong: right up until 1800, the levels of development in Western Europe and East Asia were almost identical. More generally, in the period 1000–1800, much of Eurasia was characterized by the 'advanced organic societies' that I have already mentioned above (Goldstone 1998, 266–267). These were well organized societies with efficient markets that often put extant technology to the fullest use. Such societies first developed in China and the Islamic states, then made an entry in Europe, the first instances being the large Italian city-states, followed by the territorial states in Western Europe.

In historical perspective, this was a remarkable development. Nonetheless, these societies hit an upper ceiling for development due to their limited ability to exploit fossil fuels. According to Goldstone, this barrier was breached surprisingly quickly, as England in the period 1689–1848 transformed itself into the first truly modern society. The rest of Western Europe and a number of British settler colonies followed suit, after which the balance of power shifted decisively in favour of the Europeans, who as late as the mid-eighteenth century had been unable to conquer other advanced organic societies (268–269). In other words, it is misleading to talk about a progressive European development in the period 1500–1800 or, *a fortiori*, 1200–1800. The reality was more a sudden spurt led by England in the eighteenth century.

Compared to Pomeranz and Bin Wong, Goldstone accordingly focuses on the English development. His explanation of the European – or, rather, English – miracle emphasizes a series of minor coincidences. First, Goldstone dates the beginning of the English transition to modernity to the Glorious Revolution in 1688. This was a decisive juncture in the sense that it limited the power of the king, introduced official acceptance of religious tolerance, and created a greater protection of the fundamental freedoms of – at least – the elite than what we find elsewhere in Europe and Eurasia at the time. Goldstone refers to this as a 'liberalizing regime'. Here, England distinguishes itself from Southern Europe, where the Counter-Reformation fostered the opposite development, famously illustrated by the Inquisition. In England after 1688, the Anglican Church instead subscribed to Isaac Newton's new mechanistic worldview, which turned the existing Christian worldview on its head. More generally, secular science and its belief in the ability of humankind to alter living conditions by understanding the laws of nature was promoted by other institutions, including the Royal Society.

Goldstone sees the Glorious Revolution in 1688 as a necessary but not sufficient condition for the English breakthrough. Similar political and social conditions had characterized the Netherlands after the hard-won independence from the Spanish Hapsburgs (see the previous chapter). In fact, the English 'liberalizing regime' was imported directly from the Netherlands, which provided the royal pretender, William of Orange, who was crowned king in 1688. The Dutch version of the 'liberalizing regime' had fostered the so-called 'Dutch Golden Age' in the seventeenth century, but it did not lead to a transition to modern industrial society. In fact, the Industrial Revolution was slow to make inroads in the Netherlands.

So, given this advantageous political context, what explains the advent of the Industrial Revolution in England in the eighteenth century? According to Goldstone (1998, 271–274; 2000, 183), this development was a remarkable coincidence that can be attributed to a combination of cultural, technological, and environmental circumstances. We have already touched upon the cultural factor, that parts of northern Europe after the Reformation had quite open and tolerant societies that urged individuals to try to do things in new ways in order to improve material conditions, despite the major risks this often involved.

The technological and environmental or geological circumstances had to do with the presence of abundant and easily accessible coal deposits in England. England did not have enough forests, and coal had therefore largely replaced wood for heating in the sixteenth century. This shift was eased by the English coal seams running close to the surface. Coal could therefore be mined without particularly advanced means. However, everything has its time, and eventually it became necessary to dig deeper mine shafts in order to access coal. These shafts tended become filled with water, which had to be pumped out, and in 1712 Thomas Newcomen developed the first, extremely primitive, steam-based pump. This machine was only feasible because it was to be used in places with direct and abundant access to coal and water. A good fifty years later, James Watt improved Newcomen's invention, thereby clearing the path for the modern steam engine that could power locomotives and ships.

This brings us to the third circumstance: the environmental or geological factor. The location of the English coal deposits is an important part of the explanation for why it made sense to use them on a large scale, and above all coal was easy to transport to England's economic centre via waterways. In contrast, the Chinese coal deposits were concentrated in relatively isolated parts of northern China, far from the most advanced economic areas along the lower Yangtze.[5] This unique combination of circumstances – the character of coal resources being the most important – triggered the Industrial Revolution, the first leap toward modern society.

Revisiting the disagreement between the Eurocentrists and the revisionists

I have painted a picture of 'Californian' revolutionaries who have done everything they can to overturn the idolatry of past generations (the findings of the Eurocentrists). There is a lot of truth in this as the California School represents a deliberate challenge to the conventional wisdom. But how deep does this disagreement actually run?

We can begin by noting that the scholars referred to as Eurocentrists by Goldstone, Pomeranz, and Bin Wong have accepted many of the arguments presented in this chapter. Even Eric Jones (2000, 856) admits that there are more similarities between Western Europe and East Asia in the years up to 1800 than claimed in previous research, including his own prior work (Jones 2008[1981]). And Hall (2001, 493) concedes this point completely, acknowledging his past mistakes (Hall 1985).

Second, it is worth noting that the research question addressed by the two schools is largely the same, namely what caused the great divergence between the West and the Rest? While the California School might well claim that the rise of Europe occurred later than previously thought, this does not change the fact that it is this rise that must be explained. Hall (2001, 494) points out that the two schools are not as far apart as they initially appear – or at least that the two ventures are not necessarily in opposition to one another. The disagreement between the Euro-centrists and the California School does not alter the fact that all aforementioned analyses concur on three things: that the story about the long-term economic development is a story about Eurasia, that Europe at some – not clearly speci-fied – point in time within the last five hundred years broke away, and that this can be explained only by comparing Europe with China, India, and Islam (Jones (2008[1981]), 153–159). In other words, what the British historian John Darwin (2008) refers to as a Eurasian perspective is needed. Anderson (1990, 60) makes the same point when he objects to Michael Mann's great attempt at explaining the evolutionary leap in *The Sources of Social Power*. Anderson draws attention to Mann's focus on the West, adding that:

> true difference can only be established by contrast. Avoiding all compara-tive analysis of Chinese or Arabo–Turkic civilizations, among others, Mann would seem to deprive himself of any basis for a causal explanation of West-ern specificity.

Third, a partial criticism of the California School is that the image of the sud-den European spurt as coincidental is somewhat overdrawn. In a review of *The Great Divergence*, Jones (2000, 859) criticizes Pomeranz for ignoring that the north-western part of Europe had more responsive political institutions than East Asia. As we shall see in the next chapter, the main current in the literature places crucial emphasis on this factor in its attempt to explain the rise of Europe. But so does Goldstone. In his eyes, England's 'liberalizing regime' is a necessary but not suf-ficient condition for the Industrial Revolution. Similarly, Bin Wong (1997), Gold-stone (1998), and Pomeranz (2000) all end up emphasizing the significance of the geopolitical competition within the European multistate system. As Bin Wong (1997, 73–101, 277) observes, this was the great difference between the contexts in which the state-builders in Western Europe and China were navigating. For Gold-stone, this also seems to be a necessary condition for the Industrial Revolution, as the competition explains why a Catholic conformity did not make inroads into the Protestant European north. More generally, with Hall (2001, 494), we can note that most scholars from the California School end up emphasizing the importance of political factors – in the best Weberian style.

Conclusions

The California School's criticism of past research reminds one of British historian A.J.P. Taylor's (1972, 210) famous verdict on the origins of World War I:

> Men are reluctant to believe that great events have small causes. Therefore, once the Great War started, they were convinced that it must be the outcome of profound forces. It is hard to discover these when we examine the details.

The rise of Europe is arguably the biggest event in the social sciences; it is certainly the event that modern social science was conceived to explain (see the introduction). According to Pomeranz, Bin Wong, and Goldstone, this 'Great Divergence' was triggered by a number of rather insignificant and arbitrary differences. That is, this dramatic difference must be attributed to apparently inconspicuous events during a *critical juncture*. Goldstone's explanation is obviously the purest example of this logic, as he singles out a series of small coincidences which in combination made England able to make the leap to the Industrial Revolution – with major consequences for world history.

In this chapter, I have presented the California School's argument that, all the way up to 1800, the world was characterized by multiple, equally prosperous economic centres. I have examined Pomeranz' and Goldstone's explanations of this subsequent diversity, which can be documented in earnest only after 1800. Finally, I have presented a couple of critical comments against this new revisionist research agenda, drawing on arguments made by scholars labelled as Eurocentrists by the California School.

However, I will conclude with an example of how the message of the California School has become quite widespread, namely aforementioned historian John Darwin's (2008) *tour de force* through the history of the last six hundred years in *After Tamerlane: The Rise and Fall of Global Empires, 1400–2000*. Darwin's account largely echoes the main messages of the California School. Europe was, we are told, for long the most backward of the four major cultural areas of Eurasia: the countries surrounding the Mediterranean Sea, the Fertile Crescent, the Indian Subcontinent, and East Asia. Indeed, as late as the Age of Discoveries, Europe was, at most, in third place economically and technologically, clearly lagging behind China and the Islamic kingdoms in the Middle East, possibly slightly ahead of the Indians. Darwin points out that it took almost three centuries from the arrival of the Portuguese in the Indian Ocean until the Europeans were able to colonize anything other than maritime points of support. As late as the mid-eighteenth century, the Europeans were little more than a minor irritant for the major Asian states.

These are, Darwin adds, not the only areas in which Europe had little to boast about in comparative perspective. Around the year 1700, the Japanese capital Edo (with its one million inhabitants) was double the size of London; in 1650, Delhi matched Paris in size; Europe struggled to compete with the Indian textile industry; and the Chinese were uninterested in low-quality European-made goods. Only the silver deposits in Peru and Bolivia made it possible for the Europeans to trade in earnest with these areas. Europe was also vulnerable militarily. As late as the seventeenth century, the Ottoman Empire threatened Central Europe: the Turks were standing at the gates of Vienna in both 1529 and 1683. And for long periods, the Chinese emperors as well as the Indian Mughals possessed stronger land forces than the European powers.

Seen from the higher ground, the years 1620–1740 were therefore characterized by a Eurasian equilibrium – the expression is Darwin's (2008) – as the Western Europeans were merely one of several players. Darwin's point is important in the sense that the next steps can easily blind us to the frailty of the European situation for several centuries after the beginning of the Age of Discoveries. Add to this that we easily come to think of the European colonization process in terms of the later African pattern, according to which decision-makers in London, Berlin, and Paris would divide vast lands among them with the stroke of a pen (see Chapter 15). This was never the case in Asia. In the eastern part of the continent, China and Japan remained independent states. While they might well have had to sign humiliating treaties with the Europeans in the nineteenth century, they nevertheless maintained control over their internal affairs. Nor were the core Ottoman areas ever colonized, and Iran/Persia also maintained its independence. The Europeans did position themselves firmly in Southeast Asia. But India, which became incorporated into the vast British Commonwealth, is actually the exception that confirms the rule that colonization in Asia was at most indirect. Darwin's book thus in many respects confirms the insights one gets from the California School. More precisely, his account shows the advantages of examining the interactions between the various centres of Eurasia shorn of considerations about Europe's ultimate triumph.

That said, the reader is left with a sense that Darwin exaggerates his case. For example, it is difficult to accept wholesale the claim about military equality until the mid-eighteenth century. It was Europeans who positioned themselves firmly along the shores of the Indian Ocean and in what was to become Indonesia – not Asians conquering maritime points along the European Atlantic coast. To be sure, the Ottomans won major military victories over European armies in parts of this period. However, in the seventeenth century, this occurred with the help of technological support from Europe, especially concerning firearms. In addition to these episodes, it is difficult to find major European defeats after the year 1400.[6] In the next chapter, I will take a closer look at alternative explanations of the rise of Europe with focus on these earlier stages of European expansion.

Notes

1 These labels have been found in the respective attempts to categorize their opponents and therefore have negative connotations. Eurocentrism is thus the accusation made by revisionists, while the latter label captures a tendency to exaggerate the criticism of the established literature.
2 I focus on these three scholars who are commonly regarded as forming the core of the California School (see, e.g., Goldstone 1998; Hall 2001, 489).

3 And Siberia, if we include the Russian colonizations.

4 I have left out a more detailed discussion of Bin Wong's (1997) writings, as he does not provide a clear explanation of how we can explain the ascent of Europe.

5 In fact, the Chinese (see next chapter) had large-scale, semi-industrial use of coal dating all the way back to 1000 AD. This was an age in which northern China played a more important role economically and politically, meaning that it was easier to exploit the coal deposits in the north. At that time, the Chinese were also familiar with advanced smelting techniques, including some in which coke was blasted in furnaces (see McNeill 1982, 45).

6 On the contrary, we can adduce a number of examples of major European victories, such as the first great European land victory in Asia: the conquest of Bengal following the Battle of Plassey on 23 June 1757. The Bengali forces were betrayed by commander Mir Jafar, who led approximately one-third of the total forces and simply stayed away from the battle. But the fact remains that Robert Clive's one thousand Europeans (assisted by approximately two thousand Indian support troops) defeated an adversary who numbered some fifty thousand – and that with only slightly more than twenty casualties (see Landes 1998, 160).

12

EUROPE AND THE EMERGENCE OF THE MARKET ECONOMY

This chapter addresses the literature referred to in the previous chapter as 'Eurocentrism'. The most important name within this tradition is surely Douglass North (e.g., North and Thomas 1973; North 1981; 1990; 2005), but I will cast the net a little more broadly. Instead of limiting the chapter to a specific author, I will summarize and discuss what I regard as the main current in the economic literature on the rise of Europe: institutional theories about the emergence of the modern market economy.

Europe versus the rest of Eurasia

Many economic historians (e.g., North and Thomas 1973; Landes 1998; Bernstein 2008; Jones 2008[1981]) have attempted to explain why the Industrial Revolution and the subsequent economic miracle[1] took place in Europe and not elsewhere. Combined with accounts from some historians (e.g., McNeill 1982), these analyses allow us to draw the outline of an explanation of why Europe distanced itself economically from the rest of Eurasia.

The premise: The primate of political institutions

I have already mentioned the key claim of the 'Eurocentrists' in the previous chapter: that European institutions were superior to those found in Asia in terms of providing the stimulus for economic growth. More precisely, the claim is that property rights were more secure in Europe – or at least in the west (or possibly only north-west) of Europe. In what follows, we will look more closely at how this facilitated economic development. However, before doing so, we need to take a step back. While the Douglass North tradition does indeed identify these 'economic institutions' as the proximate cause of the European increases in wealth and

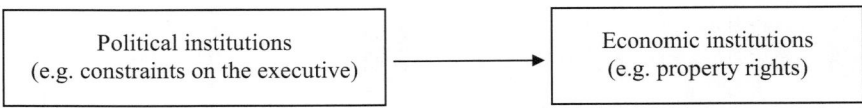

FIGURE 12.1 The primacy of political institutions

prosperity, scholars within this tradition emphasize that the economic institutions depend on something else, something more important: on political institutions (see Figure 12.1).

The political institutions, including the regime form (e.g., the presence or absence of institutions constraining the executive), thus stand out as the deeper explanation for the variation in the economic development. In slightly more technical terms, the claim is that property rights are endogenous to the political regime form (Robinson 2002, 510–511). It is only where power is held in check, limited by countervailing power, that it is possible to systematically prevent transgressions against property. To be effective, this countervailing power must in turn be anchored in political institutions. Indeed, in some of his later writings, North (2005) goes so far as to argue that it is ultimately the *belief systems* in society that make the difference. The North tradition therefore faces a triple challenge: to explain why the arbitrariness of power in Europe was reined in by political institutions such as parliaments and courts; to show that this political development safeguarded private property; and to demonstrate that these economic institutions were conducive to economic growth.

Competition as the locomotive of history

Within the Eurocentrist camp, there is widespread agreement on an admittedly very general explanation for the advent of propitious institutions (cf. Ertman 1997, 4).[2] It was the political fragmentation of Europe and the subsequent competition between the European states – religiously, politically, militarily, and economically – that created the framework for the European miracle (McNeill 1982, 68–69, 112–116; Hall 1985, 139; Landes 1998, 37–38; Jones 2008[1981], 239–245; Mann 1986, 397–99).

'States' here refer to the minimalist state definition introduced in Chapter 2. The state apparatuses in the High and Late Middle Ages remained a good distance from the Weberian ideal type, towards which they would gradually develop after the sixteenth-century military revolution (Downing 1992; Parker 1996[1988]). However, the absence of modern states does not equate an absence of competition. We find a harbinger of the multistate system all the way back to the twelfth century (Hintze 1975[1906]; Tilly 1990; Schumpeter 1991[1917/1918]; Ertman 1997, 23–28; Stasavage 2011, 9). As Hall (1985, 15) points out, the emphasis on the favourable economic effects of competition between the European states can be traced back to Adam Smith and David Hume. Jones (2008[1981], 104–108) adds that a multistate system like the one in Europe is a historical exception (see also Nexon 2009; Møller 2014). Empires have instead been the rule, and empires prevent competition between entities.

But Europe is the historical exception. Since the fall of the Roman Empire, no power has proved able to subdue the most important parts of the European continent. Or, rather, all attempts – from Justinian to Charlemagne via the Hofenstaufen emperors to the Habsburgs to Napoleon and Hitler – have fallen short. China once again serves to put the European situation in perspective. In 1450, Europe would not have been the region of Eurasia most likely to achieve a competitive edge, economically (see, e.g., Diamond 1999[1997], 409). As already mentioned in Chapter 11, should an unbiased observer venture a guess in 1450 as to where a forthcoming industrial revolution would take place, China would have been the best bet. In the preceding chapter, I mentioned various Chinese technological and economic advantages that, according to the California School, lasted for centuries after the beginning of the great overseas explorations. We have also repeatedly noted that China, as a single empire, dwarfed the European states in most important respects.

Somewhat paradoxically, it is this latter circumstance that some researchers see as a possible explanation for the European advance. According to this vein of thinking, China's political advantages around the year 1450 would prove a curse. The unchallenged position of the Chinese emperors made it possible to halt the otherwise impressive economic development (McNeill 1982, 48–49). Hall (1985, 46–50) observes that the greatest technological progress occurred during the Sung Dynasty (960–1269), where China was marked by internal disorder, while the well-consolidated Ming Dynasty that followed (1369–1644) formed a political obstacle to further technological development. The iron industry was practically strangled, ocean-going shipping was abandoned, and the Ming Dynasty transited from a cash economy to a bartering-based economy. More generally, Hansen (2000, 95, 189, 414) describes how innovation marked the periods of China's history in which the country was not united and observes that Chinese thinkers throughout these periods lamented the internal divisions without realizing this.

The situation was very different in Europe, where, as touched upon in the chapters above, competition was the rule. The significance of religious conflict in Europe is difficult to exaggerate in this context (cf. de Ruggiero 1927, 19). The Roman Catholic Church has been in conflict with the Orthodox Church since the Early Middle Ages (culminating in the Great Schism in 1054), and, since the Reformation, Western Christianity has been divided internally in competing churches. Moreover, at least[3] since the Gregorian reforms of the eleventh century, the Roman Catholic Church formed a counter-pole to secular rulers (see Fukuyama 2011). Hall (1985, 113) refers somewhat lyrically to this clash as the *trahison des clercs* of the West. The absence of a single, general religious and political authority and the associated military competition meant that the European great powers constantly had to embrace new technology and political institutions (Hall 1985, 135; Zakaria 2003, 34).

For long periods, the situation was different in Asia, China in particular. The rigid ideological uniformity of Confucianism and the unchallenged power of the emperor meant that conservatism reigned, which quenched the thirst for new knowledge. A telling example is the decision of the Ming Dynasty to stop the major maritime voyages of discovery in the middle of the fifteenth century and later to prohibit ocean sailing entirely. In the period 1405–1433, enormous Chinese fleets had sailed the Indian Ocean. These fleets, led by a eunuch, Zheng He, had visited what is today Indonesia, Sri Lanka, the Arabian Peninsula, and East Africa. The sources refer to more than three hundred enormous ships manned by some twenty-eight thousand sailors in the first expedition. By comparison, the fleet led by Portuguese Vasco da Gama that rounded the Horn of Africa in 1497 and reached the Indian Ocean consisted of four ships and 170 sailors. The Chinese were thus in an entirely different technological and economic league as far as state-organized voyages of discovery were concerned (Hansen 2000, 381). However, the Ming emperors suddenly prohibited ocean-going shipping, and a genuine technological setback occurred, as the existing knowledge about how to build these ships was lost (Hall 1985, 50) – precisely when the European maritime nations started the expeditions that were to conquer the seven seas, without any opposition from China.

China was not the only part of Asia affected by such conservatism. Consider the decision made by the Japanese shogun to shut the country off from the rest of the world in the seventeenth century, a decision which included a ban on modern weapons technology. Or take the long, persistent, and ultimately successful – but, from an economic and a geopolitical perspective, extremely unwise – campaign by the Ottoman sultans against the printing of books (Landes 1998, 401–2). Comparison with Europe is again illustrative.[4] In the Middle Ages, the Roman Catholic Church banned the use of the crossbow on the grounds that it enabled simple peasants with little training to bring down armour-clad knights. This was not cricket. However, the crossbow was efficient, and, because of the constant competition, none of the European armies dared do without it (Bartlett 1993). Similarly, the great European powers could not get away with putting ocean-going sailing on the shelf.

E Pluribus Unum

However, the European diversity is only half of the equation. Consider here Jones' (2008[1981]) aforementioned emphasis on the European multistate system. Such a system requires relatively independent states (the units), but they must interact with one another (the system). The reason the European inter-state competition became an efficient spur on development was the highly integrated nature of the system (Hall 1989, 553; Bartlett 1993; see also Weber 1981[1927], 337; Mann 1986, 397–99). Impulses crossed borders extremely fast, and the European state system was interwoven in an entirely different manner than the civilizations in Asia. In fact, medieval Europe was marked by a high degree of cultural uniformity. Or, rather, the part of Europe that referred to the Pope in Rome was characterized by such uniformity. Even though the Catholic Church did not have a monopoly on secular power, it created a common mental frame of reference and a shared clerical infrastructure, which eased the exchange of technology and political ideas (Hall 1985,

123–124; Poggi 1990, 38). Latin served as a *lingua mundi* in this area – even the national alphabets were marginally modified versions of the Latin alphabet – and the European nobility and princely families arranged marriages across the nascent state borders.

Some researchers have also argued that certain aspects of the religious doctrine of Western Christianity favoured political and economic development and that the Catholic Church contributed to the weakening of clan and family ties in Europe, which also eased the European miracle (Hall 1985, 130–131; Fukuyama 2011). We have already touched on these arguments in the discussion of Weber in Chapter 4. Jones (2008[1981], 111) points out that the existence of a common calendar demarcates the (Western) European cultural community. In his analysis of European state formation, which we discussed in the previous chapter, Thomas Ertman (1997, 4) specifically limits his attention to Western and Central Europe in order to keep the community impact constant.

A rather curious observation illustrates the uniqueness of the European system. Without pursuing the point further, Finer (1997b, 1269) notes that it is only in Europe that the later territorial states were normally created through marriage or bequeathing of entire regions; just think of the ability of the Hapsburgs to expand their empire in this manner.[5] This uniquely European way of constructing states was probably due to the combination of a competitive state system and a cultural community. The more general point is that it was the combination of constant competition and the cultural community that set the economic development in Europe in motion. Here we can also refer to Jared Diamond (1999[1997], 430), who formulates an 'optimal fragmentation principle'. 'Optimal' refers specifically to how the European degree of fragmentation was perfect – neither too much nor too little, if you will – for creating development.

Combating arbitrariness

The cultural community making up Western Christendom and the constant competition, respectively, represent the two deep causes singled out by the Eurocentrists in their institutional theories about the emergence of the modern market economy. This cocktail created a distinctive political development, marked by institutions that limited the arbitrary power of the authorities, including representative institutions. A general illustration of the explanatory model proposed by the Europeanists would therefore look something like Figure 12.2.

However, this does not alter the fact that the European miracle was indeed something of a miracle. For it was premised on solving a fundamental problem. Here, I am thinking of the vicious circle that English economist Thomas Malthus described more than two hundred years ago: that technological progress inevitably leads to population growth, which in turn means that incomes remain at subsistence level.

Clark (2007) describes this 'Malthusian' era as a world in which 'good governance' in reality was 'bad governance'. Only regular visits by the four horsemen

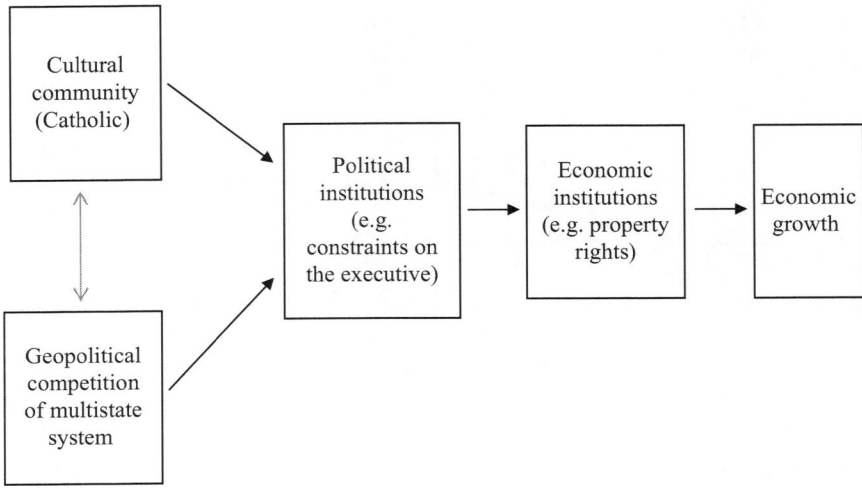

FIGURE 12.2   The full causal chain

of the Apocalypse – defeat, war, hunger, and death – could lead to higher living standards – at least for those fortunate enough to survive. In other words, propitious institutions led to economic misery. For the result of political stability and efficient market interaction was always population growth, which in turn depleted society's resources and reduced the individual's standard of living. According to Clark (2007), it was only in the nineteenth century that the income of the average English labourer exceeded the earnings in the golden years following the catastrophe of the Black Death. In that sense, just three centuries ago – and in antiquity, for that matter – common humans lived under material conditions that were no better than those of their ancestors in the Stone Age (but see Fukuyama 2008). The writings of the classic economists nicely exposed the nuts and bolts of this world. We have already touched upon this point when noting that the classic liberal economists were painfully aware of the limits of economic growth (see Chapter 11). This was even true for Adam Smith, but, above all, it pervades the writings of Malthus and Ricardo – particularly the 'iron law of wages', which offers a brilliant description of the Malthusian trap.

The economic uniformity in the world prior to the Industrial Revolution is thus rather simple to explain. It is the diversity in our age – the great divergence separating the developed and developing countries – that is surprising. This divide is due precisely to Europe and its offshoots in North America and Oceania having experienced unprecedented economic growth over the last five hundred years – and to certain other regions (most recently in East Asia) imitating the Europeans on this point. The causal chain is only convincing if we can explain why Malthus would prove to be wrong in his own lifetime (and certainly after his death in 1834).

Here, we can return to the observation that the Chinese emperors in the fifteenth century implemented measures to slow down economic development. The crucial institutional breakthrough in Europe consisted of limiting the arbitrariness of power – which, seen from this perspective, allowed the short-sighted Chinese policies. It was above all else the introduction of constitutional barriers – including freedom rights, the enforcement of law, and political representation – that put Europe on a different track (North and Thomas 1973; Landes 1998; Gress 2007; Jones 2008[1981]).

This is the very point made by Douglass North and Robert Paul Thomas (1973) in *The Rise of the Western World: A New Economic History*, their famous analysis of the emergence of the Western market economy. North and Thomas focus on property rights and show how the European countries in which these rights were most effective (particularly England and the Netherlands) pulled away from the countries in which the opposite was the case (particularly Spain). North and Thomas made a new contribution to economics with this historical account, which emphasized the significance of institutions for economic development. In itself, however, the explanation is rather unsatisfactory, as North and Thomas do not really explain why the effective institutions developed. The most they do is to forward an explanation based on population growth.

North has since continued along the designated trail, thereby contributing to the establishment of the 'New Institutional Economics' approach and ultimately receiving a Nobel Prize for his work. In some of his more recent work (1981; 1990; 2005), he digs much deeper into the foundations of the European miracle. However, since we have already discussed such deeper causes, we will only concern ourselves with the proximate causes here – that is, the development of constitutional systems that limited the arbitrary exercise of power.

A couple of examples illustrate the importance of this factor. In *A Splendid Exchange*, economic historian William Bernstein (2008) describes what is possibly the greatest success story as far as trade is concerned: seventeenth-century Netherlands. In the beginning of the seventeenth century, all roads led to Amsterdam. The Dutch East India Company managed a vast colonial empire in Asia, ruled the seas, and accounted for the lion's share of global shipping. Meanwhile, the Netherlands was the workshop of Europe. Wool from Leiden had practically strangled the textile industry in southern Europe; the English sent raw sugar, tobacco, and diamonds to the Netherlands for processing and refinement; housewives throughout the continent demanded porcelain from Delft; and even the paper industry – which the French and Italians had long dominated – was now in the hands of the enterprising Dutch (Bernstein 2008). The Dutch achievements are reflected in the interest rates for savings and loans. The interest rate in London was around 10% in 1600; the corresponding rate on the Amsterdam financial market was a mere 4%. It was thus far cheaper to raise capital for investments in the Netherlands, which made it possible to exploit new business opportunities (Bernstein 2008).

Why were the Dutch interest rates so low? The answer is found in the superior institutional formula of the Netherlands. The political power was in the hands of a representative institution dominated by the townsmen (the merchant class), a constellation that restrained abuses of public power (see also Chapter 10). The Dutch state always serviced its debt, refrained from suddenly increasing customs and duties, and generally ensured the framework that allowed the market mechanism to function. In other words, the Dutch replaced the Portuguese and Spaniards as the masters of the seas because they created an institutional formula that promoted trade instead of plunder (Bernstein 2008).

Landes (1998, 265) offers a telling example of the other side of the coin: the perverse economic effects of unrestrained power. When the first important Russian rail link, between Moscow and St. Petersburg, was to be established, the Tsar was to set the route. He supposedly did so by placing a ruler between the two cities and drawing a straight line. However, his fingertip was in the way, and the otherwise straight rail line was interrupted by a single, large curve. We have already touched upon some more glaring examples in the cases of China and Japan, and Hall (1985, 99–100) adds a number of equally telling examples from the Islamic world (see also Landes 1983, 27–28).

The general message is thus that the Western European competition – within a cultural community rooted in the Western church – paved the way for a superior institutional formula, or, rather, for political institutions promoting growth. In many ways, the research agenda promoted by Daron A. Acemoglu and James Robinson – which is addressed in the next chapter – can be read as an offshoot or even a specification of this literature.

Criticism

Chapter 11 reviewed the California School's criticism of the Eurocentrists. However, a number of other aspects of the Eurocentrists' description of Europe in the High Middle Ages have come under fire. For example, Epstein (2002, 6–7) criticizes Douglass North for having an ahistorical approach to medieval Europe. Epstein begins with a rather simple observation: a basic assumption in North's research agenda is that authorities *de facto* hold power. This is exactly why the powers-that-be are the villains for Douglass North and those who have followed his lead; if they are not held accountable, they will use their power to enrich themselves by seizing their subjects' property. Such arbitrary and therefore uncertain property rights undermine economic activity – and therefore also economic prosperity.

Epstein objects that North projects an image of the strong state power of the nineteenth and twentieth centuries, with coherent legal systems, back in time. The problem is that such centralization and legal integration was only genuinely achieved in Europe in the nineteenth century. The medieval states were very different. They were based on a fragmented sovereignty, and there was no common law, but rather privileges for specific estate groups such as the nobility, clergy, and townsmen. Under these circumstances, Epstein points out, economic growth was inhibited by the absence of central power and legal uniformity – not by the abuse of central power. Modern growth required centralization. Miguel Centeno (2003) makes a similar point in his analysis of political and economic development in Latin America over the latest two hundred years (see Chapter 15). Here, too, it is the absence of a state power rather than the transgression of power that has been touted as the greatest suppressor of economic development.

Conclusions

The answer presented above as to why Europe pulled away economically from East Asia, the Indian Subcontinent, and the Middle East singles out the combination of political fragmentation and an integrated cultural community. We have seen how all of this – paradoxically – would appear to be rooted in both the common frame of reference of Western Christianity and its fundamental fragmentation, partly between religious and secular authorities in general and partly between the various secular authorities. This led to institutional breakthroughs that paved the way for economic growth by limiting the arbitrary exercise of power.

I return to several of these points on the following pages. First, however, a caveat. As spelled out in the previous chapter, Western Europe was merely one of several combatants in the great Eurasian rivalry in recent millennia – a combatant that over the course of the nineteenth century proved to be the strongest without ever becoming strong enough to completely subjugate the other centres of power. Hence, as recently as a few centuries ago, it seemed anything but certain that Europe would take the economic lead. The 'Eurasian' focus that ties together almost all analyses presented in Chapters 11 and 12 is so enriching because it conjures up an image of a completely open beginning – an image that the later European domination has tended to overshadow. As should be clear to the reader at this stage, this book is permeated by this kind of Eurasian perspective.

Notes

1 The title of Jones' (2008[1981]) book is *The European Miracle*. One might argue that the wording is rather unfortunate insofar as 'miracle' suggests something that cannot be explained (Anderson 1990, 71).
2 Clark (2007) is an exception, as he instead emphasizes how modern man, imbued with a Puritan work ethic and long time horizons, replaced short-sighted traditional man, who prefers leisure over work. This happened, Clark claims, through a gradual Darwinian selection process that spread 'middle class values' in society and occurred faster in Western Europe, especially in England, than in East Asia, as the middle class in the former had relatively more children (in relation to the lower class) than in the latter.
3 In fact, the doctrine about papal supremacy (over secular rulers) dates all the way back to Pope Gelasius in the fifth century (see Cantor 1993[1963], 86–87, 177).
4 Needless to say, it is also possible to find examples of similar conservatism and narrow-mindedness in Europe. What is important here is the general – one is tempted to write *systematic* – difference between Europe and the rest of Eurasia on this point.
5 As the famous saying goes, *bella gerant alii, tu felix Austria nube* ('let others wage war: you, happy Austria, marry').

13

COLONIZATION PROCESSES, ECONOMIC GROWTH, AND POLITICAL DEVELOPMENT

In recent decades, economists have invaded political science, armed to the teeth with formal theoretical models and sophisticated econometric methods (see, e.g., Robinson 2006). Among the stormtroopers is the duo Daron A. Acemoglu and James Robinson. In a series of articles, Acemoglu and Robinson have demonstrated that much of the variation in economic prosperity in our time – the difference between developed countries and developing countries as well as differences within the latter category – must be attributed to the existence or absence of a specific kind of political institution – that is, institutions that limit the power of the authorities (see Acemoglu et al. 2001; 2002a; 2008). Such '*constraints on the executive*' are conducive to economic growth because they provide a shield against legal arbitrariness – a shield that guarantees private property and thereby the willingness of ordinary citizens to take risks.

It is no exaggeration to talk of an 'Acemoglu-Robinson research agenda',[1] which in many ways has helped transform the thoughts of economists and political scientists alike regarding the causes of economic growth and democratization. Acemoglu and Robinson's work has had an impact on how we theorize the causes of economic growth and regime change and on the techniques we use to apply these theoretical arguments empirically. It is particularly striking how quickly it has become commonplace to deduce claims about macro-correlations from micro-economic models that have been ingeniously constructed using assumptions borrowed from economics, and how fast IV-estimation has become the industry standard. Both parts have a lengthy history in economics and have been used for quite some time in certain areas in political science, including the study of American politics. However, it is really only in connection with and as a result of Acemoglu and Robinson's work that they have become part of the comparative historical analyses reviewed in this book. This chapter examines the Acemoglu-Robinson research agenda more closely. To avoid straying too far from the subject matter of this book, I focus on the relationship between institutions and, respectively, economic growth and regime change.

Colonization processes and the spread of institutions

Acemoglu and Robinson's first forays into the subject investigate the relationship between institutions and economic development in former European colonies (Acemoglu et al. 2001; 2002a). Acemoglu and Robinson elegantly weave together two different threads: they present a theory about the transplantation of institutions and a test of the impact of these institutions on economic growth.

Let us go step by step. Acemoglu and Robinson note how institutions that limit power were exported – or, rather, transplanted – to the colonies in which Europeans settled in large droves, including the United States, Canada, Australia, and New Zealand, as well as a number of South American colonies, such as Argentina, Chile, and Uruguay. The Europeans brought with them the institutions they knew from home – hence the expression *neo Europes* that has been used to refer to these 'settler colonies'. In colonies where Europeans settled in limited numbers, such as most of Sub-Saharan Arica (the Cape Province is an exception) and Southeast Asia, they instead established or maintained what Acemoglu and Robinson refer to as *extractive* institutions.

What explains the extent to which Europeans settled? This is where we find the first of Acemoglu and Robinson's contributions. To make a long story short, the Europeans stayed away from places that were marked by either high mortality rates for colonialists or a high population density (or both) in the colonial period (see Acemoglu et al. 2001; 2002a). As illustrated in Figure 13.1, these factors make it possible to isolate the impact of the institutions. Let us look at this in detail.

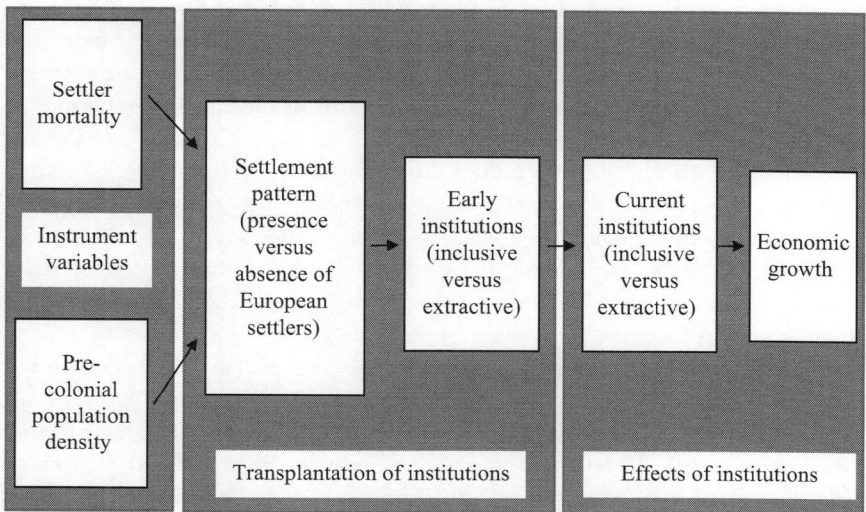

FIGURE 13.1 Colonial transplantation of institutions and economic growth

Note: Based on Acemoglu, Johnson, and Robinson (2001, 1370).

Mortality rates among Europeans

The disease environment varied considerably in the different colonies. In the temperate climates in North America, Australia, New Zealand, Argentina, Chile, and Uruguay, the environment was at least as good as in Western Europe. However, in large parts of Sub-Saharan Africa and in parts of Southeast Asia, Europeans died at abnormally high rates, particularly due to malaria and yellow fever.[2] Europeans were well informed about the potentially fatal prospects of moving to the subtropical regions. For instance, British and French newspapers reported the mortality rates in the various colonies (Acemoglu et al. 2001, 1373–1374).

Acemoglu and Robinson make a rather convincing case that this had consequences for which political and economic institutions were developed in the respective colonies. European colonists generally avoided areas with a high risk of dying prematurely. Where the numbers of European colonists were limited, the most rational colonization strategy was to establish or take control of existing, *extractive* institutions, the aim of which was to exploit the natives – e.g., via heavy taxation and forced labour. Europeans thus established a kind of indirect rule, using existing structures. For instance, they would make local chiefs the henchmen of colonial power in order to demand tribute – or they would create similar positions and let Europeans fill out these roles. This extractive strategy was used by the English, the French, the Belgians, the Dutch, and the Portuguese in most of the African colonies and in parts of Southeast Asia, as well as by the Spanish in parts of Latin America. Acemoglu and Robinson single out Belgian king Leopold's 'private' colony in Congo as the archetypical – and most terrifying – example of the extractive model (1375).

Conversely, the 'European' institutions were transplanted to the healthier areas where large-scale European colonization took place. Or, rather, the European colonists were prepared to fight to introduce such institutions. They demanded the rights they were familiar with from home, including political rights and property rights (1374). Here, it is important to remember that Acemoglu and Robinson see no difference between Europeans colonizers. Whether French, British, or Iberian, they imported their institutions if they settled down in large numbers. The European colonies therefore developed along two very different tracks depending on the pattern of colonization. Moreover, these tracks were difficult to change once they had been set. Seen from this vantage point, European colonization constituted a *critical juncture*, which was followed by path dependence. It follows that former colonies were unable to switch tracks in connection with de-colonization. They therefore retained the institutions established upon the initial encounter with the Europeans (1376).

This brings us to Acemoglu and Robinson's major innovation and their second major contribution. They use mortality rates as an instrument for the character of institutions today. The reasoning is that mortality rates affected whether or not Europeans settled down and, hence, brought their own institutions with them – but that past mortality rates for Europeans have no impact on economic growth in our time, with the exception of the indirect effect that goes via institutions (Acemoglu et al. 2001, 1370–1371). The latter might seem counter-intuitive, but the point is that the locals, who were immune, did not die of illnesses such as malaria and yellow fever, meaning that these illnesses have not directly impeded or dampened economic growth (1371).

Acemoglu and Robinson measure settler mortality by taking the fatality rates among posted soldiers, sailors, and in some places bishops at different points in time between the seventeenth and the nineteenth centuries (1370). Their dataset covers sixty-four former European colonies for which fatality rates can be found. Acemoglu and Robinson show that mortality among colonists accounts for upwards of 25% of the variation in institutions in our time, measured in terms of respect for private property and limitations on executive power (1370–1371). They also demonstrate that mortality rates correlate strongly with a measure for institutions in 1900, which is a necessary condition for their path dependency argument (1378). Bearing this in mind, they investigate the extent to which the mortality rates can account for differences in economic prosperity in our time. The conclusion is clear: there is a statistically significant relationship that explains a substantial part of today's variation in economic wealth.

This correlation survives regardless of what Acemoglu and Robinson throw at it. For example, they carry out the analysis without the countries referred to above as *neo Europes* and without African countries. They also control for a series of potential confounders – variables that could have an effect on both mortality rates and economic development. Indeed, many of the common explanations for economic differences between colonies turn out to be insignificant when mortality rates are accounted for (1388–1391). This applies to the impact of the differences between *common law* and *civil law* systems, religion, the percentage of the population that is of European descent, and the incidence of malaria. Finally, the effect of being a British colony is almost negligible when mortality rates are factored in.

Population density at the time of colonization

The mortality rates among European settlers is not the only variable to shape the institutional development in the former colonies. In a later article, Acemoglu and Robinson introduce another factor: population density at the time of colonization (Acemoglu, Johnson, and Robinson 2002a). Acemoglu and Robinson begin with the rather interesting observation that the colonies that were the wealthiest at the time of colonization became the poorest over time – and vice versa. For example, contemporary Canada, the United States, Argentina, and Australia were dirt-poor before the Europeans arrived, whereas Aztec Mexico, Inca Peru, and certain African and Southeast Asian states were far more prosperous.

This 'reversal of fortune' is interesting for several reasons. First, it undermines geographical explanations for prosperity. In comparative perspective, the tropical areas were prosperous when the Europeans reached them, whereas, today, they are poor in relation to the temperate regions (1231–1232). It therefore makes little sense to use bio-geographical explanations to account for the income disparities that have appeared in the world since the great overseas explorations. Acemoglu and Robinson again argue that institutions rather than geography are key. In brief, the European colonization caused an *institutional reversal*: where the Europeans met poor societies, they would settle down and import their own institutions; where they found themselves amid plenty, it made more sense to establish or take control of existing *extractive* institutions in order to skim the cream (1235).

Acemoglu and Robinson first and foremost measure prosperity in terms of the degree of urbanization. The reasoning is that a large urban population demands a societal surplus when measured up against subsistence levels. They add a measure for population size, which as we know from Chapter 10 is often used as a proxy for development in historical periods for which we have no reliable economic data (1232). *En passant*, Acemoglu and Robinson show that there is a very strong empirical correlation between urbanization and income levels and that there is a negative correlation between the degree of urbanization and population size in the year 1500 and income levels today (1232, 1244) – but only in the sample of former European colonies, mind you. If we run the same analysis on non-colonies, prosperity in 1500 predicts high levels of wealth today (1253, see Table 13.1).

The Europeans settled in sparsely populated (and hence underdeveloped) regions distant from the unhealthy tropical climes. They brought their institutions with them, thereby planting sustained growth rates in this previously impoverished soil. Possibly the most illustrative example is the thirteen English colonies in North America that would eventually liberate themselves and establish the United States of America. As Finer (1997b) has pointed out, even before independence a larger part of the population had the right to vote in the colonial parliaments than in the motherland (Great Britain) – and the legal system protected private property. The opposite was the case in areas that were relatively prosperous around 1500. Here, the Europeans took over the existing exploitative institutions, which explains why these areas were never really able to achieve sustained economic growth. Over time, the two groups of colonies therefore traded places with respect to prosperity levels.

One of Acemoglu and Robinson's interesting points is that the economic effects of institutions were not really felt until after the Industrial Revolution in the second half of the eighteenth century. Until around the year 1500, the tropical areas were clearly the most prosperous. But as late as 1700, India, Indonesia, Brazil, and

TABLE 13.1 Urbanization rates in 1500 (unit: contemporary states)

0.0–2.99%	3.0–5.99%	6.0–8.99%	9.0–11.99%	12.00–14.99%	>15.0%
Argentine, Australia, Brasil, Canada, Guyana, Paraguay, Uruguay, USA, Venezuela	Dominican Republic, Hong Kong, Haiti, Jamaica, New Zealand, Singapore	Bangladesh, Colombia, Indonesia, India, Laos, Sri Lanka, Malaysia, Pakistan, Vietnam	Belize, Bolivia, Costa Rica, Ecuador, Guatemala, Honduras, Nicaragua, Panama, Peru, El Salvador	Algeria, Egypt, Mexico, Tunisia	Morocco

Source: Acemoglu, Johnson, and Robinson 2002a.

Mexico were more prosperous than the United States based on the very limited information we have concerning income levels. The United States only surpassed these countries around 1820 – after which it and the other *neo Europes* never looked back (Acemoglu et al. 2002a, 1256).

Acemoglu and Robinson show that this is consistent with the negative correlation between the level of affluence in 1500 and the quality of contemporary institutions, above all measured in terms of limitations on executive power. They also demonstrate that this correlation disappears if we introduce the aforementioned instrument for the transplantation of institutions, namely European settler mortality (1271). Finally, Acemoglu and Robinson control for alternative explanations, including more specific factors such as coal deposits (1261).

We are thus left with the following story: the institutional development was the result of what the Europeans met *in situ*, in turn deciding which colonization strategy was the most profitable; but it was only with industrialization that this led to the dramatic differences in income levels we know today.

Economic development and democratization

We find the most telling illustration of how Acemoglu and Robinson have brought economic instruments into political science in a couple of articles that would appear to be spinoffs of their work on institutions and economic growth (Robinson 2006; Acemoglu et al. 2008). Here, Acemoglu and Robinson use their research agenda as a lever to examine one of the most renowned relationships in the social sciences: so-called modernization theory. The modernization perspective saturates most of nineteenth-century sociology. The modern interpretation of this relationship dates back to the decades following World War II. The claim is that all countries will develop along the same path, which leads to economic prosperity and modern democracy. We find a good example of this line of thought in Walt Rostow's (1960) *The Stages of Economic Growth* (see Møller and Skaaning 2013, Chapter 7). Acemoglu and Robinson focus on a more specific claim made in the literature, however: that either economic growth or a high level of prosperity is conducive to a transition to democracy and/or to democratic stability. This relationship received its modern formulation with Seymour Martin Lipset (1959).

As Robinson (2006, 524–525) points out, this is one of the strongest relationships identified by political scientists. However, Acemoglu and Robinson candidly declare that political scientists have never properly tested it (Acemoglu et al. 2008). Existing analyses have primarily enlisted cross-case variation and have neglected to account for 'reverse causality' (i.e., that democracy could be conducive to economic growth) and the challenges related to the *omitted variable bias* (i.e., that unaccounted third variables might affect both the level of modernization and democracy). In a nutshell, the strong empirical relationship that surely exists between levels of prosperity and levels of democracy does not in itself say anything about whether or not there is also a causal relationship. Acemoglu and Robinson suggest two ways of correcting these problems.

First, the analysis can be refined by 'fixed effects', which control for country-specific factors that do not change over time. In other words, such a test examines whether or not *changes* in the level of prosperity tend to produce *similar changes* in the level of democracy in the individual countries. Conversely, such an investigation does not harness cross-case variation. In other words, with fixed effects we are merely analysing whether or not countries have a tendency to become more democratic as they get richer.

Second, one can examine the relationship by instrumenting for levels of wealth. This requires an instrument variable that affects economic growth without affecting democracy (with the exception of the indirect effect that goes via economic growth). Acemoglu and Robinson acknowledge that finding such instruments is no mean feat. However, they argue that it makes sense to use measures for the savings rate and changes in the income levels of trading partners (810).

Regardless of whether they use 'fixed effects' or instrument variables, the following record stands: the correlation between modernization and the level of democratization disappears. To repeat the staggering conclusion – the modernization relationship that generations of political scientists have identified breaks down when it is attacked by these econometric methods! Or, more precisely, the relationship disappears when we study the latest one hundred years in general and the period since 1945 in particular. This begs a particular question. If increases in wealth do not lead to increases in levels of democracy, what explains that – in today's world – richer countries have a greater tendency to be democratic than poorer ones? Surely there must be a connection, considering that all countries in the world were poor five hundred years ago, prior to modern increases in wealth (812)?

Acemoglu and Robinson suggest two possible answers to this question. Either there is indeed a modernization correlation that simply works over a longer period – that is, centuries instead of decades – or, alternatively, economic and political development goes hand in hand as a result of underlying factors that affect both (812). It goes without saying that Acemoglu and Robinson lean towards the second explanation. More specifically, they claim that the *institutions of constraint* that Europeans transplanted during colonization processes have contributed to increases in wealth since the Industrial Revolution and to democratization since the French Revolution (see Figure 13.2).

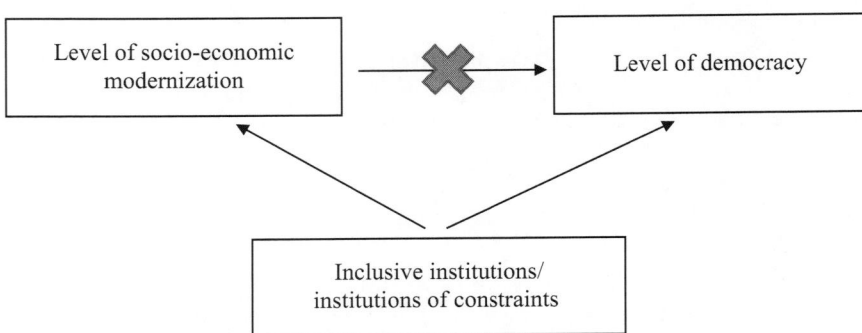

FIGURE 13.2 The spurious modernization relationship

Acemoglu and Robinson investigate if existing data supports this – or if it rather corroborates the *longue durée* interpretation of modernization theory. They code the so-called POLITY dataset, which measures the extent of *constraints on the executive*, back to the year 1500. Initially, they find a clear statistical correlation between changes in income and changes in the level of democracy[3] in the period 1500– 2000 (832), but this correlation practically disappears when a series of historical factors that might plausibly create institutional differences are taken into account (835). Furthermore, Acemoglu and Robinson note that the relationship disappears completely if they run the analysis in a sample comprising former European colonies. This is important, as they are able to use their earlier results to control for the character of institutions. More precisely, the relationship disappears as soon as population density in 1500 is introduced as a control (836).

It is important to keep in mind that Acemoglu and Robinson are only investigating the relationship between income *levels* and democracy *levels* in the article referred to above. Modernization theory also includes a claim about the levels of prosperity affecting democratization and democratic stability. However, in another article Acemoglu and Robinson have demonstrated that there would not appear to be any relationship between income and the transition to democracy – or for that matter democratic breakdown (813).

One final detail is worth mentioning. In a separate article, Robinson (2006) argues that the most considerable progress in modernization theory in recent years has been made with respect to theory and not empirical investigation. Political scientists have finally endeavoured to provide a decent explanation for how modernization leads to democratization and/or democratic stability – that is, to identify convincing causal mechanisms on the micro-level. According to Robinson, political scientists have achieved these breakthroughs by drawing on insights from economics, including micro-economics. This point effectively frames the picture painted in this chapter, namely that economists have successfully invaded political science (see Møller and Skaaning 2013, Chapter 7).

Criticism

Understanding the Acemoglu-Robinson research agenda requires an appreciation of their historical point of departure. Boiled down to a single sentence – economically and politically auspicious institutions emerged in Western Europe and were subsequently transplanted to some of the European colonies. Over time, these institutions stimulated increases in wealth and democratization in Western Europe as well as in the colonies where they were exported – and *vice versa* with the colonies in which European institutions did not make inroads. Acemoglu and Robinson repeatedly emphasize that institutional change also occurs today (e.g., Acemoglu et al. 2001, 1395). Nevertheless, their assumption is that this is the exception. Institutions are sluggish; once a particular track has been laid, it is not easily changed, and it affects the behaviour of individuals, including their behaviour as economic agents.

Exactly what kinds of institutions are associated with these beneficial effects? Here, we are touching on a paradox in the research agenda. Especially in their earlier work, Acemoglu and Robinson were very nonchalant when describing these institutions, and when it comes to the origins of these institutions their work is marked by an almost deafening silence.

With respect to the former point, we are merely informed that, at their core, these institutions concern the inviolability of property rights and the presence of *constraints on the executive* (e.g., Acemoglu et al. 2001). Robinson (2002, 511) explains and defends this nonchalance, arguing that the best strategy in cross-national analyses is to capture equilibrium outcomes rather than the specific institutions that sustain these outcomes. Such a strategy is agnostic about which institutions ensure stable property rights. The important point is that institutions – as described above – can be measured using the mortality rates for European colonists or the population density in the colonies when the Europeans arrived. The closest Acemoglu and Robinson come to identifying the character of the relevant institutions is their repeated references to the prior work of North and Jones, which we presented in the previous chapter (e.g., Acemoglu et al. 2001, 1369; 2008, 813). In other words, they envisage a combination of political institutions (restrictions on the authorities) and economic institutions (property rights).

This insouciance creates a two-fold vagueness.[4] First, because we are dealing with two different kinds of institutions, in theory a dictatorship could display great respect for property rights, as is the case with contemporary Singapore and many European monarchies in the nineteenth century. Second, it is unclear whether there is a hierarchy between the two different kinds of institutions. For example, they could conceivably affect each other or one could be a consequence of the other (cf. Mazzuca 2010a).

In one of their recent works, *Why Nations Fail*, Acemoglu and Robinson (2012) attempt to alleviate the conceptual confusion by distinguishing between two different forms of institutions: political and economic. Both assume the same forms: inclusive versus extractive. The former category is favourable for economic growth and democratization; the latter, unfavourable. More specifically, inclusive political institutions are defined by the limitations on arbitrary power that we have already touched upon in this chapter. Similarly, the inclusive economic institutions are above all defined by respect for property rights.

However, instead of merging the two, Acemoglu and Robinson argue that it is the political institutions that determine the economic institutions. Inclusive economic institutions can be established and maintained only when inclusive political institutions exist: limited power is prior to effective property rights. Acemoglu and Robinson's new position thereby solves a problem in their earlier research (but see Robinson 2002). Yet, the fact remains that they have never seriously tested whether this hierarchy or sequence can be corroborated empirically. In this sense, the new argument would appear to be more of a postulate.

Next, it is striking that Acemoglu and Robinson's scholarship hardly addresses the European emergence of favourable institutions (see, however, Acemoglu,

Johnson, and Robinson 2002b). All we are told is that they emerged in the western part of Europe over the latest five hundred years. The contemporary variation in income levels and democracy must therefore – as Acemoglu and Robinson non-chalantly remark – be traced back to 'some *critical junctures* during the last 500 years' (Acemoglu et al. 2008, 813; emphasis in the original). Indeed, in some papers, it is only phrases such as 'European-like institutions' (Acemoglu et al. 2001, 1374) that suggest the origins of the key factor behind economic growth.

Acemoglu and Robinson's nonchalant treatment of the historical origins of the factors they analyse can to some extent be attributed to the fact that they write into a particular debate (e.g., Acemoglu et al. 2001; 2002a). They are first and foremost interested in the economic impact of geography versus institutions. The relevant institutions (inclusive institutions or constraints on the authorities) emerged endogenously in Europe, but they are exogenous in the colonies because they were transferred there directly by the Europeans. Whether or not this occurred varies based on the factors that determine whether or not the Europeans could settle down, which means that the causal effect of the institutions can be isolated and gauged. Note in this context that the analyses carried out by Acemoglu and Robinson make no attempt at identifying the configuration of factors that created economic growth. The aim is solely to isolate and investigate the economic effects of a specific causal factor, namely institutions.

However, the neglect of the European emergence of favourable institutions is problematic for at least two reasons. First, it means that Acemoglu and Robinson do not attempt to trace their causal chain back in time. This is contrary to the point, celebrated in the philosophy of science, that '[t]he further away we can get from the outcome in question, the better (ceteris paribus) our explanation will be' (Gerring 2001, 142; see also Kitschelt 2003). To the contrary, Acemoglu and Robinson's institutions constraining the executive power emerge as a kind of *deus ex machina*, at least in Europe.

Second, Acemoglu and Robinson neither date the timing of these institutional innovations nor demarcate the area they have historically characterized. This is problematic because, in their model, the transplantation of favourable institutions occurs via colonization. Throughout history, there have been numerous large-scale acts of colonization, including large-scale settlements – from the Han-Chinese colonization of southern China to the Austronesian colonization of Southeast Asia to the African Bantu colonization of the southern part of Africa (see Diamond 1999[1997]). Only European colonization is relevant for Acemoglu and Robinson, but not all European countries have historically had favourable institutions that could be transplanted. Russia in particular, which became an integrated part of the European state system in the seventeenth and eighteenth centuries, was never characterized by inclusive institutions or institutions of constraints (Myers 1975; Finer 1997b). Russian colonization was therefore unable to spread auspicious institutions, whether based on large-scale settlements (which was often the case, e.g., in many regions of what is now Russia) or more indirect take-overs (e.g., in the Caucasus and Central Asia). In order to know which colonial powers are relevant, we must demarcate the emergence of the relevant institutions in time and space. However, other than some very vague remarks concerning their emergence in the western part of Europe some five hundred years ago, Acemoglu et al. offer very little help in drawing these limits.

To be sure, in *Why Nations Fail*, Acemoglu and Robinson (2012) present a number of more explicit considerations about this issue. They trace an early difference between Western and Eastern Europe all the way back to the Black Death, which intensified serfdom in Eastern Europe while weakening it in Western Europe (see also Chapter 7). Moreover, in their eyes, the Glorious Revolution in England and the French Revolution are the two most important breaking points. These revolutions are construed as contingent events triggered by chance that have occasioned *critical junctures* with crucial significance for the course of history.

Acemoglu and Robinson might thereby be said to try their hand at an actual historical analysis of the origins of the institutions. Nevertheless, Jared Diamond (2012), in his review of *Why Nations Fail*, can take Acemoglu and Robinson to task for failing to provide a systematic explanation of why inclusive political institutions emerge – and thus a prediction of where this is most likely to happen. Diamond points out that Acemoglu and Robinson's notion that small differences and contingent choices at *critical junctures* are crucial for institutional development has some rather extreme implications. The logical inference must be that favourable institutions emerge randomly over time and space, 'depending on who happened to decide what at some particular place and time'. In Diamond's eyes, this fits poorly with favourable institutions making inroads throughout the western part of Europe – and the fact that they never emerged in Sub-Saharan Africa.

Acemoglu and Robinson (2012) counter by arguing that the development of institutions is a systematic result of historical processes, which can be studied systemically – which they claim to do in their own book. But Diamond has rightly responded that the way they describe historical developments (propitious in England since the High Middle Ages, with a breaking point around the Glorious Revolution in 1688, and in Japan after the Meiji Revolution; unpropitious in Spain after the great voyages of discovery, in Imperial Russia, and in Ethiopia) leaves an impression of randomness. This would also appear to follow from Acemoglu and Robinson's (2012, 271) suggestion that other areas might have undergone their own Glorious Revolutions had the Europeans not interfered. However, we find no such randomness when we look at a historical atlas.

Diamond sees an early transition to agriculture as a necessary condition for the successful development of institutions, meaning that geography casts long shadows, even into our time (see Diamond 1999[1997]). Note in this connection the following observation: Hariri (2012) shows that an early transition to agriculture outside of Europe helped prevent the European transplantation of the very kinds of political and economic institutions that Acemoglu and Robinson regard as crucial for democratization and economic development. This is one among many examples of how the past casts its shadow in a much more deterministic manner than indicated by Acemoglu and Robinson's focus on contingency and *critical junctures*.

Finally, some scepticism is in order with respect to Acemoglu and Robinson's all-out rejection of modernization theory. As described above, they go to great lengths to show that this relationship does not stand up to a proper empirical analysis, but they conclude that there is actually an effect of income in the period before 1875 (see also Robinson 2006). This is important as it is in this specific period that we would expect to find a relationship, considering that this was when the first genuine democratizations took place (Boix and Stokes 2003; Boix 2011).

Conclusions

This criticism of Acemoglu and Robinson should not cloud the fact that their research agenda has provided a breath of fresh air to the literature on the Rise of Europe. Their influence in both economics and political science in recent years is well deserved. They have had a wealth of ideas, their empirical research is solid, and the relevance is beyond doubt. Acemoglu and Robinson's work illustrates how the import of econometric techniques has turned political science upside-down in some respects. This input has undoubtedly strengthened the literature on state formation, regime change, and economic development.

That said, Acemoglu and Robinson's research agenda is also vulnerable because of its origins in economics. Above all, the analyses reviewed in this chapter have a tendency to become ahistorical in the sense that the effects of institutions are traced across time with little understanding of their historical origins, contextual variations, or historical specificities. A telling example, which might be said to frame the research agenda in a more general sense, is that Acemoglu and Robinson (2012) identify inclusive political institutions in the Roman Republic, medieval Venice, England after the Glorious Revolution, and many other places without any appreciation of the essentially different nature of these institutions.

Notes

1 Several of Acemoglu and Robinson's seminal articles have been written together with other authors; among them Simon Johnson. But Acemoglu and Robinson's (2006; 2012) two books do not include other co-authors, and, more generally, they appear to 'own' the research project. In this chapter, I therefore only refer to Acemoglu and Robinson in the text itself, while the other co-authors are mentioned in the references.

2 These two mosquito-borne diseases account for upwards of 80% of European fatalities in the colonies (Acemoglu et al. 2001, 1380).

3 There were no genuine democracies before 1800, but the point made by Acemoglu and Robinson is that we are nevertheless able to distinguish between the degree of democracy around the world prior to that date, including the extent to which the authorities are limited by institutional barriers, such as parliaments (see also Knutsen et al. 2016).

4 At the same time, the institutional limitations on the authorities are sometimes measured with the level of democracy, which increases the confusion.

14

WAR AND STATE FORMATION IN ANCIENT CHINA

The European multistate system is an important part of the equation that produced the modern state, modern democracy, and the modern market economy. But the fact of the matter is that the European state system is not as unique as the previous chapters – implicitly or explicitly – have made it out to be (see Møller 2014). This chapter discusses the multistate system that is most similar to the one later found in Europe: the Chinese state system in the period 656–221 BC (Hui 2001; 2004; 2005).

In Chinese history, these centuries are known as the 'Spring and Autumn Period' (722–479 BC) and 'the Warring States Period' (475–221 BC), respectively. The second term is apt. In fact, the Chinese word for China, *Zhongguo*, which is normally translated as 'the Middle Kingdom', literally means the 'central states' (Hui 2005, 1). The term is a reminder of the Warring States Period. In these centuries, Chinese state formations along the Yellow River competed within a rather stable state system where geopolitical balance prevented any individual state from getting the upper hand. Indeed, the number of state entities declined from around 170 in the beginning of the Warring States Period to eight towards the end of the period (Bradford 2001, 136). Nevertheless, until the second half of the third century BC, the state system ensured a general equilibrium between the competitors. This changed in the third century BC. From the year 284 BC (and particularly after the year 257 BC), the western state in the system, Qin (hence the various European words for 'China'), gained superiority, and in 221 BC the Qin-ruler Zheng united China, creating the empire that, with some interruptions, has remained a reality all the way into the twentieth century.

The first part of this chapter will examine how the Chinese state system sparked an early consolidation of state powers and the granting of certain legal and social rights. In other words, mechanisms that previous chapters have identified in Europe can be identified in ancient China. The main emphasis is on the way geopolitical competition has augmented state power, as the political and economic effects are less striking than the bureaucratization found in the Chinese multistate system. Scholars have noted that the ancient Chinese states displayed an early form of Weberian bureaucratization, including meritocratic employment practices (e.g., Hui 2005; Fukuyama 2011). Conversely, the other features of the Weberian state definition introduced in Chapter 1 were lacking, particularly attributes pertaining to the rule of law. In other words, this chapter primarily applies a minimalistic definition of the state.

Below, I present and discuss a fascinating contribution to the state-formation literature, namely political scientist Victoria Hui's *War and State Formation in Ancient China and Early Modern Europe* (2005). This book is a daring and thoughtful comparison of the state system in the Warring States Period and the later European system, and there is much to learn from Hui's comparison. However, I will also make a number of critical points.

War and state formation in China

If we apply a minimalist definition of the state, most scholars agree that the first modern states developed in China in the Warring States Period. Francis Fukuyama's book *The Origins of Political Order* (2011) offers a good example. Fukuyama draws a distinction between three different forms of development: the development of state power, political development in the form of democratization, and the development of rule of law. According to Fukuyama, China is interesting because 'the Middle Kingdom' developed strong state power very early but never democratized nor developed the rule of law. This fundamentally distinguishes China from Western and Central Europe, where the tradition for rule of law emerged prior to the modern state and democracy. As the great historian of the Middle Ages Joseph Strayer (1970, 23–24) once observed, the states in the west of Europe were bound by law at creation; and even though the legalistic ideal was often broken, the legitimacy of the European states always rested upon this ideal (see also Finer 1997a, 870).

Victoria Hui (2004; 2005) has recently attempted to explain why China and Europe developed in different directions – and, more specifically, why China set the stage for the first modern states in the Warring States Period. Hui (2005, 1) begins by posing the following question: why did Europe become characterized by a separation of political powers (*checks and balances*), while China developed a state that dominated society completely (*coercive universal empire*)? This is one of the biggest questions of comparative historical analysis. It is striking that Europe after the fall of the Roman Empire has been marked by political fragmentation, constitutionalism, and in time democracy, while China has been characterized by centralized state power, which has been extremely conservative in terms of admitting rights to its subjects.

Hui starts with a simple observation: in the most important areas, the Chinese state system in the period 656–221 BC resembled the European state system we know from the period 1494–1815. Both systems were characterized by independent entities that were not subjected to a higher authority and that interacted (2005, 5). This is why it is so interesting to compare the two systems, Hui reasons (2004, 176). She does not resort to the logic of comparative control; in fact, she emphasizes that controlled comparisons are rarely meaningful in large-scale comparative historical analysis. Instead, she focuses on uncovering the causal mechanisms that operate in both systems, and she makes points about timing and path dependency that she has drawn from the historical institutionalists (2005, 7–8).

Hui's dynamic theory of international politics

Hui uses the comparison of China and Europe to establish a 'dynamic theory of international politics' capable of explaining how relatively similar state systems can pave the way for different political outcomes (Hui 2004, 176; 2005, 224). Her basic point is that such systems are characterized by two opposing mechanisms: a *logic of domination* and a *logic of balancing*. As the term itself implies, the logic of domination eliminates competition from the system, culminating with one state swallowing up the others. Conversely, the logic of balancing works to maintain competition, particularly because the other states form alliances against the strongest state. Because the two mechanisms work at cross-purposes, it is not possible *a priori* to predict whether domination or balancing will prevail in the long run (Hui 2004, 176–177; 2005, 34). Hui's point is that it is necessary to study the historical case – with the help of these mechanisms – to explain why, for example, the state of Qin was able to unite China, whereas even Napoleon's grand project ran aground in Europe.

Hui draws the logic of balancing from the dominant theory in International Relations: Kenneth Waltz' (1979) so-called neorealism. But the addition of the logic of domination renders her theory a fundamental challenge to Waltz. The neorealistic logic dictates constant balancing – that is, a strong state's attempt to expand will be met by reactions from the other states, after which equilibrium is (at some point at least) restored to the system. In contrast, Hui argues that competition can be removed via the logic of domination. In fact, she goes even further in her challenge to Waltz and argues that domination will normally trump the balancing dynamic. The centripetal force is facilitated by the opportunity to carry out reforms that strengthen the capacity of the state and the military, by divide-and-conquer strategies (*divide et impera*) and, finally, by the opportunity to act ruthlessly against competitors, whereas the centrifugal force is complicated by collective action problems (Hui 2005, 27). In other words, the European balancing outcome is actually quite surprising, while the Chinese result of domination is only to be expected.

To better understand these processes, Hui embeds a state theory in her theory of international relations. She elegantly argues that both the balancing and domination dynamics also operate *within* the individual states (2005, 41). The centrifugal dynamic leads to negotiations between authorities and subjects, and therefore often to the granting of rights, whereas the centripetal dynamic strengthens the resources of the state and therefore its ability to suppress. Hui draws both of these mechanisms from Tilly (Hui 2004, 181–182; 2005, 38–41; see Chapter 9) and argues that the logic of domination will also have a tendency to prevail over the logic of balancing in the domestic arena.

How, then, do we explain that balancing triumphed in Europe, both internally (constitutionalism) and in interstate relations (maintenance of the multistate system)? Hui's rather simple interpretation is that the European state-builders missed their chance to dominate. Instead of implementing reforms aimed at strengthening the state, such as direct taxation, building a bureaucracy based on meritocracy, and the introduction of conscription, both the French monarchs and the Austrian Hapsburgs carried out reforms that weakened the state. Hui singles out the use of mercenaries and the sale of offices (e.g., judgeships and the right to collect taxes) as the most important of these 'self-weakening reforms'. We have already touched upon this development in the review of Thomas Ertman's *Birth of the Leviathan* (1997) in Chapter 9. However, in contrast to Ertman, Hui largely sees these developments as contingent – that is, as a product of actors' choices. She specifically describes how the European economy (in contrast to the Chinese economy) was commercialized prior to large-scale statehood. This tempted the European monarchs and princes to choose short-sighted solutions, such as the sale of offices and the right to farm taxes. But Hui is unapologetic that the European monarchies could have chosen more long-term solutions. This point also extends to military strategy. The European kings and emperors neglected to be sufficiently ruthless in times of war. Even Napoleon did not practice the mass execution of defeated enemy soldiers (Hui 2005, 109, 136).

The Chinese experience was very different, although the balancing dynamic was also evident here. In fact, the period 656–284 BC was generally characterized by international balance à la Waltz. Domestically, this led the Chinese princes and (later) kings to introduce civil rights, including freedom of expression, legal protection, and certain economic rights (Hui 2001; 2005, 168–169). But the Chinese competition was far more intensive and brutal than the European one (2005, 149–156). The Chinese authorities and statesmen were far more cunning and conniving, and the tendency was therefore towards domination. The smaller states were initially swallowed up by larger states, and, in the course of the third century BC, Qin succeeded in subjugating the other (warring) states. This was possible because Qin authorities did not miss their chance. They carried out extensive reforms, often by borrowing effective models from the other, more developed states. Moreover, Qin's foreign policy was completely shorn of any moral considerations; for example, the Qin generals practiced the mass execution of defeated enemies, and Qin diplomats cheated the other states in negotiations.

In 221 BC, when Qin had finally conquered the other states, the balancing dynamic disappeared on the interstate level. At the same time, the new power monopoly made it possible for King Zheng of Qin – who took the title as the first Chinese emperor – to do away with the balancing tendencies domestically. This is almost by definition the ambition of absolute rulers, as it becomes easier to suppress opposition (cf. Holmes 2004, 21). The civil rights that had previously been granted were withdrawn, and the Chinese found themselves with an early forerunner of totalitarianism instead of the separation of powers and constitutionalism (Hui 2005, 184, fn. 89).[1]

The European princes, kings, and emperors were far less effective. Only Prussia in the seventeenth century and Great Britain in the eighteenth century chose the path that led to effective state power. France under Napoleon did the same, and for some time it appeared as though Napoleon was going to repeat Zheng's feat (Hui 2004, 197–198). However, the self-weakening reforms of the past – particularly the enormous state debt – weighed Napoleon down and prevented his large-scale attempt to dominate Europe. Meanwhile, Great Britain was a worthy competitor, albeit one whose superior domestic institutional formula rested on checks and balances. The eventual British victory therefore did not pave the way for the logic of domination but instead reinforced the tendency to separate powers, domestically and internationally.

Criticism

It was thus actors' choices that made the difference between China and Europe – although these choices were constrained by factors such as the timing of commercialization (more on this below). This is Hui's main explanation for why the two relatively identical state systems experienced such very different fates. The analysis is fascinating as is Hui's (2005, 169) conclusion that the European development of constitutionalism and civil rights was far more coincidental than previous research would lead us to believe.

That said, Hui's analysis leaves a number of questions unanswered. As Kitschelt (2003) has argued, actor-centred explanations must be analysed in relation to the underlying structures that constrain which choices are possible (and conceivable) in a specific situation. The obvious objection to Hui's analysis is that the underlying structural conditions might have shaped the choices made by actors in China and Europe, respectively, in the periods under investigation. One of the strengths of Hui's analysis is that she actually picks up the gauntlet on this point. She expressly rejects two possible structural confounders: that geography have made life more difficult for the European would-be empire builders (Hui 2005, 90–91, 163, see also Chapter 12) and that the cultural homogeneity was simply greater in China, which made it easier to form a single integrated state (2005, 165).

The only underlying factor that Hui seriously grants significance is, as mentioned above, the timing of the commercialization of the economy. In Europe, the economy was commercialized *before* the multistate system emerged, whereas this occurred *after* the onset of geopolitical competition in China. Commercialization made it easier for the European authorities to indulge in short-sighted fiscal measures – especially the sale of offices – when it became necessary to finance warfare (Hui 2005, 141–142; see also Vu 2010, 157). There was simply money to be had from the urban bourgeoisie. This shortcut to military prowess proved to be a detour on the way to becoming a powerful state. But Hui maintains that even the temptation of commercialization could be overcome by effective state-builders – and was therefore not a decisive factor.

In the course of the analysis, it becomes clear that Hui feels compelled to consider further differences. She raises the potential objection that a form of inter-state *checks and balances* was already present in medieval Europe – that is, before the emergence of the multistate system – while the same was not the case in ancient China (Hui 2005, 195–196). Or, to specify the question, did European feudalism and/or medieval representative institutions in themselves strengthen the logic of balancing at the expense of the logic of domination? Hui's answer to both questions is 'no'. With respect to the former, she argues that the so-called 'Zhou feudalism' that existed in China before the Warring States Period largely corresponded to European feudalism (2005, 195–205), for which reason this could not have made the difference (see also Hui 2001).[2] Regarding the latter, Hui acknowledges that China had no counterpart to the European representative institutions (2005, 198). However, she argues that these institutions did not make much difference, as most European authorities proved able to undermine them after the competitiveness of the state system had become a reality.

According to Hui, the more important difference was that numerous privileged estate groups existed in Europe – the church, the nobility, and the cities – whereas in China there was only the nobility. The medieval representative institutions were merely a consequence of the existence of these privileged groups rather than an independent factor[3] (2005, 202–203). With respect to the peculiar development of Europe, Hui therefore ends up attributing considerable significance to the independent church and the free cities (Hui 2005, 203–204, 211–214; Vu 2010, 161). As Vu (2010, 161) emphasizes, Hui's analysis appears to show that competition created by war and preparation for war might well lead to a consolidation of state power but not necessarily to representative institutions. This requires a certain balance of power in society between the significant social groups, including the church and the emperor.

However, this is precisely where Hui's understanding of feudalism proves superficial. As I have argued elsewhere, recent historical research shows that ancient China is fundamentally different from medieval Europe with respect to the context within which the state-builders had to operate, particularly with respect to the need to negotiate with the masses (Møller 2014; 2015a). Hui (2005, 196, fn. 143) bases her reading of Zhou feudalism on relatively dated work – namely Creel (1970, 319–320). In so doing, she ignores that more recent research has largely rejected the notion that ancient China was characterized by feudalism as we know it from Western Europe (see e.g., Cook 1997, 253–255, 282–284; Feng 2003; 2006; 2008; Von Falkenhausen 2006).

The more general criticism of Hui can be summarized as follows: despite the premise that historical differences should be taken seriously and that path dependency has an impact on state formation processes, Hui ultimately ignores that China and Europe distinguish themselves from one another on crucial points that affect the logics of balancing and domination (see also Finer 1996, 442–444). A way of driving this point home is to once again return to Fukuyama's (2011) recent attempt to contrast China and Europe. Fukuyama observes that the precocious development of the modern state in Warring States China was followed by neither rule of law nor democratization. According to Fukuyama, the European development was the exact opposite. In Europe, the rule of law – and a primitive forerunner of democracy in the form of constitutionalism and representative institutions – preceded the contemporary state formation process (see also Møller 2015b).

The crowned heads of Western Europe were entangled in a web of legal privileges and contractual relations all the way back to the High Middle Ages. They were unable to levy taxes without the approval of representative institutions, they could not force the nobility to do much, and they could not interfere in church matters. In fact, according to Fukuyama (2011), the European notion of the rule of law stems from the work of the Catholic Church in the Middle Ages. It was medieval Church Law that laid the foundations for the rule of law, and the separation of secular and religious power ensured that the authorities did not merely abolish the legal privileges of the various estate groups. Fukuyama thereby traces the rule of law back to the Gregorian Revolution in the eleventh century and the subsequent Investiture Controversy between the church in Rome and the Holy Roman Emperor. With reference to Finer (1997a, 863), we might view the Gregorian Revolution as a 'rediscovery' of the old Jewish notion of the 'limited monarchy', in which rulers do not pass laws but merely administer pre-existing law based on a religious source.

According to Fukuyama (2011), this conflict resulted from a concatenation of historical coincidences. But it determined the fate of the West. The medieval development of the rule of law meant that kings and emperors of Western and Central Europe were forced to consolidate state power under considerable legal restrictions. The rule of law thus predates the Reformation, the Renaissance, and the Industrialization. Even in absolutist states such as France and Spain, the authorities could not disregard the historical liberties of the nobility and the bourgeoisie (as the Chinese emperors did). And it was out of this balance of power that the modern constitutional systems in the United Kingdom and Scandinavia emerged, which over time spread to the rest of Western Europe and became the forerunner of modern liberal democracy.

If we accept Fukuyama's main point, Europe was fundamentally different from China. Hall (1985, 102) describes how the European states were forced to provide infrastructural services for two reasons: the prior existence of a civil society and the need to raise taxes for warfare. Hui fails to capture these connections, and this is a significant flaw in her analysis.

Conclusions

The golden age of Chinese philosophy – with renowned figures such as Confucius, Mencius, and Laozi – coincided with the Warring States Period. This chapter has described how the Chinese multistate system of the day in many ways resembled the multistate system that is such an important part of the equation behind the European development of the modern state, modern democracy, and the modern market economy. If we bear this in mind, it is hardly surprising that ancient China set the stage for the first modern states, the bureaucratic and military capacities of which far surpassed anything we know from Europe in the Middle Ages. Nor is it surprising that the continual competition led to the granting of rights, including a certain amount of freedom of expression, which was a precondition for the work of the Chinese philosophers.

These rights were rescinded after the first Qin emperor (in the year 221 BC) and the first Han emperor (in the year 206 BC) had unified China. China never experienced another philosophical golden age and eventually also fell behind Europe militarily and economically, although this history brings us two thousand years further ahead (see Chapters 11 and 12). The Europe-China comparison is instructive, as it indicates that the European path towards the modern state, modern democracy, and the modern market economy was more coincidental than suggested in this book thus far. In other words, using China to create a 'counterfactual Europe' (Hui 2004, 194) is both provocative and a bit of an eye-opener.

Where does this leave us? Competition between independent entities would appear to be a historical prerequisite for political and economic dynamism. But we have also seen that there is a caveat. In her otherwise formidable analysis of China in the Warring States Period, Hui overlooks some important contextual features of Europe. The absence of these contextual features clearly did not prevent the emergence of a modern state in Warring States China. However, it is plausible that their absence helped prevent the development of the rule of law and political constitutionalism – both of which came about in Europe prior to the rise of the modern state. As Vu (2010, 164) points out and as already touched on above, it is telling that Western and Central European countries developed representative institutions *before* the modern state began to form in earnest in the sixteenth century. Part V further addresses this development.

Notes

1 Hui expressly uses the term 'totalitarism'. Most would argue that this is 'stretching' the concept, as actual totalitarism requires a modern state and economy.
2 Note that Hui here appears to draw specifically on the logic of control, which she has otherwise declared irrelevant in large-scale historical comparisons between China and Europe (see also Møller 2015a).
3 In other words, Hui argues that representative institutions are epiphenomenal.

15

WAR AND STATE FORMATION IN LATIN AMERICA AND SUB-SAHARAN AFRICA

Readers of this book are by now painfully aware that the story about the advent of the modern Weberian state is by and large a story about Europe. This one-sided focus on a particular region – Centeno (2003, 275) talks about 'empirical Euro-centrism'[1] – is one reason the nexus between war and state formation figures so prominently in the literature. As has been argued *ad nauseam*, from the High Middle Ages onwards, Europe constituted an international system in which the threat of war was ubiquitous and state-builders had to strengthen the centre to survive the ruthless competition. Just think of the misfortune of Poland, not to mention formerly sovereign states such as Burgundy, Naples, Bavaria, and Saxony, which all disappeared in the maelstrom of war.

In many other places, the situation looks nothing like this – especially not since the end of World War II. That is the starting point for a recent body of literature that analyses state formation processes in Latin America, Africa, and Asia before and after decolonization. There is consensus in this literature that geopolitical pressure has not been nearly as important as in Europe. Conditions for state-building have therefore been very different – and so have the outcomes of state-building processes. Above all, many states outside of Europe and the European settler colonies are ineffective, plagued by corruption, transgressions of rights, and the absence of basic public services; indeed, some of them belong in the category of failed states. The only major exception is East Asia, where first Japan and later also South Korea, Taiwan, and China have developed powerful states, and Southeast Asia, where countries such as Singapore, Malaysia, Thailand, and – to a lesser extent – Indonesia have fared well on these parameters. However, there are scattered individual success stories across South America and Africa, including countries such as Botswana, Chile, and Uruguay, all of which developed relatively effective states while they were still poor. With these observations in mind, the literature examined in this chapter has two aims:

*   to understand the consequences of the fact that state-builders outside of Europe have navigated under conditions in which the threat of war has been rather limited.
*   to explain why effective state apparatuses have nevertheless been established in some countries.

The chapter addresses two works in particular: Jeffrey Herbst's (2000) *States and Power in Africa* and Miguel Centeno's (2003) *Blood and Debt* – spiced with a few references to the work of other researchers. These two works examine state formation processes outside of Europe through a dialogue with the established literature on Europe (see also Kurtz 2013). The purpose of this chapter is similar – that is, to identify how the state formation processes in Latin America and Africa differ from the earlier processes in Europe discussed in this book. This can be understood as an implicit use of logic of comparative control. More technically, the chapter compares Europe with Sub-Saharan Africa and Latin America, respectively. The point is that an integrated multistate system and the geopolitical competition that accompanies it cannot be found outside of Europe and that the effects – primarily effective state formation – are therefore also absent.

The East Asian exception

Before we delve into these two regions, a few words on East Asia, a part of the world that is otherwise not covered in this chapter. As mentioned above, this region distinguishes itself from Latin America and – even more – Sub-Saharan Africa by the many examples of effective state-building in the twentieth and twenty-first centuries. A series of deep historical causes has contributed to East Asia finding itself in another category than the rest of the former Third World. In Chapter 14, we saw how a harbinger of the modern state first saw the light of day in this area, specifically in China in the Warring States Period. Similarly, in Chapter 11 we learned that, until around 1800, East Asia was one of the most prosperous and urbanized areas of the world. Finally, East Asia took part in the Eurasian development, which, according to geographer Jared Diamond (1999[1997]), explains why this huge area, spanning the distance from Ireland in the West to Japan in the East, was historically most advanced. It seems plausible that these 'deep' developments have been conducive to the grand modernization project in East Asia in recent generations.

However, East Asia is also the major exception in the period after 1945 in one other respect: it has featured a generalized geopolitical pressure on state-builders. Several scholars have argued that some of the European war and state formation mechanisms have operated in this setting, and that they thereby shed light on, for example, the spectacular development of effective state apparatuses in South Korea and Taiwan. Doner et al. (2005) thus associate the merits of the East Asian Tigers with their exposed geographical position. Wedged between the United States / Japan on one side and China on the other, they were forced to enlist their own citizens in a grand state-building project. Without a steady flow of tax revenue, they were unable to maintain a credible defence. In return, an effective and incorrupt state apparatus was established and maintained, which in turn paved the way for the respective economic miracles.

If this is true, then the East Asian Tigers are an example of how the historical link between geopolitical pressure and state development and political development, respectively – as we know it from Europe and partly also from ancient China – continue to operate in the contemporary world. The question then becomes whether the Tigers are an exception or whether these mechanisms have also manifested themselves in other regions in our time?

Sub-Saharan Africa

Jeffrey Herbst's (2000) response to this question is a resounding 'no', at least in relation to Sub-Saharan Africa.[2] Herbst begins with an often-heard observation: most African states are unable to complete even basic tasks, such as enforcing laws, building roads and other infrastructure, and giving the population access to education. Instead, the state apparatuses are riddled with corruption and nepotism, and most of the limited services they deliver go to insiders, particularly in the national capitals. Indeed, the state is often completely absent in the rural areas (see also Bratton and Van de Walle 1997). The other side of the coin is that many African states are unable to tax their residents systematically and are instead forced to finance their activities via indirect taxes on trade and via development aid, coupled with income from natural resources such as oil and diamonds.

The genesis of the modern African states

Herbst links this disheartening development to basic structural conditions that distinguish Africa from Europe. First and most important is population density – or rather lack thereof (11). Compared with, e.g., Western Europe, population density in Africa has always been very low. As recently as one hundred years ago, there were virtually no cities of significance south of the Sahara and hardly anything that deserves to be called roads. Rural areas were not valuable possessions – it was not worthwhile defending them systematically – because the spread of intensive agriculture was limited and because goods were difficult to trade (35–38).

This does not equate an absence of war, but it means that war was aimed at capturing people rather than conquering territory – as had also been the objective of many wars in medieval Europe (Bartlett 1993). The main aim of African war was to capture slaves who could either be sold to Europeans or Muslims or used to sweeten one's own life. A secondary goal was to make tribes outside of one's area pay tribute, preferably in the form of slaves. In Herbst's words, power in Africa was 'non-territorial' (2000, 35); African 'states' assumed the form of concentric circles in which the powers-that-be only exercised direct control over the centre itself. The consequent states can hardly even be said to live up to the minimalist definition introduced in Chapter 1, as they did not actually have priority over other forms of organization within a demarcated territory. Herbst makes the interesting observation that African authorities rarely tried to draw maps of their areas – a striking illustration of their indifference towards territory.

This was the situation that met the European colonial powers after the beginning of the great voyages. For the same reasons, the Europeans were long reluctant to become engaged in Africa. The Portuguese already sailed along the African coast in the fifteenth century, but in the following centuries the Europeans merely established maritime strongholds along the coast from which they could purchase slaves and precious goods such as metals and ivory (hence, the 'Ivory Coast' and the former 'Gold Coast', now Ghana). As recently as 1885, Africa was therefore left to the Africans, with the important exception that the European triangular trade reinforced the tendency of African authorities to capture slaves (to sell to the Europeans) instead of consolidating territory. In fact, most European decision-makers agreed that Africa simply was not worth the bother, partly because the inland areas did not represent any particular value.

However, this suddenly changed with the so-called *Scramble for Africa*. Towards the end of the nineteenth century, Africa was one of the few places where it was still easy to establish colonies, and the Germans and Belgians entered the fray at this time. Meanwhile, established colonial powers such as France and the United Kingdom began vying for East Africa. An enabling factor was the development of modern malaria medicine (64–65). Traditionally, as described in Chapter 13, African areas plagued by malaria and yellow fever had been regarded as the 'white man's coffin'. The high mortality rates among Europeans explain why only what is now South Africa, which had a healthier climate, had at this time been settled by considerable numbers of Europeans. But in the nineteenth century, modern medicine permitted a European presence in the areas around the equator.

However, the Europeans were not inclined to fight over African colonies. At the Berlin Conference in 1884/1885, they drew lines on the map on the basis of a few simple principles, the most important being that a colonial power had the right to the inland area behind the outposts that had been established in the coastal areas. The European colonial powers were not interested in going to war against one another over rather worthless African territory, and peaceful co-existence was therefore secured through treaties and agreements. In 1898, things almost went wrong at Fashoda, when British and French soldiers suddenly found themselves at gun point. But conflict was avoided, and the result of what Herbst refers to as the Berlin Principle was that the French, British, Portuguese, Belgians, and Germans were able to conquer very large areas without having to make major efforts to control them.

It is often argued that European colonization radically transformed Africa, but, according to Herbst, this is incorrect. For the Europeans confronted the very same problems as the African state-builders prior to European colonization, namely that territory was not particularly valuable and that it was difficult to control. Due to the Berlin Principle, which reduced the risk of war, the Europeans were not forced to invest in physical or administrative infrastructure. They could concentrate on establishing a capital where they were genuinely present, while the rural areas were often ruled indirectly through cooperation with tribal chiefs (83). Very small groups of Europeans therefore 'ruled' or at least 'managed' enormous areas with millions of Africans. On this point, the European colonies point towards the limited range of the state apparatus in current African countries (95).

Only in one respect did the Europeans genuinely turn the African reality on its head: they established territorial borders between their colonies. While these lines were drawn on a map in Berlin without much consideration to geographical or ethnic realities, the concerted efforts of the great powers rendered these artificial limits real in the sense that no military power was ready to violate them. This brings us to the second crucial difference between African and European conditions. The vast majority of the borders established by the Europeans proved durable, and the authorities in the individual capitals did not have to worry about neighbouring countries attempting to make inroads into their territory. Such was the situation for the European colonial powers, and such has the situation been since the decolonization in the 1960s and 1970s. The African independence movements took over the states and the state apparatuses that the Europeans had established. Few borders have been altered since independence – the establishment of Eritrea in 1993 and South Sudan in 2011 are the only really good examples – and wars between states have been few and far between and have generally concerned political influence more than the re-drawing of borders.

The realist notion of an anarchic international system simply has little traction in Africa (100–105). On the contrary, the situation has been one of international harmony, which in many African states goes hand-in-hand with internal disharmony (109–110). Herbst links these two circumstances. The easy external sovereignty has made it possible to make do with a low degree of internal sovereignty. In Africa, one who controls the national capital is recognized as the leader of the country by the outside world – no matter how limited this person's control is in the countryside (110–111). In a nutshell, the external protection of the state system has enabled weak states and weak regimes to survive – and rulers to cater to their personal interests instead of economic growth and citizens' rights. The situation has been the exact opposite of what we know from the European past, where such states would have been swallowed up by stronger neighbours (113). Without its *raison d'être* – to protect the population against external enemies – the African states have struggled to be recognized internally. The lack of external pressure has undermined two of the most basic functions of the modern state: to create legitimacy among the population and to collect taxes.

The consequences for state capacity in our time

Herbst devotes a number of chapters to the hangovers that this cocktail has given Africans. A telling illustration is found in what Schumpeter describes as the very core of the state (see Chapter 5): the ability to tax its citizens. Ever since decolonization, most African states have been unable to tax their citizens directly. Instead, they have relied on indirect taxes on trade and foodstuffs and external sources such as development aid (116–124).

One major reason for the absence of direct taxation is that the legitimacy of African states has been so limited. After decolonization, the new leaders attempted to create a sense of nationalism based on independence from European colonial powers. However, as soon as the external threat from the Europeans disappeared, it became difficult to maintain this source of legitimacy (116–130). Furthermore, the absence of an external threat has meant that the African authorities have rarely needed to engage in bargaining with their citizens. They have been free to use state revenue on unproductive ventures, including grandiose but economically hopeless prestige projects and bribing important groups. The international system has basically prompted a political order based on cronyism and corruption. The result has been that – just as during the European colonization – the African states have assumed the form of concentric circles. The state has only really been present in the capital – which has also received the public services that are left after the corrupt politicians and bureaucrats have taken their cut – while the rural areas and smaller urban centres have generally been left to fend for themselves (131–135).

There is little to envy here, but it is important not to lump all African countries together. This brings us to the variation in state capacity that we find in Africa. Herbst here returns to his starting point, namely that geography in itself contributes to the creation of a power vacuum in the African states. He points out that there are major differences in terms of how hard the African states are hit on this point. The situation is worst for countries with 'difficult political geography' – that is, large countries with population centres separated by great distances. At the opposite end of the spectrum we find countries with 'favourable geography' – i.e., countries of a manageable size with a single population centre, normally around the capital. Countries such as the Sudan, Nigeria, and the Democratic Republic of Congo (formerly Zaire) belong in the former category, while countries such as Botswana and Eritrea are in the latter. Herbst also operates with two other categories. One is so-called hinterland countries, which are large, just like the countries in the unfavourable category, but where half or more of the country consists of virtually uninhabitable lands that the state-builders are free to ignore. This category includes countries with large desert areas, such as Chad and Mauritania. Finally, there are countries with a neutral geography which have several different centres but with surmountable distances between them (see Table 15.1).

Herbst shows that these distinctions account for much of the variation in African state-building. For example, countries with favourable geography have been

TABLE 15.1 Herbst's classification of African states, based on their geography

Difficult geography	Hinterland countries	Neutral geography	Favourable geography
Angola,	Chad	Cameroon	Benin
Democratic Republic	Mali	Ghana	Botswana
Congo	Mauritania	Ivory Coast	Burkina Faso
Ethiopia	Niger	Kenya	Burundi
Mozambique		Malawi	Central African
Namibia		Uganda	Republic
Nigeria		Zambia	Congo-Brazzaville
Senegal			Equatorial Guinea
Somalia			Eritrea
Sudan			Gabon
Tanzania			Gambia
			Guinea
			Guinea Bissau
			Lesotho
			Liberia
			Rwanda
			Sierra Leone
			Swaziland
			Togo
			Zimbabwe

Note: Edited version of Herbst (2000, 161).

better at building networks of roads even though they are actually the countries that depend the least on investments in infrastructure (166). Herbst also reveals that much of the variation can be traced back to the colonial period. In other words, states with favourable geography had an initial advantage (167), and they have generally capitalized on that advantage. Herbst demonstrates that, on average, states with favourable geography have better citizenship policies and have been better at establishing effective property rights over land.

The former accomplishment is particularly important. As in Europe, citizenship policy in the African states rests either on *jus soli* or *jus sanguinis* – that is, where one is born (*soli*, 'soil') – or on ancestry (*sanguinis*, 'blood'). Herbst argues rather convincingly that *jus soli* offers great advantages for state legitimacy, as citizenship is one of the few things that African states have to offer population groups outside the capital. This is extra important in countries with unfavourable geography, where the power of the capital has a limited reach and where salient ethnic cleavages exist. This makes it that much more paradoxical that states with unfavourable geography overwhelmingly tend towards the *jus sanguinis* principle (239–243). This principle has contributed to civil wars in countries such as the Democratic Republic of Congo, where the large Tutsi population in the eastern part of the country has had difficulty obtaining citizen status.

Once again, geography accounts for the general differences, although the choices made by state-builders explain why we also find variation within the individual categories. One of the absolute stars in the African context, Botswana, has thus distanced itself from the other countries in the favourable category – and not all of the countries with an unfavourable geography have managed as poorly as the Democratic Republic of Congo or Sudan.

Herbst ends his book by calling for alternatives to the contemporary African states. He encourages the international community to acknowledge that many of the African states are empty shells – fictive entities created in Berlin almost 150 years ago – which will never become efficient. Against that background, he suggests a number of measures, some of which are rather straightforward, such as channelling development aid down to the regional level instead of allowing it to go via the central level. Others are far more radical, including dividing states with unfavourable geography into more manageable parts or even thinking in alternatives to the nation–state with respect to Sub-Saharan Africa (see also Krasner 2005).

Latin America

Miguel Centeno's book *Blood and Debt* (2003) is of the same ilk as Herbst's (2000). It focuses on Latin America, but Centeno also analyses a non-European continent through a dialogue with the European war-makes-states literature. In fact, his starting point is very similar to Herbst's. Compared to Western Europe and the British settler colonies in, for example, North America, Latin America is characterized by states that have never really won institutional autonomy for themselves, suffer low legitimacy among the citizenry, and have a limited institutional capacity. This even holds when we take the level of development into account: the Latin American states are less effective than state apparatuses in countries at comparable levels of wealth. The manifestation of this is states that are incapable of providing basic services such as health care and education, have never fostered a sense of national togetherness or managed to regulate the economy (with high inflation and massive public deficits as a result), and in many places are unable to maintain law and order (3–6). The situation might not be as bad as in Sub-Saharan Africa, but it is bad enough – for millions and millions of Spanish- and Portuguese-speaking men and women south of the Rio Grande.[3]

However, these millions of people have been more fortunate than Western Europeans in at least one respect. Latin America has been a remarkably peaceful place with respect to inter-state relations. While there were a number of wars in the decades after independence from Spain in the beginning of the nineteenth century, conflicts have generally been brief, involved limited numbers of troops, and at most caused minor changes to national borders. And the twentieth century was practically one long period of peace. It is telling that the borders of 1840 roughly correspond to the borders of today (9).

Two questions must be answered. Why have the Latin American countries been so weak? And why has Latin America largely been spared from war? Centeno, like Herbst, finds the answer by coupling the two queries. The Latin American states have been too weak to wage war and therefore also too weak to maintain law and order. To make matters worse, the military has often been more occupied with fighting domestic than foreign enemies – which is reflected in civil wars being more common than inter-state wars (66–84). This is rather similar to Herbst's story, but Centeno draws a slightly different conclusion. In his view, the development of Latin America since the beginning of the nineteenth century illustrates that the relationship between war and state formation in Europe – Centeno calls this literature the 'bellic' theory – is not universal. According to Centeno, it rests on specific conditions that we can identify by holding Latin America up as a mirror (18, 165). This mirror reveals above all else that the form of warfare and the social context in which it takes place determine its impact – at least on the character of the state.

Centeno maps the character and the frequency of wars in Latin America, and he analyses the consequences of warfare for the development of the state apparatus, national sentiment, and citizenship rights. He draws on data sources that are meaningful to measure in (most of) the Latin American states, including articles in military journals, national monuments, and symbols on currencies and stamps. Centeno uses these data to address the war-makes-states relationship.

His analysis reveals that, over the last two hundred years, Latin America has generally seen only *limited* wars – as opposed to the *total* wars in Europe in the first half of the twentieth century and the American Civil War in the 1860s (35–43). The sole exception is the War of the Triple Alliance (1864–1870), where a thoroughly mobilized Paraguay lost more than half of its population in a war of attrition in which the regional great powers, Argentina and Brazil, fought the small landlocked country.[4] Virtually all other military disputes have been of limited scale, normally of short duration, and often decided after the first couple of battles. Most of these conflicts are concentrated in specific periods in the nineteenth century. Regardless of how we measure, the South Americans have largely been spared the scourge of war.

This development is reflected in the core indicator of the bellic theory: taxation (see Chapters 5 and 9). The Latin American wars have not fostered a broader and/ or more efficient taxation of the population. Instead, the wars of the nineteenth century were financed by printing money (an inflation tax), via taxes on international trade, and by borrowing, particularly in Europe (116–135), none of which stimulated the construction of a powerful administrative apparatus. According to Centeno, this shows that war sparks taxation only under certain conditions, notably strong political institutions, which again can be realized only if the elites agree on boosting the capacity of the state (106–107). Centeno notes that this combination first occurred in Europe after the military revolution around 1600. In Latin America, these conditions did not exist in the nineteenth century. The first real states emerged later, particularly in the southern half of the continent (Chile, Argentina, Uruguay, and Brazil), and their creation largely coincides with the beginning of the sustained period of peace in the twentieth century. Warfare therefore did not contribute to strengthening these states, which – with Chile and Uruguay as partial exceptions – never attained the capacity and efficiency we know from the Western world.

Why were the Latin American countries not geared to state-building as a result of the warfare that did take place in the nineteenth century? Above all else because they were internally divided and both elites and masses therefore unable to find common ground. Centeno lists a number of factors, such as regionalism (the capital cities often had limited control over the rest of the country, which was ruled by self-appointed *caudillos*), racial segregation between the white upper class and the Indian or Afro-American lower classes, and finally disputes between elites – for example, conflicts between conservative and liberal groups (141–159). These cleavages reflect how the Latin American states won their independence from Spain – as well as the fact that they were planted in the midst of large territories that were difficult to manage. The resulting social conflict prevented war from creating states. For example, the elite were able to avoid taxation and feared the underclass more than they feared foreign powers.

Nor has war contributed to national sentiment in Latin America – with some partial exceptions, which we will return to below. Internal divisions once more stood in the way. The elites have not been interested in creating a sense of inclusive nationalism, which would grant the indigenous underclass citizenship rights on a par with the whites. Moreover, we find little evidence of hostility between the peoples of Latin America (170). With the exception of Portuguese-speaking Brazil, the elites on the continent were characterized by considerable homogeneity upon winning independence from Spain. Coupled with the absence of a strong identity as Argentinian, Peruvian, or Columbian, it is unsurprising that national unity has not been established (173). As far as national monuments, street names, and symbols on currency and stamps, the same heroes are celebrated across the continent (most importantly the heroes of Latin American independence, such as Simón Bolívar).

The absence of hostile imagery and the presence of internal divisions have also prevented wars from expanding citizenship rights. In Europe, conscription played a role in fostering such rights, as the sons of peasants who were called up left the military as citizens. Having a duty to give one's life to the state has tended to increase self-esteem and self-awareness, and the military often trained and educated its recruits. The limited wars in Latin America did not require universal conscription, and the military therefore – with Argentina as a partial exception – never contributed to integrating the lower classes (237–238). Moreover, the lengthy Latin American peace in the twentieth century rendered it difficult to justify conscription, which the elites in any case had no interest in maintaining.

Centeno's story is not quite as simple as I have made it out to be above. Certain Latin American states have actually become relatively efficient and have been relatively successful at fostering national unity – and war has stimulated both in some places. Centeno's most curious example is Paraguay, which developed a despotic state in the nineteenth century that was able to mobilize the entire society for warfare. As referred to above, the War of the Triple Alliance laid much of the country to waste, but the sense of nationhood shared by the elites and masses persisted, and Paraguay emerged victorious from one of the few other serious wars in Latin America, the so-called Chaco War against Bolivia in 1932–1935. The most obvious exception to the rule, however, is Chile. Not only did this peripheral state along the Pacific coast develop an efficient state very early, it also established a basic consensus between the elites and the masses. Crucially, war facilitated both. The Chilean exceptionalism can be traced all the way back to independence. The second major national hero of Latin American independence, José de San Martin, liberated the area and installed state structures, and a series of subsequent wars with Peru and Bolivia further boosted the Chilean state apparatus and its legitimacy in the population. It also gave Chile, which emerged victorious from these conflicts, important territorial gains. Argentina, Brazil, Uruguay, and Mexico have similarly undergone periods in which warfare has had favourable effects on state-building and helped foster a sense of national unity, albeit without this elevating them into the Chilean category.

These exceptions are obviously important, but they do not alter the general diagnosis. The conclusion of *Blood and Debt* is that the inter-state peace of Latin America has created weak states that have been unable to protect their own citizens internally. The military has focused on fighting internal enemies as social cleavages have crippled state-building throughout the continent. Centeno therefore concludes that the European development, where warfare and state formation were mutually reinforcing, is the exception rather than the rule. The established literature has been blinded by the aforementioned empirical Eurocentrism – a blindfold that the study of Latin America removes.

More precisely, *Blood and Debt* shows that the war-makes-states relationship is based on a number of scope conditions, including the following: that an administrative core exists before the geopolitical pressure intensifies; that at least part of the ruling elite sees the development of the state capacity as being in their interest; and that there is general agreement as to who is included in the nation (275–276). For Latin America, the European analogy is not monist Prussia but rather fragmented Austria-Hungary, where war exposed the frailty of the regime and the absence of a common sense of nationhood (116). Another interpretation of Centeno's work is that wars must be frequent and concentrated (and occur at the right time) to lead to state formation. The study of Latin America shows that path dependency and sequences or timing are crucial for understanding the consequences of war (278–279).

According to Centeno, *Blood and Debt* is a book about the costs of peace (17). He points out that the disheartening corollary of his findings might well be that we have either strong states that fight each other but run a tight ship internally (Europe) or weak states that are peaceful externally but create internal misrule (Latin America) (264) – the classic choice between a rock and a hard place.

Criticism

Herbst's (2000) and Centeno's (2003) works shed light on the on-going state-building processes in Africa and Latin America, respectively. They do so with the existing literature on Europe as their frame of reference. *States and Power in Africa* and *Blood and Debt* show that states have been forged and reshaped differently in Africa and Latin America than in Europe. In both books, the character of the international system is presented as the underlying cause. In contrast to the situation in Europe, the African and Latin American systems have not been characterized by general and sustained geopolitical competition, meaning that the authorities have not been incentivized to create efficient states. In that sense, peace has come at great cost.

The two books clearly contribute to our knowledge about state-building processes. Nonetheless, they are not without blemish. If we refer back to the distinction made in this book between the state and the regime form, it is difficult to pothole Herbst. He indicates that his book is about states and state formation in Sub-Saharan Africa. But in that case, 'state' is to be understood quite broadly as Herbst incorporates elements of the regime form in his analysis, including the ability of the population to hold the authorities accountable.

Next, Herbst's otherwise thought-provoking assertion that European colonization – aside from establishing permanent borders – did not radically transform the African states and societies is somewhat problematic. As Robinson (2002, 515–516) notes in a review of the book, it is rather artificial to only consider the actual European colonization after 1885. Herbst himself mentions that the Europeans had an impact on the African states for centuries before the *Scramble for Africa*, particularly due to the demand for slaves. Numerous researchers regard this as extremely important for explaining the character of the African political institutions and state apparatuses that developed after the encounter with the Europeans in the fifteenth century. The triangular trade contributed to establishing what Acemoglu and Robinson (2012) call *extractive institutions*, as these institutions provided opportunities to capture and sell slaves (see Chapter 13). At the same time, the slave trade had a direct impact on population density, which is the most important variable in Herbst's analysis. No fewer than ten million Africans were shipped out of Africa as part of the triangular trade – a population drain that helps explain why the Europeans took over states with a low population density after 1885 (see Robinson 2002, 515–516).

Centeno's (2003) splendid book also has some weak points. He deliberately situates *Blood and Debt* in the Weberian tradition, where general theory is used to explain while the particularities of the individual cases are identified (19). For this very reason Centeno never attempts to present a general model explaining the variation he identifies in Latin America. As mentioned above, Centeno shows that war has had beneficial effects in a number of instances. Likewise, he emphasizes that the states in the southern cone of the continent (Chile, Argentina, Uruguay, and Brazil) are more efficient than those in the northern half of the continent. As Domínguez (2003, 510) points out in a review of *Blood and Debt*, almost half of Centeno's cases are thus in the 'exception' category, at least for certain periods. Centeno makes some interesting observations about these exceptions in general and about Chile in particular, but he never presents a more systematic explanation for why some Latin American states are more efficient than others.

This problem might stem from Centeno analysing Latin America through a dialogue with the literature on Europe. At times, it seems somewhat odd to use so much ammunition – if the reader will pardon the metaphor – on analysing the effects of war on a continent with so little of it. It follows that a systematic explanation of the Latin American variation probably has to take into account factors that are at most indirectly associated with geopolitical competition. Kurtz (2013) has recently made attempts at just such an internal analysis – in his own words, social dynamics rather than international dynamics – and in doing so he criticizes Centeno (2003) for having eyes only for the geopolitical dimension.

A panoramic view

This chapter has addressed state-building processes outside of Europe by delving into the work of Herbst (2000) on Africa and Centeno (2003) on Latin America. It makes sense to conclude the chapter by applying a more general perspective. In a review article, Tuong Vu (2010) has attempted to summarize recent decades' efforts to analyse state formation processes outside of Europe. Like Herbst (2000) and Centeno (2003), Vu's frame of reference is the established literature on Europe (2010, 151–154). More specifically, he emphasizes two of the ground-breaking findings of this literature: the claim that the modern, centralized state, with its formidable bureaucracy, is a consequence of warfare and preparation for war (see in particular Chapters 5 and 9) and, further along these lines, that this battle for survival over time forced the European monarchs to negotiate with their citizens. This initially led the monarchs to grant the economic elite political representation and civil rights. When mass armies later became necessary (and with them conscription), this bargain was extended to ordinary people – and this *quid pro quo* ostensibly sowed the seeds for modern democracy.

What do recent decades' analyses of non-European countries tell us about the generalizability of these two relationships? So sounds Tuong Vu's ambitious question. To answer it, he takes stock of a number of large-scale analyses of state formation in Latin America, Africa, and Asia – with detours to the recent literature on Europe.

As regards the emergence of the centralized state, Vu makes two general conclusions, which will be unsurprising after examining the work of Herbst and Centeno. First, there are many places where warfare has not led to bureaucratization and centralization. Second, there would appear to be alternative routes to this destination – routes that do not involve generalized geopolitical pressure. In South America, wars have been few and far between, too short and limited to consolidate the state. And in parts of East Asia, it seems that it has been the strategic choices of the elites – more than pressure from external enemies – that have resulted in centralized and efficient bureaucracies (158). The Asian Tigers, which since the 1950s have taken the path from a level of prosperity reminiscent of African developing countries to something resembling European conditions, are a good example of the importance of the elites in society.

Vu points out that a variant of this point is also relevant in parts of Western Europe. The Netherlands were thus able to construct one of the most well-oiled war machines and one of the strongest economies on the continent in the seventeenth century without any strong central state – simply because the Protestant merchants developed an effective 'private' network that served as a functional equivalent (155–156). This issue will be pursued further in Chapter 16.

Conclusions

The state formation literature has traditionally revolved around European developments. The first attempts to look beyond this context were burdened by this legacy. In his book, Herbst mentions how much of the political science research on African state-building processes has struggled to study Africa on its own terms. Above all, scholars have tended to overestimate the African states' ability to regulate and manage society because they have taken European states as the implicit or explicit baseline.

Only in recent decades have researchers really managed to apply a more unbiased perspective on areas of the world such as Africa. The classic war-makes-states relationship rests on specific conditions that existed in Europe after the military revolutions of the sixteenth century but which have not applied in most other regions of the world in recent centuries. In areas in which a single power prevailed or where the warring parties were too weak for large-scale wars of conquest, the classic relationship between war and state formation simply has little traction.

If we shift our focus to the consequences of geopolitical dynamics, the simple message is that the mechanisms we know from Europe have not (or only to a limited extent) recurred outside of Western Europe and the British settler colonies. That might sound like bad news as a modern state and liberal democracy are something people everywhere yearn for (Chu et al. 2008). But there is another side of the coin. Since World War II, the global community has largely removed the threat of war between states. Some scholars have pointed out that the global community is thereby undermining the survival mechanisms that led to the rule of law and democracy in Europe – principally by eliminating the need for bargaining between the authorities and subjects. I already referred to this point in the introduction. Here we can make an important point: if the literature reviewed in this chapter is to be believed, these mechanisms are not to be expected outside of Europe. Should that be the case, it is an unmitigated good that the global community has restrained the international anarchy of the past.

Notes

1   Centeno uses the adjective 'empirical' to distinguish his observation from the accusation of normative Eurocentrism that we met in Chapter 11. Centeno's point is solely that the literature has primarily dealt with Europe and that the most prominent contexts outside of Europe have therefore been ignored.

2 In his book, Herbst (2000, 5) covers all Sub-Saharan African countries, with the exception of island states such as Cape Verde. I follow Herbst in simply using 'Africa' when referring to this area.
3 Centeno analyses all formerly Iberian colonies in South America and also includes Mexico, but he does not include the other Central American countries (1).
4 According to some – probably exaggerated – accounts, a mere twenty-eight thousand Paraguayan men survived the war. In any case, for a few generations after 1870 the gender balance was skewed in this small country.

16

NEO-WEBERIAN PERSPECTIVES ON STATE FORMATION AND REGIME CHANGE

Earlier in this book, I argued that both the Barrington Moore research agenda and the more recent contributions to the literature discussed in the previous chapters are inspired by Max Weber's pioneering work. It is all the more remarkable that Weber's most significant contribution, his sociology of religion, has played such a modest role in post-1945 research on state formation, regime change, and economic development, at least within comparative historical analysis. The 'Weberist' insight about the political and economic significance of ideas has largely been ignored in the comparative historical analyses covered in Parts III and IV of this book. The literature instead emphasizes material factors, particularly war and class struggle. Above all, it is striking that Weber's notion that Protestantism was the sledgehammer of modernity has not really been picked up by most of the literature that has followed in the German sociologist's footprints.

This would appear to be about to change (see also Capoccia and Ziblatt 2010). This chapter addresses two recent attempts to return to Weber's focus on Protestantism: Philip S. Gorski's (2003) *The Disciplinary Revolution* and Robert D. Woodberry's 'The Missionary Roots of Liberal Democracy' (2012). Gorski and Woodberry are both American sociologists. They deliberately revisit Weber, but they also go beyond his classic work by focusing on other dependent variables. Where Weber first and foremost links Protestantism (or, more specifically, Calvinism) to the emergence of modern capitalism, Gorski links it to state formation, and Woodberry to democracy and democratization.

Gorski: Calvinism, social discipline, and state formation

Gorski starts out with the following observation: the Reformation paved the way for large-scale social discipline in the sixteenth and seventeenth centuries. This social disciplining increased the power of the emerging state apparatuses throughout

Western and Central Europe, but these developments were much more intense in areas marked by Calvinism. These states (England, the Netherlands, and Prussia are the best examples) therefore reaped more benefits from social discipline than both Lutheran and Roman Catholic states. Like Weber, Gorski thus focuses squarely on the peculiar significance of Calvinism. In fact, *The Disciplinary Revolution* can be seen as an attempt to combine Weber's focus on the Calvinist secular ethic with French philosopher Michel Foucault's notion of disciplining through the systematic observation of behaviour (x).

The result is a ground-breaking work consisting of three parts. In the first, Gorski situates his argument within the literature, in the second he analyses the relationship between disciplining and state formation in the Netherlands and Prussia, and, in the third and concluding part, he makes a panoramic comparison of the intensity of religious discipline in Calvinist, Lutheran, and Catholic parts of Europe.

Gorski sets the stage by pointing out that most of the literature on state-building has focused on two 'revolutions': the military revolution of the sixteenth century and the bourgeois revolutions of the seventeenth and eighteenth centuries. This neglects a third revolution, namely the disciplinary revolution triggered by the Reformation.

Gorski sweepingly declares that discipline meant just as much for the modern state as the steam engine meant for the Industrial Revolution (xvi). But in order to understand the impact of discipline, it is necessary to do away with the top-down study of state formation. Disciplining largely seems to have come from below, bottom-up, via the work of church leaders in local communities. According to Gorski, this explains why some of the least centralized states of the sixteenth century – England, the Netherlands, and Prussia – would prove to be the most powerful in the centuries to follow (xvii).

Gorski touches upon a number of the works that we have covered in Parts III and IV. He criticizes the analyses carried out by Wallerstein, Downing, and Ertman for suffering from one and the same problem: they are unable to explain the cases that are actually the most important for their theories (10–13), precisely because they have neglected the significance of religious conflicts (15). This is where Gorski proposes his Weber-Foucault synthesis. Weber was actually incredibly close to linking Calvinism to state formation, but, according to Gorski, Weber's bellic focus on war and state formation (see Chapters 4, 5, 9, 14, and 15) prevented him from going all the way (26–28). Gorski finds the pieces missing from Weber's puzzle in Foucault's theory about the 'micro-political' effects of the systematic observation of behaviour (28).

The Weber-Foucault synthesis points towards two ways in which Calvinism could create a sense of discipline that promoted state capacity: first, a disciplinary revolution from below, which strengthened the societal infrastructure, thereby making it easier for the state to regulate society; and, second, a disciplinary revolution from above that rendered the state apparatus more autonomous, thereby enabling it to carry out reforms at the expense of elite interests.

Netherlands and Prussia

The Netherlands and Prussia illustrate these two relationships. In both countries, Calvinism contributed to increasing state capacity, but it did so in fundamentally different ways. The Netherlands offers an example of a disciplinary revolution from below, while Prussia is an example of a disciplinary revolution from above. The consequences of these differences are important: where the former revolution increased the capacity of the state to regulate society, the latter first and foremost increased the state's administrative capacity (114, see Table 16.1).

Let us touch on the two countries in turn. Earlier in the book, we have seen how the seventeenth century belonged to the Netherlands. Gorski points out that the Dutch achievements cannot be explained on the basis of the bellic focus on war and state formation. To be sure, the Netherlands developed into a great power militarily, but the Dutch state never centralized and bureaucratized in the way the literature would expect – and would see as a prerequisite for military might. Nor did it need to, Gorski points out, because the Dutch state was strong on the local level. It was better at taxing its citizens than France and England; it was better at maintaining law and order; and it was also less corrupt than other European states.

The fact that the Dutch acted in such an exemplary manner in the absence of a strong central state watching over them was due to Calvinist discipline. In the course of the seventeenth century, Calvinism became the religion of the majority of the Dutch. Gorski documents numerous examples of the systematic disciplining from below that ensued. One of the more curious is the so-called *Tuchthuis*, where lost souls learned to behave properly and to appreciate an honest day's work (63–64). This was a system of observation and sanctions in the best Foucauldian style, orchestrated by the church, not the state. In short, the church community raised its members to value the Protestant ethic, which we have already met in Chapter 4.

Gorski argues that disciplining subsequently spread like rings in the water in Dutch society. For example, he links this disciplining to what is possibly the most important set of reforms in the military revolution: Dutch military commander John Maurice of Nassau's 're-discovery' of the Romans' use of military drill exercises towards the end of the sixteenth century (72–73). The Dutch troops actually behaved in such a disciplined manner that the cities of the Netherlands competed to have garrisons – whereas similar garrisons in, for example, France were used to punish obstinate cities.

TABLE 16.1 Disciplinary revolutions and state formation in the Netherlands and Prussia

		Increase of the ability of the state to	
		Regulate	*Administrate*
Character of disciplinary revolution	Bottom–up	The Netherlands	
	Top–down		Prussia

Source: Based on Gorski (2003).

The history of the surprising Dutch secession from the Spanish Habsburgs during the Eighty Years' War (1568–1648) and the subsequent Dutch Golden Age in the 1600s is the story of a state that grew strong from the bottom up through religious and social discipline. Even though the Dutch political regime and the Dutch state remained fragmented, the public infrastructure was so strong that formidable armies could be raised and financed via efficient tax collection and borrowing at the lowest interest rates in Europe – all within the context of a highly ordered society in which crime, idleness, and corruption were rare phenomena.

Moving on to Prussia, we find a different but equally interesting paradox. Prussia in the seventeenth century was not just one of Europe's backwaters politically and economically; it was also one of the continent's weakest and most fragmented states. This is not the normal image we have of Prussia; we tend to associate it with the state that by the eighteenth century stood as the most centralized and rationalized in Europe (79). In fact, Max Weber's renowned definition of the bureaucratic state, introduced in Chapter 1, builds largely on Prussia. How was it possible to make this transition in the course of a single century?

To a great extent, the Prussian reforms were triggered by geopolitical pressure. However, as in the Dutch case, this pressure does not explain why the Prussian reaction was so much more efficient than those of neighbouring countries (84). According to Gorski, we can solve this paradox only by understanding the unique political rationality of the Prussian Hohenzollerns and the political autonomy that came to characterize the Prussian state (82). Gorski links both to Calvinism. In contrast to the Netherlands, Prussian society never became 'Calvinized' in earnest. It had been placed solidly in the Lutheran fold from early times, and the Prussian nobility were stubborn supporters of Luther's teachings. But Gorski points out that Prussia nevertheless underwent two reformations: first, the Lutheran in the period 1520–50, but then a second, 'Calvinist' reformation, which started with the conversion of the Prussian ruler in 1613 (86).

Although Calvinism remained a minority religion in the vaster part of the Prussian domains, it became the religion of the crown, the court, and, over time, the state apparatus. This created a decisive religious cleavage between the crown and the Lutheran elites in the Estates, and it is precisely this conflict that explains why the Prussian monarchs broke the power of the Estates and created the renowned, autonomous Prussian state. Gorski finds important evidence for this claim in the way the most important Prussian reformer, the Great Elector Frederik William, who ruled from 1640–1688, dealt with the Estates in different parts of the Prussian possessions. After multiple clashes with the Lutheran elites in the Brandenburg and East-Prussian Estates, Frederik William simply stopped calling these institutions and started taxing compulsorily rather than based on consent. What is less well known is that Frederik William at the same time strengthened the Estates in some of his western possessions, including Cleve-Mark in the Rhineland.

The reason was simple. In the western possessions, the elites in the Estates were Calvinist, and they could therefore find a common ground with their Calvinist monarch (90–91). In Prussia proper, the religious conflict between Lutheran elites and a Calvinist monarch rendered a similar accord impossible. Frederik William reacted by 'Calvinizing' his state apparatus, primarily by recruiting Calvinists from abroad, who were looking for a place to practice their religion or merely for career opportunities. In 1650, around 15% of the Prussian civil servants were Calvinists – in 1680 the corresponding figure was almost 80% (89). This new Calvinist elite owed nothing to the Lutheran elites but everything to the Crown. This was the formula that made it possible to create an autonomous state apparatus, which enabled the Prussian monarchs to carry out a disciplinary revolution from above.

It has been said of Prussia that it was an army with a state and not the other way around, and the primary emphasis of the revolution from above was on the military. More specifically, after his accession to the throne in 1713, Prince Frederik William's grandchild and namesake, King Frederik William I, carried out a series of military reforms.[1] Most important was national conscription, and the disciplining of the recruits had an impact on the rest of society (97–98). Frederik William also reformed the state administration so that it came to resemble Weber's meritocratic bureaucracy even more (99–100). These efforts were aided by a specific current within Lutheranism, namely Pietism, which shared a number of features with Calvinism. Frederik William actively encouraged the pietistic influence that, Gorski argues, led to a disciplinary revolution from below similar to what occurred in the Netherlands (105) – albeit a revolution that was less important than the Calvinist revolution from above.

A comparative perspective

In the final chapter, Gorski investigates whether the link between Calvinism, discipline, and state formation in Europe after the Reformation has a broader resonance (114). Here, Gorski displays an ability possessed by few sociologists and political scientists. He is able to absorb – but also nuance and criticize – recent historiography on religion and discipline. In contrast to the state formation literature, historians have not ignored the relationship between religion and discipline. But the predominant perspective among historians emphasizes that such discipline occurred in Calvinist, Lutheran, and, after the Counter-Reformation, Catholic areas alike. Gorski accepts much of this work but convincingly argues that historians have had problems seeing the forest for the trees. The historians' work has primarily taken the form of isolated case studies of circumscribed areas that have made it difficult to compare the degree or intensity of the discipline across the respective confessions. This criticism is similar to Marc Bloch's criticism of monographic studies of representative institutions (see Chapter 5), and Gorski's corrective also resonates with Blochs's advice: instead of examining only the individual cases, we need to analyse distributions to get the full picture (154–155).

Gorski reviews this historiographic literature and concludes that while disciplining did take place in all of Western Christianity after the Reformation, it was most intense in Protestant areas in general and Calvinist areas in particular (114). Just as in his analysis of the Netherlands and Prussia, Gorski shifts back and forth between the societal level and the state apparatus. As regards the former, the book contains a lengthy analysis of alms giving and poverty relief in the three religions (125–137).

With respect to the latter, Gorski focuses on the relationship between religion and patrimonialism versus bureaucracy. He begins with the geographic distinction that Thomas Ertman presented in Chapter 9 (see Table 9.2). Gorski makes the simple observation that almost all of Ertman's cases of bureaucracy are found in Protestant states, while patrimonialism is for the most part found in Catholic states (140–141). This, he argues, is no coincidence. Gorski points out that it was the Roman Church itself that, in connection with the Great Schism (1378–1417), introduced patrimonial techniques such as the sale of offices. These then spread geographically to nearby areas, including France and Spain. This influence could also be felt in Northern Europe, but it was initially weaker, and it was cut short by the Reformation (142–147). Protestant reformers fought against the patrimonial tendencies within the church, and the Protestant churches were therefore organized bureaucratically: the Protestant minister, in Gorski's eyes, was the first modern bureaucrat (148–150). Over the years, these techniques were spread to the state apparatuses in the Protestant states (150–153).

The Disciplinary Revolution ends with a call to integrate the study of religion and the study of state formation. Gorski introduces a number of sweeping claims to the effect that religion has affected regime development, revolutions, nationalism, and the emergence of the welfare state. But these speculations should not overshadow his main message: that the modern states that emerged in Europe did much more than repress and tax – and that only a sense of religious discipline from below can enable us to understand the causes that led to the emergence of the rational-legal state.

Method and criticism

It is somewhat difficult to grasp exactly which methods Gorski uses. There are some clear instances of controlled comparison – for instance, the contrast between the Lutheran-dominated Estates in Brandenburg and East-Prussia and the Calvinist-dominated Estates in Cleve-Mark. However, the analyses of Netherlands and Prussia, respectively, mainly seem to build on a kind of in-depth case study. The validity of these analyses is supported by Gorski's attempt to understand the disagreements in historiography. He refers interchangeably to works in Dutch, German, French, and Italian, and he has conducted his own archival studies in the Netherlands.

More generally, one always has the feeling that the conclusions are underwritten empirically. In Hall's (2004, 573) words, Gorski's analysis is based on a fundamental use of logical thoughts and considerations rather than any specific research techniques. Early in his book, Gorski (2003, x) clarifies that his cases are not countries but rather religions or denominations. However, he concedes (38) that we can also understand the analyses as a series of comparisons between countries. More precisely, the comparison of the Netherlands and Prussia can be viewed as a MDSD, which renders it possible to focus on the effects of Calvinist discipline in very different contexts, while the comparison of Protestant and Catholic areas can be understood as a MSSD, which – within a common European framework – makes it possible to identify the effects of various denominations. Finally, Gorski emphasizes that the logic of comparative control must be taken with a grain of salt, as diffusion and imitation are constantly going on, both within the Calvinist states and across the denominations (38).

This is all rather convincing. Two points of criticism are nevertheless worth emphasizing. The first follows from the somewhat nebulous use of methods. Gorski starts (and finishes) his book with a number of rather categorical claims about the significance of Calvinism for state formation: recall his cheeky declaration that the Calvinist discipline meant just as much for the modern state as the steam engine did for the Industrial Revolution. In the course of the analysis, the reader gets the sense that this was primarily talking cheap, as Gorski keeps back-pedalling. The Calvinist discipline was not the only important factor; precisely how much it contributed in relation to geopolitical pressure is unclear, and the disciplining also occurred in Lutheran and Catholic areas – just to name a few qualifications. The lack of transparency is further increased by Gorski's almost excessively detailed conceptual distinctions: he identifies four types of disciplining (32), two types of disciplinary revolutions (34), four types of state powers (35), and four types of patrimonialism. The reason these fine-grained distinctions have received scarce attention above is that they make it difficult to focus on the main claims. In other words, they make it more difficult to capture the extent of the impact of Calvinism. We do not really know how important the disciplining impact of Calvinism was for state formation, although Gorski establishes that scholars ignore it at their peril.

Next, Gorski's comparative analysis has a surprising blind spot. As far as Calvinism and Pietism are concerned, he confines attention to Great Britain, the Netherlands, Switzerland, and Prussia (and to a lesser extent Sweden). This is a catalogue of the places where efforts to build the state were most effective after the Reformation. However, Gorski ignores that Calvinism also had a great impact in East-Central Europe. More precisely, an aborted or at least arrested Calvinist reformation took place in both Poland and Hungary, something Gorski merely mentions in passing once (159).[2]

As we know from earlier chapters, neither of these countries underwent a systematic bureaucratization and strengthening of state power. Indeed, Poland is the example of patrimonialism and state fragmentation *par excellence*. This is interesting considering that up to 20% of the Poles were at some point in time supporters of Calvin's teachings. And among the political elite – the nobility, *szlachta*, who steered Poland via the *Sejm* – almost half were Calvinists in the sixteenth century, and there were even periods when a majority of the members of parliament were Calvinists. This majority pushed through legislation on religious tolerance in 1573, which attests to the significant influence of Jean Calvin's teachings. More generally, the Calvinist share of the Polish population in general and the Polish nobility in specific is higher than what we find in Lutheran Prussia, for example. The Counter-Reformation reduced the Calvinist influence considerably – and closed most of the space for religious tolerance that had been created. Nevertheless, we have to wonder why Poland, if only temporarily, did not experience some of the processes we find in the Netherlands and Prussia.

In Hungary, a similar reformation took place. Even today, the Calvinist (reformed) church is the second largest in the country, second only to the Roman Catholic Church. But Hungary is yet another partially Calvinized place where Gorski's mechanisms fail to have played out. It would have been refreshing to get Gorski's thoughts on these ostensible exceptions. Relevant questions include whether Polish Calvinism did not last long enough for it to make a difference; whether we actually find some of the Calvinist mechanisms operating, just without the same influence on the character of the state; and in this case what would explain the dissimilarities with the Netherlands and Prussia. Gorski exposes his flank to an attack because *The Disciplinary Revolution* is silent on all of this.

Woodberry: Missionaries and democracy

Gorski has not been alone in revisiting Weber. Robert D. Woodberry's (2012) article 'The Missionary Roots of Liberal Democracy', which appeared in the most prestigious political journal, *American Political Science Review*, does so too. Woodberry focuses not on state formation but on regime change, or more specifically on the advent of modern, representative democracy and its subsequent dissemination around the globe. His point of departure is strikingly similar to Gorski's. That is, he claims that the tendency in the democratization literature to emphasize material factors such as class struggle at the expense of cultural and religious interests has resulted in a simplistic view of human motivations (244).

Woodberry's Weberian alternative is stark: in his eyes, Western modernity has been formed by religious factors, which have subsequently also affected the spread of this modernity (244). However, Woodberry is not quite as ambitious as implied in these sentences. Above all, his story is about Protestantism and democracy in general – and Protestant missionaries and democratization in particular.

The Protestants' primary objective was to spread (their reading of) the Gospel. *Reading* is to be taken entirely literally, as one of the core tenants of Protestantism was that common people should be able to read the Bible (and other key texts, such as Luther's Small Catechism) in the vernacular, and that every man is his own priest. This had a number of unintended consequences, which turned out to be important for the emergence of modern democracy and its subsequent spread. The Protestants thus fought for religious tolerance, which facilitated the printing of books and education for commoners, they established newspapers and founded voluntary associations, and they forced colonial powers to treat the colonized peoples better. The Protestants thereby left a changed world in their wake. All these developments promoted the emergence and dissemination of modern democracy, regardless of how many actually converted to Protestantism (244–245).

Historical analysis

That is Woodberry's basic claim. His empirical investigation consists of two steps: a qualitative historical analysis and a quantitative statistical analysis. The point of departure for the historical analysis is a simple observation: modern representative democracy emerged in Protestant countries, and the early democratic theorists (men such as English John Locke) drew on religious justifications rather than, for example, French Enlightenment-inspired thought[3] or ideas from classical Greece (245, 249).

Woodberry is painfully aware that earlier research has challenged the link between Protestantism and early democratization. The main objection has been that it is spurious – that it follows some deeper factors that promoted Protestantism as well as democracy in specific parts of Europe (246). However, these objections lose their strength as we move beyond Europe, Woodberry reasons. He points out that a similar relationship exists in several, radically different contexts: among European settler colonies, among post-communist countries, and even among the remaining countries in Africa, Asia, and Latin America (246–247).

In all three instances, we can raise new objections. For example, it is possible that it was British colonization rather than Protestantism that promoted democratization in the settler colonies (246). But the fact that the relationship is so robust to changing context speaks to its advantage. If the relationship is valid, what was it that the Protestants did in and outside of Europe? For Woodberry, the key is the Protestant struggle for ordinary people to be able to read religious texts – an effort that proved to be a catalyst for the spread of book printing, education, and voluntary associations. The Protestants also fought for religious freedom because they often stood in opposition to the powers-that-be. Notice in this connection that the education of common people was not necessarily in the interests of the elites (it is easier to subdue the unenlightened), and Protestantism thus became a political battering ram for the masses.

It is particularly telling that illiteracy was first eliminated in a series of economically backward but deeply Protestant areas, such as Scandinavia and parts of Scotland, while the Catholic Church did not begin massive investments in education until it felt the Protestants breathing down their neck (251–252). The Protestant penchant for voluntary associations had a similar effect, both in and outside of Europe. For example, the Indian National Congress Party can be seen as a direct reaction to the competition from Protestant missionary associations (253). This observation illustrates a crucial point: these mechanisms operated even in areas where relatively few people converted to Protestantism. Non-Protestant elites (including Catholic, Hindu, and Muslim elites) thus made concessions with respect to mass education and mass media in areas where they found themselves competing with the Protestant missionaries (250).

Statistical analysis

As indicated by the title of the article, a significant part of Woodberry's story revolves precisely around the influence of Protestant missionaries under foreign skies. His provocative claim is that the variation in the levels of democracy outside of Europe must above all be attributed to the influence of these Protestant missionaries.

Woodberry tests his claim using a large-scale statistical analysis of 142 countries. He omits European countries as well as British settler colonies, which makes the test of the relationship between Protestantism and democracy conservative. Woodberry's dependent variable is the average levels of democracy since World War II (in the periods 1950–1994 and 1955–2007, respectively). He measures the influence of the Protestant missionaries using two different specifications of the same variable:

- Protestant missionaries per ten thousand residents in 1923.
- the number of years an area has been the target of Protestant missions.

Woodberry furthermore investigates the effect of a related variable, namely the percentage of Evangelical (Protestant) residents in 1900. In addition, his analysis includes control variables that cover virtually every other conceivable cause of democracy. What does the analysis show?

To make a long story short, the two first specifications of Protestant influence are statistically significant, and their effect is substantial. Woodberry shows that the danger of endogeneity – that is, levels of democracy promoting the missionary work and not the other way around – is minor, precisely because the Protestant variables are measured in 1923 at the latest, where there were hardly any democracies outside Europe and the European settler colonies (259). In addition, the explanatory power of the model increases dramatically when the missionary variables are introduced. In fact, these variables explain almost half of the variation in the levels of democracy outside Europe (268).

At least as interesting is the fact that all other variables in the model become insignificant (259–260). For example, Woodberry's variables destroy the effect of the two most important colonization variables in Acemoglu and Robinson's study: the mortality rates for settlers and population density in 1500 (see Chapter 13) (263). However, the results also show that the percentage of Protestants in 1900 becomes insignificant in several of the models (263). Woodberry takes this as indication that it is not the conversion to Protestantism as such that is decisive but rather the Protestant missionaries' influence *in situ*. Finally, two measures of the influence of Catholic missionaries are also insignificant.

As a final step, Woodberry repeats the analysis with a series of instrument variables. He concedes that none of them unto themselves are particularly convincing but finds consolation in his findings proving robust whatever he throws at them (266). He also concedes that the analysis is vulnerable to the suspicion of spuriosity, but he uses a couple of simple arguments to strengthen the validity of the results. For an unidentified third variable to be behind the massive correlation, it would have to explain almost completely the variation in the work of the Protestant missionaries as well as the levels of democracy (268). It is difficult to imagine that such a 'magic variable' would remain overlooked. Furthermore, this hypothetical variable would have to render all other explanations in the literature insignificant. In other words, if Woodberry has a problem, it applies *a fortiori* to the rest of the literature (268).

Criticism

Woodberry emphasizes that he has identified a relationship that is valid for a particular historical period. Today, the impact of Protestant missionaries is not a requirement for democracy, among other things because since the 1960s, the Catholic Church has adopted a new policy and actively aided democratization (268–269). However, this historic turn, too, Woodberry attributes to the competition from the Protestants.

Woodberry's analysis is almost painfully thorough. His list of references is overwhelming; he has spent years merely coding his key variables; and, even though the statistical analysis encounters certain problems, Woodberry does everything possible to undermine his main findings – without success. The reader is left practically breathless, with a feeling that every conceivable objection to Woodbury's history has been swept from the table.

However, a single point of criticism is worth mentioning. Woodberry's 'evangelizing Protestants' is a bit of a residual category. Particularly in the historical analysis, it is quite clear that – as in the case of Weber and Gorski – it is the Calvinists who feature as most important (see, e.g., Woodberry 2012, 249). However, in contrast to Gorski's work, no possible hierarchy between the Protestant denominations is explicated by Woodberry. This might be due to the narrow framework provided by an article, but it makes it a little more difficult to grasp the otherwise rather convincing mechanisms that he presents.

Conclusions

Weber has of course been lurking beneath the surface throughout Woodberry's article, but only in the very last paragraph does he show his true colours. Woodberry concedes that Weber's specific arguments about the impact of Protestantism might not have stood the test of time. According to Woodberry, however, Weber's fundamental insights remain: religious convictions and religious institutions are the source from which European modernity – and thus modernity more generally – sprang. A bit of a *crescendo*, and one that could also have been made by Gorski.

This statement is a direct challenge to the existing literature on state formation. As mentioned, the basis for the work carried out by Gorski and Woodberry is that Weber's link between religion and the development of society in general and Protestantism and the rationalization process in the West in particular has largely been ignored by the very literature which Weber sparked. Instead, this literature has revolved around the effects of class structures, state structures, and international structures.

Gorski and Woodberry provide a corrective that emphasizes cultural factors or merely ideas (see also Capoccia and Ziblatt 2010). It is liberating how, in this manner, Weber's sociology of religion is again being taken seriously. As with Weber himself, the focus is above all else on the effects of Calvinism on the societies in which it made inroads. Weber primarily linked these effects to modern capitalism, but in this chapter it has been convincingly established that Protestantism has also affected state formation and regime change. Or, in other words, it has paved the way for the triumph of the modern world over the course of the latest five hundred years.

Notes

1 Frederik William I lived like a monk; his ascetic way of life is practically a caricature of the secular Calvinist ethic we have already met in Weber's writings.
2 In contrast, Gorski has explicit reservations regarding Scotland, which is commonly known as one of the areas in Europe that was most influenced by Calvinism. According to Gorski, however, this country was too poor to survive as an independent state, despite the disciplinary revolution (76).
3 Here, Woodberry is invoking the conventional distinction between the radical French Enlightenment, which was anti-clerical, and the moderate Scottish–English, which was influenced by Protestant thought. According to Woodberry, the latter promoted democracy while the former did not (249).

PART V

Explaining the rise of representative institutions

17

THE THEORETICAL ARGUMENT

Introduction

The European development of 'constraints on the executive' has long been seen as critical in explaining global disparities in the quality of political and economic institutions – and hence differences in state formation, regime change, and economic development (North and Thomas 1973; North 1990; Acemoglu et al. 2001, 2002a, 2008; Jones 2008[1981]; Hariri 2012; cf. Stasavage 2010; Blaydes and Chaney 2013). The contention of the last part of this book is that we need to understand the origins of these institutions of constraints to understand the context in which the modern state, modern democracy, and the modern market economy arose (see Møller 2015b). The following four chapters are therefore devoted to pursuing these origins, an endeavour which requires that we delve into medieval Europe.

The point of departure for this pursuit is simple: representative institutions are increasingly identified as the core of the European development of constraints on the executive (Hintze 1975[1931]; Myers 1975; Downing 1992; Ertman 1997; Stasavage 2010; Van Zanden et al. 2012; Blaydes and Chaney 2013; Abramson and Boix 2014). As we have seen in earlier chapters, these institutions – Estates or parliaments or diets – were the only ones that could systematically constrain monarchs (Ertman 1997, 19). It is against this background that we find a teeming new literature which has attempted to explain various aspects of the rise of representative institutions (Ertman 1997; Stasavage 2010, 2011; Blaydes & Chaney 2013; Abramson and Boix 2014; Møller 2014, 2016a; Boucoyannis 2015; cf. Stasavage 2016).

However, this prior scholarship has had very little to say about the origin of these institutions (Stasavage 2016, 2). The main insight of a large body of work is that Europe's unique political and economic development, including the rise of representative institutions, owes much to the European multistate system, which generated a ubiquitous pressure on state-builders to augment their bureaucratic capacity and develop the wherewithal for warfare (Hintze 1975[1906]; 1975[1931]; Poggi 1978; Weber 1981[1927]; Hall 1985; Mann 1986; Tilly 1990; Schumpeter 1991[1917/1918]; Ertman 1997, 4; Jones 2008[1981]; see also Bisson 1966, 1199; Finer 1997a, 1026). This explanatory factor has featured extremely prominently in this book. But prior chapters have also demonstrated that multistate systems characterized by generalized geopolitical competition have existed elsewhere without producing representative institutions (see also Watson 1992; Hui 2005; Kaufman et al. 2007; Møller 2014; Stasavage 2016, 10–11). Indeed, as we have seen in Chapter 14 and as I shall further detail below, in other contexts a similar geopolitical pressure has facilitated an intensification of absolutism. In the words of Otto Hintze (1975[1931], 308–309), what is so peculiar about the geopolitical competition of the nascent European multistate system is that it simultaneously prompted increasing political rationalization and 'triggered its opposite: a corporate reaction'.

Any account of the rise of representative institutions that accepts the causal importance of geopolitical pressure must solve this paradox. The literature contains several contributions that attempt to deal with the European side of it by emphasizing particular aspects of the setting in which representative institutions arose (Vu 2010, 159). Harking back to an older literature on feudalism, Blaydes and Chaney (2013) argue that feudal military organization bolstered local aristocracies at the expense of the rulers and thereby shored up representative institutions (see Ganshof 1952[1944], 154; Bloch 1971[1939], 228; Hintze 1975[1931]; Strayer 1987[1965], 29). Van Zanden et al. (2012, 847) – stressing a point earlier made by Poggi (1978, 36–42) and ultimately by Max Weber (Bendix 1962[1946]) – instead posit that the key to the advent of representative institutions is to be found in the medieval communal revolution – i.e., in the rise of autonomous towns (see also Abramson and Boix 2014).[1] Finally, a number of scholars have associated the origins of representative institutions with the work of the Catholic Church, including the Catholic clergy, after the revival of Roman Law in the eleventh century (Hintze 1975[1931]; Tierney 1982; see also Finer 1997a).[2]

These explanations are unsatisfactory because they fail to observe what has been identified as the key requirement of any attempt to deal with medieval and early modern European patterns of state formation: to systematically combine the mechanical pressures of the international system with the character of the state-society relations within the units of this system (Tilly 1990; Downing 1992; Spruyt 1994; Ertman 1997; Hui 2004; 2005; Møller 2014; see also Nexon 2009, 353–354). Though virtually all scholars agree that warfare had something to do with the rise of representative institutions, we find no systematical attempt to account for the consequences of geopolitical pressure – for regime change – in the context of different kinds of state-society relations. In other words, we find no attempt to genuinely solve the paradox that geopolitical pressure seems to have had completely different effects on regime change in different empirical contexts.

A main reason for this is that most of the recent work on representative institutions has been remarkably Eurocentric (see also Mann 1986; Tilly 1990; Downing 1992; Ertman 1997). To genuinely solve the puzzle that geopolitical pressure seems to have been conducive to the development of representative institutions in Europe but not elsewhere, we need to return to the macro-historical comparisons that we find in the classical work of Max Weber (Bendix 1962[1946]) and Otto Hintze (1962[1929]; 1962[1930]; 1975[1931]), reviewed and discussed earlier in this book (see Chapters 4–5).

This work is pervaded by an emphasis on the importance of the autonomous groups that were a ubiquitous feature of medieval Europe (see also Poggi 1978; Finer 1997a; 1997b; Sabetti 2004). This chapter presents an explanation of the European development of institutions of constraints which draws insights from this classical work – and the focus on autonomous societal groups in particular – but embeds these insights in a more analytical model that combines system-level and domestic-level features. The basic argument, which is developed and operationalized below, is that the onset of geopolitical competition interacted with state-society relations to produce either representative institutions or an intensification of absolutism. In the chapters that follow, historical case studies of medieval Leon-Castile, medieval Aragon-Catalonia, and medieval England, on the one hand, and ancient China and early modern Russia, on the other hand, are enlisted to probe this argument. This last part of the book thereby sheds new light on the historical dynamics of regime change in general and the origins of representative institutions in particular.

The argument

The argument can be summarized as follows: representative institutions arose and later became institutionalized as a result of the onset of geopolitical pressure in contexts that were characterized by multiple autonomous social groups, while the absence of such groups instead provoked an intensification of absolutism. In other words, as illustrated in Figure 17.1, geopolitical competition is the operative variable that produces regime change, but its effects are conditioned by pre-existing state-society relations.

Definitions

The key concepts in this conditional relationship are representative institutions, generalized geopolitical competition, and multiple autonomous social groups. When defining these concepts, we need to steer between the poles of generality (where the concepts become trivial)[3] and specificity (where they simply become a description of state of affairs in medieval Europe or even just parts of medieval Europe). In other words, we need to strike the exact same balance as when formulating the explanatory argument where the poles navigated between are the completely analytic claim about the uniform effects of geopolitical competition, on the one hand, and the contextual explanations of representative institutions emphasizing a particular within-unit aspect of Western Europe, on the other hand.

With respect to *representative institutions*, we can first note the virtue of the decision to scope down from vague and composite concepts such as 'medieval

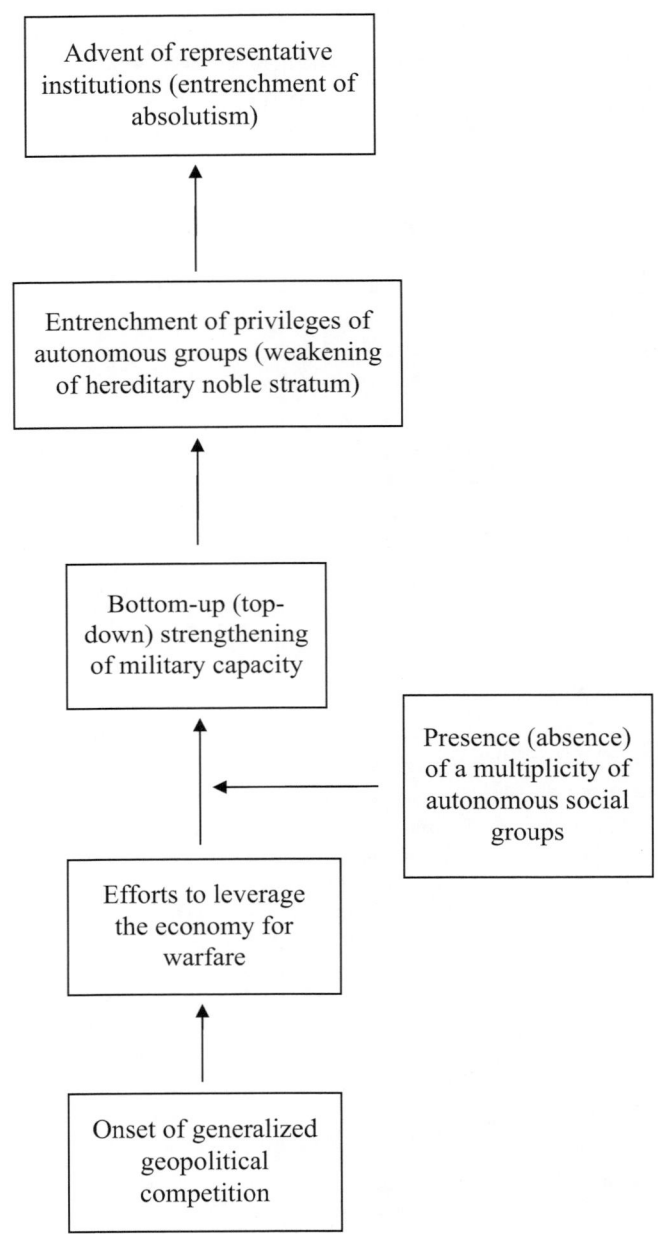

FIGURE 17.1   Regime change as a function of the onset of geopolitical competition and the presence (absence) of a multiplicity of autonomous groups

constitutionalism' (Downing 1992, 10; Sabetti 2004) and 'institutions of constraints' (Acemoglu et al. 2008). But even with the more specific and more easily measurable concept of representative institutions, we still need to walk the line between the poles of generality and specificity. Stasavage's (2010, 630) definition falls close to the overly general pole: 'a collective body at the level of the state that met with some regularity and had at least a consultative role in decision making'. At the other end of the spectrum, Van Zanden et al. (2012, 837) adopt a definition which basically describes medieval European parliaments, including their membership (three or four estates) and their functions (granting of taxation, etc.).[4] We need a definition that carves out a position between these two extremes. Such a definition must, on the one hand, distinguish representative institutions from the assemblies of notables we find in many historical societies and, on the other hand, be so general that it can potentially travel beyond medieval Europe. Poggi (1978, 47–48) provides such a definition, which he summarizes in three criteria: *representative institutions* can be defined as institutionalized assemblies (not *ad hoc* gatherings) that represent the people in a particular territory (they are not a gathering of personalities), and that are independent bodies (not subject to the rulers). Representative institutions thereby create a regime form where an estate pole representing the community of the realm confronts a monarchical pole representing the Crown (Hintze 1962[1930], 122; Poggi 1978, 47–48; Finer 1997a, 1029). This can be contrasted with the regime form of absolutism, where the ruler makes up the sole pole (cf. Ertman 1997, 19).

With *generalized geopolitical competition*, we face a similar challenge. On the one hand, warfare has been ubiquitous in the history that has come down to us, and it has repeatedly sparked state formation and political development (Bradford 2001; Morris 2014). On the other hand, many scholars working on Europe have provided a very restricted definition of this variable, centred on the presence of a fully formed multistate system such as that which characterized Europe after the French invasion of Italy in 1494 or after the Peace of Westphalia in 1648 (Hui 2004, 176; 2005; Levy and Thompson 2005, 15). A fully formed multistate system will necessarily create generalized geopolitical competition, whereas this is not the case with simple warfare. But we also find generalized geopolitical competition in what might be termed nascent state systems such as those which characterized medieval Europe or ancient China before the Warring States period. The key point is that *generalized geopolitical competition* refers not to episodic but to repeated warfare – and the constant threat of warfare – between relatively stable political units interacting in the absence of a higher authority, meaning that rulers must repeatedly mobilize their economies (cf. Hintze 1975[1906]; Tilly 1990; Schumpeter 1991[1917/1918]; Ertman 1997, 23–28; Stasavage 2011, 9).

Finally, there are the *multiple, autonomous social groups*. Here, the contextual danger is to define these in terms of the historically very peculiar estate society of medieval Europe, where a myriad of different groups – the most important being the nobility, the clergy, the townsmen, and in some areas the free peasantry – retained judicial privileges (see, e.g., Poggi 1978, 43; Finer 1997a, 1028–1029; Sabetti 2004). At the same time, we need to avoid simply identifying the existence of a privileged order as some form of hereditary nobility is present in virtually all stratified societies. To steer a middle course, two aspects must be clarified: the autonomy of the social groups and their functions. More analytically, the point is that these groups are not servitors of the rulers as in the traditional form of domination that Weber termed patrimonialism[5] but autonomous (Bendix 1962[1946], 360–384) and that there exists not only the nobility but other social groups with a different kind of autonomy covering distinct social domains. *Multiple, autonomous social groups* are thus characterized by having particular rights ('immunities'/'privileges') recognized by rulers and by being not functionally equivalent but rather differentiated (Hintze 1962[1930], 122–123; Bendix 1962[1946], 360–384). That is, there exists not only the hereditary nobility that is present in virtually all stratified societies but other social groups with a different kind of autonomy covering distinct social domains – for instance, 'free' townsmen and an independent clergy.

Fleshing out the argument

These definitions pave the way for elaborating the general argument about the advent of representative institutions provided above. The basic building block of this argument is that generalized geopolitical competition has one universal effect: it sparks the political rationalization and centralization necessary to bring about the wherewithal for warfare. However, under a particular set of circumstances, namely the presence of multiple autonomous groups, these reforms trigger the corporate reaction Hintze identifies. This condition is exogenous to the theoretical argument. In other words, the ambition of the argument is to capture the political consequences of the onset of generalized geopolitical competition given the presence or absence of multiple autonomous groups, not to explain the origins of these groups.

As illustrated in Figure 17.1, the concatenation of geopolitical pressure and multiple autonomous groups creates a bottom-up strengthening of military capacity via a logic of bargaining. This is a matter of both incentives and power. In the face of multiple autonomous groups, bargaining is the most efficient way to prepare for warfare for rulers who lack a well-developed bureaucracy because the autonomous groups can reach into most domains of society and can transmit government authority within these domains at their own expense. The autonomous groups are able to mobilize for warfare on a scale that meets the demands created by geopolitical competition – for instance, by increasing the size of armies via the use of organized militias and due to their ability to tap landed, commercial, and clerical wealth. But the need to bargain also follows from the fact that the multiple autonomous groups are able to balance and subsequently challenge the ruler due to their ability to bar him/her from these very domains, and it therefore has some important longer-term consequences.

In this situation, efforts to leverage the economy for warfare consistently spark political grievances. For instance, any attempt to rationalize law in a top-down manner produces a demand for an official recognition of the customary law that guarantees established immunities. More generally, as a concession for contributing to warfare, the autonomous social groups demand – and extract – an *institutionalized* recognition of their traditional privileges, normally via collective charters of liberties granted by the ruler. This further strengthens the autonomous groups and makes the extraction of taxes and financial aid even more cumbersome because some of the privileges entail exemptions from taxation and because the privileges prevent the ruler from directly governing most social domains. The ruler therefore convokes representative institutions to secure a more institutionalized forum for consenting to taxation. These institutions are at first convoked *ad hoc* to serve the rulers' interests. But gradually – as a *quid pro quo* for consenting to taxation – they obtain independent constitutional prerogatives, including the right to be summoned with regularity, the right to veto taxation, and possibly also the right to audit spending or occasionally even appoint officials and settle successions to the throne. The results are different degrees of institutionalized constraints on rulers.

The political repercussions of geopolitical competition are completely different where no multiplicity of autonomous groups exists. Once again, the onset of geopolitical competition forces the ruler to leverage the economy for warfare. But in this scenario no strong bargaining partners with the ability to mobilize broad swatches of the economy and to work as transmission belts to channel authority exists. The one strong group present in virtually all historic settings – the ranked nobility – simply cannot provide the wherewithal necessary to meet the external challenges produced by generalized geopolitical competition. For instance, while the nobility can tap landed wealth and field aristocratic forces (say, knights or chariots), it does not have the means to mobilize commercial or ecclesiastical wealth and to create mass armies. The ruler is therefore forced to strengthening military capacity top-down via bureaucratic and political centralization.

Once again, incentives and power are mutually reinforcing, but this time they bring about what is emphatically a top-down strategy. The catalogue of top-down reforms includes measures such as universal conscription, carrying out censuses, administrative restructuring of the realm, and direct taxation. More generally, customary law is displaced in favour of royal law. This strengthening of monarchical authority does not spark the kind of organized resistance that must be countered by concessions because the ruler is able to sideline the hitherto strong nobility by leveraging the economy for warfare directly. This, in turn, undercuts the nobility's traditional importance in warfare and weakens it to the extent that it no longer poses any constraints on the ruler. The general result of this process is an intensification of already-existing absolutism.

This second scenario places the importance of a multiplicity of strong groups in relief. In itself, an array of groups is a liability and not a strength as it makes it easier for monarchs to use divide-and-rule tactics. For instance, if a strong nobility is internally divided (e.g., into high and low nobility), it is possible to use these divisions to weaken it. But if the groups are differentiated and cover distinct societal domains, the ruler will be unable to tap the resources needed for warfare in a top-down manner in order to sideline, e.g., the nobility. In a nutshell, the associational and organizational characteristics of group autonomy make it possible to either acquire or block access to resources. This is why the number of groups matter.

Operationalizing the argument

To corroborate the conditional relationship illustrated in Figure 17.1, we must identify two different sequences of events, sparked by the same impulse, namely the onset of generalized geopolitical competition.

In the scenario that brings about representative institutions, it must first be established that this occurs in a societal context where multiple autonomous groups – the exogenous condition of the theoretical argument – exist and bar the ruler from mobilizing broad swatches of the economy for warfare via the very weak state apparatus at his/her disposal. Instead, the ruler is forced to bargain with the autonomous social groups. As part of this bargaining, the ruler grants concessions in the form of repeated recognitions of privileges. Furthermore, to make this bargaining effective by committing the groups, the ruler turns from convoking the usual assemblies of notables to convoking representative institutions. When the groups represented in these institutions consent to financial aid – e.g., in the form of taxation – they demand and obtain an institutionalized recognition of their right to partake in the government of the realm. This includes an institutionalization of representative institutions, which creates the regime form where the community of the realm confronts the crown.

More particular observable implications of the argument include the following: first, efforts to leverage possessions for warfare – including attempts to create royal law and demands for military service and taxation – spark grievances among the autonomous groups that force the ruler to recognize and often enlarge customary rights. Second, instead of creating a state apparatus that can extract resources directly, the ruler relies on the autonomous social groups to transmit government authority at their own expense – e.g., by collecting taxes themselves. Third, the ruler depends on military forces from several groups – e.g., in the form of noble knights and their retainers, knights from monastic military orders, and urban militias. Fourth, the strength of the autonomous social groups mean that on key decisions concerning taxation, succession, and warfare, the ruler turns from relying on a consultative assembly of notables toward convoking broader representative institutions to seek the consent of the 'community of the realm'. Fifth, over time the autonomous groups extract concessions in the form of institutionalized constraints on rulers.

It follows from this that the developments that culminate in representative institutions are likely to be most conspicuous when an intensification of external pressure places the autonomous groups in a situation where the ruler depends on their assistance for his/her very survival or when the ruler's position is internally weak – e.g., due to minorities or rival claimants for the throne. If the autonomous groups can present a united front in these situations, the ruler has little alternative but to give in to their demands because s/he has direct control only over a minor part of the economy and because the autonomous groups can potentially shift their alliance to royal pretenders.

In the scenario that creates an intensification of absolutism, it must first be established that the onset of generalized geopolitical competition occurs in a context where no multiplicity of autonomous social groups hinders the ruler from extracting resources from society. The ruler proceeds by extracting these resources via direct taxation of the population and by amplifying military might via the introduction of conscription. Also, customary law is displaced in favour of royal law. This strengthening of military capacity and the bureaucracy further skews the balance of power between the ruler and social groups, paving the way for the weakening of even the hereditary nobility.

More particular observable implications of the argument include the following: first, in response to the onset of geopolitical pressure, the ruler carries out censuses of the population, implements direct taxation (e.g., head taxes), and introduces conscription and a standing army. Second, this strengthening of monarchical authority does not spark the kind of organized resistance that must be countered by concessions. Third, the nobility loses its traditional ability to restrain the ruler via assemblies of notables and direct influence at the court. Fourth, important matters of state concerning taxation, warfare, and succession are increasingly dealt with only by the ruler.

It follows from this that the developments that ultimately produce an intensification of absolutism are likely to be most conspicuous when an intensification of external pressure triggers intense reforms needed to secure the very survival of the ruler and/or when rulers are internally strong. The consequent increase in the sway of central power makes it possible to further roll back the privileges of the nobility.

Conclusions

This chapter can be set against the many chapters that precede it. In effect, I have used the scholarship that I have reviewed in this book as a stepping stone for formulating a new argument about what – based on this very scholarship – emerges as the key issue of European state formation, regime change, and economic development. This key issue concerns the origins of representative institutions. More particularly, I have presented an explanation of the origins of representative institutions that is based on a systematic attempt to integrate systemic influences with domestic factors. The core postulate is that representative government was the (bottom-up) product of a concatenation between external geopolitical pressure and the internal balance caused by the existence of a multiplicity of autonomous groups. In the absence of a multiplicity of autonomous groups, geopolitical pressure instead paved the way for a top-down strengthening of autocracy.

This conditional relationship has been operationalized above. First, I have carefully defined the key concepts that go into the conditional relationship, navigating between the two poles of trivial generality and contextual specificity. Second, I have identified a number of observable implications of the causal argument, and I have identified the causal sequences that are sparked by an intensification of geopolitical pressure in the context of either multiple autonomous groups or in the absence of such groups. These sequences in general and the associated implications in particular must be identified in the analysed cases for the argument to be corroborated. This is the aim of Chapter 19. However, before we can apply the argument, it is necessary to discuss some of the methodological challenges that face scholars probing the origins of representative institutions. This is the purpose of Chapter 18.

Notes

1 Related to this, Hui (2004; 2005) proposes that the monetization of the European economy in the period 1000–1300 affected the way rulers interacted with and extracted resources from society (see also Tilly 1985; Downing 1992; Stasavage 2011, 9).
2 Some scholars take these factors to reflect more general causal dynamics. For instance, the rise of towns is sometimes seen as part and parcel of a more general process of economic development, whereas the impact of the Church and Roman Law is sometimes seen as reflecting the role of political ideas (cf. Stasavage 2016, 2).
3 To illustrate, we find some kinds of assemblies of notables in most societies, and we also find some kind of privileged orders and some kind of warfare.
4 For Van Zanden et al. (2012: 837) a parliament is only a parliament if the towns are represented, a conceptual delimitation that to some extent makes their claim that the emergence of towns were the cause behind the convocation of parliaments true by definition.
5 Weber contrasted this form of rule with a different kind of traditional domination, which he termed 'feudalism' and which contains the multiple autonomous social groups my definition emphasizes (Bendix 1962[1946], 360–384).

18

THE METHODOLOGICAL CHALLENGES

Introduction

The point of departure for Part V of this book is that a logical next step for the literature on the 'institutions of constraints', which scholars have singled out as a key factor in explaining global disparities in wealth and democracy levels into the present, is to analyse the origins of medieval representative institutions. This can be seen as a way of pushing the causal chain of the work on the institutionalist origins of comparative development one step further back. A new research agenda centred on representative institutions has indeed gotten off the ground in recent years, and it seems a safe bet that these endeavours will be intensified in the future (Stasavage 2016).

However, the attempt to analyse the origins of representative institutions confronts scholars with a fundamental problem. Diffusion of political institutions means that the notion of unit independence is tenuous in a situation where we do not have the kind of detailed quantitative or narrative data that allows us to remedy this. That is, as I shall argue below, the problem of diffusion is especially acute in the context of medieval Western and Central Europe. Three ways of dealing with this problem are presented in this chapter, and the case is made for combining several of these strategies when analysing the origins of representative institutions. On this basis, I set out the guidelines that I will use to empirically apply the theoretical argument presented in Chapter 17.

Diffusion of institutions in medieval Europe

Let us define diffusion as a spread of innovations among the units of a social system and let us note that such innovations diffuse easiest if a system is tight knit – that is, when multiple and overlapping networks pervade the system. On this basis, we can note two reasons why medieval Europe was saturated by diffusion of political ideas and institutions (see also Møller 2016c).

First, the political units that we find in Western and Central Europe in the Middle Ages in themselves facilitated diffusion. These were loose and bundled units, which historians refer to as 'composite states' (Te Brake 1998). They had often been created by testament or marriage, and they therefore tended to contain a number of relatively independent sub-units, which had their own laws and political institutions (Poggi 1990). Often these subunits did not make up a coherent territorial block but were separated by other units that fell under the formal sway of other monarchs. Indeed, the space of Western and Central Europe made up a patchwork of such subunits. Borders were fungible and loose, and the result was that impulses would spring across subunits within a composite realm and across subunits of different realms. Ideas were therefore quickly transported over great distances (see Bartlett 1993). To illustrate this, we can turn to one of the most well-known events of the Middle Ages, namely the granting by King John of the Magna Carta in 1215. As Vincent (2012, 62) points out, the great charter was inspired by similar charters in 'those parts of Spain and southern France where King John had been diplomatically most active in the years before 1215'. This example is important for our story because the Magna Carta, which John quickly annulled, was repeatedly reissued by Plantagenet rulers over the following century, and because it has been identified as one of the key drivers of the development of the English parliament under John's son and grandson (Maddicott 2010; Vincent 2012, 62).

Second, and perhaps even more importantly, the Catholic Church provided a common mental frame of reference that towered above anything else in medieval Europe. The church was an international institution, and it was present in virtually every locality of Western and Central Europe (Hall 1985; Mann 1986; Finer 1997a, 857). Indeed, the clergy took care not only of religious functions but – until the advent of the universities – also of the monarchs' administrative tasks (Ertman 2005). Almost a hundred years ago, Otto Hintze (1975[1931], 318) noted that the fact that 'the whole primitive machinery of state were in the hands of ecclesiastics, and that the procedures and ideas of these chancelleries passed from country to country, from court to court' meant that 'a certain uniformity of thinking about politics and administration was established'. This kind of diffusion is obviously important for our purposes. It spread a series of key notions across Latin Christendom, such as the use of political representation and the notion of corporate groups, which were to play an important role in the advent of representative institutions (Hintze, 1975[1931], 318; Proctor 1980; Tierney, 1982, 11–25; Finer, 1997a, 863–864; Maddicott 2010).

Taken together, the impact of the composite structure of states and of the church means that it is flawed to treat the political units of Western and Central Europe as independent entities in comparative analysis when probing the origins of representative institutions (cf. van Zanden et al. 2012, 839; see also Marongiu 1968, 53). This is illustrated in Figure 18.1.

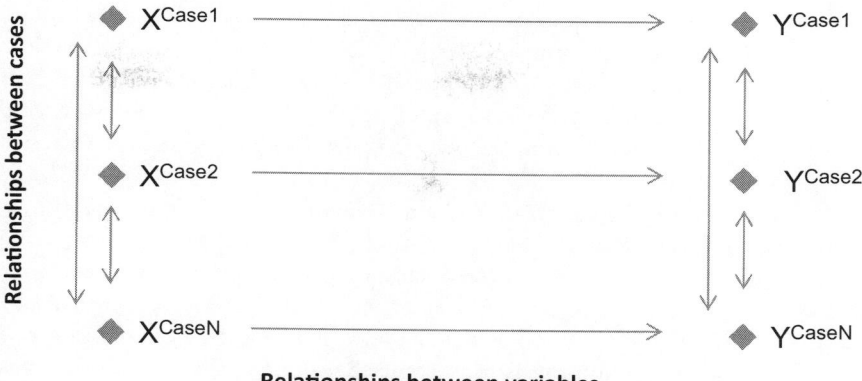

FIGURE 18.1 Diffusion and cross-spatial autocorrelation

Note: Adapted from Møller (2016c).

Illustrating the problem of diffusion: Recent research on the development of representative institutions

Two of the most important recent attempts to analyse the origins and character of representative institutions illustrate these problems. Both of these analyses are premised on the political units of Western and Latin Christendom being independent, and both enlist large-N data on representative institutions as well as a number of control variables (see also Abramson and Boix 2014).

Blaydes and Chaney (2013) argue that changes in military technology – more precisely the advent of feudal military organization based on the aristocratic warrior – produced representative institutions. They corroborate this claim in a statistical analysis where they use ruler duration (based on numismatic data) as a proxy for the process that brought about representative institutions. I have already pointed out that in medieval Europe diffusion of political institutions was pervasive. As we know from earlier chapters, the interstate competition in Europe was likewise an effective spur of the spread of military innovations (Hall 1985, 135, 553; Tilly 1990; Bartlett 1993; Ertman 1997; Jones 2008[1981], 45). The situation might therefore be that both military technology and political institutions diffused according to a similar pattern but with a time lag between them, creating a strong but spurious statistical relationship between the two (and between military organization and ruler duration if the latter proxies strong political institutions).

Stasavage (2010) argues that in medieval and early modern Europe there were geographical barriers to representation, meaning that the smaller the political unit, the more frequent were convocations of representative institutions. This he tests using a dataset of European political units that includes Russia. As pointed out in Chapter 10, the main spatial problem here is that representative institutions could not emerge in medieval and early modern Russia because their spread was bound by the community of the Catholic Church or Western Christendom. By including Russia into the statistical analysis, Stasavage's (2010) analysis is prone to suffer from confirmation bias as a geographically large unit that could not plausibly develop representative institutions will inevitably strengthen any relationship between size and representation.

In different ways, the two analyses therefore illustrate how diffusion of institutions create problems that are difficult to handle in statistical analysis. Now, there are a series of standard ways to address the problem of diffusion in quantitative analysis, and many of these do in fact enter the analyses of Blaydes and Chaney (2013) and Stasavage (2010). These techniques include clustering standard errors on regions, modelling diffusion as convergence by controlling for the initial scores of the political institutions, using regional fixed effects, and including a variable measuring institutions in neighbouring countries. While these techniques mitigate the problem, they cannot substitute for a genuine control for diffusion. That is, unless a variable actually measuring the diffusion of political institutions is enlisted, any empirical relationship will remain vulnerable. This applies, *a fortiori*, to the two reviewed examples for the simple reason that, as I have argued, it is easy to object that diffusion might drive the results.

Three ways of dealing with diffusion when analysing representative institutions

How can scholars probe origins in the face of such pervasive diffusion of political institutions? An alluring reaction would be to focus on the process itself by operationalizing mechanisms of diffusion of political institutions in medieval Europe and mapping out the empirical evidence (see, e.g., Weyland 2009; 2010). This line of research would surely be valuable and would probably tell us much about how representative institutions spread. However, it would not tell us much about their origins.

In what follows, three ways of tackling diffusion when analysing the rise of representative institutions are proposed. First, we can displace focus from general patterns to the *first recorded incidences* of representative institutions. Focusing on first incidences removes at least the most direct diffusion – that is, the demonstration effects unleashed by the initial advent of representative institutions. Within-case analysis of the developments that first brought them about should thus enable scholars to avoid some of the problems that arise from diffusion. Furthermore, if it is possible to analyse several near-simultaneous early incidents in this way, we would still stand a good chance of identifying more general causal dynamics (see Figure 18.2).

This way of approaching origins is not bullet-proof, however. It has already been hinted that the Magna Carta, which historians construe as a cornerstone in the development of the English parliament (Maddicott 2010), was to some extent itself a product of diffusion. More generally, charters of liberties are found throughout Western and Central Europe in the Middle Ages (Bloch 1971a[1939], 1356), and many of these charters predate the first representative institutions (see Proctor 1980;

FIGURE 18.2   Analysing first incidences

Note: Adapted from Møller (2016c).

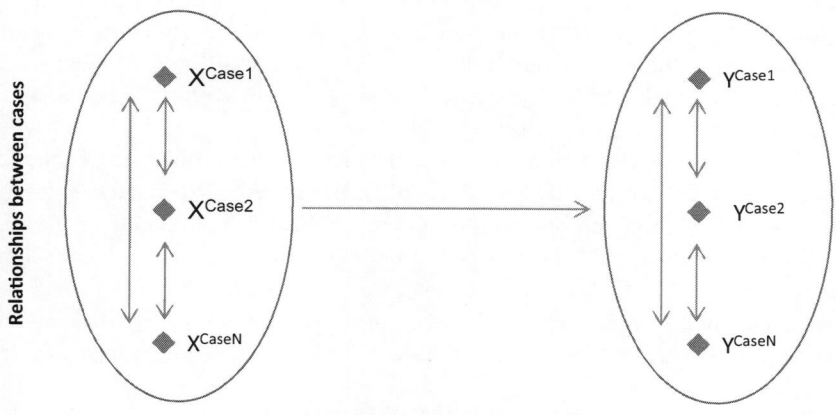

FIGURE 18.3   Scoping up in comparisons

O'Callaghan 1989; Maddicott 2010). Tellingly, in 1215 the English barons directly pointed to and used Henry I's coronation charter from 1100 as a precedent (Vincent 2012, 10–11, 59–63). So, the norms and practices about charters of rights and about representation might have diffused prior to the first convocations of genuine representative institutions.

The second suggestion – *scoping up in comparative analyses* – provides a more coherent solution to the problem of diffusion (see Figure 18.3). This construes as one case the entire area within which representative institutions and the norms and practices behind them diffused. It is anchored in the more general insight that diffusion is normally confined to (or at the very least much more pervasive on) a regional level than across regions because the requisite mechanisms of transmissions are much more effective between neighbouring countries and/or culturally related countries than between culturally distinct countries large distances apart (Kopstein and Reilly 2000; Mainwaring and Perez-Linan 2005). Any such 'regional effects' were probably much stronger in the past when transmitting information across large stretches of land was very difficult. This means that it is possible to circumvent the methodological problems created by diffusion by scoping up from non-independent political units such as composite states to independent units in the form of more general regions.

In the case of representative institutions, this is relatively straightforward. Exactly because the Catholic Church was the main engine of diffusion, it is Latin or Western Christendom that demarcates this 'regional' case. Until modern times, we find no representative institutions outside this zone (Hintze 1962[1930]; Myers 1975; Poggi 1978; Stasavage 2010). In the Middle Ages, this area made up the unit of comparison that Marc Bloch (1954[1949]; see also Chirot 1984, 25–26) terms a 'civilization' – i.e., a culturally relatively tight-knit region (Hall 1985; Bartlett 1993; Jones 2008[1981]).[1] To reiterate, the main integrative force of this area was the Catholic Church (see also Southern 1970; Hall 1985; Finer 1997a). But on top of this, Latin functioned as the *lingua mundi* of the educated few and completely dominated the rudimentary state apparatuses, royal and noble houses intermarried across the borders of the 'composite states', and these elites often had possessions which cut across borders (see Bisson 2009, 293–294).

The very notion that Latin Christendom can be separated out in the European space implies the existence of a residual case, namely Orthodox Eastern Europe – after the fall of Constantinople to the Ottoman Turks in 1453 mainly represented by Russia (Southern 1970; Finer 1997b, 1409). Other cases include ancient China and the Islamic World (see Hui 2005; Blaydes and Chaney 2013; Møller 2014). When applying a comparative logic to analyse the origins of representative institutions, it is other cases of this ilk that Western and Central Europe can be contrasted with (see Figure 18.4).

Finally, if we are to make any intra-Latin Christendom comparisons, it makes most sense to do so over time rather than across space. Here, we are confronted not with spatial autocorrelation but with possible autocorrelation over time (historical multi-colinearity). What must be tested in this situation is not the general cross-temporal development of the unit of Western and Central Europe described above 'but rather the deviation(s) from it, that is, the cross-unit synchronic variance in terms of relative earliness, lateness, presence, absence or intensity' (Bartolini 1993, 159). That is, we can *analyse the timing* of representative institutions, posing questions such as why these institutions arose relatively early in the Iberian Peninsula, England, and France and relatively late in Scandinavia and East-Central Europe. Though such an analysis would still be vulnerable to problems created by diffusion, it gives scholars some leverage in testing whether some explanatory factors were more important than others, based on their onset across space and the timing of

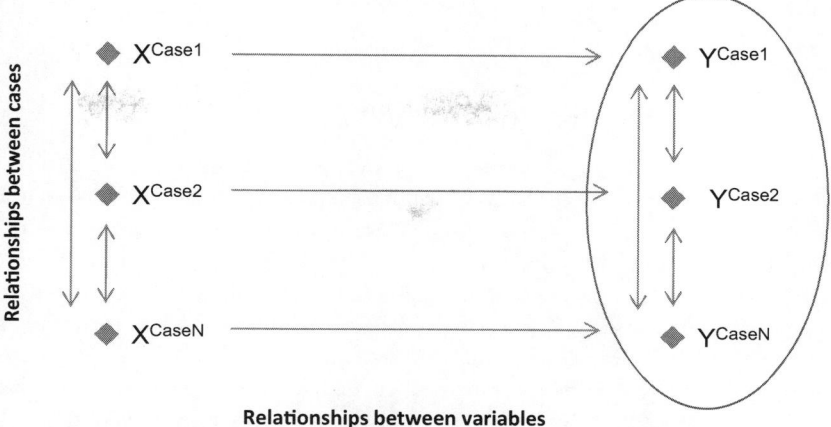

Relationships between variables

FIGURE 18.4 Analysing timing

the representative institutions (Bartolini 1993; see also Blaydes and Chaney 2013, 29–30).

None of these three strategies are easy fixes, and as with all analytical techniques we encounter a series of tradeoffs. The best way to avoid cross-spatial autocorrelation is to contrast cases where the scrutinized developments arose in virtual isolation of each other – that is, by scoping up in our comparisons. But doing so, we surrender an appreciation of the nuances within the constituent units of these macro-cases, and we are also confronted by the problem that it can be very difficult to employ controlled comparisons between cases that are relatively dissimilar in many regards exactly due to this isolation (Sewell 1996, 248–259).

Fortunately, the three strategies are not mutually exclusive, and the most convincing analysis of the origins of representative institutions is – insofar as this is practically feasible – one which combines several of them. Here, it is important to note that each of them can be used in a partial way. Having carried out a more general comparison based on scoping up, one could select one early incidence of representative institutions (say, England or Aragon-Catalonia, see more below) rather than selecting several as suggested above, and/or one could use a more general form of congruence analysis rather than in-depth process tracing. *Vice versa*, a controlled comparison based on scoping up could be employed simply as a more general check on an analysis that is mainly based on in-depth process tracing of early incidents. Similarly, though timing is best analysed using a large-N dataset that scores political units in Latin Christendom across both space and time, it would still be profitable to more qualitatively contrast the early rise of representative institutions in one or a few cases with the late rise in one or a few cases, say the Iberian cases with Scandinavia or Poland and Hungary. This could be couched in an analysis mainly based on analysing first incidences or on scoping up (or even one that does both).

Guidelines for the empirical analysis

These considerations can be converted into more specific methodological advice for how to empirically apply the argument presented in Chapter 17. It follows from the point made in this chapter that a large-N statistical analysis of the origins of representative institutions runs up against the problem of autocorrelation and a dearth of data. Invoking the strategies presented above, I will instead empirically apply the argument by contrasting and analysing a series of carefully chosen historical cases.

More specifically, I will combine the strategies of scoping up in comparative analysis and of analysing first recorded incidences. The former strategy serves to harness the logic of comparative control in a way that is relatively immune to the problem of diffusion. Here, the most obvious counterfactual for the European multistate system is ancient China up until the Imperial unification in 221 BC (Hui 2005; see also Hsu 1999; Lewis 1999; Møller 2014). As pointed out in Chapter 14, the Chinese case is appealing as a device for control in that it is the *sole* well-attested multistate system that developed in isolation from other historical systems and because it is characterized by dissimilar state-society relations (Watson 1992, 22, 85). However, a different case allows us to make an even more controlled comparison exactly because it did not occur in isolation: Russia (Hosking 2001, xi). In the seventeenth and eighteenth centuries, Russian state-builders were directly affected by the very same geopolitical pressure as obtained in the rest of Europe but faced a very different societal landscape (Anderson 1974b; Finer 1997b, 1405–1423; Hosking 2001; Møller 2015b). As in the case of ancient China, the comparison with Western European cases thus serves to bring out the different effects of geopolitical pressure, depending on the character of initial state-society relations, insofar as such exist.

On the European side, I use the strategy of analysing first incidences as a way to tackle the problem of diffusion. As illustrated in Table 18.1, the first representative institutions arose in the Iberian kingdoms in the twelfth and thirteenth centuries, followed by England and then the rest of Western Europe (Stasavage 2010; Van Zanden et al. 2012; see also Marongiu 1968; Myers 1975, 24; Poggi 1978). The most obvious choices for in-depth analysis are the early instances in the Iberian Peninsula where it seems plausible that the main impetus behind political developments was endogenous. As Van Zanden et al. (2012, 839) point out, it is unclear if the adoption of similar representative institutions across the rest of Western and Central Europe is the result of the 'copying of this institution, or of parallel evolution under similar circumstances' (see also Marongiu 1968, 53).

However, as Table 18.1 indicates, the English case represents a near-simultaneous instance. In England, the impetus behind representative institutions arguably goes back to the events that produced the Magna Carta in 1215 (see Maddicott 2010). Marongiu (1968, 76) accordingly observes that the Spanish and English cases deserve scrutiny because they throw light on the origins of representative institutions. In the chapter that follows, I will therefore analyse the two major Iberian

TABLE 18.1 First attestations of 'national' representative institutions in Western and Central Europe, 1100–1599

1100–1199	1200–1299	1300–1399	1400–1499	1500–1599
Leon-Castile	France	Scotland	Württemberg	Austria
Aragon	Portugal	Ireland	Saxony	Sweden
Catalonia	England	Hesse	Palatine	
Navarra	Hungary	Bavaria	Brandenburg	
	Sicily	Bohemia	Belgium	
	Valencia	Poland	Netherlands	
		Piedmont	Switzerland	
			Denmark	
			Sardinia	
			Napoli	

Note: Based on van Zanden et al. (2012). Van Zanden et al. code Russia as having representative institutions in the sixteenth century, but, as argued in the case study of Russia below, this cannot be sustained based on other sources (cf. Myers 1975, 34–37).

cases of Leon-Castile and Aragon-Catalonia as well as England. Afterwards, the cases of ancient China and early modern Russia are analysed in order to provide comparative contrast by scoping up.

Conclusions

I have argued that a fundamental problem confronting the new research agenda on the origins of representative institutions is that diffusion of political institutions undermines unit independence. In the face of this problem, it is difficult to use a logic of comparative control – whether quantitatively or qualitatively – to contrast cases within Western and Central Europe. I have also noted that the most important recent attempts to probe at the origins and character of representative institutions are vulnerable to this problem. Against this background, three strategies for probing into the origins of representative institutions have been identified: *analysing first recorded incidences*, *scoping up in comparisons*, and *analysing timing*. Two of these strategies guide my empirical analysis of the argument presented in Chapter 17.

Finally, it is worth noting that the advice for tackling autocorrelation due to diffusion presented in this chapter has a more general relevance. The three identified strategies would probably be relevant whenever diffusion undermines unit independence in comparative analyses. However, the problem of non-independence applies *a fortiori* to the attempt to explain the origins of representative institutions due to the pervasive diffusion of political institutions in medieval Europe.

Note

1 Ertman (1997, 4) confines his attention to this area for this very reason, arguing that this allows him to hold constant a series of potential confounders of the relationships he is investigating.

19
THE EMPIRICAL EVIDENCE

Introduction

In this chapter, the theoretical argument presented in Chapter 17 is applied on five cases: medieval Leon-Castile, medieval Aragon-Catalonia, medieval England, ancient China, and early modern Russia. In the three Western European cases, I take the intensification of geopolitical pressure in the late twelfth century described in earlier chapters of the book as the starting point. Against this backdrop, I trace the development of representative institutions from the first recorded incidences around 1200 up until the early institutionalization in the decades after 1300. In the Chinese and Russian cases, I take a similar intensification of geopolitical pressure as the starting point and attempt to understand why, at most, it led to aborted attempts to create equivalents to representative institutions – and ended up strengthening autocracy instead.

Leon-Castile

The kingdom of Leon-Castile was split into two in 1157, only to be reunified in 1230. In both this period and the century that followed, the kings of Leon, Castile, and Leon-Castile confronted persistent geopolitical pressure, particularly from the Muslim *taifas* in *el-Andalus* – often backed by forces in Morocco – but also from the other Christian Spanish realms and from France (O'Callaghan 1975).

The on-going *Reconquista* empowered the monarchy, both by shoring it up financially and by making the church, which accepted the king's position as leader of an on-going crusade against the Muslims, relatively subservient (O'Callaghan 1975, 263; 1989, 10; Procter 1980, 202). But the Reconquista also shored up several other groups (O'Callaghan 1989, 10–12). A noble class defined by heritable fiscal privileges, descent, and knightly service had existed since at least the eleventh century, and self-governing municipalities mushroomed from the eleventh century onwards (O'Callaghan 1975, 267–271; Procter 1980, 30). To consolidate conquests, a large number of frontier tenancies were awarded to magnates (O'Callaghan 1975, 288, 467–469; Stacey 1999, 23–24; Bisson 2009, 97–100), and charters (*fueros*) of communal autonomy were granted to annexed towns to attract Christian settlers from the north (O'Callaghan 1975, 240). This further strengthened both the nobles and the towns, which around the end of the twelfth century probably had a more pronounced autonomy than anywhere else in Western Europe, save Flanders (Procter 1980, 30, 94, 100, 103; O'Callaghan 1989, 10–12).

More generally, the clergy, the nobility, and the townsmen constituted coherent classes from early on, each with their own privileges enshrined in their respective *fueros* (O'Callaghan 1989, 41–59). Throughout the late twelfth, thirteenth, and fourteenth centuries, they jealously guarded these *fueros*. A recurring pattern was that the king reconfirmed these, often upon ascending the throne or as a concession for taxation (O'Callaghan 1989, 125). This pattern owed much to the geopolitical pressure described above, as the kings could not tax arbitrarily and as repeated wars against the Muslim south and Christian neighbours necessitated raising extraordinary funds for warfare and mobilizing noble knights and their retainers, urban militias, and the monastic military orders. It is against this backdrop that we find the first convocations of representative institutions in Leon-Castile (O'Callaghan 1975, 277–278; O'Callaghan 1989, 130–131).

In the twelfth century, all Christian Spanish rulers convoked king's councils (*curia*, vernacular *corte*), a consultative body attended by notables to discuss matters of the realm. The standard formula was that kings acted 'with the counsel of the chief men of my curia' (O'Callaghan 1975, 264–265, 287; Procter 1980, 1–18). It is very difficult to attest when these curies turned into *cortes*, genuine representative institutions (Marongiu 1968, 63; Procter 1980, e.g. 46, 51–52, 107–108; Cerda 2011, 62). In what follows, I will embed two landmark episodes in a more general narrative to tease out what occasioned the initial convocation and the later institutionalization of the *cortes* in Leon-Castile.

We begin with the three first assemblies to which townsmen definitely sent their representatives: Leon in 1188, 1202, and 1208 (Procter 1980, 45). The first convocation followed immediately after Alfonso IX's accession to the Leonese throne. The new king faced a perilous situation. His father Ferdinand II's misrule had emptied the royal coffers and stoked opposition among both nobles and towns across Leon. On top of this, there was a latent threat – which erupted into genuine warfare in the 1190s and again in 1204 – from Castile, which claimed the border region of Tierra de Campus and harboured a rival claim on the Leonese throne, as well as a threat from Portugal over Galicia (Bianchini 2012, 22–23, 39–43). Finally, the Popes repeatedly excommunicated Alfonso due to marriages that transgressed the rules of consanguinity (O'Callaghan 1975, 242–245; Procter 1980, 49). Alfonso was thus pressured both externally and internally when he summoned townsmen to Leon in April 1188. The main reason for convening the early assemblies in 1188, 1202, and 1208 was to gain consent to taxation, more explicitly to the aptly termed *moneda,* which was granted by the towns in exchange for a pledge not to debase the currency[1] for a seven-year period, the first time in 1202 (O'Callaghan 1975, 267; Procter 1980, 54). But the admittedly scarce evidence also indicates that it was an alliance between Leonese nobles and towns that forced Alfonso's hand (Marongiu 1968, 62).

The *cortes* was slower to develop in Castile, but after the unification between Leon and Castile in 1230, and especially after 1250, the *cortes* was regularly convoked (Marongiu 1968, 64–65; Procter 1980, 167). The voting of taxes at the *cortes* seems to have been premised on the king first addressing the grievances of towns, nobles, and clergy (O'Callaghan 1989, 75). The most important tax came to be the direct tax of the *servicio,* first levied at a *cortes* at Burgos in 1269 (Procter 1980, 190–194), but over time the *cortes* granted a bewildering variety of taxes (O'Callaghan 1989, 130–151). Often, these subsidies were intended to pay stipends (*soldades*) to magnates for military service, propped up by town militias as stipulated in the communal *fueros* and by the monastic military orders (O'Callaghan 1975, 456; 1989, 51). Changes in conditions for military service – both for nobles and for town militias – could also be altered only at the *cortes* (e.g., at Segovia in 1256, Seville in 1264, and Burgos in 1338), as consent from those affected was necessary (O'Callaghan 1989, 109).

The most frequent convocations of the *cortes* occurred during succession conflicts (Marongiu 1968, 64–65; O'Callaghan 1975, 334–335), the most protracted of which was that which began with the challenge against Alfonso X in 1272 and in a sense continued up through the minorities of Fernando IV (who was six years old when he succeeded to the throne in 1295) and of Alfonso XI (who was eleven years old when crowned in 1312). The backdrop of these conflicts was the attempt of Alfonso X (1252–1284) to rationalize law and taxation in Castile, based upon the framework of the revived Roman law.[2] This was a general pattern in thirteenth- and fourteenth-century Castile, and the repeated attempts to impose uniform territorial law at the expense of the traditional *fueros* nearly always stoked opposition, especially from the nobility (O'Callaghan 1975, 450, 467–469). It certainly did so under Alfonso X as the magnates rebelled in 1272 (Linehan 1999, 693). The conflict threatened Alfonso X's ambition to win the imperial crown as Holy Roman Emperor, and he was therefore forced to come to an agreement. At the *cortes* in Burgos in September 1272, Alfonso reconfirmed the traditional privileges of both the nobility and the towns (the *Fuero antiguo*), at the cost of arresting his own attempt at judicial rationalization and centralization (the *Fuero real*) (O'Callaghan 1975, 372–373; 1989, 22–24, 117–120; Procter 1980, 133–143, 180; Linehan 1999, 694).

To make matters worse, Alfonso's son, Sancho, who had played a key role in keeping a Moroccan invasion at bay in 1275, fell out with his father, who was still very unpopular among both the nobility and the townsmen. Most of the nobles and town accordingly sided with Sancho, who called a *cortes*-like assembly[3] at Valladolid in the spring of 1282 to usurp power (Linehan 1999, 695). The succession strife of 1282–1284 placed the autonomous groups of Leon-Castile at the centre of politics.

A number of so-called *hermandades* – associations of towns, nobles, or clergy – were formed in these turbulent years (Procter 1980, 103; O'Callaghan 1989, 24–26). These associations normally convoked their own regular assemblies and presented a forceful way of defending their rights (O'Callaghan 1975, 448). For almost half a century, the *hermandades* – mostly those of the towns – would dominate political affairs of Leon-Castile (Linehan 1999, 621).

At the 1282 assembly, Sancho accepted both annual convocations of the *hermandades* that supported him and recognized their right to resistance if traditional *fueros* were not respected (O'Callaghan 1989, 86). Sancho's premature death in 1295 was followed by the minority of his son, Fernando IV (1295–1301). During this period, the *cortes* was convoked nearly annually. The *hermandades* repeatedly used their power to dominate the crown, perhaps most spectacularly at Fernando's first *cortes* at Valladolid 1295, where the towns insisted that the king could not demand forced loans without consent, in effect equating loans with extraordinary levies (O'Callaghan 1989, 29, 133). Even during Fernando's later reign (1301–1312), the *cortes* was used to control and weaken the monarchy (O'Callaghan 1989, 30–33). For instance, the *cortes* of Valladolid in 1307 demanded the right to audit the king's expenses (a practice that was repeated at Burgos in 1315) (O'Callaghan 1989, 139–141, 200). Finally, there were also very frequent convocations of the *cortes* during the subsequent minority of Alfonso XI (1312–1325) as towns and nobles often allied to keep the regency checked (O'Callaghan 1989, 34). In fact, the power of the *hermandades* and the *cortes* might be said to have climaxed during the regency after 1312 (O'Callaghan 1989, 90–92). At the *cortes* of Palencia in 1313, the regency even promised biannual convocations. Although this promise was not fulfilled, it testifies to the institutionalized place in the government of the realm that the *cortes* had achieved (O'Callaghan 1989, 196).

The crown of Aragon

The *Reconquista* also embroiled the crown of Aragon – which included Catalonia (after 1137), the Kingdom of Valencia (after 1238), and a series of Mediterranean possessions (e.g., Sicily after 1282) – in generalized geopolitical pressure throughout the eleventh, twelfth, and thirteenth centuries (O'Callaghan 1975). Meanwhile, the crown of Aragon faced a series of other threats, sometimes from neighbouring Leon-Castile, sometimes from north of the Pyrenees as the kings of Aragon confronted the French royal house over Provence and, later, Sicily.

As in Castile, conquered Muslim towns were resettled by Christians who were granted charters (*fueros*) of self-government in exchange for military service and paying taxes (Kagay 1981, 17; Bartlett 1993). As early as 1077, the old capital city of Jaca was granted a charter of liberties (Bisson 1986, 13). More generally, the conquered Muslim towns were resettled by Christians who were granted *fueros* of self-government against promising military service and taxes (Kagay 1981, 17). Reconquered Zaragoza had achieved such privileges by the 1130s, with Daroca following in 1142, and Tereul in 1171. The Catalonian development was a bit tardier, but, in the twelfth and thirteenth centuries, many Catalonian towns also achieved charters (*furs*) as part of the same process. Tortosa received a charter in 1148, Lerida in 1149, and Barcelona in 1163. More generally, by 1200 many Catalan towns had gained municipal autonomy, codified in their respective *furs* (Bisson 1986, 32–33, 42–45).

A recurring pattern was that Aragonese count-kings,[4] upon succession to the throne, would promise to uphold *fueros* and *furs* in return for the towns declaring their allegiance to the crown (Kagay 1981, 37–38).

The Aragonese nobility was historically very strong. As described below, it revolted against the king on repeated occasions – e.g., in 1283, 1287, and 1348 (Kagay 1981, 8). The potency of this nobility can also to be traced to the *Reconquista,* as the kings of Aragon established powerful tenants-in-chief in the new areas south of Old Aragon (O'Callaghan 1975, 358; Bisson 1986, 17). Likewise, charters were awarded to the clergy as part of the resettlement, including to the military orders of the Temple and the Hospital, which were an active force in the wars with the Muslims (Bisson 1986, 42–45). Similar developments occurred in Catalonia (Bisson 1986, 33).

Royal councils of magnates had been assembled from at least the eleventh century. Townsmen were present as early as the assembly at Jaca in 1134, where the Aragonese nobility managed to extract one of Europe's earliest 'great charters' of customary rights from Alfonso I (Bisson 1986, 18). But it was during James's long reign (1213–1276) that, first, the Catalan *corts* and, later, the Aragonese *cortes* came to take the form of a genuine representative institution (Kagay 1981, 152–153, 356; Bisson 1986, 80–81; Møller 2016a). In both Aragon and Catalonia, James called frequent assemblies during the first part of his reign, which were used to secure subsidies, mainly from the towns (as nobles and clergy were exempted from direct taxation) (Kagay 1981, 67–73, 77–82; Bisson 1986, 79–80; Abulafia 1999, 645–646). James came to be known as the Conqueror; signal victories include the conquest of the Balearic Islands in 1229–35 and the conquest of the kingdom of Valencia in 1238. Thus, many of his assemblies were convoked to prepare for campaigns against the Muslims – e.g., an assembly at Barcelona in December 1228 to prepare an attack on Muslim Majorca and a general *cort* (comprising both Catalans and Aragonese) at Monzon in December 1232 to prepare a campaign against Muslim Valencia (O'Callaghan 1975, 342–347; Kagay 1981, 96–105; Bisson 1986, 64–66).

However, both *corts* and *cortes* only became institutionalized parts of the regime after the death of the conqueror and the revolutionary events of the 1280s. The prelude is to be found in James I's military campaigns. Though these were generally successful, James' attempt to leverage his possessions for warfare repeatedly antagonized the Aragonese nobility and towns, who felt that he violated his customary rights by rationalizing legislation and taxing without consent. Moreover, they were dissatisfied that James consulted the magnates and towns less often in the second part of his reign (Abulafia 1999, 660). The nobles countered this by creating the so-called *Union.* As early as 1265, the Union forced James to grant new *fueros* to the Aragonese nobility and to establish the ombudsman office of *Justicia* (O'Callaghan

1975, 366–367; Kagay 1981, 135–137). By the end of James' reign, the Aragonese nobles were in virtual revolt (Bisson 1986, 73)

James' successor, Peter the Great, started his reign with a spectacular foreign policy triumph when he wrested Sicily from the House of Anjou following the Sicilian Vespers in 1282. But this acquisition came at a heavy price, as it embroiled the crown of Aragon in conflict with the French Angevins in Naples, the French pope Martin IV, and ultimately the French kings, later backed by Castile (O'Callaghan 1975, 387–388; Kagay 1981, 213). This situation represented the gravest threat to its existence that the crown of Aragon was to experience in the Middle Ages (Bisson 1986, 88). The pope excommunicated Peter and released his subjects from fealty (O'Callaghan 1975, 388), the Angevins counterattacked in Southern Italy, and, in 1285, the French king marched across the Pyrenees and invaded Catalonia.

Peter also faced unrest at home. At a *cortes* at Tarazona in September 1283, the Aragonese magnates protested that they were being unlawfully taxed and that they had not been consulted over Sicily. The Union was formed again and gained the support of a number of important Aragonese towns. As always, the main aim of the Union was to secure the Aragonese *fueros*, but this time it also attempted to secure more general control over the king's administration via the *cortes* (Kagay 1981, 164–166). The Aragonese towns and nobles had an effective weapon: the refusal to aid Peter militarily against the French and Angevin threat until their grievances had been addressed. Peter responded by summoning the Aragonese nobles and townsmen to Zaragoza, where, in October 1283, he granted the *Privilegio General*. Besides reconfirming customary rights at the expense of Roman law, the privileges included a pledge to invoke the *cortes* annually, to reconfirm the ombudsman office of *Justicia*, and to take counsel in the *cortes* about future wars. This transformed the *cortes* from an assembly convoked at the king's initiative to a permanent public institution (O'Callaghan 1975, 388–389; Kagay 1981, 169–177).

The Union kept up the pressure by itself becoming a permanent institution meant to check the king. It even began to convene its own assemblies, and it deliberately used the French threat to press further demands on first King Peter and, later, his successor Alphonse III (1285–91) (Kagay 1981, 192–197). When Philip III invaded Catalonia in 1285, the Aragonese refused to aid Peter militarily. In 1287, the Union openly rebelled against Alphonse III, threatening to recognize the French prince of Valois as their sovereign. This challenge occasioned the aptly termed *Privilegios de la Union* at the *cortes* of Zaragoza in January 1288 (O'Callaghan 1975, 394–395). These privileges guaranteed that nobles and members of town councils could only be tried by the *Justicia* and that the *cortes* had to be consulted in all matters of royal government. Finally, the king accepted that those who pledge a tax also collect it (Kagay 1981, 216–243).

The Aragonese monarchs faced similar restive forces in Catalonia. These were easier placated, albeit at a cost comparable to that paid in Aragon. At the Catalan *corts* at Barcelona in December 1283, Peter confirmed customary law (including the *furs*) at the expense of royal law and promised an annual convocation of the *corts*, which were to be endowed with legislative powers (Marongiu 1968, 68–69;

O'Callaghan 1975, 389; Kagay 1981, 189). The *corts* responded by granting Peter extraordinary funding for the French wars, but this was to be collected by members of the *corts* itself. This was a harbinger of the so-called *Generalidat*, a committee of the *corts* that came to collect and audit taxes in the second part of the fourteenth century (O'Callaghan 1975, 443–444; Kagay 1981, 212).

The concessions of the 1280s can be seen as the birth certificate of representative institutions under the Crown of Aragon (Kagay 1981, 1189). More generally, the result of the upheavals between 1282 and 1287 was that the constitutional balance of power was altered, with the *corts* and the *cortes* now institutionalized as an estate pole confronting the monarch (Bisson 1986, 90).

England

Twelfth-century England was but one of several units of a composite Plantagenet realm, which also included other parts of Great Britain and huge tracts of continental possessions from Normandy to the Pyrenees. By the end of the twelfth century, this realm had become embroiled in generalized geopolitical competition as the Plantagenet kings attempted to expand their influence in Ireland, Wales, and Scotland, while also defending their position in France (Carpenter 1999; Maddicott 2010).

The Plantagenet kings' need to leverage their possessions for warfare came to provide a rallying point for opposition against the crown (Maddicott 2010, 97–103). To track the establishment of the English Parliament, three particular episodes of opposition against the English kings should be examined: the events that produced the Magna Carta of 1215, the stormy years of 1258–1259 and 1264–1265, and the protracted conflict between 1311 and 1327 (see Marongiu 1968, 79; Maddicott 2010).

The magnates constituted the most powerful social group in England, deriving from the Norman conquest of 1066, and were a group that, even before the advent of Parliament, had exerted a key influence on the crown (Finer 1997a, 1039). The clergy constituted another important group. Henry I had issued a charter of liberties to the barons and to the church upon his coronation in 1100, and it was also Henry who abandoned lay investiture in 1106 (Bisson 2009, 175; Maddicott 2010, 69). Finally, there were towns with self-government and charters, but (with London as the exception) these were of much less consequence than the self-governing Spanish towns discussed above (Vincent 2012, 61–62).

In the last decades of the twelfth century and the first decades of the thirteenth century, Plantagenet England experienced what was probably the most systematic increase in royal power and royal financial extortion anywhere in Western Europe at the time (Carpenter 1990, 7–8; 1999, 320). The Plantagenet kings had first increased financial exploitation due to the threat from Capetian France; further hikes occurred to recoup the French possessions following King John's (1199–1216) string of defeats in 1204 (Carpenter 1999, 322–323; Vincent 2012, 38–39, 43). This financial exploitation sparked opposition from among the English magnates (Bisson

2009, 515–516). John also fell out with the Church over investiture, and, in the period 1208–1213, England became placed under interdict and John excommunicated (Carpenter 1999, 319). The final strain came when John's attempt to reconquer the Plantagenet possessions in Normandy and Anjou came to naught in his defeat at the battle of Bouvines in Northern France on 27 July 1214. This sparked a rebellion led by the magnates but at least tacitly supported by the clergy and with the townsmen of London also playing an important role. The result of the ensuing confrontation was King John's issuing of the Magna Carta in June 1215. The Magna Carta can be seen as a general attempt by the magnates to restore their customary rights in the face of an arbitrary royal centralization (Carpenter 1999, 322; Maddicott 2010, 127; Vincent 2012, 60, 78). Most important in the present context is Clause 14, which emphasized the need for consent for extraordinary taxation (Maddicott 2010, 119).

The Magna Carta was in a sense a failure, as John – supported by the Pope – immediately rescinded it. However, it was to become a focal point for the development of the English Parliament in the following century (Maddicott 2010, 228). From 1216 onwards the Popes backed the Charter, and, throughout the period analysed below, the magnates consistently maintained – normally with reference to the Magna Carta – that a public tax required consent from the realm, i.e., from the magnates. This principle had become accepted by the 1230s at the latest (Carpenter 1999, 337–338).

In the first part of his long reign, John's son Henry III (1216–1272) repeatedly turned to the magnates to secure consent for taxation (Carpenter 1990, 54–63). For instance, in 1225, at a 'great council' in London, the magnates granted Henry a subsidy for warfare against France on the condition that the Magna Carta be reissued (Maddicott 2010, 109). During the second part of the thirteenth century, this was to transform the consultative assemblies of notables, which English kings had long called, and which as early as the 1170s were sometimes referred to as *parlements*, into genuine representative institutions.

Henry did not repeat John's arbitrary financial demands, but he nevertheless managed to alienate both a large part of the nobility and a large part of the clergy. During the first part of his reign, Henry repeatedly asked his assemblies to grant extraordinary levies to assist him in regaining the lost lands in France. The magnates frequently disputed whether such taxes were necessary or the result of vainglorious ambition (Marongiu 1968, 83; Hariss 1975, 36–38; Maddicott 2010, 170–175). Yet the main reason for the final fallout was Henry's attempt to place his second son Edmund on the Sicilian throne. Henry first alienated the English church by making it pay huge amounts to the Pope between 1254 and 1259 in exchange for having Sicily awarded as a fief to Edmund (Carpenter 1999, 333–335). Tapping clerical wealth was necessary for Henry's design, but it was not sufficient. In 1258, he requested a grant of taxation to fulfil his Sicilian ambitions, which triggered a baronial challenge. The magnates had been opposed to the Sicilian business from the start, and they now opposed the tax, which they did not deem necessary. Henry had no chance of collecting the tax without support from the magnates, who – supported by the clergy – used this to force the so-called Provisions of Oxford upon him (Maddicott 2010, 235–236).

The Provisions included a clause about the regular convocation of parliaments. For the first time, Parliament had gained a formal place in the English body politic (Maddicott 2010, 234). Other clauses concerned the provision of justice and reforms to the law. Henry partly rolled back these reforms in 1261, but only to pave the way for an even more tangible challenge, which culminated with Simon de Montfort's victory over Henry at Lewes on 14 May 1264 (Carpenter 1999, 340). Montfort proceeded to call parliaments in 1264 and 1265, which included both elected representatives of the shires and burgesses. Montfort was then defeated and killed at Evesham in August 1265, but, at the Marlborough Parliament of November 1267, the reinstated Henry essentially confirmed the provision of 1258–9 (Maddicott 2010, 263–264).

Fast-forward to the late 1290s, where the soldiers in English armies were increasingly paid directly by the crown and where renewed wars with Scotland and France hugely increased the financial needs of the crown (Omrod 2000, 281–282). Edward I (1272–1307) and Edward II (1307–1327) responded by raising large amounts of extraordinary taxation and increasing duties on trade. These significant demands, in turn, bred a political challenge that would define the role of Parliament (Ormrod 2000, 295–296). Even at this stage, the English king had no standing army, no police force, and no local royal administration. The king's ability to raise revenue relied on cooperation from the strong groups that penetrated English society in general, and from the magnates in particular (Omrod 2000, 284–285).

Edward I had been adept at handling this relationship but during Edward II's tenure, the magnates recurrently challenged his authority during confrontations over the need for extraordinary taxation. In the February Parliament of 1310, the magnates forced Edward to accept the appointment of twenty-one Lord Ordainers. These then presented the so-called 'New Ordinances' in the autumn of 1311, which established that consent must also be secured for military service (Hariss 1975, 90; Omrod 2000, 286). More generally, during Edward II's reign, taxes were only granted provided that the king addressed the grievances presented by the magnates on behalf of the community of the realm (Hariss 1975, 105–108).

Edward II was to defeat the magnates and annul the Ordinances in 1322. But his chosen medium for this annulment was Parliament. Moreover, Edward's actions sparked renewed opposition, which in 1327 led to his deposition and murder as a magnate coalition headed by the queen and her lover, Mortimer, defeated him. Crucially, the acts were formally transacted in Parliament, where Edward abdicated before he was killed (Omrod 2000, 287–288). His son, Edward III, ascended the throne in January 1327 and in 1330 sidelined the queen and Mortimer. But rather than challenging the nobility, Edward III tried to placate them via a combination of capable administration and political concessions. This was once again necessary due to warfare, this time in the form of the Hundred Years' War with France (the beginning of which is normally dated to 1337). In April 1341, Edward was forced to accept that nobles could be tried only by peers. The working relationship established between king and nobility was so effective that there were no armed rebellions against Edward III during his long reign between 1330 and 1377 (Ormrod 2000, 289–290).

Edward III's reign was characterized by a broadening of the political community, as the local representatives of shires and towns increasingly partook in rule via Parliament. Elected representatives from the shires had first appeared at Parliament in 1254. By the 1290s, they had become a mainstay, and, after 1327, townsmen also attended all Parliaments (Ormrod 2000, 291). By the beginning of the Hundred Years' War, this had brought into being a bicameral representative institution, and, during Edward's reign, the Commons gradually took over the power to consent to taxation and as the main forum for presenting petitions to the king (Hariss 1975, 98). The coming of age of the Commons can be attested by the so-called Good Parliament of 1376, where the Commons refused to grant Edward III a direct tax before grievances had been addressed (Ormrod 2000, 292–295).

The English case, in spite of the role played by the citizenry of London, shows that the communal revolution is not sufficient to explain the advent of representative institutions. In England, the magnates played the key role, but the church and the English localities also weighed in. England is also rather idiosyncratic with respect to the absence of privileges such as exemptions from taxation for the nobility. Nonetheless, the English kings needed to tap ecclesiastical wealth to be able to muster forces of sufficient size to take on the French kings but often were unable to do so due to opposition from English bishops and the pope. In that sense, the English development also very much testifies to the importance of multiple strong social groups that could balance rulers in the context of geopolitical competition.

Ancient China

As we know from Chapter 14, for more than five hundred years – during the so-called Spring and Autumn Period (771–476 BC) and the ensuing Warring States Period (475–221 BC) – ancient China was characterized by a multistate system. By 656 BC, this system was characterized by generalized geopolitical competition (Hsu 1999; Hui 2005, 57), which further intensified in the Warring States period (481–221 BC) (Hsu 1999, 545–586; Lewis 1999, 587–650). In the early part of the period, there were approximately 150 states, many of them very small. By the end of the Warring States Period, less than ten states were left (Hsu 1999, 567; Bradford 2001, 136). This process is remarkably similar to that described by Charles Tilly (1975, 15) in medieval and early modern Europe (cf. Hui 2004; 2005).

The remaining states vied for hegemony, but they did so in a context that was very different from what we have seen in the analysis of medieval Spain and medieval England. Even Hui (2005), who makes an assertive case for the similarities in state-society relations in early modern Europe and ancient China, concedes that a big difference is to be found in the absence of a multiplicity of autonomous social groups in the latter and its presence in the former (Hui 2005, 202–203). The only important social group in Spring and Autumn and early Warring States China was the hereditary nobility. This nobility had grown immensely strong in the Western Zhou Period (1046–771 BC), and well into the Spring and Autumn Period it was able to provide important checks on the rulers (Li 2006, 127). No independent clergy existed alongside this nobility, and there is no documentation that cities had a communal autonomy similar to that of medieval Europe (Bodde 1956, 60–62; Elvin 1978).

There is some evidence of convocations of assemblies of notables (*gou ren*) by ancient Chinese rulers during the Spring and Autumn Period (Hsu 1999, 572; Hui 2005, 196–197). But these never developed into anything like representative institutions. To understand why this was so, we first need to more closely examine the effects of the generalized geopolitical competition of ancient China. After 656 BC and especially towards the end of the Warring States Period, we find an explosion in the intensity and scope of warfare (Lewis 1999; Hsu 1999; Hui 2005, 242–248). This was premised upon a rationalization of the state apparatus, including the military (Hsu 1999; Lewis 1999; Hui 2004; 2005). Chinese states such as Qin repeatedly adopted institutions and techniques that had proven effective in neighbouring states. Most important was the transition from aristocratic chariot warfare to mass infantry armies, which began in the Spring and Autumn Period and produced huge armies into the Warring States Period (Hsu 1999, 573; Lewis 1999, 601, 612–620; Hui 2005, 58–65; von Falkenhausen 2006, 8). This, in turn, necessitated additional reforms such as the introduction of conscription, censuses of the population, and direct taxation of the peasantry.

This shoring up of state power as a response to geopolitical competition largely undermined the nobility because it lost its military function, which had been based on chariot warfare (Hsu 1999, 573; Lewis 1999, 97–599, 620–621; von Falkenhausen 2006, 8–9). Archaeological findings document that the ranked elite was weakened severely after the onset of sustained geopolitical pressure in the seventh century BC (Li 2006; von Falkenhausen 2006; cf. Hsu 1999, 564). Around the mid-fourth century BC, power was concentrated in the person of the rulers who had developed from the 'highest representatives of the ranked elite' in the Spring and Autumn Period to the despotic kings of Warring States China, the formerly strong nobility now completely marginalized politically (Lewis 1999, 602–603; von Falkenhausen 2006, 326–328, 365–369, 391–395). For instance, office-holding changed from being a hereditary privilege for nobles to an annex of royal power (Lewis 1999, 597, 603–604, 611).

This development was a general one (see Lewis 1999; von Falkenhausen 2006, 8–9, 326–328, 365–369), but it was most conspicuous in the state of Qin, which as we know from Chapter 14 would eventually roll up the system entirely and establish the first Chinese Empire in 221 BC. It is therefore worthwhile to look a bit closer at Qin's trajectory and development. The career of the statesman Shang Yang in Qin from 356 onwards is often used to illustrate the political and administrative reforms that were implemented in Warring States China (e.g., Hui 2005, 80–84). Shang Yang was a nobleman who first served as an official in the state of Wei but then moved to Qin. Here, he rose to pre-eminence at the court of Duke Xiao and carried out a set of ambitious reforms designed to increase taxation and mobilize the citizenry for military service. Borrowing from other warring states (including Wei), the catalogue of reforms included a detailed legal code with draconically tough penalties, administrative reforms creating direct rule at the local level, a hierarchy of titles to reward meritorious state service, agricultural reforms, and the introduction of a head tax (Lewis 1999, 612–615). These reforms produced a significant increase in the state's ability to steer the economy and in its administrative reach into localities.

Shang Yang's reforms weakened the privileges of the hereditary nobles, who were removed from state service and became superfluous militarily due to the mass armies that could now be mustered (Hui 2005, 102–103). Nonetheless, these reforms sparked no significant revolts against the centralization of princely power. They did, however, produce a court rebellion against Shang Yang when Duke Xiao died in 338 BC, though this was primarily because the former Crown Prince had been a victim of some of Shang Yang's policies. Upon ascending the throne as King Huiwen, he got rid of Shang Yang. But, crucially, he maintained the reforms.

Shang Yang's reforms were important for Qin's ability to roll up the multi-state system in the third century BC. The final Qin rise lasted more than a century, from 356 BC to 221 BC (Hui 2004). By 300 BC, Qin had consolidated its territorial situation: after 284 BC it was clearly the strongest Chinese state, and after 256 BC there was an obvious Qin superiority. Throughout this period, the Qin rulers were able to consolidate their conquests due to the reforms described above. Annexed territories were divided into administrative districts directly governed by officials, who extracted taxes from the population and organized their military service (Lewis 1999, 614–615). One reason that this was possible was that the conquered areas did not contain strong autonomous groups that had to be co-opted (Hui 2005, 97–98). It is telling that – scanning the 135-year period where Qin rose to pre-eminence – we find little evidence that the aggressive attempt to leverage the Qin domains for warfare stoked domestic opposition. More generally, the frequency of civil wars seems to have decreased dramatically from the Spring and Autumn Period to the late part of the Warring States Period, where the Chinese rulers had consolidated their position at the expense of the nobility (Hsu 1999, 568; Lewis 1999, 598; Hui 2005, 206).

Early modern Russia

For centuries after the Mongol invasions in the 1230s, Russia was isolated from the warfare of Western and Central Europe. But by the 1550s, Russia had become embroiled in geopolitical pressures on two fronts: against the Tartar khanates in the southeast and against Poland and Sweden in the northwest. This pressure further increased as a consequence of Peter the Great's humiliating defeat against the Swedes at Narva in 1700 (Riasanovsky 1969, 245; Finer 1997b, 1413; Hosking 2001, 185). There is consensus in the literature that Russia's intense state-building and military build-up after 1700 was elicited by war (Finer 1997b, 1413; Taylor 2003, 29).

What was the nature of the Russian society that was affected by this exogenous geopolitical impulse? It is often observed that Muscovite Russia contained no strong societal groups (Hintze 1975[1931], 341; Downing 1992, 38–43), but it is more correct to say that medieval Muscovy was characterized by a very simple pattern of social stratification. The landowners were strong, ecclesiastical landholding was relatively important, the middle class was weak or virtually non-existent, and the large mass of the population were peasants (Riasanovsky 1969, 129–131; Hosking 2001).

Traditionally, the Russian nobility, the Boyars, were strong vis-à-vis the rulers (first Grand Princes, later Tsars, later Emperors), not least because the rulers relied on them militarily (Riasanovsky 1969, 163–164). The more specific political manifestation of this was that the Boyars – via the so-called Boyar Duma – participated in ruling the realm (Ostrowski 2006, 215). In the seventeenth century, the Duma contained between 28 and 153 members, with membership largely hereditary (Evtuhov et al. 2004, 175). The Duma was continually in session, and the proclamation of state policies was based on the formula 'The Grand Prince decrees with the Boyars' (Ostrowski 2006, 224–225). It has been pointed out that the Duma almost qualified as a court of law, one that also helped the rulers legislate (Evtuhov et al. 2004, 105).

The Boyar Duma was emphatically an advisory body, and it shared many similarities with the kings' courts or magnate assemblies that we find in the medieval Iberian states prior to the convocation of representative institutions. Though the Boyars were often able to balance the Grand Princes, they did so as members of clans or families, not as an autonomous societal group (Finer 1997b, 1411). More generally, it was not laws and institutions that empowered the high nobility politically but simply closeness and personal ties to the ruler (Evtuhov et al. 2004, 167; Lieven, 2006, 228). The Boyars 'lacked any formal, corporate, or legal means of checking him, unlike their Western counterparts' (Evtuhov et al. 2004, 105–106; Lieven, 2006, 239). The same can be said about a second important social group, the clergy. The Russian relationship between church and state was based on the Byzantine tradition of symphony – or at least harmony – and there was no crisp distinction between the secular and the religious spheres (Ostrowski 2006, 224–225). The clergy was therefore not an autonomous group, and it had little formal ability to constrain the rulers.

The Boyar Duma was not alone in advising the tsars. In 1549, Ivan the Terrible convened what came to be known as the *Zemskii Sobor*, a gathering where the monarch met with primarily the Boyar nobility and the Orthodox clergy but occasionally also freemen more generally. In the first decade of Romanov rule, the *Zemskii Sobor* can be said to have participated in the government of Russia (Riasanovsky 1969, 193; Evtuhov et al. 2004, 131). Whereas the Boyar Duma had little to do with representative institutions, the status of the *Zemskii Sobors* is more disputed in the literature. Some have accepted it as a representative institution (e.g., Van

Zanden et al. 2012, 842).[5] The bulk of scholarship disagrees with this and stresses that membership was not based on representation and that the assembly had no institutionalized position in rulership (Myers 1975, 34–37; Downing 1992, 38–43). Ivan's *Zemskii Sobor* was made up of 'servitors of the tsar rather than delegates of constituencies' (Bogatyrev 2006, 251).

However, in the previous case studies, we have seen that the development of representative institutions was everywhere a gradual process. The convening of *Zemskii Sobors* was probably partly an attempt to imitate the Western European representative institutions, which were well-known in early modern Russia. But as opposed to what occurred in Leon-Castile and Aragon-Catalonia (and elsewhere in Western Europe) in the thirteenth and early fourteenth centuries, the *Zemskii Sobor* never developed into a genuine representative institution with independent prerogatives. Why was that?

To answer this question, it makes sense to zoom in on the events sparked by the intensification of geopolitical competition. The external pressure impelled Ivan the Terrible to expand the army and invite foreign expertise on military matters (Riasanovsky 1969, 161–163; Parker 1996[1988], 38). The most important aspect of Ivan's rule was not the convocation of the first *Zemskii Sobor* in 1549 but a ruthless centralization of power. Ivan reformed the state apparatus, established the first standing army (the so-called *Streltsy*), and introduced the first laws restricting the mobility of peasants. Moreover, using what at times amounted to a reign of terror, Ivan severely weakened the Boyar nobility. In 1564, Ivan forced the Boyars to grant him absolute powers and started a ruthless campaign against internal enemies (the so-called '*oprichnina* terror') (Riasanovsky 1969, 157–172; Evtuhov et al. 2004, 123–126, 132–138; Bogatyrev 2006). Ivan's policies severely destabilized Russia, but, by rolling back the power of the Boyars, they also paved the way for the creation of a much stronger autocracy.

This development continued when geopolitical competition further intensified during the reign of Peter the Great. Peter introduced universal conscription and a direct poll tax on peasants and townspeople, issued internal passports, carried out censuses, and introduced the meritocratic Table of Ranks (Hosking 2001, 196–219). The two most important reforms were the introduction of general conscription and the introduction of a direct head tax on all peasants and townspeople (Riasanovsky 1969, 252–259; Taylor 2003, 29). Peter also completely reorganized central government along lines inspired by Western European states in general and Sweden in particular.

All of the listed reforms were carried out in a top-down manner: by intensifying coercion (Hosking 2001, 176; Taylor 2003, 40; Evtuhov et al. 2004, 221). This was possible because Peter faced such limited restraints on his power (Taylor 2003, 40). But it was also required, as neither prior institutions nor strong groups were available as the building blocks that state-builders could use to create and staff new structures. There was simply no extant 'transmission belt for government authority' (Hosking 2001, 215–216). The result was that the traditional constraints on the power of Muscovite grand princes and later tsars were removed by Peter. He had no use for an independent church, the Boyar Duma, or convening *Zemskii Sobors*, and, by ignoring these institutions, he largely escaped the traditional barriers against absolute power in Muscovy (Riasanovsky 1969, 254–255; Finer 1997b, 1414–1416).

The nobility Peter brought under his thumb via his establishment of a new Table of Ranks. This made rank – especially military rank – much more meritocratic and much less dependent upon noble status (Evtuhov et al. 2004, 215–217; cf. Finer 1997b, 1415). Peter similarly short-changed the church – or at least its ability to restrain him politically. In 1721 he went so far as to abolish the Patriarchy and replace it with a 'Holy Synod'. The Synod was staffed by clergy, but it was overseen by a secular official, normally an officer. This new arrangement gave Peter – and subsequent emperors – virtual control of church possessions, church organization, and church policies (Riasanovsky 1969, 257; Finer 1997b, 1416; Hosking 2001, 198–199). The *de facto* constraints on the rulers that existed before the onset of geopolitical competition were thus swept away as Peter created an autocratic regime that differed conspicuously from the contemporary Western European cases of absolutism (Hosking 1997, 78–92; Finer 1997b, 1419).

Conclusions

Table 19.1 summarizes the empirical evidence, substantiated in the case studies above, on how the two medieval Iberian cases and medieval England, on the one hand, and ancient China and early modern Russia, on the other hand, can be ordered on the variables shown in Figure 17.1. The five cases are all characterized by the onset of geopolitical competition. But this occurred in the context of radically different state-society relations. In the Iberian cases and in England, multiple autonomous groups were in existence prior to the advent of representative institutions, whereas only the ranked nobility was important in ancient China and early modern Russia. The case studies thus corroborate the argument summarized in Figure 17.1: a relatively similar geopolitical pressure produced representative institution in the former context but an intensification of absolutism in the latter context, including a weakening of the hitherto strong ranked nobility.

The empirical analysis has been restricted to three among the many realms of medieval Latin Christendom. But the explanatory model arguably has a general relevance for all of Latin Christendom. As Hintze (1975[1931], 346), Ertman (1997), and Stasavage (2011) point out, a nascent state system was in existence in Western Europe after the twelfth century (see also Myers 1975, 56; Maddicott 2010, 106). With respect to the autonomous groups, the clergy had established its autonomy following the Gregorian reforms in the second half of the eleventh century (Southern 1970), a majority of the European cities which were to gain their political autonomy (meaning that they had institutions for self-governance, the officials filling which were elected or chosen by lot) had done so before 1200, and most of the remaining free cities followed before 1300 (Bartlett 1993; Stasavage 2014, 14–17).

TABLE 19.1 Summary of scores on the variables of geopolitical competition, state-society relations, and regime change

	Leon-Castile, Aragon-Catalonia, and England	Ancient China	Early modern Russia
Onset of geopolitical competition	12th century AD	7th century BC	16th century AD
Initial state-society relations	Multiple autonomous groups (nobility, clergy, and townsmen)	Hereditary nobility	Hereditary nobility
Development in state-society relations	Privileges of autonomous groups entrenched	Nobility weakened	Nobility weakened
Regime change	Assemblies of notables superseded by representative institutions 1200–1300 AD	Entrenchment of absolutism in 4th and 3rd century BC, including the disappearance of assemblies of notables	Entrenchment of absolutism in 17th and 18th century AD, including the disappearance of assemblies of notables

Finally, the nobility had an independence that was recognized in the eleventh and twelfth centuries (Stacey 1999). In the period after 1050, these privileges were increasingly codified in charters, which defined privileges collectively (Bisson 2009, 351). Finally, as reported in Table 18.1, representative institutions ultimately came to characterize all of Latin Christendom.

It therefore seems plausible that the argument about the advent of representative institutions has a wider empirical purchase – i.e., that it is valid for all of Western Christendom. On top of this, we can also adduce some additional evidence from the medieval Iberian Peninsula. This peninsula contained a residual case – the Muslim area of *el-Andalus* – that was equally affected by generalized geopolitical competition. This pressure contributed to create deep internal rivalries among Muslim *taifas* in an area hitherto ruled by one power centre in Cordoba. Indeed, as the outcome of the *Reconquista* was to demonstrate, the very existence of the Muslim states was threatened. In this light, it seems puzzling that no attempt to introduce charters of self-government for frontier cities or to increase tax intakes via consultation at representative institutions occurred, even in hard-pressed Grenada. Demonstration effects must have been pervasive across the constantly shifting borders of Christian and Muslim Spain. The fact that the Muslim societies retained the absolutist regime form established by the Caliphs in Cordoba to the very end is difficult to explain without reference to the lack of the kind of autonomous groups that we find in the Spanish marcher kingdoms (O'Callaghan 1975, 137–162, 271, 432; Kagay 1981, 399).

Notes

1 As elsewhere in Western Europe, coinage was a customary regalian right in Leon-Castile (Procter 1980, 26).
2 Crucially, the new Roman law legitimized the king's right to legislate, rather than simply recognizing already-existing customary law (O'Callaghan 1989, 113).
3 It was not a genuine *cortes*, which could only be summoned by the king – that is, by Alfonso X.
4 The composite nature of the Crown of Aragon was such that the monarch was count of the county of Catalonia and king of Aragon and, later, Valencia, hence the title count-king (Bisson 1986).
5 Though it obviously does not qualify as such based on their rather demanding definition (Van Zanden et al. 2012, 837).

20

THE GENERAL CONCLUSIONS

Recall the main claim presented in Chapter 17: that representative institutions were the product of a conditional relationship. More specifically, I have argued that representative institutions arose and later became institutionalized as a result of the onset of generalized geopolitical pressure in a context characterized by multiple autonomous social groups, whereas a similar geopolitical pressure in contexts not characterized by a multiplicity of autonomous groups instead worked to intensify absolutism.

The case studies presented in Chapter 19 largely corroborate this claim, based on the methodological guidelines introduced in Chapter 18. More particularly, the Russian and Chinese cases show that even a strong nobility can be sidelined if the king can mobilize the rest of the economy directly. Can we say something more particular about the combination of social groups necessary to spark representative institutions? There is no doubt that the most powerful opposition against medieval European rulers came from the nobility (Blaydes and Chaney 2013). The most clear-cut example is England where the magnates played the key role, although the church and the English localities also weighed in. England is also rather idiosyncratic in the absence of privileges such as exemptions from taxation for the nobility. The strong English monarchy was simply able to sanction what turned into the common law, instead of having to rely on more particularistic charters for different groups. Nonetheless, the Plantagenet kings needed to tap ecclesiastical wealth to be able to muster forces of sufficient size to take on the French kings but were often unable to do so due to opposition from English bishops and the pope.

The Iberian cases testify to the importance of the towns, but they also show that the European development was much affected by the existence of an independent church that cut across borders. While the church played a hugely important role both as a material force and by spreading the notion of representation (based on Roman Law) (see, e.g., Kagay 1981, 359; Maddicott 2010, 208–209), it could have done little on its own. What mattered was the papacy's ability to use excommunication and interdict to get other autonomous groups to challenge rulers (Southern 1970).

The empirical analysis further illustrates an important theoretical point. It was not the number of autonomous groups that was critical but the fact that they were differentiated. The European case studies provide clear evidence that rulers did in fact attempt to divide the autonomous groups, normally by allying with the towns against the nobility (see also Poggi 1978, Chapter 3). But the fundamental problem was that – as opposed to an internally divided nobility – these groups inhabited functionally different social domains. Rulers faced a situation where it was not possible to mobilize for warfare without the backing of several groups. For instance, they needed the military assistance of magnates and the taxes (and sometimes militiamen) of towns – while also often depending on extraordinary levies on the church and, at least in the Iberian cases, on the knights of the monastic military orders. This not only placed the individual groups in a strong bargaining situation; it also ensured that an alliance between groups would effectively corner the monarch, at least in a context of acute external pressure or when several claimants for the throne vied for support.

The Aragonese case illustrates these points. The Aragonese nobility was an important source of high-quality soldiers as were the military orders of the Temple and the Hospital. But one of the traditional privileges of the Aragonese nobility and clergy was that they were exempted from regular taxes (though they still contributed to extraordinary levies on all property owners) (O'Callaghan 1975, 129). This meant that Aragonese count-kings mainly had to rely on the towns to secure the wherewithal needed for warfare. This in itself provided an impetus for summoning towns to the royal assemblies, where they would sometimes counterbalance hostile nobles (Kagay 1981, 152–153; Bisson 1986, 52–57). But what the story about the Aragonese Union in the 1280s shows is that in the context of an external threat, monarchs were checkmated if the towns and the nobility could find common ground (Marongiu 1968, 72–73).

Thus, the towns' function as a third force was not an unmitigated blessing for the monarch – it would have been easier to face off only the nobility, insofar as funding from the towns could be secured based on direct rule via royal officials. This point travels well to the case of Leon-Castile, where we again encounter the claim that the towns were summoned to the *cortes* to counterbalance the nobles (e.g., O'Callaghan 1969, 1515). But here, too, the historical investigation shows that it was when the towns and nobles (and to a lesser extent the clergy) sided against the crown – via their *hermandades* – that the *cortes* won most concessions. Furthermore, this often happened in circumstances where the kings were under acute pressure because they encountered hostile popes who used interdict and excommunication to free their subjects from their allegiance to the crown, faced external pressure, or competed with rival claimants for the throne.

Let us scope up from these three cases and identify the general differences between the medieval European developments and the prior Chinese and later

Russian developments – with particular emphasis on the dissimilar effects of the intensification of geopolitical pressure. In a nutshell, the empirical analysis shows that Western European rulers faced a societal context where any important undertaking – be it fiscal or foreign policy – was likely to flounder without the active collaboration of the strong autonomous groups they faced. As elsewhere, the onset of generalized geopolitical competition incentivized rulers to carry out reforms to strengthen state capacity at the centre. But these reforms provoked resistance from the autonomous groups who feared (correctly, as the Chinese and Russian case shows) that their customary privileges were being endangered. This spurred the bargaining pattern of taxation and military service in exchange for political concessions that we have repeatedly seen in the case studies above. Representative institutions were convoked by rulers to provide a forum for such negotiations and to secure the commitment of domestic groups. As Bisson (2009, 559) points out, assemblies were thus originally implements of lordships. But eventually they took on a life of their own, becoming constraints on lordship. The ultimate product of this bargaining was a regime form in which representative institutions were co-legislators with the monarch.

The more contextual implication of the model is that early modern regime change in Europe was contingent on the prior existence of a multiplicity of autonomous groups. Turning our attention to ancient China and to early modern Russia, the arrangements that made constraints on the rulers a possible outcome in medieval Europe were simply not present. In the absence of a multiplicity of autonomous groups covering distinct social domains, rulers faced completely different incentives, as the economy had to be mobilized in a top-down way. The opposite logics of the two paths of regime change are illustrated by the transformations of the historically ubiquitous king's councils or assemblies of notables, which advised monarchs on matters such as legislation, justice, taxation, and war. In the former scenario, this council was ultimately transformed into a parliament that achieved independent prerogatives with respect to the listed policy areas. In the latter scenario, the assemblies of notables disappeared.

Stasavage (2016) has recently proposed an explanation for the advent of representative institutions which shares important similarities with, but also differs from, the one forwarded in Part V of this book. Stasavage stresses two factors: the weakness of medieval European monarchs and the fact that they often ruled relatively small realms. According to Stasavage (2016, 12–14), the first factor (weakness) forced monarchs to negotiate with social groups, and the second (small distance) lowered the transaction cost of convening at assemblies to carry out this bargaining. The analysis in this book similarly illustrates how the absence of a central bureaucracy forced Iberian rulers to turn to the social groups who could transmit government authority throughout the realm. Moreover, we have seen that representative institutions were normally convoked at the level of constituent units (say, Aragon and Catalonia) rather than the level of composite units (say, Aragon-Catalonia).

But Stasavage's focus on the weakness of rulers and geographical size is nonetheless unconvincing in itself. As with the direct effects attributed to geopolitical pressure, the problem with the first factor is that we find numerous instances of weak rulers historically but very few instances where this produced representative institutions.[1] With respect to distance, my analysis indicates that what mattered was not geographical size itself (after all, the Spanish possessions of the Crown of Aragon were not large enough to make travel cumbersome). The important thing was that the rights of strong social groups were anchored on this local level, meaning that, say, Aragonese groups – most notoriously the Aragonese Union – fought for Aragonese institutions that would cater to Aragonese interests, rather than for more general institutions of the entire realm of the Crown of Aragon (see also Møller 2016a). More generally, the gist of the argument proposed in Chapter 17 is that what matters is not the characteristics of the rulers' positions (weakness and small realms) but rather the characteristics of the social groups they confronted.

Based on the analysis, we can take issue with two other points in the recent literature on the origins and development of representative institutions. The first concerns the *data* that enter the myriad statistical analyses of the origins and the character of these institutions. The datasets coded by Stasavage (2010; 2011), Van Zanden et al. (2012), and most recently Abramson and Boix (2014) are premised on the ability to distinguish genuine representative institutions – which are independent of the monarch – from their forerunners in the form of assemblies of notables. Here, a couple of caveats are in order. Even simply attesting when a royal curia is no longer an assembly of notables but a genuine representative institution is very difficult – a point long ago noted by Marongiu (1968, 85). Two issues are particularly testing. First, all over Western Europe, representative institutions were the product of a gradual evolution, and it is often difficult to pinpoint a particular assembly or even a delimited time period as demarcating the transition. Second, the historical sources are very fragmentary, meaning that we often do not know whether particular assemblies took place and, if they did, whether or not representatives of, e.g., the towns were summoned to them (see O'Callaghan 1975, 266–267; Procter 1980; Kagay 1981; Maddicott 2010). Though the long-term cross-case patterns of the datasets might be robust, the point in time at which cases enter the datasets is likely to be spurious. But the more general problem is that these tallies begin very 'late', by the time assemblies had become genuine representative institutions (see Møller 2016a). To this we can add the massive problems of autocorrelation across the European space noted in Chapter 18. In this situation, it probably makes more sense to carry out in-depth qualitative analysis of particular cases than to do statistical testing, at least if the objective is to elucidate origins.

Next, the analysis carried out above also testifies to the importance of a broad *comparative scope* of analysis. An apt way to illustrate this point is to return to Blaydes and Chaney's (2013) interesting account of how feudal military organization was conducive to the creation of representative institutions. Blaydes and Chaney (2013, 19) recognize that a comparative perspective is necessary to elucidate the origins of representative institutions. But they delimit the comparison to one between Latin Christendom and the Islamic world. They thereby ignore that relatively similar forms of military organization and, more particularly, strong aristocracies based on land ownership and military service have existed in other periods without producing representative institutions.[2] Ancient China is one such example; Russia, another.

Returning to the main storyline, the causal chain proposed in this chapter could be pushed further back by accounting for the European development of multiple autonomous groups prior to the intensification of geopolitical pressure in the late twelfth century. This development probably owes much to the secular-religious struggles of the eleventh century, which opened up quasi-independent social domains that first the clergy and subsequently the nobility and townsmen could fill (cf. Southern 1970; Finer 1997a). Accounting for these prior developments lies beyond the scope of this book, but historical analysis devoted to understanding whether this was a product of pure contingency or a more systematical consequence of features of early medieval relations between church and state could be a next step for those interested in the origins of representative institutions.

Notes

1   We can make a similar observation about the initial absence or presence of bureaucratic power. Russia also lacked a strong central bureaucracy as it became embroiled in geopolitical pressure. But due to the absence of strong autonomous groups, Russian tsars had no alternative to the top-down state building strategy (see Møller 2015b). Much the same can probably be said about the situation of Chinese rulers when geopolitical pressure arose in the Spring and Autumn Period, though the historical evidence is very scarce for this period.

2   Blaydes and Chaney do in fact discuss the effect of feudalism in Japan in an online appendix and even show that it, too, impacts their variable of ruler duration (see also 2013, 26, fn. 28). But this serves to make problematic the contention that longer ruler duration was triggered by the same mechanisms that produced representative institutions, in that no such institutions arose in medieval Japan (or in ancient China or early modern Russia).

CONCLUSIONS

One of the most spectacular developments within political science in the new millennium has been the advent of the literature on the Origins of Comparative Development. This scholarship traces present-day divergences in economic and political trajectories to the European 'institutions of constraints' that arose in the Middle Ages and were transplanted to a series of European colonies following the overseas voyages after 1500 (Downing 1992; Acemoglu et al. 2001; 2002a; 2002b; 2008; Jones 2008[1981]; Acemoglu and Robinson 2012; Hariri 2012). The key observation of this literature is that these institutions, by placing constraints on executives, were conducive to both economic growth and democratization.

It is no exaggeration to say that this research agenda has been among the most influential in political science in the new millennium. Nonetheless, so far there has been no attempt to cover it in a coherent way. The aim of this book has been to do so. But one of the book's main arguments is that the new literature on the origins of comparative development can be genuinely appreciated only by relating it to an older body of scholarship, which deals with the Rise of the West (Hall 2001) – i.e., the Western or European development of the trinity of the modern state, modern democracy, and the modern market economy (cf. Mills 1959, 152–153; Skocpol 1984a, 1; Goldstone 1998, 250; Pomeranz 2000, 3). One of the most important contributors to this older scholarship is Max Weber, whose entire authorship has been construed as an attempt to answer the question, 'Why Europe?' (Chirot 1985). A series of other authors, including Alexis de Tocqueville, Otto Hintze, Joseph A. Schumpeter, and, more recently, Barrington Moore, Charles Tilly, Perry Anderson, and Theda Skocpol have wrestled with more particular aspects of this general question.

This classical literature thus deals with exactly the same research question as the new literature on the origins of comparative development, only with a more Eurocentric focus. The preceding chapters have reviewed and discussed the most important contributions to this classical literature, beginning with Max Weber, before moving on to the new research agenda on the colonial transplantation of European 'institutions of constraints' and the origins of these institutions. More particularly, the book has structured the material by dividing it into three clusters: classical comparative historical analyses, the Barrington-Moore research programme, and the recent literature on the origins of comparative development.

Throughout the book, the theoretical, methodological, and empirical contributions of the relevant authors have been singled out and discussed, and the way the different authors write into older debates has been emphasized. The aim of these *Conclusions* is to, first, synthesize some of the scholarship that has been dealt with in the book and to, second, identify the likely future direction of this research and the challenges that must be faced in order for it to progress.

Main themes

The key theme that emerges from this book can be summarized in one word: 'Europe'. The story about the advent of the modern state, modern democracy, and the modern market economy remains a story about Western and Central Europe and its colonial offspring in the Americas and Oceania. This is where the breakthrough to administrative, political, and economic modernity occurred and where today's state-centred international system came into being. In order to understand the processes that produced state-building, regime change, and economic development, we therefore need to understand what is peculiar about the European context. However, as Weber, who insisted on the occidental origins of modernity, knew, the distinctiveness of Europe can be genuinely appreciated only in comparative perspective. While some of the works treated in this book mainly address variation within Europe, many go one step further and compare Europe or parts of Europe with other parts of the world.

Hence the second great theme of the book – the need for historical comparisons, either across large stretches of time or by including long periods in cross-spatial analysis. Harnessing historical variation serves to mitigate a number of problems that follow from analysing shorter periods of time, including the problem of truncated samples and the long shadow of the past – that is, the fact that many historical developments are path-dependent. Furthermore, a historical perspective is needed to identify and understand the causal mechanisms of, e.g., state-building that are generic. Even if the context shapes how these mechanisms play out, we can learn quite a lot about the drivers of processes of state formation, regime change, and economic development by analysing historical contexts (see Møller 2016b).

One of the key variables we can learn about in this way can be said to make up the third theme of the book. This is warfare or, more generally, generalized geo-political pressure. Warfare and the threat of warfare has been history's great state-builder, and it has also had important knock-on effects on regime change and economic development. This equals saying that the absence of generalized geopolitical pressure in many developing countries in the period after 1945 in general and after 1989 in particular operates as a scope condition of present-day processes of state formation, regime change, and economic development. More generally, we can note that the effects of warfare have not been invariant across space and time. An important insight that emerges from this book is that, in Europe, generalized geopolitical pressure has had different effects than elsewhere. It not only increased state capacity but also sparked the 'corporate reaction' that Otto Hintze referred to (see Chapter 17). Only by understanding this corporate reaction can we understand why the European multi-state system saw the advent of the modern state, modern democracy, and the modern market economy.

This can be phrased in more generic terms, which brings us to the fourth theme of the book: external-internal interactions. The point is that geopolitical pressure interacts with domestic conditions to produce secular change. Though warfare triggers a general set of mechanisms, the outcome plays out differently in different contexts. In Europe, generalized geopolitical pressure brought about state-building from below and political constraints on rulers, thereby also facilitating the development of the market economy. In other historical contexts, such as ancient China and early modern Russia, it instead brought about a pattern of top-down state-building which removed rather than increased constraints on rulers. Finally, in places such as Sub-Saharan Africa and to a lesser extent Latin America, very different domestic conditions have meant that warfare – when it took place – did little to increase state capacity.

In other words, to genuinely understand the first – and most general – theme of the book, the distinctiveness of Europe, we must understand what Alexis de Tocqueville termed the *point de départ*. More directly, we need to understand the way the social and political context of medieval Europe conditioned state-building, regime change, and economic development following the sixteenth-century military revolution. This also serves as a frame of reference for understanding the colonial transplantation of European institutions after the onset of the great overseas voyages. In the final part of the book, I presented my own attempt to get at these medieval developments. The core postulate of the argument presented in Part V of the book is that representative government was the product of a causal interaction between external geopolitical pressure and the internal balance caused by the existence of a multiplicity of autonomous groups. This brought about a political system characterized by institutions of constraints, and it further shored up a social milieu where strong groups were able to balance rulers. In the absence of these initial conditions, the effects of the sixteenth-century military revolution are likely to have been significantly different – probably more in line with what we find elsewhere, including in ancient China and early modern Russia.

The way forward

These are the main themes of this book. Future scholarship is likely to further expound them. Based on what has been discussed in the twenty preceding chapters, two separate tracks must be followed to achieve genuine progress.

First, we need more disaggregated, high-quality data for more political units over more years. The present dearth of quantitative historical data has hugely impeded empirical research. Here, there is room for optimism as a number of new data-gathering initiatives are under way. First, and most generally, the so-called 'Varieties of Democracy' (V-Dem) project has been coding numerous aspects relevant to democratization, state formation, and economic development back to 1900 for all relevant political units in the world. An offspring – the so-called 'Historical V-Dem' – is presently coding selected indicators all the way back to 1789. These new data will cover what has been termed the 'Long 19th century', the period between the French Revolution and World War I. A series of other data ventures have coded additional or overlapping empirical indicators for the same period (for an overview, see Knutsen et al. 2016).

These new data will enable scholars to refine analysis of the breakthrough to the modern state, modern democracy, and the modern market economy. One of the great advantages of much of the new data is its disaggregated nature, which will allow scholars to probe the interrelationships between, e.g., aspects of the state and aspects of democracy as well as the sequencing of different components of the state, democracy, and the market economy (see Møller 2015a). However, to understand the prerequisites of these developments, we need similar data covering medieval and early modern Europe. Here, too, there is some room for optimism as scholars have made great headway coding, for instance, aspects of representative institutions (Stasavage 2010; Van Zanden et al. 2012; Abramson and Boix 2014). Nonetheless, many other features of political regimes could be coded, and it seems fair to say that large-N data relevant to state formation, regime change, and economic development for the period before 1789 is likely to remain scarce in the years to come (Knutsen et al. 2016).

Second, we need more in-depth historical analysis of key cases. There is much that cannot be captured by large-N cross-case analysis, even if these analyses span longer time periods and include a large number of cases. The general problem here is the well-known one that correlation is not causality. To understand causal relationships, we often need to get closer to actors' choices, which means that we must favour depth over breadth. Furthermore, some historical cases are simply more interesting than others. Most important here are the 'first-movers' or 'early incidences' where a particular historical development, say representative institutions or modern bureaucracy, first emerged (see Chapter 18). Many of these developments afterwards spread via historical diffusion, something that makes it difficult to identify the causes of their initial advent using cross-case analysis. Only by genuinely going historical in the form of in-depth qualitative studies can we probe these origins.

In the best of worlds, scholars will combine these two approaches, as has hitherto been a key characteristic of comparative historical analysis (Lange 2012). However, a certain division of labour is probably to be expected. Division of labour has its advantages – in science as well as in market relations. Yet the important thing is that scholars interact across such boundaries. That is, the story of state formation, regime change, and economic development should not turn into a 'tale of two cultures' (Mahoney and Goertz 2006). In this connection, one final issue is worth mentioning. As recently as the 1980s and 1990s, a number of attempts at 'philosophic history' had an important impact on the study of state formation, regime change, and economic development (e.g., Hall 1985; Gellner 1988). While these works do not belong within the tradition of comparative historical analysis, they provide valuable inspiration to scholars engaging in empirical analysis. It is a pity that few such works seem to be produced today. The recent attempts to go empirical in the study of state formation, regime change, and economic development are to be applauded. But they need not crowd out arm-chair speculation, which attempts to understand the broader picture liberated from the straightjacket of having to assess causal effects empirically. Then we would be throwing the baby away with the bath water.

BIBLIOGRAPHY

Abbott, A. (1991). History and sociology: the lost synthesis. *Social Science History*, 15:2, 201–238.

Abramson, S. and Boix, C. (2014). The Roots of the Industrial Revolution: Political Institutions or (Socially-Embedded) Know-How? Working paper, Princeton, NJ: Princeton University.

Abulafia, D. (1999). The Rise of Aragon-Catalonia. In *The New Cambridge Medieval History V*, edited by D. Abulafia, 644–667, Cambridge: Cambridge University Press.

Acemoglu, D., Johnson, S. and Robinson, J.A. (2001). The colonial origins of comparative development: an empirical investigation. *American Economic Review*, 91:5, 1369–1401.

Acemoglu, D., Johnson, S. and Robinson, J.A. (2002a). Reversal of fortune: geography and institutions in the making of the modern world income distribution. *Quarterly Journal of Economics*, 117:4, 1231–1294.

Acemoglu, D., Johnson, S. and Robinson, J.A. (2002b). The Rise of Europe: Atlantic Trade, Institutional Change and Economic Growth. Working paper no. 02–43, Cambridge, MA: Department of Economics Massachusetts Institute of Technology (MIT).

Acemoglu, D., Johnson, S., Robinson, J.A. and Yared, P. (2008). Income and democracy. *American Economic Review*, 98:3, 808–842.

Acemoglu, D. and Robinson, J.A. (2006). *Economic Origins of Dictatorship and Democracy*. Cambridge: Cambridge University Press.

Acemoglu, D. and Robinson, J.A. (2012). *Why Nations Fail: The Origins of Power in Prosperity and Poverty*. London: Profile.

Almond, G. and Powell, G.B. (1966). *Comparative Politics: A Developmental Approach*. Boston: Little, Brown & Company.

Alsted, J. (2001). *De menneskelige samfunds udvikling: En kritisk introduktion til historisk sociologi*. Roskilde: Roskilde University Press.

Alsted, J. (2008). Teorier om statsdannelse in historisk sociologi – styrker og svagheder. *Politica*, 40:4, 395–409.

Anderson, P. (1974a). *Passages from Antiquity to Feudalism*. London: Verso.

Anderson, P. (1974b). *Lineages of the Absolutist State*. London: Verso.

Anderson, P. (1990). A culture in contraflow – I. *New Left Review*, 180, 41–78.

Aron, R. (1965). *Main Currents in Sociological Thought: Montesquieu, Comte, Marx, Tocqueville.* Harmondsworth: Penguin.

Bartlett, R. (1993). *The Making of Europe: Conquest, Colonization and Cultural Change 950–1350.* Princeton, NJ: Princeton University Press.

Bartolini, S. (1993). On time and comparative research. *Journal of Theoretical Politics,* 5:2, 131–167.

Bendix, R. (1962[1946]). *Max Weber: An Intellectual Portrait.* Garden City, NY: Anchor Books.

Bendix, R. (1978). *Kings or People: Power and the Mandate to Rule.* Berkeley, Los Angeles, London: University of California Press.

Berman, S. (1997a). Civil society and political institutionalization. *American Behavioral Scientist,* 40:5, 562–574.

Berman, S. (1997b). Civil society and the collapse of the Weimar republic. *World Politics,* 49:2, 401–429.

Bernstein, W.J. (2008). *A Splendid Exchange: How Trade Shaped the World.* Berkeley, CA: Atlantic Monthly Press.

Bianchini, J. (2012). *The Queen's Hand: Power and Authority in the Reign of Berenguela of Castile.* Philadelphia: University of Pennsylvania Press.

Bisson, T.N. (1966). The military origins of medieval representation. *The American Historical Review,* 71:4, 1199–1218.

Bisson, T.N. (1986). *The Medieval Crown of Aragon: A Short History.* Oxford: Clarendon Press.

Bisson, T.N. (2009). *The Crisis of the Twelfth Century: Power, Lordship, and the Origins of European Government.* Princeton, NJ: Princeton University Press.

Blaydes, L. and Chaney, E. (2013). The feudal revolution and Europe's rise: political divergence of the Christian west and the Muslim world before 1500 CE. *American Political Science Review,* 107:1, 16–34.

Bloch, M. (1954[1949]). *The Historian's Craft.* New York: Knopf.

Bloch, M. (1967). *Land and Work in Medieval Europe: Selected Papers by M. Bloch* (transl. Anderson, J.E.). London: Routledge & Kegan Paul.

Bloch, M. (1971a[1939]). *Feudal Society, Volume I: The Growth of Ties of Dependence* (transl. from French by Manyon, L.A.). London: Routledge & Kegan Paul.

Bloch, M. (1971b[1939]). *Feudal Society, Volume II: Social Classes and Political Organization* (transl. from French by Manyon, L.A.). London: Routledge & Kegan Paul.

Bobbit, P. (2002). *The Shield of Achilles: War, Peace, and the Course of History.* New York: Alfred A. Knopf.

Bodde, D. (1956). Feudalism in China. In *Feudalism in History,* edited by R. Coulborn, 49–92, Princeton, NJ: Princeton University Press.

Bogatyrev, S. (2006). Ivan IV (1533–1584). In *The Cambridge History of Russia, Volume I: From Early Rus' to 1689,* edited by Maureen Perrie, 240–263, Cambridge: Cambridge University Press.

Boix, C. (2011). Democracy, development, and the international system. *International Political Science Review,* 105:4, 809–828.

Boix, C. and Stokes, S. (2003). Endogenous democratization. *World Politics,* 55:4, 517–549.

Boucoyannis, D.A. (2015). No Taxation of Elites, No Representation: State Capacity and the Origins of Representation. *Politics and Society,* 43, 303–332.

Bradford, A.S. (2001). *With Arrow, Sword, and Spear: A History of Warfare in the Ancient World.* New York: Fall River Press.

Bratton, M. and van de Walle, N. (1997). *Democratic Experiments in Africa: Regime Transitions in Comparative Perspective.* Cambridge: Cambridge University Press.

Brewer, J. (1989). *The Sinews of Power: War, Money and the English State, 1688–1783.* London, Boston, Sydney & Wellington: Unwin Hyman.

Brogan, H. (2006). *Alexis de Tocqueville: A Life.* New Haven: Yale University Press.

Burckhardt, J. (1987[1860]). *Renaissancens Kultur i Italien*. Viby J.: Kimære.

Burke, P. (1992). Preface in Bloch, M. (1954[1949]). *The Historian's Craft*. Manchester: Manchester University Press.

Cantor, N. (1993[1963]). *The Civilization of the Middle Ages*. New York: Harper Perennial.

Capoccia, G. and Kelemen, R.D. (2007). The study of critical junctures: theory, narrative and counterfactuals in historical institutionalism. *World Politics*, 59:3, 341–369.

Capoccia, G. and Ziblatt, D. (2010). The historical turn in democratization studies: a new research agenda for Europe and beyond. *Comparative Political Studies*, 43:8/9, 931–968.

Carothers, T. (1998). The rule of law revival. *Foreign Affairs*, 77:2, 95–107.

Carpenter, D.A. (1990). *The Minority of Henry III*. Berkeley, CA: University of California Press.

Carpenter, D.A. (1999). The Plantagenet kings. In *The New Cambridge Medieval History V*, edited by David Abulafia, 314–357, Cambridge: Cambridge University Press.

Centeno, M.A. (2003). *Blood and Debt: War and the Nation-State in Latin America*. University Park: Pennsylvania State University Press.

Cerda, J.M. (2011). The assemblies of Alfonso VIII of Castile: Burgos (1169) to Carrión (1188). *Journal of Medieval Iberian Studies,* 3:1, 61–77.

Chandler, A.D. (1971). Business History as Institutional History. In *Approaches to American Economic History,* edited by G.R. Taylor and L.F. Ellsworth, 17–24, Charlottesville: University Press of Virginia.

Chirot, D. (1984). The Social and Historical Landscape of Marc Bloch. In *Vision and Method in Historical Sociology,* edited by T. Skocpol, 22–46, Cambridge: Cambridge University Press.

Chirot, D. (1985). The rise of the West. *American Sociological Review*, 50:2, 181–195.

Chu, Y., Bratton, M., Lagos, M., Shastri, S. and Tessler, M. (2008). Public opinion and democratic legitimacy. *Journal of Democracy*, 19:2, 74–87.

Clark, G. (2007). *A Farewell to Alms: A Brief Economic History of the World*. Princeton, NJ & Oxford: Princeton University Press.

Collier, D. and Levitsky, S. (1997). Democracy with adjectives: conceptual innovation in comparative research. *World Politics*, 49:3, 430–451.

Collier, D. and Mahon, J.E. (1993). Conceptual 'stretching' revisited: adapting categories in comparative analysis. *American Political Science Review*, 87:4, 845–855.

Collins, R. (1986). *Max Weber: A Skeleton Key*. Beverly Hills: Sage Publications.

Collins, R. (2000). *Max Weber – personen og forfatterskabet*. København: Hans Reitzels Forlag.

Cook, C.A. (1997). Wealth and the western Zhou. *Bulletin of the School of Oriental and African Studies*, 60:2, 253–294.

Coppedge, M. (2012). *Democratization and Research Methods*. Cambridge: Cambridge University Press.

Creel, H. (1970). *The Origins of Statecraft in China*. Chicago: University of Chicago Press.

Dahl, R.A. (1956). *A Preface to Democratic Theory*. Chicago: University of Chicago Press.

Dahl, R.A. (1989). *Democracy and Its Critics*. New Haven: Yale University Press.

Dahl, R.A. and Tufte, E.R. (1974). *Size and Democracy*. Stanford: Stanford University Press.

Darwin, J. (2008). *After Tamerlane: The Rise and Fall of Global Empires, 1400–2000*. London: Penguin.

Davies, J.C. (1962). Toward a theory of revolution. *American Sociological Review*, 27:1, 5–19.

de Ruggiero, G. (1927). *The History of European Liberalism*. Boston: Beacon Press.

de Tocqueville, A. (1955[1856]). *The Old Régime and the French Revolution*. New York: Doubleday Anchor Books.

de Tocqueville, A. (1970). *Recollections*. New York: Doubleday Anchor Books.

de Tocqueville, A. (1984[1835/1840]). *Democracy in America*. New York: Penguin Books.

Diamond, J. (1999[1997]). *Guns, Germs, and Steel: The Fates of Human Societies*. New York & London: W.W. Norton & Company.

Diamond, J. (2012). What makes countries rich or poor? *The New York Review of Books*, June 7.

Domínguez, J.I. (2003). Review of blood and debt: war and the nation-state in Latin America. *Political Science Quarterly*, 118:3, 509–510.

Doner, R.F., Ritchie, B.K. and Slater, D. (2005). Systemic vulnerability and the origins of developmental states: northeast and southeast Asia in comparative perspective. *International Organization*, 59:2, 327–361.

Downing, B.M. (1988). Constitutionalism, warfare, and political change in early modern Europe. *Theory and Society*, 17:1, 7–56.

Downing, B.M. (1989). Medieval origins of constitutional government in the West. *Theory and Society*, 18:2, 213–247.

Downing, B.M. (1992). *The Military Revolution and Political Change: Origins of Democracy and Autocracy in Early Modern Europe*. Princeton, NJ: Princeton University Press.

Doyle, M. (1986). Liberalism and world politics. *American Political Science Review*, 80:4, 1151–1169.

du Boulay, F.R.H. (1967). Foreword. In *Land and Work in Mediaeval Europe: Selected Papers by Marc Bloch* (transl. Anderson, J.E.), edited by M. Bloch, London: Routledge & Kegan Paul.

Dunning, T. (2012). *Natural Experiments in the Social Sciences: A Design-Based Approach*. London: Cambridge University Press.

Eisenstadt, S.N. (1963). *The Political Systems of Empires*. New York: Free Press of Glencoe.

Elman, C. (2005). Explanatory typologies in qualitative studies of international politics. *International Organization*, 59:2, 293–326.

Elster, J. (2006). Tocqueville on 1789: Preconditions, Precipitants, and Triggers. In *The Cambridge Companion to Tocqueville*, edited by C.B. Welch, 49–80, Cambridge: Cambridge University Press.

Elster, J. (2009). *Alexis de Tocqueville: The First Social Scientist*. Cambridge: Cambridge University Press.

Elvin, M. (1978). Chinese Cities since the Sung Dynasty. In *Towns in Societies: Essays in Economic History and Historical Sociology*, edited by P. Abrams and E.A. Wrigley, 79–90, Cambridge: Cambridge University Press.

Epstein, S.R. (2002). *Freedom and Growth: The Rise of States and Markets in Europe, 1300–1750*. London: Routledge.

Ertman, T. (1997). *Birth of the Leviathan. Building States and Regimes in Medieval and Early Modern Europe*. Cambridge: Cambridge University Press.

Ertman, T. (2005). Building States – Inherently a Long-Term Process? An Argument from Comparative History. In *States and Development: Historical Antecedents of Stagnation and Advance*, edited by M. Lange and D. Rueschemeyer, 165–182, London: Palgrave Macmillan.

Evans, P.B., Rueschemeyer, D. and Skocpol, T. (eds.) (1985). *Bringing the State Back in*. Cambridge: Cambridge University Press.

Evtuhov, C., Goldfrank, D., Hughes, L. and Stites, R. (2004). *A History of Russia: Peoples, Legends, Events, Forces*. New York: Houghton Mifflin Company.

Femia, J.V. (1972). Barrington Moore and the preconditions for democracy. *British Journal of Political Science*, 2:1, 21–46.

Feng, L. (2003). Feudalism and western Zhou China: a criticism. *Harvard Journal of Asiatic*, 63:1, 115–144.

Feng, L. (2006). *Landscape and Power in Early China: The Crisis and Fall of the Western Zhou, 1045–771 BC*. Cambridge: Cambridge University Press.

Feng, L. (2008). *Bureaucracy and the State in Early China: Governing the Western Zhou*. Cambridge: Cambridge University Press.

Finer, S.E. (1996). *The History of Government I: Ancient Monarchies and Empires*. Oxford: Oxford University Press.

Finer, S.E. (1997a). *The History of Government II: The Intermediate Ages.* Oxford: Oxford University Press.

Finer, S.E. (1997b). *The History of Government III: Empires, Monarchies, and the Modern State.* Oxford: Oxford University Press.

Fukuyama, F. (2008). The eighteenth-century hockey stick. *SAIS Review*, 28:1, 187–189.

Fukuyama, F. (2010[1968]). Foreword. In *Political Order in Changing Societies*, edited by S.P. Huntington, xi–xvii, New Haven: Yale University Press.

Fukuyama, F. (2011). *The Origins of Political Order: From Prehuman Times to the French Revolution.* London: Profile Books.

Fulbrook, M. and Skocpol, T. (1984). Destined Pathways. In *Vision and Method in Historical Sociology*, edited by T. Skocpol, 170–210, Cambridge: Cambridge University Press.

Ganshof, F. L. (1952[1944]). *Feudalism* (transl. Philip Grierson). London: Longmans.

Gellner, E. (1988). *Plough, Book and Sword: The Structure of Human History.* London: Collins Harvill.

Gellner, E. (1994). *Conditions of Liberty: Civil Society and Its Rivals.* London: Hamish Hamilton.

George, A. and Bennett, A. (2005). *Case Study and Theory Development.* Cambridge, MA: MIT Press.

Gerhard, D. (1970). Otto Hintze: his work and his significance in historiography. *Central European History*, 3:1/2, 17–48.

Gerring, J. (2001). *Social Science Methodology: A Criterial Framework.* Cambridge: Cambridge University Press.

Gerring, J. (2004). What is a case study and what is it good for? *American Political Science Review*, 98:2, 341–354.

Gerschenkron, A. (1962). Economic Backwardness in Historical Perspective. In *Economic Backwardness in Historical Perspective: A Book of Essays*, edited by A. Gerschenkron, 5–30, Cambridge: Harvard University Press.

Gilbert, F. (1975). Introduction. In *The Historical Essays of Otto Hintze*, edited by F. Gilbert, 3–30, New York: Oxford University Press.

Gill, G. (2003). *The Nature and Development of the Modern State.* New York: Palgrave Macmillan.

Goertz, G. and Mahoney, J. (2005). The possibility principle: choosing negative cases in comparative research. *American Political Science Review*, 98:4, 653–669.

Goldscheid, R. (1958[1925]). A Sociological Approach to Problems of Public Finance (transl. Henderson, E.). In *Classics in the Theory of Public Finance,* edited by R.A. Musgrave and A.T. Peacock, 202–213, London: MacMillan Press Ltd.

Goldstone, J.A. (1998). The problem of the 'early modern' world. *Journal of the Economic and Social History of the Orient*, 41:3, 249–284.

Goldstone, J.A. (2000). The rise of the west – or not? a revision to socio economic history. *Sociological Theory*, 18:2, 175–194.

Goldthorpe, I. (1991). *The Uses of History in Sociology: Reflections on Some Recent Tendencies.* Oxford: Nuffield College.

Gorski, P.S. (2003). *The Disciplinary Revolution: Calvinism and the Rise of the State in Early Modern Europe.* Chicago & London: University of Chicago Press.

Gress, D. (2007). *Velstandens kilder: Om den europæiske økonomis udvikling.* København: Borgen.

Hall, J.A. (1985). *Powers & Liberties: The Causes and Consequences of the Rise of the West.* Oxford: Basil Blackwell.

Hall, J.A. (1989). They do things differently there, or, the contribution of British historical sociology. *British Journal of Sociology*, 40:4, 544–564.

Hall, J.A. (2001). Confessions of a Eurocentric. *International Sociology*, 16:3, 488–497.

Hall, J.A. (2004). Review of the disciplinary revolution: calvinism and the rise of the state in early modern Europe. *Contemporary Sociology*, 33:5, 573–574.

Hall, P.A. (2003). Aligning Ontology and Methodology in Comparative Research. In *Comparative Historical Analysis in the Social Sciences*, edited by J. Mahoney and D. Rueschemeyer, 373–406, Cambridge: Cambridge University Press.

Hansen, M.H. (1998). *Polis and City-State: An Ancient Concept and Its Modern Equivalent*. Copenhagen: Munksgaard.

Hansen, V. (2000). *Open Empire: A History of China to 1600*. New York: Norton.

Hariri, J.G. (2012). The autocratic legacy of early statehood. *American Political Science Review*, 106:3, 471–494.

Hariss, G.L. (1975). *King, Parliament, and Public Finance in Medieval England to 1369*. Oxford: Clarendon Press.

Hawthorn, G. (1992). Schumpeter the superior. *London Review of Books*, 14:4, 15–16.

Held, D. (2006[1987]). *Models of Democracy*. Cambridge: Polity Press.

Herbst, J. (2000). *States and Power in Africa: Comparative Lessons in Authority and Control*. Princeton, NJ: Princeton University Press.

Herlihy, D. (1970). *The History of Feudalism*. New Jersey, NJ: Humanities Press.

Hintze, O. (1962[1929]). Wesen und Verbreitung des Feudalismus. In *Staat und Verfassung, vol. I*, edited by O. Hintze, Göttingen: Vandenhoeck & Ruprecht.

Hintze, O. (1962[1930]). Typologie der ständischen Verfassungen des Abenlandes. In *Staat und Verfassung, vol. I*, edited by O. Hintze, 120–139, Göttingen: Vandenhoeck & Ruprecht.

Hintze, O. (1975[1906]). Military Organization and the Organization of the State. In *The Historical Essays of Otto Hintze*, edited by F. Gilbert, 178–215, New York: Oxford University Press.

Hintze, O. (1975[1931]). The Preconditions of Representative Government in the Context of World History. In *The Historical Essays of Otto Hintze*, edited by F. Gilbert, 302–353, New York: Oxford University Press.

Hirschman, A.O. (1970). The search for paradigms as a hindrance to understanding. *World Politics*, 22:3, 329–343.

Hobsbawm, E. (1997[1969]). What Do Historians Owe to Karl Marx? In *On History*, edited by E. Hobsbawm, 186–206, London: Abacus.

Hobsbawm, E. (1997[1978]). British History and the Annales: A Note. In *On History*, edited by E. Hobsbawm, 178–185, London: Abacus.

Holmes, S. (2004). Lineages of the Rule of Law. In *Democracy and the Rule of Law*, edited by J.M. Maravall and A. Przeworski, 19–61, Cambridge: Cambridge University Press.

Hosking, G. (1997). *Russia: People and Empire, 1552–1927*. London: HarperCollinsPublishers.

Hosking, G. (2001). *Russia and the Russians: A History*. London: Allan Lane, The Penguin Press.

Hsu, C. (1999). The Spring and Autumn Period. In *The Cambridge History of Ancient China*, edited by M. Loewe and E.L. Shaughnessy, 545–586, Cambridge: Cambridge University Press.

Hughes, H.S. (1958). *Consciousness and Society*. New York: Knopf.

Hui, V.T. (2001). The emergence and demise of nascent constitutional rights: comparing ancient China and early modern Europe. *Journal of Political Philosophy*, 9, 272–403.

Hui, V.T. (2004). Toward a dynamic theory of international politics: insights from comparing the ancient Chinese and early modern European systems. *International Organization*, 58:1, 175–205.

Hui, V.T. (2005). *War and State Formation in Ancient China and Early Modern Europe*. Cambridge: Cambridge University Press.

Hume, D. (1987[1777]). Of the Study of History. In *Essays Withdrawn, Essay VI, Essays Moral, Political, and Literary*, edited by D. Hume, 563–569, Indianapolis: Liberty Fund, Inc.

Hunt, L. (1984). Charles Tilly's Collective Action. In *Vision and Method in Historical Sociology,* edited by T. Skocpol, 244–275, Cambridge: Cambridge University Press.

Huntington, S.P. (1968). *Political Order in Changing Societies.* New Haven, CT:Yale University Press.

Huntington, S.P. (1991). *The Third Wave: Democratization in the Late Twentieth Century.* Norman: University of Oklahoma Press.

Jardin, A. (1988). *Tocqueville: A Biography.* London: Peter Halban.

Jaume, L. (2013). *Tocqueville: The Aristocratic Sources of Liberty.* Princeton, NJ: Princeton University Press.

Jones, E.L. (2000). Time and chance in the old-world economies. *The Journal of Economic History,* 60:3, 856–859.

Jones, E.L. (2008[1981]). *The European Miracle: Environments, Economies and Geopolitics in the History of Europe and Asia.* Cambridge: Cambridge University Press.

Kagay, D.J. (1981). The Development of the Cortes in the Crown of Aragon, 1064–1327. *ETD Collection for Fordham University.*

Kant, I. (1995[1795]). *Til den evige fred.* København: Gyldendal.

Kaufman, S., Little, R. and Wohlforth, W. (2007). *The Balance of Power in World History.* New York: Palgrave.

Keating, M. (2009). Putting European political science back together again. *European Political Science Review,* 1:2, 297–316.

Kestnbaum, M. and Skocpol, T. (1993). War and the development of modern national states. *Sociological Forum,* 8:4, 661–674.

Kiernan, V.G. (1980). Review of states and social revolution: a comparative analysis of France, Russia, and China. *The English Historical Review,* 95:376, 638–641.

Kitschelt, H. (1992). Political regime change: structure and process-driven explanations? *American Political Science Review,* 86:4, 1028–1034.

Kitschelt, H. (2003). Accounting for postcommunist regime diversity: what counts as a good cause? In *Capitalism and Democracy in Central and Eastern Europe: Assessing the Legacy of Communist Rule,* edited by G. Ekiert and S.E. Hanson, 49–86, Cambridge: Cambridge University Press.

Knudsen, T. and Rothstein, B. (1994). State-building in Scandinavia. *Comparative Politics,* 26:2, 203–220.

Knutsen, C.H., Møller, J. and Skaaning, S.-E. (2016). Going historical: measuring democraticness before the age of mass democracy. *International Political Science Review* (forthcoming).

Kokkonen, A. and Sundell, A. (2014). Delivering stability – primogeniture and autocratic survival in European monarchies 1000–1800. *American Political Science Review,* 108:2, 438–453.

Kopstein, J.S. and Reilly, D.A. (2000). Geographic diffusion and the transformation of the postcommunist world. *World Politics,* 53:1, 1–37.

Kornhauser, W. (1959). *The Politics of Mass Society.* Glencoe: Free Press.

Krasner, S.D. (2005). The case for shared sovereignty. *Journal of Democracy,* 16:1, 72–76.

Kundera, M. (2004[1984]). *The Unbearable Lightness of Being.* London: Faber and Faber.

Kurtz, M.J. (2013). *Latin American State-building in Comparative Perspective: Social Foundations of Institutional Order.* London: Cambridge University Press.

Lachmann, R. (2002). Comparison within a single social formation: a critical appreciation of Perry Anderson's lineages of the absolute state. *Qualitative Sociology,* 25:1, 83–92.

Landes, D. (1983). *Revolution in Time: Clocks and the Making of the Modern World.* Cambridge: Harvard University Press.

Landes, D. (1998). *The Wealth and Poverty of Nations: Why Some Are So Rich and Some So Poor*. New York: W. W. Norton.

Lange, M. (2012). *Comparative-Historical Methods*. London: Sage.

Lederer, E. (1940). *State of the Masses: The Threat of the Classless Society*. New York: W. W. Norton and Company.

Levitsky, S. and Way, L. A. (2010). *Competitive Authoritarianism: Hybrid Regimes after the Cold War*. New York: Cambridge University Press.

Levy, J. S. and Thompson, W. R. (2005). Hegemonic threats and great-power balancing in Europe, 1495–1999. *Security Studies*, 14: 1–33.

Lewis, M. E. (1999). Warring States: Political History. In *The Cambridge History of Ancient China*, edited by M. Loewe and E. L. Shaughnessy, 587–650, Cambridge: Cambridge University Press.

Lieberman, E. S. (2005). Nested analysis as a mixed-method strategy for comparative research. *American Political Science Review*, 99:3, 435–442.

Lieven, D. (2006). The Elites. In *The Cambridge History of Russia, Volume II: Imperial Russia, 1689–1971*, edited by D. Lieven, 227–244, Cambridge: Cambridge University Press.

Li, Feng. (2006). *Landscape and Power in Early China: The Crisis and Fall of the Western Zhou, 1045–771 BC*. Cambridge: Cambridge University Press.

Linehan, P. (1999). Castile, Portugal and Navarre. In *The New Cambridge Medieval History V*, edited by D. Abulafia, 668–699, Cambridge: Cambridge University Press.

Lipset, S. M. (1959). Some social requisites of democracy: economic development and political legitimacy. *American Political Science Review*, 53:1, 69–105.

Lipset, S. M. (1963). *The First New Nation: The United States in Historical and Comparative Perspective*. New York: W. W. Norton and Company.

Lipset, S. M., Trow, M. A. and Coleman, J. S. (1956). *Union Democracy: The Internal Politics of the International Typographical Union*. Glencoe: Free Press.

Luebbert, G. M. (1991). *Liberalism, Fascism, or Social Democracy: Social Classes and the Political Origins of Regimes in Interwar Europe*. Oxford: Oxford University Press.

Lustik, I. S. (1996). History, historiography, and political science: multiple historical records and the problem of selection bias. *American Political Science Review*, 90:3, 605–618.

Maddicott, J. R. (2010). *The Origins of the English Parliament*. Oxford: Oxford University Press.

Mahoney, J. (2000). Path dependence in historical sociology. *Theory and Society*, 29:4, 507–548.

Mahoney, J. (2003a). Knowledge Accumulation in Comparative Historical Research: The Case of Democracy and Authoritarianism. In *Comparative Historical Analysis in the Social Sciences*, edited by J. Mahoney and D. Rueschemeyer, 131–174, Cambridge: Cambridge University Press.

Mahoney, J. (2003b). Strategies of Causal Assessment in Comparative Historical Analysis. In *Comparative Historical Analysis in the Social Sciences*, edited by J. Mahoney and D. Rueschemeyer, 337–372, Cambridge: Cambridge University Press.

Mahoney, J. (2004). Comparative-historical methodology. *Annual Review of Sociology*, 30:1, 81–101.

Mahoney, J. and Goertz, G. (2006). A tale of two cultures: contrasting quantitative and qualitative research. *Political Analysis*, 14:3, 227–249.

Mahoney, J. and Rueschemeyer, D. (2003). Comparative historical analysis: achievements and agendas. In *Comparative Historical Analysis in the Social Sciences*, edited by J. Mahoney and D. Rueschemeyer, 3–38, Cambridge: Cambridge University Press.

Mainwaring, S. and Perez-Linan, A. (2005). Why Regions of the World Are Important. Regional Specificities and Region-Wide Diffusion of Democracy. Paper 9/12/05.

Manin, B. (1997). *The Principles of Representative Government*. Cambridge: Cambridge University Press.

Mann, M. (1986). *The Sources of Social Power: A History of Power from the Beginning to AD 1760.* Cambridge: Cambridge University Press.

Mansfield, H.C. (2010). *Tocqueville: A Very Short Introduction.* Oxford: Oxford University Press.

Marongiu, A. (1968). *Medieval Parliaments: A Comparative Study.* Vol. 32. London: Eyre & Spottiswoode.

Martoccio, M. (2013). Review of states of credit: size, power, and the development of European polities. *Journal of Interdisciplinary History,* 43:3, 471–473.

Mazzuca, S. (2010a). Access to power versus exercise of power: reconceptualizing the quality of democracy in Latin America. *Studies in Comparative International Development,* 45:3, 334–357.

Mazzuca, S. (2010b). Macrofoundations of Regime change: democracy, state formation, and capitalist development. *Comparative Politics,* 43:1, 1–19.

McAdam, D., Tarrow, S. and Tilly, C. (2001). *Dynamics of Contention.* Cambridge: Cambridge University Press.

McDonald, T.J. (1996). *The Historic Turn in the Human Sciences.* Ann Arbor: University of Michigan Press.

McDonald, P.J. and Sweeney, K. (2007). The Achilles' heel of liberal IR theory? globalization and conflict in the Pre-World War I era. *World Politics,* 59:3, 370–403.

McNeill, W.H. (1982). *The Pursuit of Power: Technology, Armed Force, and Society since A.D. 1000.* Chicago: University of Chicago Press.

Merton, R.K. (1968). *Social Theory and Social Structure.* New York: Free Press.

Mill, J.S. (1843). *A System of Logic.* New York: Harper & Brothers.

Mills, C.W. (1959). *The Sociological Imagination.* Oxford: Oxford University Press.

Møller, J. (2007). Wherefore the liberal state? post-soviet democratic blues and lessons from fiscal sociology. *East European Politics and Society,* 21:2, 294–315.

Møller, J. (2012). When one might not see the wood for the trees: the 'historical turn' in democratization studies, critical junctures, and cross-case comparisons. *Democratization,* 20:4, 693–715.

Møller, J. (2014). Why Europe avoided hegemony: a historical perspective on the balance of power. *International Studies Quarterly,* 58:4, 660–670.

Møller, J. (2015a). Composite and loose concepts, historical analogies, and the logic of control in comparative historical analysis. *Sociological Methods & Research,* online first: 1–27.

Møller, J. (2015b). The medieval roots of democracy. *Journal of Democracy,* 26:3, 110–123.

Møller, J. (2016a). The birth of representative institutions: the case of the crown of Aragon. *Social Science History* (forthcoming).

Møller, J. (2016b). Putting the civil conflict-regime nexus in historical perspective. *APSA Comparative Democratization Newsletter,* 14:2, 3, 20–22.

Møller, J. (2016c). A framework for congruence analysis in comparative historical analysis of political change. *Quality and Quantity,* online first.

Møller, J. and Skaaning, S.-E. (2010). From each according to his need, to each according to his ability: a comparative analysis of post-communist corruption. *Acta Politica,* 45:3, 320–345.

Møller, J. and Skaaning, S.-E. (2013). *Democracy and Democratization in Comparative Perspective: Conceptions, Conjunctures, Causes, and Consequences.* London: Routledge.

Møller, J. and Skaaning, S.-E. (2016a). *Alexis de Tocqueville.* København: DJØFs Forlag.

Møller, J. and Skaaning, S.-E. (2016b). Explanatory typologies as a nested strategy of inquiry: combining cross-case and within-case analysis. *Sociological Methods & Research,* online first: 1–31.

Montesquieu, C.-L.S. (1989[1748]). *The Spirit of the Laws.* Cambridge: Cambridge University Press.

Moore, B. (1991[1966]). *Social Origins of Dictatorship and Democracy: Lord and Peasant in the Making of the Modern World*. London: Penguin.

Moore, M. (2004). Revenues, state formation, and the quality of governance in developing countries. *International Political Science Review*, 25:3, 297–319.

Morris, I. (2014). *War! What Is It Good For? Conflict and the Progress of Civilization from Primates to Robots*. London: Palgrave Macmillan.

Munck, G. and Snyder, R. (2007). *Passion, Craft and Method in Comparative Politics*. Baltimore: The Johns Hopkins University Press.

Myers, A.R. (1975). *Parliaments and Estates in Europe to 1789*. London: Thames and Hudson.

Nexon, D. (2009). The balance of power in the balance. *World Politics*, 61:2, 330–359.

North, D.C. (1981). *Structure and Change in Economic History*. New York: W.W. Norton.

North, D.C. (1990). *Institutions, Institutional Change and Economic Performance*. Cambridge: Cambridge University Press.

North, D.C. (2005). *Understanding the Process of Economic Change*. Princeton, NJ & Oxford: Princeton University Press.

North, D.C. and Thomas, R.P. (1973). *The Rise of the Western World: A New Economic History*. Cambridge: Cambridge University Press.

North, D.C., Wallis, J. and Weingast, B. (2009). *Violence and Social Orders: A Conceptual Framework for Interpreting Recorded Human History*. New York: Cambridge University Press.

O'Callaghan, J.F. (1969). The beginnings of the cortes of Leon-Castile. *The American Historical Review*, 74:5, 1503–1537.

O'Callaghan, J.F. (1975). *A History of Medieval Spain*. Ithaca, NY & London: Cornell University Press.

O'Callaghan, J.F. (1989). *The Cortes of Castile-Léon 1188–1350*. Philadelphia: University of Pennsylvania Press.

O'Donnell, G. (2010). *Democracy, Agency, and the State: Theory with Comparative Intent*. Oxford: Oxford University Press.

Omrod, M. (2000). The reign of Richard II. In *The New Cambridge Medieval History VI*, edited by M. Jones, 273–296, Cambridge: Cambridge University Press.

Ostrom, E. (1990). *Governing the Commons: The Evolution of Institutions for Collective Action*. New York: Cambridge University Press.

Ostrom, E. (2000). The future of democracy. *Scandinavian Political Studies*, 23:3, 280–283.

Ostrowski, D. (2006). The Growth of Muscovy (1462–1533). In *The Cambridge History of Russia, Volume I: From Early Rus' to 1689*, edited by M. Perrie, 213–239, Cambridge: Cambridge University Press.

Oxhorn, P. (2003). Social Inequality, Civil Society, and the Limits of Citizenship in Latin America. In *What Justice? Whose Justice? Fighting for Fairness in Latin America*, edited by S. Eckstein and T. Wickham-Crowley, 35–63, Berkeley: University of California Press.

Palmer, A. (1970). *The Lands Between: A History of East-Central Europe since the Congress of Vienna*. New York: The Macmillan Company.

Parker, G. (1996[1988]). *The Military Revolution: Military Innovation and the Rise of the West, 1500–1800*. Cambridge: Cambridge University Press.

Parsons, T. (1937). *The Structure of Social Action*. New York: McGraw-Hill.

Perry, E.J. (1980). Review of states and social revolution. *The Journal of Asian Studies*, 39:3, 533–535.

Petersen, M.B. and Skaaning, S.-E. (2010). Ultimate causes of state formation. *Historical Social Research / Historische Sozialforschung*, 35:3, 200–226.

Pierson, P. (2000). Increasing returns, path dependence, and the study of politics. *American Political Science Review*, 94:2, 251–267.

Pocock, J.G.A. (2003[1975]). *The Machiavellian Moment: Florentine Political Thought and the Atlantic Republican Tradition*. Princeton, NJ: Princeton University Press.

Poggi, G. (1978). *The Development of the Modern State: A Sociological Introduction*. Stanford: Stanford University Press.

Poggi, G. (1990). *The State: Its Nature, Development and Prospects*. Stanford: Stanford University Press.

Poggi, G. (1991). Max Weber's Conceptual Portrait of Feudalism. In *Max Weber: Critical Assessments 1, vol. III,* edited by P. Hamilton, 79–93, London & New York: Routledge.

Poggi, G. (2006). *Weber: A Short Introduction*. Cambridge: Polity Press.

Poggi, G. (2013). The Nation-State. In *Introduction to Comparative Politics,* edited by D. Caramani, 85–107, Oxford: Oxford University Press.

Pomeranz, K. (2000). *The Great Divergence: Europe, China, and the Making of the Modern World Economy*. Princeton, NJ: Princeton University Press.

Prak, M. (2012). Review of Europe: early modern and modern. *American Historical Review,* 117:5, 1650–1651.

Procter, E.S. (1980). *Curia and Cortes in León and Castile 1072–1295*. Cambridge: Cambridge University Press.

Przeworski, A. (2009). Conquered or granted? a history of suffrage extensions. *British Journal of Political Science,* 39:2, 291–321.

Putnam, R.D. (1993). *Making Democracy Work: Civic Traditions in Modern Italy*. Princeton, NJ: Princeton University Press.

Putnam, R.D. (2001). *Bowling Alone: The Collapse and Revival of American Community*. New York: Simon and Schuster.

Ragin, C. and Zaret, D. (1983). Theory and method in comparative research: two strategies. *Social Forces,* 61:3, 731–754.

Riasanovsky, N.V. (1969). *A History of Russia*. Oxford: Oxford University Press.

Richter, M. (2006). Tocqueville on Threats to Liberty in Democracies. In *The Cambridge Companion to Tocqueville,* edited by C.B. Welch, 245–275, Cambridge: Cambridge University Press.

Robinson, A. (2009). *Writing and Script: A Very Short Introduction*. Oxford: Oxford University Press.

Robinson, J. (2002). States and power in Africa by Jeffrey I. Herbst: a review essay. *Journal of Economic Literature,* 40:2, 510–519.

Robinson, J. (2006). Economic development and democracy. *Annual Review of Political Science,* 9:1, 503–527.

Ross, G., Skocpol, T., Smith, T. and Vichniac, J.E. (1998). Barrington Moore's Social Origins and Beyond: Historical Social Analysis since the 1960s. In *Democracy, Revolution, and History,* edited by T. Skocpol, 1–27, Ithaca, NY & London: Cornell University Press.

Ross, M. (2001). Does oil hinder democracy? *World Politics,* 53:3, 325–361.

Rostow, W. (1960). *The Stages of Economic Growth: A Non-Communist Manifesto*. Cambridge: Cambridge University Press.

Rothman, S. (1970). Barrington Moore and the dialectics of revolution: an essay review. *American Political Science Review,* 64:1, 61–82.

Rueschemeyer, D., Stephens, E.H. and Stephens, J. (1992). *Capitalist Development and Democracy*. Chicago: University of Chicago Press.

Rustow, D. (1970). Transitions to democracy: toward a dynamic model. *Comparative Politics,* 2:3, 337–363.

Sabetti, F. (2004). Local roots of constitutionalism. *Perspectives on Political Science,* 33:2, 70–78.

Sartori, G. (1984). Guidelines for Concept Analysis. In *Social Science Concepts: A Systematic Analysis,* edited by G. Sartori, 15–85, Beverly Hills: Sage.

Sartori, G. (1987). *The Theory of Democracy Revisited*. Chatham: Chatham House.

Sartori, G. (1991). Comparing and miscomparing. *Journal of Theoretical Politics,* 3:3, 243–257.

Schumpeter, J.A. (1911). *Theorie der wirtschaftlichen Entwicklung.* Leipzig: Duncker & Humblot.

Schumpeter, J.A. (1974[1942]). *Capitalism, Socialism and Democracy.* London: Unwin University Books.

Schumpeter, J.A. (1991[1917/1918]). The Crisis of the Tax State. In *The Economics and Sociology of Capitalism,* edited by R. Swedberg, 99–140, Princeton, NJ: Princeton University Press.

Schumpeter, J.A. (1991[1919]). The Sociology of Imperialisms. In *The Economics and Sociology of Capitalism,* edited by R. Swedberg, 141–219, Princeton, NJ: Princeton University Press.

Sewell, W.H. (1967). Marc Bloch and the logic of comparative history. *History and Theory,* 6:2, 208–218.

Sewell, W.H. Jr. (1996). Three Temporalities: Toward an Eventful Sociology. In *The Historic Turn in the Human Sciences,* edited by T.J. McDonald, 245–280, Ann Arbor: University of Michigan Press.

Skinner, Q. (1989). The State. In *Political Innovation and Conceptual Change,* edited by T. Ball, J. Farr, and R.L. Hanson, 90–131, Cambridge: Cambridge University Press.

Skocpol, T. (1973). A critical review of Barrington Moore's 'Social Origins of Dictatorship and Democracy'. *Politics and Society,* 4:1, 1–34.

Skocpol, T. (1979). *States and Social Revolutions: A Comparative Analysis of France, Russia and China.* Cambridge: Cambridge University Press.

Skocpol, T. (ed.) (1984a). *Vision and Method in Historical Sociology.* Cambridge: Cambridge University Press.

Skocpol, T. (1984b). Sociology's Historical Imagination. In *Vision and Method in Historical Sociology,* edited by T. Skocpol, 1–21, Cambridge: Cambridge University Press.

Skocpol, T. (1984c). Emerging Agendas and Recurrent Strategies in Historical Sociology. In *Vision and Method in Historical Sociology,* edited by T. Skocpol, 356–391, Cambridge: Cambridge University Press.

Skocpol, T. (1985). Bringing the State Back In: Strategies of Analysis in Current Research. In *Bringing the State Back In,* edited by P.B. Evans, D. Rueschemeyer, and T. Skocpol, 3–37, Cambridge: Cambridge University Press.

Skocpol, T. (2003). Doubly Engaged Social Science: The Promise of Comparative Historical Analysis. In *Comparative Historical Analysis in the Social Sciences,* edited by J. Mahoney and D. Rueschemeyer, 407–428, Cambridge: Cambridge University Press.

Skocpol, T. and Somers, M. (1980). The uses of comparative history in macrosocial inquiry. *Comparative Studies in Society and History,* 22:2, 174–197.

Smelser, N. (1976). *Comparative Methods in the Social Sciences.* Englewood Cliffs: Prentice-Hall.

Smith, D. (1984). Discovering Facts and Values: The Historical Sociology of Barrington Moore. In *Vision and Method in Historical Sociology,* edited by T. Skocpol, 313–355, Cambridge: Cambridge University Press.

Snyder, R. (2001). Scaling down: the subnational comparative method. *Studies in Comparative International Development,* 36:1, 93–110.

Sørensen, G. (2008). *Democracy and Democratization: Processes and Prospects in a Changing World.* Boulder: Westview Press.

Southern, R.W. (1970). *Western Society and the Church in the Middle Ages.* New York: Penguin Books.

Spruyt, H. (1994). *The Sovereign State and Its Competitors.* Cambridge: Princeton University Press.

Stacey, R. (1999). Nobles and Knights. In *The New Cambridge Medieval History V,* edited by D. Abulafia, 13–25, Cambridge: Cambridge University Press.

Stasavage, D. (2007). Cities, constitutions, and sovereign borrowing in Europe, 1274–1785. *International Organization,* 61:3, 489–525.

Stasavage, D. (2008). *Public Debt and the Birth of the Democratic State*. Cambridge: Cambridge University Press.

Stasavage, D. (2010). When distance mattered: geographic scale and the development of European representative assemblies. *American Political Science Review*, 104:4, 625–643.

Stasavage, D. (2011). *States of Credit: Size, Power, and the Development of European Polities*. Princeton, NJ: Princeton University Press.

Stasavage, D. (2014). Was Weber right? the role of urban autonomy in Europe's rise. *American Political Science Review*, 108:2, 337–354.

Stasavage, D. (2016). Representation and consent: why they arose in Europe and not elsewhere. *Annual Review of Political Science*, 19, 145–162.

Stephens, J.D. (1989). Democratic transition and breakdown in Western Europe, 1870–1939: a test of the Moore thesis. *American Journal of Sociology*, 94:5, 1019–1077.

Stephens, J.D. and Kümmel, G. (2003). Class Structure and Democratization. In *Authoritarianism and Democracy in Europe, 1919–1939: Comparative Analysis*, edited by D. Berg-Schlosser and J. Mitchell, 39–63, Gordonsville: Palgrave MacMillan.

Stone, L. (1967). News from Everywhere. *New York Review of Books,* IX, 24 August.

Strayer, J.R. (1970). *On the Medieval Origins of the Modern State*. Princeton, NJ: Princeton University Press.

Strayer, J.R. (1987[1965]). *Feudalism*. Malabar, FL: Krieger Publishing Company.

Swedberg, R. (1991). *Joseph A. Schumpeter: His Life and Work*. Cambridge: Polity Press.

Swedberg, R. (1998). *Max Weber and the Idea of Economic Sociology*. Princeton, NJ: Princeton University Press.

Swedberg, R. (2009). *Tocqueville's Political Economy*. Princeton, NJ: Princeton University Press.

Tawney, R. H. (1912). *The Agrarian Problem in the Sixteenth Century*. London: Longmans.

Tawney, R. H. (1941). The Rise of the Gentry. *Economic History Review*, 11:1, 1–38.

Taylor, A.J.P. (1972). *The First World War*. New York: Perigee.

Taylor, B.D. (2003). *Politics and the Russian Army: Civil-Military Relations, 1689–2000*. Cambridge: Cambridge University Press.

Te Brake, W. (1998). *Shaping History: Ordinary People in European Politics, 1500–1700*. Berkeley: University of California Press.

Thelen, K. (1999). Historical institutionalism in comparative politics. *Annual Review of Political Science*, 2:1, 369–404.

Therborn, G. (1977). The rule of capital and the rise of democracy. *New Left Review*, 103:3, 3–41.

Tierney, B. (1982). *Religion, Law, and the Growth of Constitutional Thought, 1150–1650*. Cambridge: Cambridge University Press.

Tilly, C. (1975). *The Formation of National States in Western Europe*. Princeton, NJ: Princeton University Press.

Tilly, C. (1984). *Big Structures, Large Processes, Huge Comparisons*. New York: Russell Sage Foundation.

Tilly, C. (1985). War Making and State Making as Organized Crime. In *Bringing the State Back In,* edited by P.B. Evans, D. Rueschemeyer, and T. Skocpol, 169–187, Cambridge: Cambridge University Press.

Tilly, C. (1990). *Coercion, Capital, and European States AD 990–1990*. Cambridge: Basil Blackwell.

Tilly, C. (1997). Democracy, Social Change, and Economies in Transition. In *Transforming Post-Communist Political Economies,* edited by J.M. Nelson, C. Tilly, and L. Walker, 403–411, Washington, DC: National Academy Press.

Tilly, C. (2006). Why and how history matters. In *The Oxford Handbook of Contextual Political Analysis*, edited by R.E. Goodin and C. Tilly, 422–423, Oxford: Oxford University Press.

Tracy, J. (2013). Review of states of credit: size, power, and the development of European polities. *Social History*, 38:2, 240–241.

Turgenev, I. (1972[1861]). *Fathers and Sons*. London: Penguin Classics.

van Zanden, J.L., Buringh, E. and Bosker, M. (2012). The rise and decline of European parliaments, 1188–1789. *The Economic History Review*, 65:3, 835–861.

Vincent, N. (2012). *Magna Carta: A Very Short Introduction*. Vol. 321. Oxford: Oxford University Press.

von Falkenhausen, L. (2006). *Chinese Society in the Age of Confucius*. Los Angeles: University of California, The Cotsen Institute of Archaeology Press.

Vu, T. (2010). Studying the state through state formation. *World Politics*, 62:1, 148–175.

Wallerstein, I. (1974). *The Modern World-System: Capitalist Agriculture and the Origins of the European World-Economy in the Sixteenth Century*. New York: Academic Press.

Waltz, K.N. (1959[1954]). *Man, the State, and War: A Theoretical Analysis*. New York: Columbia University Press.

Waltz, K.N. (1979). *Theory of International Politics*. Reading, MA: Addison-Wesley.

Watson, A. (1992). *The Evolution of International Society: A Comparative Historical Analysis*. London and New York: Routledge.

Weber, E. (1982). About Marc Bloch. *The American Scholar*, 51:1, 73–82.

Weber, M. (1981[1927]). *General Economic History*. New Brunswick: Transaction Books.

Weber, M. (1995[1904–05]). *Den protestantiske etik og kapitalismens ånd*. København: Nansensgade Antikvariat.

Weber, M. (2003[1927]). *General Economic History* (transl. Knight, F.H.). Mineola, NY: Dover.

Welch, C.B. (2000). *De Tocqueville*. Oxford: Oxford University Press.

Welch, C.B. (2006). Introduction: Tocqueville in the Twenty-First Century. In *The Cambridge Companion to Tocqueville,* edited by C.B. Welch, 1–20, Cambridge: Cambridge University Press.

Weyland, K. (2009). The diffusion of revolution: '1848' in Europe and Latin America. *International Organization,* 63:3, 391–423.

Weyland, K. (2010). The diffusion of regime contention in European democratization, 1830–1940. *Comparative Political Studies,* 43:8, 1148–1176.

Wickham, C. (1984). The other transition: from the ancient world to feudalism. *Past & Present*, 103:1, 3–36.

Wittfogel, K.A. (1957). *Oriental Despotism: A Comparative Study of Total Power*. New Haven: Yale University Press.

Wong, R.B. (1997). *China Transformed: Historical Change and the Limits of European Experience*. Ithaca, NY & London: Cornell University Press.

Wong, R.B. (2002). The search for European differences and domination in the early modern world: a view from Asia. *The American Historical Review*, 107:2, 447–469.

Woodberry, R. (2012). The missionary roots of liberal democracy. *American Political Science Review*, 106:2, 244–274.

Zagorin, P. (1982). *Rebels and Rulers, 1500–1660*. Cambridge: Cambridge University Press.

Zakaria, F. (2003). *The Future of Freedom: Illiberal Democracy at Home and Abroad*. New York: W.W. Norton & Company.

INDEX

Page numbers in italic indicate a figure or table on the corresponding page.

state diversity in 112; tax states in 60–1; use of term 8n4; *see also* Europe
Western civilization: as failure 8n2; rationalization of 47
Western Europe: absolutism in 93–4, *94*, 95; communist revolution and 88, 97n1; political institutions of 147
within-case analysis 27
Wittfogel, Karl August 55
Woodberry, Robert D.: criticism of 205; on missionaries and democracy 202–5

work ethic: capitalism and 49–51; slavery and 33
working class, in democracy 85–6
World War I, origins of 148
World War II, geopolitical pressure after 6
writing systems, invention of ix

Zeitgeist, in French Revolution 40
Zemskii Sobor 240–1
Ziblatt, D. 26, 28n3